SALAAM
AMERICA

SALAAM AMERICA

South Asian Muslims
in New York

Aminah Mohammad-Arif

Translated by
Sarah Patey

Anthem Press

To the memory of Dada

This edition first published by Anthem Press 2002

Anthem Press is an imprint of
Wimbledon Publishing Company
PO Box 9779
London
SW19 7QA

© CNRS ÉDITIONS 2000
First published by CRNS ÉDITIONS, Paris, 2000
as *Salam America – L'islam indien en diaspora*
English translation ©
Wimbeldon Publishing Company 2002

This book is supported by the French Ministry for Foreign Affairs,
as part of the Burgess programme headed for the French Embassy
in London by the Institut Français du Royaume-Uni.

Liberté • Égalité • Fraternité
RÉPUBLIQUE FRANÇAISE

British Library Cataloguing in Publication Data
Data available

Library of Congress Cataloging in Publication Data
A catalog record has been applied for

ISBN 1 84331 009 0 (hbk)
ISBN 1 84331 010 4 (pbk)

1 3 5 7 9 10 8 6 4 2

CONTENTS

ACKNOWLEDGEMENTS

This book arose out of a thesis[1] completed under the supervision of Marc Gaborieau (CNRS/EHESS), to whom my first thanks are due: his confidence in me, his valuable advice and his great kindness, together with his learning and experience, helped and guided me throughout my work. My thanks go also to the members of the thesis panel: Denis Matringe (CNRS), Christophe Jaffrelot (CNRS/CERI), Jean Heffer (EHESS), Claude Markovits (CNRS) and Constant Hamès (CNRS), all of whom were most generous with their advice and encouragement. I would also like to thank Farhad Khrosrokhavar (EHESS), who kindly and patiently re-read one chapter of my thesis, and gave me his very helpful comments. Eric Meyer (INALCO), Gérard Colas (CNRS) and Jacques Pouchepadass (CNRS) unstintingly gave their time to read and correct my manuscript, and I am most grateful to them. I am grateful as well to Jean-Michel Lacroix (Sorbonne-Nouvelle) under whose supervision I wrote my first dissertation on the Indian diaspora. His support and interest in my work encouraged me to continue to work on this subject. I am very much in debt to Françoise Pirot (CNRS/SIS) and Maurice Legrand (CNRS/SIS) who very patiently drew up the maps. I would also like to thank CNRS Publications, and particularly Annie Cadiot, my editor, who have enabled the publication of this book. Lastly, my heartfelt thanks to Crispin Bates (University of Edinburgh), Kamaljit Sood, Tom Penn and Sarah Patey, all of whom made this English edition possible.

The research for this work was enabled by a research grant from the *Ecole des hautes études en sciences sociales*. I would like to thank its school of doctoral studies in history and civilizations, and in particular the director, Jean Andreau, and Liliane Adolphe. I would also like to express my thanks to the members of the *Bibliothèque inter-universitaire des langues orientales* and the *Centre d'études de l'Inde et de l'Asie du Sud*, especially Catarina Kasi and Radhika Shaunik, who most kindly led me to every publication relevant to my subject. Mariam Abou-Zahab (INALCO) most generously supplied me with all the documents on Pakistan I might find interesting.

In America, Yvonne Haddad (Amherst University, Massachusetts) gave me the benefit of her wide knowledge of the Muslim, in particular Arab, community in the United States. My discussions with Omar Khalidi (MIT) were also most informative. I am grateful to Sucheta Mazumdar and Vasant Kaiwar (both of Duke University) for my temporary membership of the Asian-American Center of Queens College, New York, from November 1995 to January 1996. I was made most welcome by all the members of the Center, in particular by its director, Jack Tchen, and by the historian Madhulika Khandelwal. My conversations with her were most illuminating, as were others with David Lelyveld of the University of Colombia. The generosity and kindness of Usha Sanyal were most memorable. Thanks to Atheef Kabir and Naveen, I made some contacts most valuable to my research.

I would also like to thank all the members of the south Asian community in the United States, who kindly and patiently allowed me to conduct most enlightening interviews with them. Without them, this work would not have been possible.

My profound gratitude goes to the Mohan Das family, to Mohanji himself, and to his wife Kalaji and their children, Sudha, Veena and Rikesh, for their hospitality and their warm welcome in the extreme cold of New Jersey.

And what can I say of the love and moral support afforded me by my cousins, Mani and Shameem Menon, and their children Nisha and Roshen? They looked after me during all my trips to the United States and offered comforting breaks from the frenzy of New York.

I owe a great debt of thanks to my friends. My long conversations with Christine Moliner were always most stimulating, and I benefited from her wealth of knowledge on the Sikh diaspora. She kindly read whole chapters of my thesis, as did Christèle Dedebant and Alexandra Quien, and their help was most valuable.

Words cannot express my gratitude to Anne-Marie Waliullah for her unfailingly helpful comments and corrections, nor my sadness at her unexpected death.

Florence Albrecht is a childhood friend and soul sister, and she has read and corrected the manuscript of the whole book with her usual thoroughness. I thank her with all my heart.

That this book has happened at all is due in large part to my parents, whose limitless patience and infallible encouragement have sustained me through several years of research. I shall never be able to express how thankful I am to them.

Last but not least, my heartfelt thanks to my husband and lifelong friend, Khalid, for whom this book meant many sacrifices. I am all the more grateful for his unconditional support, his invaluable help, and above all for his great sense of humour, which kept me going through the difficult times.

INTRODUCTION

Like every Sunday morning, I was on my way to the Long Island mosque. At Westbury[1] station, I went to take a taxi. I gave the driver the address, without saying that I was going to a mosque. He turned to me and said, 'Ah, you're going to the church?'

'You could say so,' I replied.

An elderly Sikh couple approached, wanting to hire the same taxi.[2] 'We're going to the Gurdwara,' the old man said in broken English.

'The what?' asked the driver.

'The sikh temple'

'What's the address?'

'I don't know,' the old Sikh replied.

He turned to me and said in Hindi, 'If we see a Sardarji,[3] we can ask where the temple is.'

I refrained from replying that we were not in Delhi, nor even in Southall.[4]

The taxi driver was puzzled. He asked me, 'Surely they must be going to the same temple as you?'

'Surely not,' I replied.

The taxi set off. I exchanged a few words with the two Sikhs in Hindi, asking for details about the temple which might help the driver find it.

After a few moments, the driver turned around and asked: 'How come you're talking the same language and yet you're not going to the same temple?'

This incident, which might well be described in a thesis on communalism[5] in India, illustrates some typical characteristics of the presence of immigrants[6] from South Asia[7] in the United States: ignorance among Americans about this community and its different religions[8] as indicated by the confusion of temple and mosque, and the failure to distinguish between Sikhism and Islam. The taxi driver's last remark is also very revealing: although there are more than 200 religious denominations in the United States, each with its own church, attended by members most of whom speak English, this taxi driver perceives non-anglophone ethnic groups as a uniform religious group.

This anecdote leads us into an analysis, later in this thesis, of attendance at mosques on Sunday mornings, traditionally the 'Lord's Day' in the Christian religion. Is this a first indication that the religious practices of Muslim (and non-Muslim) immigrants to the United States from the Indian subcontinent are becoming Americanized?

Not only are Americans ignorant of the religions of the Indian subcontinent, they also fail to distinguish physically Indians, Pakistanis, and Bangladeshis from their own Hispanics.[9] The very word 'Indian' is a source of confusion in a country where this word is used mainly to describe American Indians.[10]

The Muslims of South Asia are even less well known, either to the scientific community or to the average American, as they tend automatically to associate 'Indian' with 'Hindu'.

The Muslims of the Indian subcontinent are nevertheless interesting in a number of ways: they form a very ancient grouping (eight to ten per cent of Indian pioneers in the early twentieth century were Muslim); they are diverse ethnically and culturally (Punjabi, Muhajir, Pathan, Bengali, Hyderabadi, Gujarati, and so on); as well as religiously (Sunni, Ithna 'Ashari [also known as Twelver Shi'a], Nizarian, Bohra, Memons Ahmadiyya and others); they are dynamic (amongst all the Muslims who have settled in the United States, the South Asians stand out not only by their achievement of higher social and economic standing, but also by their clear enthusiasm for setting up religious and cultural centres in the United States).

Apart from these charcteristics characteristics, the Muslim community from the Indian subcontinent is also a major player in the assertion of Islamic identity throughout the world, this assertion being a major feature of the twentieth century.

Islam in South Asia

Muslims have been present in the subcontinent since the first century of Islam (Arab invaders entered the Sind in 711, while traders and mariners sailed across the Indian Ocean). It was the second wave, however, coming from central Asia, which gave rise to the majority of South Asian Muslims. From the thirteenth century this group dominated the political life of the peninsula. This domination reached its most glorious period under the imperial dynasty of the Moghuls (sixteenth to eighteenth centuries). At its collapse the Moghul empire lay open to the British, who supplanted the Muslims and built a huge empire which culminated under Queen Victoria. The end of the nineteenth century saw the emergence of reform movements, both nationalist and socio-religious.[11] At this time, Muslims made up 20 per cent of the population; by 1941 they had reached 24 per cent.

The independence movement started in earnest after the First World War, and gathered pace after the Second. Alongside this movement, the Muslim League of Muhammad Ali Jinnah (1876–1948) exploited the fears of the Muslim urban elite – mainly came from the Ganges plains (now in the Indian Union) – who were nervous of being subjected to a Hindu hegemony in an independent India. In order to rally the Muslim population, the separatist leaders promoted Islamic religion as a main tool of ethnic identification; their campaign was crowned with success when Pakistan was created on 14 August 1947 (although a third of Muslims stayed in India).

Islam continues to be the ideological foundation of the 'Country of the Pure'. Pakistanis (97 per cent of whom are Muslim) consider themselves today as members of a distinct (Muslim) nation.

Muslims in India are now in the minority (12.2 per cent in the 1991 census, a 'minority of 100 million souls',[12] which makes them as numerous as in either Pakistan or Bangladesh) in a state which is officially secular,[13] but in which religion is one of the major components of national identity.[14] They declare their religious identity by uniting on three issues which have become symbols: the maintenance of the *Shari'ah* law, threatened by a common civil code which would apply to all the religious groups in India; the defence of Urdu, which is suffering in competition with Hindi, the language of India; and the preservation of the Islamic character of Aligarh University. Any attack on one of these three symbols is promptly interpreted by Muslims as a prelude to an assimilation into Hinduism as is indeed advocated by Hindu nationalists.

In Bangladesh, ethnic and linguistic nationalism triumphed, rather than religious nationalism, in the 1971 war of independence. However, loyalty to Bengali culture did not result in a fusion with West Bengal: this shows the persistence of the religious feeling in the country, which has witnessed a progressive Islamization of the state. The Hindu minorities have, in the process, gradually moved out of Bangladesh, and the population is now nearly 90 per cent Muslim.

Recent history and the current situation in the Indian subcontinent would therefore seem to suggest a pre-eminence of the religious sentiment among Muslims, whether they are in the minority or in the majority, both in their modes of identification and in their identity formation.

Some of these Muslims have chosen to emigrate to a country, the United States, which recognizes the individual's right, at least in part, to preserve his or her ethnic, and especially religious, identity.

Migration, religion and ethnic identity in
the United States

The United States differs on these issues from France, where total assimilation seems to be the expected goal for immigrants, either as the precondition for an equal status for individuals living in the same society, or as a cover for cultural domination.[15] France rejects the idea of community, which is seen as a precursor to ghettoization, and advocates instead an integration into the host society at the individual level. The United States endorses the coexistence of separate communities in the national whole, and in this resembles the United Kingdom, with one important difference: there is no colonial past shared between South Asia and the United States; this is important because of the existence of close links of structural dependence between immigration and colonization, since immigration is often perceived as the last avatar of colonization.[16]

Religion occupies a significant place in the United States. The First Amendment to the Constitution, ratified in 1791, guarantees religious freedom, in a way which can remind one of Indian secularism, since it implies that the state can show favour neither to the religious over the non-religious, nor to one particular religious tradition over another. In theory, religion is therefore relegated to the private sphere. And yet Americans appear to be the most religious people amongst industrialized nations, as shown by the high proportion of the population professing to a religion and being actively committed to it. The high profile of religion in public and political life is confirmed by some significant symbols: during the ceremony of investiture, the President of the United States must swear on the Bible to respect the Constitution, which proclaims that the nation is 'under the eyes of God'. Coins carry the inscription 'In God we trust'. In every electoral campaign, themes of direct or indirect religious significance feature regularly, most importantly abortion. The relationship between state and religion can thus be seen to be very ambiguous.

It is also widely agreed that Americans accept the concept of a monotheistic morality, based on Judaism and Christianity.

The religious phenomenon in the United States has its roots in the very history of the country, in which protestant evangelical and revivalist movements played a crucial part in the social organization of the pioneers, and contributed to the Church playing a central part in urban life. In time, millions of immigrants, mainly Roman Catholic, Jewish and later Orthodox Christians, swelled the American population: the first phase of the diversification of religious life in the country. The second phase came in the latter half of the twentieth century with mass immigration of Muslims, Hindus, Buddhists and others.

As early as the first phase, churches and synagogues played a role as a preferential social space. They served to promote the spiritual, social and even economic lives of immigrants. They served their needs through volunteer networks. These centres represented a strong link with the past, and provided continuity between life in the country of origin and life in the host- society. And through their central role in educating immigrants, and helping them in their social integration, they have secured a bridge to the future.

From the start, immigrants explicitly set up their own churches, with a service in their mother tongue, and celebrants from their own country. Religious freedom paradoxically promoted the emergence of ethnic solidarity and community identification. Churches and synagogues controlled by distinct national groupings were set up and strongly contributed to the preservation of clear-cut ethnic life-styles. Hence they encouraged the formation of a group conscience. In the second and third generations, when language and culture began to disappear, religious belief and the affiliation to the ethnic church remained. Thus religion became the main driving force of ethnic identity.[17]

I will define ethnic identity as a process of construction or invention which incorporates, adapts and amplifies historical memories, cultural attributes and pre-existing solidarities, in order to create an internal cohesion, and to mark out distinctive cultural territory.[18] A fundamental element of the American psyche, ethnic identity is conceptualized as the result of external pressures and mutual perceptions in the complex relationships between majority and minority social groupings.

The United States provides the ultimate paradigm of a society of immigrants. However, the hostility that is regularly displayed against recent immigrants (nativism) shows the ambivalence of Americans towards immigration, and provides furthermore a fertile ground for various forms of nationalism. This phenomenon is strengthened by the nostalgia and the feelings of insecurity often characteristic of immigrants' lives. Moreover, the experience of migration can sometimes lead to the creation of new identitifications, where communities are imagined,[19] traditions[20] and ethnicity[21] are invented, and social structures are created. For example, Indians who did not previously think of themselves as such before emigration have become Indians in the diaspora,[22] think of themselves now as a community,[23] support political bodies which invent a national history (the Bharatiya Janata party, or BJP[24]), and through a process of romantic nostalgia generally begin to idealize their former homeland.

It is worth noting that contact with other cultures in the migratory process contributes to the reinforcement of ethnic and religious identity.

Islam and migration

The very concept of migration (*hijrah* in Arabic) has a fundamental significance in Islam. The migration of the Prophet Muhammad from Mecca to Medina in 622 marks the beginning of Islamic history. It is represented as a flight from a land of infidels where Muslims are persecuted, towards a new land where the Muslim community can flourish. Through the centuries of Muslim expansion, *hijrah* became synonymous with migration from a non-Islamic to an Islamic country, to the point where the schools of law never really discussed the problems faced by Muslims living in a non-Muslim society, while the reverse situation was very thoroughly discussed.[25]

This issue was only approached by theologians in examining the case of a Muslim convert still living in a non-Muslim land: was such a person obliged to move to a Muslim country? Sunni lawyers said they were; Shi'a defended the opposite viewpoint. Later, under the expansion of Western colonialization, the question arose of what position should be taken by Muslims if their country was invaded by Christians.[26]

Different schools of Islamic law[27] took differing positions on this. The Hanafi law (to which belong the majority of immigrants from the Indian subcontinent[28]) took up the most moderate position: migration to an Islamic country was compulsory only if Muslims were subjected to forced conversions, or were unable to fulfil their religious obligations.[29] From the nineteenth century Muslims began to emigrate on their own free will to non-Muslim countries, generally Christian-dominated ones, for the purposes of higher education, employment, or permanent settlement. Learned Muslims formulated various arguments to justify this kind of migration: the concept of necessity (*zarurat*), interpreted in economic terms; as a corollary to this, a *hijrah* permitted in order to escape illness or financial insecurity; and permitted *hijrah* with a view to propagating Islam.[30]

Some learned Muslims go so far as to recommend to Muslims a migration to Europe or the United States in order to acquire education and a knowledge of modern science and technology, which they see as essential to the development of Muslim societies. Moreover, conditions in Europe and the United States are often more favourable to the practice and propagation of Islam than they are in Islamic countries themselves.[31]

It seems, in summary, that the migration of Muslims to the United States, in theory the direct opposite of *hijrah*, does not pose fundamental theological problems. It is debatable whether immigrants in the main are even aware of the legal debate or the arguments that can be adduced to justify their presence in a non-Muslim country.

Another aspect of *hijrah* is also worth pointing out: the concept of withdrawing from society and living out one's faith. Such a 'withdrawal' could arguably be achieved within the geographical boundaries of any given society, and amounts to a social, even spatial isolation. Some Christians within the United States have chosen this way of life, the Amish people being a well-known example.

This experience was also attempted in India in the sixteenth century within the *mahdaviyyah* movement: as Professor Derryl Maclean has emphasized, the disciples of Mahdi Sayyid Muhammad Jaunpuri established 'utopian Medinas', inhabited by the 'true Muslim' community, as opposed to the others, the *kafir* (the unbelievers). The idea was to create a complete and exclusive system – one which met all needs, economic, social and spiritual. The system was not perpetuated by succeeding generations, because it required a level of commitment and devotion which they were unable to maintain.[32]

Can a similar attempt at a micro-society be once again attempted in the United States? Didn't the Nation of Islam, when it was founded, advocate such separatism? Similar attempts to withdraw from society have been tried by small numbers of Muslims in Europe.[33]

Social and indeed spatial withdrawal would not ultimately lead to total isolation, however, because the fundamental Islamic concept of *da'wa* (proselytizing) requires that Muslims will be in contact with other communities. A growing number of Americans, especially black Americans, are converting to Islam. What role are South Asian Muslims playing in this process?

Alongside *hijrah* and *da'wa*, a third concept has developed during Islamic history to guide Muslims who have had to live in non-Islamic societies: *jihad*. Usually translated as 'holy war', this term means literally 'to make an effort'. This expression can either have a very precise sense of fighting for one's faith, or it can describe the efforts made by an individual to serve God in the best way he or she can.[34] To what extent are Muslims conscious of this concept, and do they try to use it in adapting their lives to modern American society?

Islamic practices are ordained by divine law. However, the first Muslim theologians and lawyers used the concept of *ijtihad* (personal effort of interpretation) to explore the questions to which the Koran and the *Sunna* (the collection of rules for behaviour based on the words and actions of the Prophet) did not provide replies. For some 900 years *ijtihad* has no longer been officially active, but it is nevertheless essential to refer to it in new or unique situations, or when both information and competent authorities are unavailable. Could this concept not be extended to the American context to allow Muslims to adapt to a non-Muslim context?

Beyond the theories on living in a non-Muslim country, there are specific problems presented to Muslims living in a society which has been designed to accommodate individuals adhering to different religions and ways of thinking.

True, Muslims benefit from a relatively tolerant attitude in the United States towards religious practice; but what could be the place of Islam in a society where Protestantism, Catholicism and Judaism are defined as three alternate expressions of a global American religion? According to Will Herberg, 'to be a Protestant, a Catholic or a Jew are today the alternative ways of being an American'.[35]

Islam does not recognize the separation of church and state, and law is an integral part of religion. Christians and Jews have also had to define the relationship between the implications of their faith and the expectations of a secular society, but the relationship between church and state has essentially been defined in Jewish and Christian terms. Judaism may on occasion have had to face problems similar to those faced by Islam, but on the whole this religion is better integrated into the American religious landscape, and it has acquired the status of 'a most favoured religion'.

The adaptation of American society to Judeo-Christian practices does not necessarily solve the problems faced specifically by Muslims. To hold and practice the Muslim faith involves specific obligations and responsibilities. Islam embraces the whole life of its adherents and regulates a large part of their behaviour. In a number of areas and places in society, Muslims face if not difficulties, at least challenges: it is not easy to pray five times a day, especially at work; if one wants to adhere strictly to dietary requirements, it becomes difficult to eat out, which in turn affects one's social life; the main religious festivals, Id ul-Fitr (the breaking of the fast) and Id ul-Adha (the feast of Abraham's sacrifice), are not treated as public holidays; a strict application of Islamic regulations concerning lending at interest would rule out any transactions by Muslims with American financial institutions.

Islam is frequently associated by the media and by the general American public with terrorism and fundamentalism, and therefore does not enjoy a good press reputation in the United States, especially since the attack on the World Trade Center in February 1993. Until then, terrorist acts perpetrated in the name of Islam were seen as a distant menace, but now Muslims in the United States are viewed with increased suspicion [see also the Afterword, p 268].

How are Muslims reacting in such a situation? What brand of Islam are they promoting? Is Islam forced to become 'domesticated', as it has had to in France?[37] Does it have to give up on its 'active community realizations'?[38] What is its position in public life? Are Muslims forced to practice their religion 'discretely' or 'in hiding'[39], or can they operate outside the confines of a Muslim neighbourhood, a ghetto or the mosque? In France, especially in the case of North Africans, Islam can be seen as a mark of 'refuge' (associated with failure and exclusion) – is this true of Muslims from the subcontinent in the

United States? Or is Islam a distinctive mark of one's bearings, not necessarily associated with rejection, but instead pointing to the means of integration[40] into American society?

Issues of identity

We shall also examine how identity is constructed. Identity is not a fixed, static, immoveable concept. It can be defined, constructed, negotiated; it can also be subject to variations or to transformations. In the case of Muslims, it is impossible to define a uniform Islamic identity even if national or ethnic affiliations are not considered. Sunni, Twelver Shi'a, Nizari isma'ili, Bohra, Ahmadiyya, all proclaim their affiliation to Islam and affirm their Islamic identity. And yet periodically they identify themselves or are identified by others more with one particular sect than with the more general Muslim community.

Indian Muslims are especially interesting in that even before they emigrated they already belonged to a minority which regularly questioned its own identity. They are different in this from Pakistanis and Bangladeshis, who do not experience this phenomenon of 'double minority' – their Islamic identity will not be, for all that, less asserted. However, Indian Muslims are in a very particular position. They lived before emigration in a society which truly enough was secular, but where the majority of the inhabitants professed a religion usually defined as polytheistic, in other words less akin to Islam than Christianity or Judaism. (However British India was declared by most Indian Muslim scholars and theologians to be *Dar ul Islam*, literally 'the Abode of Islam', as opposed to *Dar ul Harb*, 'the Abode of War'. Today, India is endowed with similar status in the eyes of Muslims.) Is this experience of 'double minority' an advantage to Indian Muslims when they seek to become integrated into American society, or does it instead encourage them to adopt the kind of withdrawing behaviour they sometimes display in India?

Do Indian Muslims, because they are accustomed to being in the minority, and Pakistanis, because Islam is the *raison d'être* of their country, stand out among other Muslims by their more pronounced religiosity? If this is the case, what happens to the relationship between Indian Muslims and other religious groups from South Asia, especially Hindus?

When the lines between the ethnicity and the religion of a particular group become blurred that group's unity and its coherence are, if not ensured, at least favoured. This is the case for example with Sikhs (the correlation between 'Sikh' and 'Punjabi' is very close, even though not all Punjabis are Sikhs), Greek Orthodox (religion and ethnicity are for them virtually synonymous in the United States) and Jews ('Judaism is organically linked to a specific people, in fact to a nation'[42]). But for Muslims there is a different situation. What effect does this have on relations with other communities? Do Muslims from the Indian subcontinent continue to define themselves primarily by their national or ethnic affiliation, or do they attempt to transcend national and ethnic barriers in order to draw closer to other Muslims, American (white and black), Arab or Iranian, with the ultimate aim of creating an ethnic group defined as Muslim? Ruby Jo Reeves Kennedy has written in defence of the idea that ethnic groups in the United States have tended to fuse together on the basis of religious affiliation rather than to form a homogenous group.[43]

Lastly, to what extent has Islam adopted characteristics from American culture and traditions? In other words, are we seeing the development of an American Islam?

The current state of research

Little has so far been published on South Asian Muslims. Five major books have been published on the Indian diaspora to the United States: Maxine Fisher, *The Indians of New York City*; Parmatma Saran (ed.), *The New Ethnics*; Joan Jensen, *Passage from India*; Arthur and Usha Helweg, *An Immigrant Success Story*; Jean Bacon, *Life Lines*. These five works, all very interesting, deal in the main with Hindu immigrants to the United States.

Studies have been done on Muslims in the United States. Yvonne Haddad has published two major works on this issue: one with Adair Lummis, *Islamic Values in the United States*; the other with Jane Idleman Smith, *Mission to America*. Haddad has also edited two other works related to the subject: *The Muslims of America*, and with Jane Smith, *Muslim Communities in North America*. Two important works have also been published on the Muslims of Canada, edited by Earle Waugh, Baha Abu-Laban and Regula Qureshi, *The Muslim Community in North America* and *Muslim Families in North America*. These works, though interesting in themselves, have little to say on South Asian Muslims, and concentrate more on Arab and African–American Muslims. There is still little that offers a picture, both global and at the same time detailed, of the integration of South Asian Muslims into North American society, and the way in which they are defining their own identity. Two books have come out simultaneously on the religious traditions of South Asian immigrants: Raymond Williams, *Religions of Immigrants from India and Pakistan*; and John Fenton, *Transplanting Religious Traditions*. Apart from a general ten-page presentation on Indian and Pakistani Muslims, Williams writes chiefly on Nizari Isma'ili Muslims, on whom there is a most interesting chapter. Fenton, in his study of the South Asians in Atlanta, focuses on Hindus, and devotes only a few pages to the religious practices of Muslims.

There is in existence a study dealing exclusively with Indian Muslims in the

United States. Edited by Omar Khalidi, it is entitled *Indian Muslims in North America*. It contains a series of papers given at a conference in 1989 by the Indian Muslim Relief Committee. However, none of the articles give any profound analysis, as the aim of the publication was to encourage Indian Muslims to organize in order to make their mark on American society.

The recent work edited by Barbara Metcalf, *Making Muslim Space in North America and Europe,* is worth noting here too. It is rare in that it offers a comparative perspective on the Muslim diasporas to Europe and America.[44] It is a most interesting work, in particular the chapters by Barbara Metcalf, Regula Qureshi and Susan Slyomovics, but the issue of South Asian Muslims is not examined both from a general perspective and in thorough detail.

In conclusion, then, I know of no in-depth study to date on Muslims from the Indian subcontinent living in the United States. This work aims to remedy this deficiency by examining the relevant issues almost from the start.

Definition and methodology

Definition

This study of South Asian Muslims in the United States will cover the period from the 1960s, when American policies on immigration were liberalized, to the present. Immigration in the early part of the twentieth century will not be included in this study, as it was closely linked with the arrival of Punjabi Sikhs, which has been thoroughly studied elsewhere.[45]

New York has been chosen as the focus of research. It is the archetypal immigrant city, where few define themselves simply as 'American'. More than anywhere else in the United States, the hyphen is *de rigueur* in New York, where one is Irish–American, Chinese–American or Mexican–American.

There is a high concentration in New York of Muslims from South Asia, and of Muslim institutions (mosques, organizations, schools, *halal* butchers, etc.). This study will evaluate the ways in which these features of New York life help preserve the ethnic heritage and sense of identity of South Asian Muslims.

Methodology and printed sources

For this research, interviews were carried out with over a hundred people over a period of eight months. Most interviewees were met in New York, some in New Jersey, in Connecticut and in Massachusetts. Others were met in India or England. I have been conducting my research officially since 1991–92 (year of my master's degree), but in fact I have for more than ten years now been observing the lives of a handful of South Asian families in the United States, since I first visited two Indian families in 1986, one in Massachusetts, one in California. These observations not only inspired my choice of subject matter, but they have also much enriched my research.

The interviews were conducted in English and Hindi/Urdu, in the homes of the interviewees, in mosques, Muslim organizations, hospitals, on the street, in shops, restaurants, on public transport, in taxis, on college campuses (in particular: Columbia University and Queens College in New York; Harvard University and the University of Massachusetts in Amherst, Massachusetts; Wesleyan College in Connecticut; Jawaharlal Nehru University in Delhi and Madras University in India), and so on. Some interviews were conducted over the telephone with subjects (especially community leaders) living in Houston (Texas), Philadelphia (Pennsylvania), Chicago (Illinois), Atlanta (Georgia), Los Angeles (California) and Washington, DC.

Interviews were in a number of formats: some were formal (completion of a questionnaire by the interviewee), some semi-formal (individual oral questionnaire, not given to the interviewee) and some informal. In order to preserve the anonymity of the interviewees, I did not resort to the technique of life stories. The only real names given are those of some community leaders and of people already known through press reports. For convenience I have given my subjects nicknames (indicated by quotation marks). Interviewees' nicknames are in the list in Appendix 1, but it should be noted that this list includes only those quoted: many more were interviewed and contributed to my research. As part of my research, I also resorted to the technique of participatory observation.

I received, on the whole, a very warm welcome from the South Asians in New York. A small number of community leaders from sectarian minorities or traditional Sunni groups were somewhat mistrustful. However, I was only refused an interview by the leaders of one sectarian minority, and the information I have on this group I owe to dissidents. Leaders of another sectarian minority group insisted that I should interview them only by telephone. I met with reluctance only in these quarters, and I may have my own origins as a Muslim Indian woman to thank for the cooperation of others as they willingly opened up to one of their own. In particular, I think some community leaders did not feel the need, sometimes observed elsewhere, to engage in the proselytizing or apologetics they customarily present to non-Muslims. That I had come from France to investigate this community provoked some curiosity, and may have increased interest in my research. My coming from France also made me slightly more of an outsider. I leave it to others to judge whether this was sufficient to make my observations objective.

I conducted in-depth perusals of 'ethnic' journals and magazines published in New York: *India Abroad* from 1992, *The Message International* from its first publication in 1989, *The Minaret* (New York), *Samar* and *Masala* from 1995.

I studied the publications of various New York Islamic organizations on the one hand and of novels and short stories written by members of the South Asian diaspora (very prolific in the United States) on the other, and these combined to form another crucial element in my primary sources. The Internet was most useful in providing complementary information.

In the absence of reliable and precise demographic information on South Asian Muslims in New York, it would have been interesting to analyse the telephone directories of the five New York boroughs. But I faced major problems: one was the size of the task (776 Khans in the 1995 Queens directory alone!), and the other the impossibility of distinguishing by surname South Asians from Arabs and other Muslims (not all Khans are South Asians, for example). There are indeed certain names that can fairly reliably be identified as South Asian: Ansari, Azmi, Bakhshi, Batt, Beg, Bilgrami, Choudhari, Kazmi, Noorani, Qureshi, Rizvi, Siddiqi and others. Moreover, some combinations are not acceptable to Arabs, either because of their meaning (Abdul Rasul, Abdul Nabi, Ghulam Ali, etc.), or because they are grammatically incorrect (Rehman Ilahi, Mohammed Ashequeen). Yet other names contain words borrowed from the vernacular (Chand, Lal, Rakha, etc.).[46] Many names, though, are difficult to identify as specifically South Asian: unlike Muslims from Iran, Africa or Turkey, South Asian Muslims have on the whole maintained the (literary) Arab spelling (though not the pronunciation) of their forenames and surnames.

Theoretical procedure

To finish, a short note on the analytical process in this work. In this introduction, I started out from the way in which Muslims at first perceived the issue of their own identity, in the light of their history on the one hand, and on the other of the Islamic understanding of the concept of emigration and of solidarity within the Muslim community.

My analysis then aims to get beyond this internal viewpoint in two ways: first chronologically, tracing the group's development as it has had increasing contact with the host society, and as the generations have succeeded each other. Second, in applying concepts of comparative study taken from the social sciences, I hope to situate this self-definition by the group in the objective landscape of social analysis of minority ethnic groups.

To achieve this, I have relied on two types of work: firstly on studies in political sociology, undertaken by researchers like Peter Van der Veer, Arjun Appadurai, Paul Brass and Jean-François Bayart; secondly on studies in religious sociology.

A series of lectures by Peter Van der Veer at the EHESS in 1993, his work

Religious Nationalism: Hindus and Muslims in India and his introduction to *Nation and Migration* have all helped me better to understand the way in which a group constructs its identity in diaspora, and his work persuaded me to explore the concept of 'double minority' which affects, in particular, the Indian Muslims. The work of Arjun Appadurai[47] has helped me to a clearer understanding of how transnational communities, defined as it were by kindred sentiment, can develop in diasporic situations. In particular, I subscribe to his view that the process promoted by globalization is usually hybridization rather than homogenization.

My debt to Paul Brass[48] and Jean-François Bayart[49] is for the instrumentalist theory, as opposed to the primordialist or culturalist theories. I do not in any way discount the cultural and religious dimensions in the groups studied. I have tended, though, to give weight to the instrumental method of analysis, which sees social and economic factors as major influences on the attitudes and behaviours of the social groups studied, both in their relations to the 'Other' and in the ways in which they seek to integrate into the host society. The following example may help to illustrate this. Arthur and Usha Helweg see British colonization as one explanation for the way in which the Indian community has prospered in the United States: the British Empire did not succeed in preventing the Indians from keeping to their traditions, and this has given them a confidence in their culture such that they are able to maintain it even when moving into a foreign country.[50] This explanation is, however, only partly satisfying to me. The migration experience of North Africans, Algerians in particular (for whom the colonization of their country by France was much more destructive for both their society and their culture), in France compared to that of Indians in the United Kingdom, tends to confirm the Helweg's thesis. But Pakistani and Bangladeshi immigrants to the United Kingdom, who also came from countries colonized by the British, are often found at the lower end of the social scale, which throws this theory into doubt. It might be possible to see Islam, the common ground between North Africans in France and Pakistanis and Bangladeshis in England, as the explanation for the difficulties these groups have experienced in becoming integrated into the host society. The social and economic success of South Asians in the United States, however, which is independent of religious affiliation, denies this explanation. It seems to me that the reasons for the success or failure of these groups to integrate, and their social behaviour as a group, date back to factors prior to migration: on the one hand the level of education received, and on the other the social and economic position enjoyed before migration. The way in which the host country welcomes and manages immigration can also play a determining part.

This examination of religious as well as ethnic minorities required also that issues in religious sociology be examined. I was much helped by the work of American researchers in the field of Muslim minorities in the United States (in particular, the work of Yvonne Haddad and Adair Lummis, *Islamic Values in the United States*, mentioned above, and the two studies led by Yvonne Haddad on the organization and religious institutions of Muslims in North America – see above). Studies in religious sociology by French researchers have helped to establish a perspective of comparison. I have found most helpful the studies regularly published in the *Archives de sciences sociales des religions* (in particular the two issues of this journal devoted to Islam in Europe, 1985 and 1995), and in *Confluences*. Sociologists Farhad Khosrokhavar, Chantal Saint-Blancat, Jocelyne Cesari, Leïla Babès and others have recently published most interesting studies on Muslims in France and/or in Europe; these have helped me to perceive both similarities and differences in the processes of migration and of developing a group identity, for Muslims migrating to France on the one hand and the United States on the other. The similarities are the products *par essence* of modernity and of globalization, beyond borders, beyond integration experiences and beyond ethnic groups. Some works of general religious sociology, for example those led by Danièle Hervieu-Léger (in particular *Les identités religieuses en Europe* with Grace Davie) have helped me to grasp the dialectic link between modernity and contemporary religious reconstructions.

At times I have taken a historian's approach in trying to situate events in their evolutive context. I have looked at the development of group identity before migration started and compared the migration experience of South Asians with that of earlier ethnic minorities.

The analytical structures and the methods used in my research work (especially in the fieldwork) have been taken from the field of social anthropology.

The difficulties I have experienced in defining this work within a specific branch of the social sciences bring to mind a quotation from Martine Hovanessian. She is a third-generation Armenian, and in her research on Armenians in France she claims to be an anthropologist; however, she comments on her position as an 'insider' researcher: 'the anthropologist who is close to his or her subjects is often unwilling to be caged within the rigidity of models and theories.'[51]

PART 1

FROM THE INDIAN SUBCONTINENT TO AMERICA

1

ISLAM IN THE INDIAN SUBCONTINENT

Historical dynamism and internal diversity

In this first chapter I shall present the most important Muslim groups in the Indian subcontinent, and their divisions along lines of sectarianism (Sunni, Twelver Shi'a, Nizari, Bohra and Ahmadiyya), and ideology (I shall focus on the most significant Sunni movements constituted from the nineteenth century in reaction to the decline of the Moghul empire and the domination of the British). This information will be crucial to understanding the life-style, the social and religious activities and the community identifications of South Asian Muslims in the United States, since this is a microcosm of the Muslim population of the subcontinent.

The Muslim ideal may describe the unity of the *umma*, but in reality the community is divided into ideological movements and different sects. In South Asia, Muslims are also characterized by such divisions, which flourish impressively. Some of these sects have a large representation in the Indian subcontinent: a quarter of the Shi'a in the world live here, and the Shi'a community itself is divided between Twelvers, Nizari and Bohra. Though the Indian Twelvers have not developed in markedly different ways from their co-religionists in Iran or Iraq, the Nizari and Bohra have really blossomed and come into their present identity in the Indian subcontinent. Some sects, such as the Ahmadiyya, are native to South Asia.

Before looking at each of these communities in detail, I would like to remind the reader that the major division within Islam is between, on the one hand, the Sunni who make up the great majority of Muslims in the Indian subcontinent and indeed in the world and, on the other hand, the Shi'a. In Indian Islam, there is a third separate category, the Ahmadiya.

The Sunni

The term Sunni is derived from the Arabic word *sunnah*, which means 'good custom', meaning that of the Prophet. Most Muslims in the world – and in the Indian subcontinent – are Sunni (85 to 90 per cent[1]). Sunni consider themselves to be the guardians of Muslim orthodoxy. Two issues distinguish them from other Muslim schools, in particular from the Shi'a: they recognize the validity of the first four caliphs, successors to the Prophet Muhammad in leading the *umma*, Abu Bakr, 'Umar, 'Uthman and 'Ali; they do not acknowledge the political or religious roles of the descendants of 'Ali, cousin and son-in-law to the Prophet.[2] They belong to one of the major schools of law (*madh'hab*): Hanafi, Maliki, Sha'fi'i and Hanbali. The religious practices of the Sunni will be examined in detail later.

Sunni in the Indian subcontinent are divided into three main bodies, which correspond to the main Islamic movements native to the region. The first of these includes two reformed movements, the second a non-reformed movement, and the third includes a political movement.

All three trace their origins to the eighteenth century, when the power of the Moghul empire began to fade as the British influence started to grow. Muslim reaction to these political stirrings started with the *ulama* (such as Shah Waliullah, 1703–62) and the Sufi. It was however in the middle of the next century, when the decline of the Muslims and the domination of the British both accelerated, after the Indian Mutiny in 1857, that Islamic movements began to emerge. They were to leave a lasting mark on the subcontinent (and on the South Asian diaspora).

These movements were in part created in reaction to the British presence (Deobandi and Barelwi[3] in the nineteenth century, Tablighi Jama'at – derived from the Deobandi – and Jama'at-i-Islami in the twentieth), and they have in common that they insist on the superiority and distinctiveness of Islam in comparison to other religions, especially Christianity, but also Hinduism. It is worth noting that during the same historical period the Hindus were engaged in a similar process of re-evaluation and redefinition of their beliefs and practices.

The Deobandi

The town of Deoband, north of Delhi, has been the home since 1867 of one of the major centres of religious teaching in the subcontinent. Founded by Muhammad Qasim Nanautawi (1833–77) and Rashid Ahmad Gangohi (1829–1905), this Islamic seminary brought together religious scholars who were conscious of the decline of the Indian Muslim community since the

British had gone into the ascendant. Using teaching methods borrowed from the British, the Deobandi banned from their syllabus the teaching of English and 'western' sciences, and taught instead the Qur'an, the Hadis and Islamic law and sciences. Urdu replaced Persian as the language of communication and of teaching.

The Deobandi movement drew its membership mainly from the Muslim elite of the day and was rooted in the tradition of some Sufi orders. It emphasized individual spiritual discipline, gained through the influence of a spiritual master, but was firmly opposed to any veneration of saints.[4]

The Tablighi Jama'at

Founded by Muhammad Ilyas (1885–1944) between 1925 and 1927, this movement and the Jama'at-i-Islami together make up the two largest Islamic organizations created in the twentieth century in South Asia.

Ilyas was a scholar (*alim*) and a Sufi, educated at Deoband, and he taught at the Deobandi seminary in Saharanpur. Wishing to continue his father's work he gave religious instruction to the Meo (Muslims in Mewat, south of Delhi), whose Islam was much influenced by Hinduism. However, as traditional teaching methods in the seminaries were not producing committed teachers, Ilyas resigned from his job in Saharanpur and began his missionary activity in Meo villages from 1925 onwards, after spending some time in Mecca and Medina. The structures of the nascent movement were defined between 1927 and 1934. Its main aim was to encourage Muslims to purify their religious practices and to create an Islamic environment.

As the devotee is supposed to concentrate entirely on deepening his faith, he is not permitted to engage in religious controversy or to discuss politics within activities organized by the movement.[5]

The Tablighi Jama'at grew under the leadership of Ilyas' son Muhammad Yusuf (1917–65), spreading not only through the subcontinent, but also to the rest of the world, and especially to North America.

The Barelwis or Ahl-i Sunnat wa Jama'at

The Barelwi movement, in contrast, embodies the popular version of Sufi tradition in the Indian subcontinent. In this sense it is an unreformed movement, and its name derives from its founder, Ahmad Riza Khan (1856–1921), born in Bareilly (Uttar Pradesh).

This movement is based on three founding principles: the importance attached to the Prophet Muhammad; the role of saints and spiritual masters as intercessors to God; and the celebration of popular festivals (in particular

Maulid, which commemorates the Prophet's birth). The Deobandi contest these principles strongly: they condemn the veneration of saints, but above all the near-divine status given by the Barelwi to the Prophet.[6]

The Barelwi are nevertheless well-entrenched in the subcontinent, as well as in England, where they engage in sometimes violent conflict with the Deobandi.[7]

The Jama'at-i-Islami

This movement was founded in 1941 by Abu'l A'la Mawdudi (1903–79). It embodies the prototype of the fundamentalist party, in the sense that it advocates a return to original Islamic doctrine. The party's ideology is in line with the tradition of the major international fundamentalist movements, in particular the Muslim Brotherhood, which indeed was inspired by the Jama'at-i-Islami in the formulation of its own philosophy.

Mawdudi, who began his career as a journalist, believed that Islam should regulate every aspect of a person's life. He was fiercely critical of the traditional *ulama*, saying that they went no further than a rigid reading of the scriptures. Most importantly, his extensive study of Islam brought him to a rejection of all Western ideologies.

The British presence in India led him to give a political dimension to his understanding of Islam. He eventually founded the Jama'at-i-Islami, a politico-religious party, made up of a disciplined elite trained according to the Mawdudian ideal. The party was to infiltrate the political and social spheres, the ultimate objective being the establishment of a divine order on Earth through an Islamic state.

It is difficult to evaluate the impact of the Jama'at-i-Islami on Pakistan: the party played a crucial role in the Islamization of the state (which however is only official and theoretical), especially in the periods of military rule – particularly under Zia ul-Haq (1979–88). It never succeeded, though, in attracting the support of large numbers among Pakistani society, and only ever achieved mediocre results in elections.

The Indian branch of the Jama'at-i-Islami (Jama'at-i-Islami Hind) developed its own philosophy in the light of the minority status of Muslims in a secular state with a Hindu majority. Its ideology is not very different from that of its Pakistani sister party, but it has adapted to the Indian context. After concentrating at first on defending the rights of the Muslim community in India, the Jama'at-i-Islami Hind has been preaching Islam since then, and encouraging social reform and spiritual renewal of the individual.

In Bangladesh there has been for some years a growth in fundamentalist movements, among them the local Jama'at-i-Islami. In 1977, when General

Zia ur-Rahman nominated himself as president (1975–81), the constitution was amended and religion reappeared in the official texts. In 1988 Islam became the state religion, and since then the Jama'at-i-Islami has repeatedly been among the coalition parties in power, and has had exercised influence on political decisions.

The Shi'a

Shi'a in the Indian subcontinent are divided into sects: the Twelver Shi'a on the one hand and the Isma'ili on the other, the latter being sub-divided into Nizari and Bohra.

Twelver Shi'a

The term 'Shi'a' means partisan, and comes from *shi'at 'Ali* or 'Party of Ali'. This was originally a handful of men who supported the claims of 'Ali, the cousin and son-in-law of the Prophet,[10] to be caliph, or successor to the Prophet. Historically, Shi'ism goes back to the period immediately following the death of the Prophet in 632. According to Shi'a tradition, Muhammad designated 'Ali to be his successor a few months before his death, but it was only in 656 that 'Ali became leader of the community. Shi'a do not accept the legitimacy of the three caliphs who preceded him.

Shi'a doctrine is based on the specific definition of the concept of the imam and his office: the legitimate political leader of the community must be a descendant of the Prophet. Among the Sunni, the imam or caliph can be drawn from a larger circle. Shi'a see a superhuman, even miraculous dimension in the function of the political and religious head of Islam.[12]

Twelvers (Ithna 'ashariyya), who form the majority of Shi'a, are called as such because they recognize the line of the twelfth imam, whereas the Isma'ili, also known as Seven-imam Shi'a, recognize the line of the seventh imam (see below). According to the Twelver Shi'a, the successor to the eleventh and the last manifested imam was his young son Muhammad, who disappeared when his father died and has been living 'in spiritual hiding' ever since.

There are few differences between the ritual practices of Sunni and Shi'a. Shi'a, when on pilgrimage to Mecca (*Hajj*), include a visit to the tombs of 'Ali at Najaf and of Husain (grandson of the Prophet) at Kerbala (*ziyara*) in Iraq. The month of Muharram, which marks the commemoration of the martyrdom of Husain in Kerbala, carries a particular significance and is the major festival celebrated by Shi'a.

More importantly, because of the events which defined the birth of the sect, the ethos of Shi'ism extols martyrdom and persecution. The fact that Husain's death is one of the central features of Shi'ism raises the emotional tone of the religion, and promotes a sense of guilt in its adherents which is foreign to Sunni Muslims. Husain's martyrdom also encourages the development of a sense of group identity, especially when Shi'a are in a minority. Their history has sometimes meant that Shi'a have had to practise *taqiyya*, or concealment of their faith, when the community is threatened. In these circumstances, they generally adopt Sunni rituals.

In India,[13] Twelver Shi'ism gradually settled in different areas, and was able to found Shi'a kingdoms in the Deccan (South India), where the influence of the Safavids of Iran was strongly felt as early as the sixteenth century.

It was in northern India, however, after the disintegration of the Moghul empire, that the Shi'a became a powerful minority. They founded a Shi'a state in 1722 in the principality of Awadh[14], between Delhi and Benares, with as its capital Lucknow (now the capital of Uttar Pradesh).

In the nineteenth century, Sunni and Shi'a in Lucknow lived together rather peaceably: mixed marriages were arranged, especially amongst the higher echelons of Muslim society; Shi'a and Sunni celebrated together the commemoration of the martyrdom of Husain. From the beginning of the twentieth century, though, extremist elements from both sides of the community began to engage in more and more violent confrontations.[15] The Muharram celebrations were declared non-Islamic by Sunni theologians because of the passions it aroused in the name of an event of the distant past.[16] The Shi'a also developed their own institutions in Lucknow: schools, cultural organizations, newspapers, and so on, all of which promoted a sense of separate Shi'a identity. New symbols of identification came up in the form of separate mosques and burial grounds. The gulf which opened up between the two major Muslim sects in the second half of the nineteenth century partly owed to the decline and impoverishment of the Shi'a aristocracy, whereas some Sunni groups were relatively prosperous. The British introduced a legal dimension to the divisions between Sunni and Shi'a (they policed conflicts, granted or refused permission for religious celebrations, regulated processions, etc.), and turned doctrinal differences into political ones.[17] Above all, this period coincided with a religious revival which was to tear Sunni from Shi'a but also Hindu from Muslim.[18]

In Pakistan, the number of Twelver Shi'a – the major group amongst Shi'a generally – is estimated at about 12 million, that is about 15 per cent of the total Muslim population. They are frequently the victims of sectarian violence. Since the mid 1980s, conflict with the Sunni community has reached alarming proportions, with hundreds of fatalities on both sides.[19]

Very much in the minority in Bangladesh, Shi'a represent in India less than 10 per cent of the total Muslim population.[20] They live mainly in the Deccan

and in even greater numbers in Lucknow where they maintain their own separate group identity within the Muslim community, with their own social and
religious institutions. They clearly favour marriages within their own community.[21] Violent conflict still occasionally opposes them to the Sunni community.
Apart from the Muharram celebrations, commemorating the Kerbala martyrdom, this hostility originates in the traditions of *madde sahaba* and *tabarru*: the
former is a Sunni tradition, a recitation declaimed to glorify the first three
caliphs after the Prophet Muhammad as the spiritual heads and temporal
leaders of the Muslim community; the second is Shi'a and takes the form of an
attack on the claims of these same three caliphs.

The tensions between Sunni and Shi'a in the subcontinent should not, however, be exaggerated. The Shi'a have certainly developed a distinct identity, but
they nevertheless include other communities (including the Sunni) in some of
their celebrations in some areas of South Asia, for example the Muharram processions in Hyderabad, in India.[22]

Nizari Isma'ili Shi'a, or Khoja

Isma'ilism, also known as Seven-imam Shi'ism, traces its origin to a debate
about the succession of Imam Ja'far al-Sadiq (died 765).

In terms of religious ideas, the doctrine of the Isma'ili seems very complex.
The imamate is accorded the highest importance (the imam's charisma is
hereditary); moreover, the outside, or exoteric character of the religion (*zahir*)
is contrasted with the interior, more esoteric reality (*batin*). *Zahir* is the apparent,
and generally accepted meaning of the revealed scriptures which ordain precepts and rituals, whereas *batin* describes the hidden, transcendent and
immutable truths which the true disciple is to discern beyond the written word,
the rites and the precepts. These truths are interpreted by the imam, a scholar
in hermeneutics, hence his high status.[23] In ritual, the symbolic meaning is
often elevated above the practice of the ritual itself.

Isma'ili missionaries from Fatimid Egypt settled in the Sind,[24] in north-west
India, from the tenth century, and converted many Hindus to their religion.[25]

Further schisms, arising out of the issue of succession, divided the Nizari
community. In the second half of the fifteenth century, two main groups
emerged: the Muhammad Shahi, whose succession of imams had been broken
about two centuries earlier, and the Qasim Shahi, forerunners of the present
Aga Khan.

The settlement in Bombay of the first Aga Khan marked the start of
modern Nizari Isma'ilism. After nearly seven centuries in Persia, the imamate
was moved to India, and Bombay became the seat of the Qasim Shahi
Nizari.

The second Aga Khan, who succeeded in 1881, established the basic principles of the political modernization of the Nizari community. The process
culminated during the long reign of the third Aga Khan (1885–1957).

Under the latter, socio-economic reforms were introduced to transform the
Nizari community into a modern self-sufficient society, highly educated, and
prosperous.[26] By means of numerous decrees (*firman*), usually read out in the
local *jama'at khana* (the place of worship of the Isma'ili), the Aga Khan encouraged his followers to innovate, to invest, and to pursue higher education. He
insisted that women should become educated and get a professional training,
and abolished the *purdah* system. After 1914, when he visited Burma for the
second time, he advocated that Nizarian should integrate into their host country, for example by abandoning Indo-Muslim names and style of clothing.[28]

The Khoja, or Nizari, a very enterprising community, chose to seek their for-
tune outside India, not only in neighbouring countries (Burma, Ceylon), but
also in eastern and southern Africa, as early as the seventeenth century. It
was, however, only in the nineteenth century that a few Khoja definitively settled in Africa.

The Isma'ili soon created a strong and prosperous community and in the
1960s there were no fewer than 50,000 in East Africa.[29] The Africanization
policy of Kenya, and especially Uganda, in the late 1960s and early 1970s,
though, led to the expulsion of the Khojas and of other Indians – mainly
Gujaratis – who had to seek refuge elsewhere, notably in America.[31]

During his two visits to his followers in eastern Africa, in 1899 and 1905, the
third Aga Khan formulated some principles and established a certain number
of rules and laws. He encouraged them to give up the 'Indian' features of
their religion, in other words those which came from Hindu influence, and to
bring their practices into line with those of other Muslims, nevertheless maintaining their Isma'ili identity. He also urged them, as he had already done for
the Isma'ili in Burma, to abandon social and cultural traditions taken from
India, and instead to integrate themselves as much as possible into the host
culture.

In effect, this led to a westernization rather than an Africanization of the
Nizari community. The Aga Khan, however, continued to exhort his followers
to maintain their religious identity. The first *jama'at khana*, true centre of the
spiritual life of Isma'ili, was built in Zanzibar as early as the first half of the
nineteenth century.

There are at present about 20 million Isma'ili across more than 25 countries;
Pakistan, home to nearly 2 million of them, now has one of the largest Khoja
communities in the world.

Musta'li Isma'ili Shi'a, or Bohra

In 1094 a division branched out from the Nizari, giving birth to the musta'li Isma'ili. In 1130, there was a new split within the musta'li Isma'ili, between Tayyibi and Hafizi. The former became the 'Bohra'.[34]

The Tayyibi, who settled originally in Yemen, have preserved many of the traditions of the Fatimid Isma'ili. They accord the same value to the *zahir* (exoteric) and *batin* (esoteric) dimensions of the religion. However, certain new features have given this branch of Isma'ili Islam its distinct character, for example the doctrine of cosmology and the system of the Ten Intellects, among others.[35]

It was in 1067 that the first Isma'ili *Da'i*, or 'propagandist', Abdallah, arrived in India. The Hindus who converted became known as Bohra.[37]

When the 25th *Da'i mutlaq* ('absolute propagandist', or 'supreme head'; spiritual leader of the Isma'ili Bohra), Jalal, came to power, this marked the end of the Yemeni phase of the sect and the start of its leaders' settlement into India.

After the death of the 26th *Da'i mutlaq*, Da'ud (1567–91)[38], the question of his succession caused a conflict which generated a schism in the Bohra community. Da'ud Burhanuddin[39] (1591–1612) was enthroned as *Da'i* in India; the Bohra in Yemen were informed. Four years later, Sulayman, grandson of the 24th *Da'i* and 'vice- *Da'i*' of Da'ud, claimed the succession himself and returned to India to assert his rights. The great majority of Bohra, and a fraction of the Tayyibi Isma'ili of Yemen, accepted Da'ud Burhanuddin as the 27th *Da'i mutlaq* and were then called the Da'udi. A minority, mainly composed of Yemenis, together with a few Indian Bohra, accepted Sulayman as their spiritual leader and were from then on known as Sulaymani.[40]

According to recent estimates, the Da'udi population of the world is about 500,000, of whom four-fifths live in India. Other Bohra live in some 30 other countries, and the majority of non-Indian Bohra live in Pakistan (33,000).

As with the Khoja Nizari, the Bohra were among the first Asian immigrants in Africa. In that continent they developed in a similar way to the Nizarian. They emigrated for identical reasons, and grew equally prosperous. They also suffered the same political fate as the Khoja at the policy of Africanization. From the start, they created ethnic enclaves where they both lived and maintained their social and cultural customs.

The religious practices of Bohra are akin to those of other Muslims, especially of the Shi'a. They observe the Five Pillars of Islam, adding two more: submission to the 'hidden imam' (*walaya*) and a strict duty of purity (*tahara*) which entails the wearing of special clothes for prayer.[42]

When it comes to canonical taxes, in addition to *zakat* Bohra pay a certain number of compulsory taxes and dues, some Islamic in nature (*khums*, also payed by other Shi'a, and *fitra*), and others specifically for the Bohra community and the family of the *Da'i* (*haqq al-nafs, sila, nazar muqam, salam*). Since the end of the 1970s, the *Da'i* has raised the amount of the taxes due by the community.[43]

The Da'udi system is based on the model developed during the Yemeni phase of Tayyibi Isma'ilism. The *Da'i mutlaq*, unique representative of the hidden imam, claims on the strength of this all privileges due to him. He exercises total power over the community and governs autocratically. Recalcitrants are excommunicated, which means that they are not only forbidden to enter all places of worship, whether mosque or sanctuary, and lose access to all cultural practices such as marriage or burial, but they are also excluded both socially and professionally.

The current *Da'i*, Muhammad Burhanuddin, who was enthroned in 1965, in 1983 banned *riba'* (lending on interest) which is indeed prohibited within Islam. The *Da'i* ordered all Bohra bankers and bank employees to leave their jobs, or else face social exclusion. He also ordered the carrying of identity cards in three colours: green, yellow and red. The green card is awarded to those who rigorously obey all the *Da'i*'s injunctions and regularly pay their taxes. Holders of this card have access to all religious shrines and are entitled to all benefits (permission to marry and marriage ceremonies, burials and so on). The yellow card is given to those who are not completely compliant with the *Da'i*'s orders and do not pay all their taxes, or pay irregularly. Those who carry this card are objects of suspicion and are carefully watched. Holders of the red card are people who defy several of the *Da'i*'s injunctions and refuse to pay their taxes. They are not forbidden to enter religious shrines but they have no right to other benefits and are reduced to social pariahs. Finally, there are some Bohra who do not hold any card. They are forbidden to enter any mosques, mausoleums or other *jama'at khana*.[45]

Reformist groups have been formed in protest but they have not met with much success to date. The movement has spread beyond the subcontinent (to East Africa, England, Canada and elsewhere), where the Bohra populations are also under the authority of the *Da'i* and his local representatives. We shall examine later how this applies in the United States.

The Ahmaddiyya

Alongside the Sunni and Shi'a, a third strand of Islam has emerged in South Asia. This sect is similar to Sunni Islam but presents certain characteristics which put it in its own category. The eponymous Mirza Ghulam Ahmad (1838?–1908), certain he had a spiritual mission, founded the Ahmadi movement in 1889 in the Punjab.

Prophetology lies at the heart of Ahmadi doctrine, and is also the main cause of hostility from its opponents. Ghulam Ahmad reckoned that he possessed the spiritual qualities required of a Prophet and considered himself to be one. This allegation contradicted sura 33:40, which calls Muhammad the 'seal of the prophets' (*khatam al-anbiya'*), and it has therefore been opposed by the Sunni from the start.

The religious thinking of the Ahmadi differs slightly from orthodox Islamic thought but, unlike the Nizari and the Bohra, they have not introduced any innovation in terms of religious practices. They continue to follow the Hanafi rite.

The movement being well-established in the Punjab, the Ahmadiyya[46] became part of Pakistan after partition. Since the 1950s they have been attacked by 'orthodox' Muslims. In 1974 they were declared in an amendment to the constitution to be non-Muslim, and since then they have been seen as a minority, and regularly persecuted. Their leader, Hazrat Mirza Tahir Ahmad, who bears the official title *Khalifatul Massih IV* ('caliph or lieutenant to the Messiah'), has taken refuge in London, from where he continues to lead the community.

Ahmadi Muslims are famous throughout the world because of the persecution they have suffered for so many years but in fact they have also gained a reputation as keen proselytizers in many countries. This started in 1901 when Ghulam Ahmad founded an English-language monthly journal, entitled *Review of Religions*,[47] so as to propagate his teaching in the West. England was the main target of the Ahmadi missionaries.[49] In 1912 the first Ahmadi mosque outside the Indian subcontinent was opened in Woking. According to the *Review of Religions*, there were 2,000 converts in England during the first decade of the twentieth century.[50]

Ahmadi activity in other European countries began after the Second World War. The first mission in France was established in 1946.[51]

The American continent was not neglected either. In fact the Ahmadiyya consider that the very first convert to Ahmadi Islam, in the 1880s, was an American called Alexander Russell Webb. Having been disappointed by Christianity, he started to study different religions and entered into correspondence with Ghulam Ahmad. According to the Ahmadiyya, following this correspondence and a trip to India in 1892, Webb converted to Islam and took part in the spread of Islam in the United States.[52] Other sources claim however that Sunni Muslims were responsible for Webb's conversion.[53]

The first Ahmadi missionary, Mufti Muhammad Sadiq, a graduate of the University of London, was officially commissioned to go to the United States in February 1920.[54] On the ship to America, he apparently converted six passengers.[55] The American authorities at first refused him entry into the United States; he was then allowed in but imprisoned in a Philadelphia detention centre because he was accused of preaching a religion which allowed polygamy. He was released after he undertook not to say anything on that sub-ject.[56] This stay in prison was 'fruitful', in that he was said to have made another 20 converts in two months.

Once out of prison, Sadiq settled at first in New York where he threw him-self into preaching. Not long after he moved to Highland Park, near Detroit, Michigan, and in July 1921 he founded a periodical, *Moslem Sunrise* (which was renamed *Muslim Sunrise* in 1950).

Sadiq came up against the Sunni, who were already established in Highland Park,[57] when it became clear to them that this Ahmadi missionary was not preaching orthodox Islam, or at least not according to Sunni doctrine.

This conflict forced Sadiq to move again in 1922, this time to Chicago. The city became the official seat of the American Ahmadi movement. It was also the place chosen by the followers of Ghulam Ahmad for the building of their first mosque, at 4448 Wabash Avenue.[58]

From the first, Ahmadi missionaries aimed their conversion efforts not only at Muslim immigrants but also at Americans, both black and white. Some Muslim immigrants who arrived leaderless turned to the Ahmadi missionaries in the hope of developing a better understanding of their faith. But it was in the African–American community that the Ahmadiyya met with the greatest success. The highest number of converts to Islam in the centre and the west of the United States were in this community.

The denounciation of racism towards African Americans by Ahmadi mis-sionaries was received favourably by the black community. Moreover, Ahmadi Islam allowed African–Americans to move into positions of leadership.

Between 1921 and 1924, more than one thousand converts joined Islam through Ghulam Ahmad's followers.[59] In the light of this success, further mis-sionaries were sent to Chicago in 1923, 1925 and 1928, to assist Sadiq in his work, and the movement spread to other American cities. In 1933 there were Ahmadi centres in Pittsburgh, Cincinnatti, Indianapolis, Detroit and Kansas City. The following decade saw similar establishments set up in New York, Saint Louis (Missouri), Dayton (Ohio), Washington, DC, Philadelphia, Teaneck (New Jersey), Waukegan (Illinois) and Baltimore (Maryland).[60]

The 1960s gave the movement a new opportunity to affirm its belief in racial equality. The Ahmadiyya fell in beside African–Americans in their strug-gle. Islam was brandished as the only religion sincerely to advocate the abolishing of ethnic and racial barriers.[61]

Today the Ahmadi movement claims some 10 million adherents[62] in 135 countries.[63] According to Yvonne Haddad[64] they have built more than 500 mosques throughout the world but the movement's own estimate is 3,000.[65]

2

ECONOMIC AND
DEMOGRAPHIC PROFILE

Growth and prosperity

A brief history: the California pioneers (1898–1965)

The presence of Muslims from the Indian subcontinent in the United States goes back to the beginning of the twentieth century. Muslims from other parts of the world had already travelled to America. According to some authors, the first Muslims arrived with the Spanish explorers. The person most widely recognized to be the first Muslim was a certain Estevanico who arrived with Marcos de Niza in 1539 to explore Arizona.[1] After him, there were Muslims amongst black slaves arriving in the country.

In the first half of the nineteenth century, a camel driver is recorded, called Hajj Ali, and known as Hi Holly. But it was not until the second half of the nineteenth century that Muslims from Europe and the Middle East began to arrive in a more systematic way.[2] They were joined a few decades later by their co-religionists from South Asia.

The South Asian Muslims arrived mostly from the Punjab, together with a small number of Pathans, to the west coast of America. This initial Punjabi wave of immigrants comprised about 85–90 per cent Sikhs, 8–10 per cent Muslims and a very small percentage of Hindus. They came mainly for economic reasons: a demographic explosion, a shortage of land, drought and epidemics had combined to weaken and ruin a number of Punjabis at the end of the nineteenth century.[3] Most of these immigrants were illiterate young peasants, unmarried (those who were married left their wives at home), and from average income families – richer folk did not need to emigrate and the poor did not have the means to buy a passage.

They were received with marked hostility in America, especially in industry, where the white workers were trying to improve their own work conditions and were under the influence of the nativist movement. The arrival of the Indian workers further increased tension in an atmosphere already violently anti-Asian, vis-à-vis Chinese immigrants in particular, whom white workers accused of disloyal competition when they accepted lower wages.

Between 1909 and 1917 a fierce campaign was led by the Asian Exclusion League (AEL),[4] which was made up chiefly of trade unionists, to deport Asians, including Indians (of whom there were still only about 6,000 in 1917).

These campaigners obtained satisfaction in 1917 when the 1917 Immigration Law was adopted, putting an end to immigration from most Asian countries. Discriminatory measures against Indians increased dramatically: between 1917 and 1924, they were excluded not only from immigration but also from naturalization procedures, and from land ownership rights. They were also persecuted for their political activities[5] and threatened with deportation.

It was not until the 1940s that the situation improved. In July 1946 an immigration law was adopted which gave Indians an annual quota of 100 entrants and the right to obtain American citizenship. These measures were confirmed in the MacCarran Walter law of 1952. And yet it was not until 1965 (when American immigration law was liberalized) that South Asians began to arrive in the United States in significant numbers. The flow has never slowed down since then.

Demographic profile of the immigrant community

As with all religious communities, especially recent ones, it is extremely difficult to establish reliably the numbers of Muslims from the Indian subcontinent in the United States. In its ten-yearly census, the United States administration does not enquire about religious affiliation. It was not until 1957 that the question was asked, in the context of a spot check by the census authorities, to a sample of the American population. This enquiry allowed one to estimate the numerical size of certain religious minorities, and especially of the Jewish community.[6] At that date, however, South Asian immigration was not yet significant.

Since 1980 there has been a specific category of 'Asian Indian' in the census classification, but Pakistani and Bangladeshi immigrants are still classified as 'other'. As Pakistan did not exist before 1947 or Bangladesh before 1971, immigrants born before these dates, especially those who did not arrive directly from those countries, can find it difficult to define themselves. As far as Indian Muslims are concerned, the figures available apply to the whole Indian population and rarely allow one to distinguish between the different religious sub-groups.

Some immigrants, moreover, arrived via East Africa, Guyana, England or Canada; the census asks about the country of origin of one's ancestors: some of those whose parents were born in the places named above (especially the first two), will tend to name these countries as their country of origin.

Illegal immigrants introduce yet another difficulty into the calculations.

Lastly, some cases are especially complicated because of political events in the Indian subcontinent. Some Kashmiri Muslims, for example, refuse to give either India or Pakistan as their country of origin and prefer to write 'Kashmir' or 'other'.

Muslims from the Indian subcontinent themselves seek to establish accurate numbers, but they tend, as do all ethnic groups, to inflate the numbers in order to magnify their political importance and to help their access to social funds.

The figures given below must therefore be seen as including a relatively large margin for error.

Demographic evolution

It would appear that in 1980,[7] in the whole United States, there were about 25,000 Indian Muslims, 50,000 in 1985[8] and 80,000[9] (150,000 according to community leaders) in 1990, as opposed in those years to 387,223, 525,000 and 815,447[10] Indians, all religious affiliations taken together. The Pakistani population was officially 40,000 in 1980, 75,000 in 1985 and 93,663 in 1990 (but according to an estimate by Arif Ghayur it reached 135,837 in 1990;[11] the Pakistani embassy estimates are between 200,000 and 400,000, which from my own observations seems highly plausible). Bangladeshis are still fewer in number: the only figure available is 11,838 in 1990.[12] The numbers of Bangladeshis have probably also been under-estimated by the census authorities. According to the Bangladeshi leadership in New York,[13] there are nearly 60,000 Bangladeshis in New York alone (though this figure seems rather high). Total figures would therefore be between 185,501 and 227,675, or indeed far more if one takes account – even with reservations – of the estimates by community leaders.

Table A South Asian population of New York and the United States

	New York City	*New York State*	*United States*
Indians	94,590	140,985	815,562
Pakistanis	13,501	17,778	93,663
Bangladeshis	4,955	5,406	11,838
Total	113,046	164,169	921,063

Source: 1990 Census of Population

Uncertainty and imprecision are increased if one seeks to establish numbers of Indians from the subcontinent within the total Muslim population, which is estimated at about 6 million at present.

According to Carol Stone, immigrants from Asia make up 11.5 per cent of the total number of Muslims living in the United States[14] as opposed to 30.2 per cent African–Americans and 28.4 per cent Arabs. However, according to the American Muslim Council (AMC), a political organization based in Washington, immigrants from South Asia alone make up 24.4 per cent of the total Muslim population, as against 42 per cent of African–Americans and only 12.4 per cent Arabs.[15]

Whatever the estimates, it appears that the South Asian group is one of the most rapidly expanding ethnic populations. It is confined to a relatively small number of states: California, New York State, New Jersey and Illinois.

New York City has the highest concentration of Indians and probably of South Asians of all the urban centres in the United States.[16] Most are grouped in the five boroughs of the city: Manhattan, Queens, Brooklyn, the Bronx and Staten Island. Long Island also has significant numbers, in particular Nassau County.

Table B South Asian population by borough

	Queens	*Manhattan*	*Brooklyn*	*Bronx*	*Staten Island*
Indians	55,601	7,395	15,641	11,051	3,902
Pakistanis	6,449	870	4,949	847	386
Bangladeshis	2,567	473	1,313	582	20
Total	65,671	8,738	21,903	12,480	4,308

Source: 1990 Census of Population

Table C South Asian population in Nassau County

	Nassau County
Indians	11,875
Pakistanis	1,123
Bangladeshis	135
Total	13,133

Source: 1990 Census of Population

It is obviously not easy to determine the exact number of South Asian Muslims in New York. I have made my calculations by adding 10 per cent[17] of the Indian population of New York, i.e. 94,590 individuals, to the total number of Pakistanis (13,501) and Bangladeshis (4,955), as given in the 1990 census. This gives a total of 27,915, so about 30,000 people. Censuses often tend to under-estimate, and immigration, both legal and illegal, has continued regularly since 1990, so the present figure can be estimated to be between 50,000 and 80,000 people.

The majority of South Asian Muslims have chosen to live in Queens, in particular in the Jackson Heights, Corona, Flushing, Jamaica, Elmhurst, Rego Park, Forest Hills and Richmond Hill neighbourhoods.

There are also a relatively high number in Brooklyn, especially Pakistanis, who have gathered in Coney Island. The Bronx also has a small proportion of South Asians. Manhattan attracts far fewer South Asians, apart from Bangladeshis who have formed a little enclave in 6th Street, between First and Third Avenue. Bangladeshis are also found in Queens, in the Astoria area, in relatively high numbers. An area at the intersection of 26th Street and Lexington Avenue, sometimes called 'Little India', has a certain number of South Asian restaurants, grocery shops and shops with eclectic merchandise (household appliances, audio and video cassettes, ethnic newspapers and so on). Few South Asians have chosen to live there, however. Staten Island has on the whole few foreigners, and the South Asian immigrant population is not high. Lastly, Long Island, located in the east part of New York and made up of a collection of residential areas and suburbs, has attracted a growing number of South Asians.

Ethnic origin of the immigrant population

Muslims from India in the United States are largely from Hyderabad: after the collapse of the princely state in 1948, one part of the Muslim elite emigrated to Pakistan, then to the Middle East and to England, and then on to North America. The next largest group is made up of Gujaratis, and in this group also not all of them have arrived directly from India: a significant number, principally the Nizari and Bohra, lived first in East Africa.[18]

In New York, as in the rest of the United States, there are also Muslims from Uttar Pradesh (in particular from Lucknow and Aligarh), from Maharashtra (especially Bombay), from Assam, Bengal, Bihar, Kashmir and Tamil Nadu.[19] Muslims from Kerala, where they make up 20 per cent of the population, are however not highly represented, as they have in the main emigrated to the Gulf.

Pakistani immigrants mainly come from the large cities (Lahore, Karachi, Rawalpindi, Faisalabad, Hyderabad and Peshawar). The majority are Punjabi (50 per cent) and Muhajir – these are Indian Muslims who left India for Pakistan after Partition, and their descendants – (30 per cent), although the latter represent only 8 per cent of the population in Pakistan (as opposed to 56 per cent Punjabis). The Sindhis, Pathans and Baluchis, being less urbanized and not as highly educated, are correspondingly under-represented.[20]

The Bangladeshia finally, are mostly from the metropolitan areas such as Dacca and Chittagong. Recently, some Sylhetis (who have a long tradition of emigration) have swelled the size of the Bangladeshi population (though I have no exact figures).

Migration flows: the search for El Dorado

South Asian Muslims have moved to the United States for a variety of reasons. Most were drawn by the exceptional opportunities in terms of work and research conditions, and by the remuneration offered by the Americans in the fields of education and employment. The late 1960s and early 1970s were marked by a lack of highly-qualified personnel, especially doctors, because of the Vietnam war and a poor distribution of doctors within the health system. Doctors tended to leave the city centres and move to the more comfortable sub-urbs to open private clinics; as a consequence, the city centre hospitals were left under-staffed.[21] In India, on the other hand, young graduates were facing chronic unemployment because the government was incapable of coordinat-ing its education and recruitment systems, and indeed did little to halt the brain drain.

Besides, the Indian government has adopted a policy of positive discrimi-nation, a preferential treatment (called 'affirmative action' in the United States, where it is also applied) which confers advantages in both education and employment on the lower social classes. The effect of this policy has been to encourage the emigration of members of the higher castes and of Muslims from the elite. Bureaucracy, favouritism and nepotism, rife in India, Pakistan and Bangladesh alike, play a non-negligible part in appointments and promo-tion. Frustrated young graduates are all the more likely to emigrate.

Social and cultural factors also contibute to these motivations: emigration is linked to ideas of prestige, and is seen as raising the social status of a family. It is encouraged by the reports of those already settled in the United States. American novels, but above all films and TV series, now accessible to all, can also increase the desire to emigrate, especially among the young. As noted by Arthur and Usha Helweg, emigration can be seen by some as a goal in itself as they become persuaded that to go abroad and work there is the *nec plus ultra* of success. The potential emigrant and his family will exaggerate the advantages of emigration and will develop unrealistic expectations of it.[22] As a result, in the last few years a distinct culture of emigration has developed in India, in which purely professional motives have become almost secondary.

It is worth noting that women can in some cases play a key role in a couple's decision to emigrate, as they hope to escape the influence of their husband's family.

Political considerations can also be a significant part of the equation. In India, many Hyderabadis were strongly tempted to emigrate after the collapse of the princely state in 1948. The current situation in Kashmir, where Kashmiri separatists and the Indian army are engaged in a violent conflict, is a ground for emigration. Other Muslims, faced by the rise of extremist Hindu parties such as the BJP, which came to power in India in February 1998, are also looking to emigration to escape an uncertain future in India. This last factor, however, is not the main reason for Indian Muslims to move to the United States.

In Pakistan, the Ahmadiyya, who were declared non-Muslim by Zulfikar Ali Bhutto's government in 1974, tend to emigrate in large numbers, especially to the United States. Some have been successful in obtaining political asylum.[23] Other Pakistanis left their country during periods of military rule. Karachi has been torn apart for several years by the violence between the Muhajir and Sindhi communities, and between rival factions within the Muhajir community. The Sindhi, from a kind of 'majority complex' – a term often used to describe the relationship between Hindus and Muslims in India, and in particular the feelings of the Hindus vis-à-vis the Muslim minority[24] – are attempting to reduce the monopoly of political and economic influence exercised by the Muhajir population on the city of Karachi. This violence has encouraged a number of the Muhajirs to emigrate, either to the Gulf or to North America. The Sindhi people, as we have seen, are mostly peasant in origin and rarely emigrate.

As for the Bangladeshis, some were drawn during the 1971 civil war to emigrate to the United States, and when economic conditions and the demographic explosion made life less certain, they made the move.

Return migration: a myth

Return migrations do happen, but there are few in the light of the numbers of students and immigrants whose plan was to move to the United States to pursue their studies, to earn some money, and then to return to their homeland. The longing to return, often called 'the myth of return'[25] is alive and well entrenched in the minds of immigrants who often discuss it, but decide to stay or postpone indefinitely their return to India, Pakistan or Bangladesh. The classic situation is the following: during the first three or four years of their stay in the United States, immigrants talk seriously about returning. Then follows a settling period which appears to be indefinite. The problem then surfaces again when retirement approaches. South Asian immigrants on the whole have not yet reached retirement age, so it is too early to know whether they will opt to stay in the United States or to return to South Asia.

A number of reasons explain the decision of students and immigrants to stay in the United States. Some are linked to the very causes of emigration: better job and career opportunities in the United States, higher earnings. In addition there is a higher standard of living, to which they become accustomed, and which is not easy to attain in the subcontinent. The arrival of children becomes another reason: parents wish to give them the opportunity to receive the best possible education in good American schools. The presence of the children in itself offsets the emotional void and sadness of being apart from family. In addition, some succeed in bringing to the United States their entire close family and even more distant relatives. The structure of the family in the homeland is therefore recreated and the desire to leave is further reduced.

More over, South Asian immigrants are increasingly offered the means to satisfy their cultural needs, especially in large American cities like New York (for example in the area between Roosevelt Avenue and 74th Street at Jackson Heights): *desi* food is available in a growing number of groceries and restaurants; clothing shops stock saris and *shalwar kameez*[26] in the latest Delhi and Karachi styles; there are many concerts of ethnic music, and tours by famous South Asian musicians; the latest commercial Hindi films are shown in at least four cinemas in New York, and the Bollywood stars regularly come on tour to visit.

There are also psychological reasons for staying out. To return to India can be perceived by family and friends in India as a failure on the part of the immigrant: he did not succeed in America so he has had to go home. When the immigrant really does face failure in the United States, it can happen that he does not dare to return home for fear of losing face. This can sometimes have serious consequences: psychological problems can in extreme cases lead the disappointed immigrant to suicide.

Some immigrants do nevertheless decide to return to India, Pakistan or Bangladesh, but the country they encounter does not necessarily match up to the image they had been treasuring: places may have changed, relatives may have died, childhood friends may have moved away, and social or political life may have developed in ways not necessarily to their liking. This can result in strong feelings of disappointment. It is only to be expected that on returning to the subcontinent various types of problems will have to be faced (corruption, pollution, shortage of water, power failures and so on) but it is the scale of these problems which can be hard to take. They also had become used in the United States, women in particular, to a certain level of intimacy and independence, which must now be abandoned in the homeland. They can easily become disenchanted, and decide to make the journey back again to the United States.

A few South Asians have nevertheless made the choice to return to their homeland for good. However, the 'ex-expatriates' generally draw attention to themselves by a rather ostentatious life-style, and do not make themselves popular among the local population. Arthur and Usha Helweg have observed that in some way they constitute their own distinct 'ethnic' group. From the professional point of view, they are considerably advantaged by having foreign qualifications (American ones are particularly highly prized). Some employers, though, hesitate to employ ex-immigrants, as they can be very demanding: they complain about work conditions, ask for higher salaries than their colleagues and so on. South Asian employers also fear (or they use this as an excuse) that the ex-immigrants will have lost touch with the reality of the work-place in India, Pakistan or Bangladesh.[27]

The situation described above is primarily that of non-Indian Muslims, Pakistanis (except the Ahmadiyya, who will be unlikely to return to Pakistan as long as they continue to be persecuted) and Bangladeshis. Indian Muslims are a particular case: the fact that they are in the minority in India, and the political context there, may not have been the chief reason for emigration to the United States, but these two factors combine to make it very unlikely that they will wish to return.

Marriage and divorce

In terms of marriage, one of the two following situations generally applies: either an immigrant is already married when he arrives in the United States, in which case he will work for a few months, indeed for a few years, and once he is reasonably settled he will arrange for his wife and any children to join him; or if he is unmarried, he will in time return to his homeland to marry a woman from the same ethnic group and religion.

Marriage is often a relief from the solitude suffered by some students and immigrants living alone in the United States. In the 1960s and 1970s, there was a 'shortage' of South Asian women, and men often asked their families to arrange a marriage for them. Nowadays the number of women in the United States of South Asian origin has significantly increased but as they are mostly second-generation, born in the United States, newly-arrived students and immigrants reject them as too 'americanized', and prefer to return to India, Pakistan or Bangladesh to find a bride.

When a woman is the first to emigrate (as yet a fairly unusual scenario) she causes her husband to join her. Such couples rarely have children, as it is most rare that a South Asian woman will leave her children for an extended time to pursue a career. If she is unmarried, she becomes highly prized as a possible marriage partner, even if she comes from a lower social class in India. Matrimonial advertisements demonstrate that being an American citizen or having a green card is a considerable asset for a woman wishing to get married. The famous green card can even be a substitute for a dowry, which still take enormous proportions[28] in the South Asian urban middle classes.

In the first generation, mixed marriages are therefore an exception. South Asians who have emigrated to the United States to study are more willing to contemplate them but this remains largely theoretical. In reality, although some do develop intimate relationships with members of different ethnic or religious groups, most – either voluntarily or under pressure from the family – return to India, Pakistan or Bangladesh to get married.

Divorce figures remain very low in the South Asian population: it is about 2–3 per cent in New York.

These figures are rising, however. Personal factors aside, immigration itself can be the reason a marriage fails. When an immigrant, especially if he is a student, has spent a number of years in the United States and marries a less well educated woman from India, Pakistan or Bangladesh, she can find herself at a disadvantage in comparison to him, and disappoint the husband's expectations. The marriage can be ended if the husband feels that his wife is unable to adapt to the American lifestyle. This situation is in no way unusual – it has been the experience of migrating minorities throughout history. Anka Muhlstein writes of immigrants to New York in the early twentieth century:

> The freedom they [the immigrants] discovered had implications for family relationships. The father, who arrived as a trailblazer, was often humiliated when his wife, with her retrograde ways, came to join him.[29]

Divorce can be requested by the wife for identical reasons: she prefers to return to her homeland if she cannot accustom herself to American life. John Y Fenton's research in Atlanta, published in 1988, shows that the great majority of divorces happen in the first five years of immigration.[30]

Economic profile of the immigrants

Qualifications and professions

It is worth pointing out to start with that there is a dichotomy in economic terms between the immigration waves. Those who arrived in the 1980s and

1990s are generally less well qualified than their predecessors in the 1960s and 1970s. They have arrived under category number two (wives or unmarried children of permanent residents) or five (brothers or sisters of United States citizens, together with their wives/husbands and children) of the immigration quotas laid down in the 1965 act; therefore they have not had to meet educational or professional requirements for immigration.

South Asian Muslims who emigrated to the United States in the 1960s and 1970s were mainly professionals, especially doctors and engineers, as well as scientists, teachers and businessmen.

South Asian physicians have succeeded particularly well in the United States. Some have even attained highly responsible positions. One of these is Faroque Ahmad Khan. Originally from Kashmir, he arrived in the United States in 1966 for an internship at Queens Hospital Center. He has been in New York ever since. He lived at first in Queens, then moved to a residential suburb on Long Island when his financial situation improved. He lives there today with his family. A specialist in pneumology and internal medicine, he has been president of the department of internal medicine at Nassau County Medical Center on Long Island since 1987, and manages 200 employees, of whom 150 are doctors. He is also professor of medicine at Stony Brook (New York University) where he was voted teacher of the year four times between 1980 and 1995. Since 1992 he has been President of the ACP–IMG (American College of Physicians–International Medical Graduates) in New York. This committee meets the needs of some 120,000 overseas medical graduates. The American College of Physicians gave Faroque Khan an award in 1993 for his services to the medical profession. In 1995 he was voted for three years onto the Board of Regents (management board) of the ACP. It was the first time an IMG had been in this position. In 1996 an American institution carried out a poll to establish a list of the best doctors in the United States. Faroque Khan was on the list (as were 31 other South Asians in New York State alone[31]). Lastly, he has been president of the Islamic Medical Association of North America (IMANA) and of the American Council of International Physicians. His wife, Arfa Khan, is also a doctor: she is head of the radiology service in the Long Island Jewish Medical Center at New Hyde Park and professor of radiology at the Albert Einstein faculty of medicine in the Bronx. The couple say they have succeeded by their own efforts but that the American system gave them the opportunities they needed.

Most Indians have arrived in the United States with university degrees (75 per cent), and continued to study on arrival to obtain American qualifications (68 per cent).[32] Among Pakistanis, in 1971 82.6 per cent of arrivals were professionals and technicians, others were teachers, scientists and businessmen.[33]

Although most of the South Asians who have emigrated for educational and professional reasons are men, the women are also educated, if not to quite the same degree as the men. There are, however, a good number of families in the United States where both spouses are professionals.

Using New York as an example, immigrants from the Indian subcontinent are markedly more highly educated than the average among Americans. According to the 1990 census, 65.7 per cent of Indian men and 47.9 per cent of Indian women over 25 (of all religious affiliations) had at the time a qualification of at least degree level, as against 26.2 per cent of men and 20.5 per cent of women in the population of New York as a whole.[34]

In addition to this educational asset, South Asians have a linguistic advantage as well. In 1990, only 24 per cent[35] of the Indians in New York had little or no English, compared to 48.2 per cent of the total Asian population.[36]

In terms of employment, 35.5 per cent of the active male Indian population in New York[37] in 1990 was in the professional and senior management category; 35.1 per cent were in technical or administrative positions, and 6 per cent were in the secondary sector. The corresponding figures for the New York population as a whole are 30 per cent, 33.1 per cent, and 9.42 per cent respectively.[38] Among the female Indian population, the percentage of professionals and senior managers is 35.3 per cent, in administration there are 41.3 per cent and in the secondary sector 1.5 per cent. The corresponding city-wide figures are 31.3 per cent, 44 per cent and 1.8 per cent.[39]

Pakistanis, and to a lesser extent Bangladeshis, may not have succeeded as well as the Indians (they arrived later), but they nevertheless occupy fairly similar positions, and are particularly noteworthy for their success in scientific occupations.

Altogether, the high standard of education – modelled on the British system – achieved by the South Asian Muslims, their good English, their exposure to Western values and their upper middle class origins all combine to equip them to structurally integrate into American society.

A tendency to diversify: 'ethnic business'

In spite of their achievements, the economic profile of the Indian subcontinental community in New York has altered over the years, as immigrants have not always been able to find work commensurate with their qualifications, except for doctors.

This is particularly the case with scientists, managerial staff and administrators, who have often seen their level of responsibilities decrease after emigration. And yet these are the people who have left their homeland not to escape poverty but to raise their social status. Some have moved into areas they thought more lucrative: in other words they have gone into business.

This diversification in occupation is also explained by work-place discrimination. Generally, immigrants do not face major difficulty in finding a job but they find that hurdles arise when there is a possibility of promotion. South Asian immigrants, and all Asians, are indeed proportionally under-represented in positions of leadership and decision-making. This leads to frustration, especially as those who arrived as students have had to work harder and gain more qualifications than (white) Americans in order to obtain the same kind of work.

A certain number of South Asians, professionals and those arrived in the more recent immigration waves, have therefore decided to go into other forms of employment: insurance, banking, restaurants, hotels, travel agency and small retail (especially groceries, 'ethnic' goods, audio and video cassettes of music and films from the subcontinent and so on).

Those who were formerly professionals have two assets: they have a starting capital from their former work and their level of education makes them more aware of and better informed about the world of business.

Those who arrived under the fifth category of the immigration quota have been crucially helped by the first group in establishing themselves in business and making the essential initial contacts.

New York has the highest number of South Asian businesses in the country, and is a particularly interesting example of the phenomenon of employment diversification leading to 'ethnic business'. In the 1960s and 1970s, other than a small handful of businesses specializing in import–export and a few restaurants, South-Asian-run companies were still very small in number and very scattered geographically. Very few had specialized in ethnic products. The shops themselves were concentrated in Manhattan (mainly between 26th Street and Lexington Avenue). Since then, successive of waves of immigration have transformed the size and nature of these businesses: insurance, travel agents, clothing shops, electronic goods, and so on, have emerged. Activity is no longer concentrated in Manhattan but has spread throughout the city.[40] Even in Manhattan, some neighbourhoods are well-known for having areas where South Asian shops are concentrated: apart from 'Little India' in Lexington Avenue, there is a series of clothing shops strung out between 30th Street and 40th Street, towards Broadway. Diamond shops can also be found between 46th Street and 49th Street and between 5th Avenue and 6th Avenue.

The best-known neighbourhood for South Asian businesses, however, is undoubtedly Jackson Heights, in Queens, at 74th Street.[41] The first shop, called 'Sam and Raj', goes back to 1976. It was set up by two Hindu friends, Subhash Kapadia and Raj Gandhi, who were working together as engineers in an American company. After five years they were made redundant, so they decided to open a shop selling electrical household goods. They opened it in Manhattan at first, in 1973, but three years later they were unable to renew their lease, 'retreated' to Queens, and opened a new shop in Jackson Heights, on 74th Street. Luck was now on their side: their initial capital came from their savings while they were working in industry. They also received financial help from family and friends. They claim never to have had to take out any bank loans. They both came from families with a business background in Bombay and this stood them in good stead, they say. Raj Gandhi left the shop to go into estate agency, while Subhash Kapadia found another partner, Nitin Vora, also from a merchant family. In 1996, during 'Asian American Heritage Month', Subhash Kapadia was given a citation of merit by the Governor of New York, George Pataki, for his contribution to the economic development of the Indian community.

At the end of the 1970s, Gandhi and Kapadia were joined by other South Asians who opened a number of shops and restaurants in the area. Since then, there has been galloping development in Jackson Heights: in 1990 there were about 100 South Asian businesses recorded there (restaurants, jewellery shops, insurance companies, sari shops and so on). The growth of this neighbourhood has coincided with the demographic expansion of the South Asian population in the United States.

Many of the shopkeepers in the area are former professionals who have moved into business, which confirms my earlier description. Now that Jackson Heights has become a major South Asian commercial area, families traditionally engaged in retail activity have settled there, some of whom have branches elsewhere in the United States as well, or even multi-national businesses. Raj Jewels of London and the Singapore Emporium fall into this category. Although most have arrived directly from the subcontinent, some 'twice-' or even 'thrice-migrants' from East Africa, Australia, Canada and Great Britain have arrived to swell the number of shopkeepers and restaurant owners. The owners of these businesses do not usually live in Jackson Heights but prefer to live in the more comfortable residential suburbs.

South Asians are often taken on as sales or general assistants, waiters and so on. Every day, apparently, unemployed men and women come to seek work in the area. Some are illegal immigrants or waiting for a green card.

The customers visiting Jackson Heights are mainly South Asian – about 10,000 shoppers per week, it is estimated. Some have travelled a long way, from New Jersey or Connecticut, for example, or even further. There is a subcontinental bazaar atmosphere in the evenings and at weekends (even snow, as I witnessed myself, does not keep shoppers or strollers away). In Manhattan shopping neighbourhoods customers come from much more varied ethnic backgrounds, in both shops and restaurants.

This picture is not dissimilar to the one in France but the difference lies in how separate ethnic groups co-exist: in France, there is a clear segregation along national lines in the South Asian shopping areas (Tamils from India and especially from Sri Lanka are mainly found in the Chapelle area, and Pakistanis in Strasbourg Saint Denis). In Jackson Heights, shops run by Indians, Pakistanis and Bangladeshis are found cheek by jowl: signs on the shops announce 'Indo-Pak-Bangla'. The Pakistani shops join in the sales during the main Hindu festivals of *Holi* and *Diwali,* out of pragmatism rather than a spirit of ecumenism.

This concentration has not been met with unalloyed enthusiasm, white Americans in particular being wary of this large concentration of South Asians. Their irritation has been reinforced as they see an increasing number of Asians and Hispanics move to the neighbouring areas. An association has even been formed, the 'Jackson Heights Beautification Group', to protect the neighbourhood. A dialogue has now been initiated between South Asian shop-keepers and residents, both white and non-white (Koreans and Chinese in particular) but this has not in any way banished ethnic tensions.

Since 1992, there has been a plan officially to rename 74th Street 'Little India', on the model of Chinatown or Little Italy: by doing this, local shop-keepers hope to attract tourists and new customers. Various suggestions have been made, such as erecting an arch at the entrance to the area which would evoke the Taj Mahal. This idea, however, is not universally welcomed. Some hold that South Asians should rather seek to become integrated than to empha-size their differences and others fear that current problems could be made worse (more traffic, more garbage and so on). On the other hand, there are calls for the neighbourhood to be renamed 'Jai Kishan Heights' or 'Jinnah Heights' . . . a few voices favour 'Little South Asia' instead of 'Little India' in respect for the non-Indians .

And yet it is not Jackson Heights that most merits the name 'Jinnah Heights': that would fit better in a neighbourhood of Coney Island between Avenue H and Newkirk Avenue in Brooklyn, not far from the Jewish quarter. Here there are nearly a hundred little shops, all Pakistani apart from one or two antique shops which will probably disappear soon. The first Pakistani grocery shop, the 'Punjab Grocery', opened in 1984, and it is owned by Abbas Rizvi. He was not keen that a shop selling *halal* meat should be run by Hindus (they left the neighbourhood some time ago now), so he decided to open a shop himself.[42] He was soon joined by dozens of other immigrants from Pakistan and their customers also hail largely from the same country.

A few Pakistanis have been already living in the area since the late 1970s. In the early 1980s they established a mosque, the Makki Masjid, which now draws sev-eral hundred for Friday prayers. The inhabitants of this neighbourhood are nearly all working-class Punjabis who often work outside the area as garage attendants, taxi drivers, labourers and so on. The women are not much visible during the day, but come out for a stroll in the evening, most of them wearing the *shalwar kameez.*

According to the policeman who for the last ten years or so has been watching the mosque on Fridays at prayer time for the past ten years ('a courtesy', he explains), the neighbourhood is known to have a low crime rate and little delinquency, which he says makes his job almost boring. When Pakistanis first settled in the neighbourhood there were a few tensions with their Jewish neighbours; however, they seem to have established a modus vivendi. Relations are not warm, but the two communities, only a few blocks apart, are cohabiting in peace.[43]

This area of Coney Island is a typical ethnic enclave (a relatively rare phenomenon among South Asians in the United States so far), and it is different from Jackson Heights in at least three ways: its social composition, its ethnic cohesion, and the fact that it is residential and well as commercial.

In both Coney Island and Jackson Heights, therefore, South Asians have made their ethnic mark on the New York landscape.

South Asians have established a solid reputation in another field: the hotel trade. I shall discuss this only briefly as this sector is less important in New York and concerns Muslims but little. According to Salim Khan, Punjabis who arrived at the beginning of the twentieth century launched themselves into the hotel trade on the Californian coast, at Stockton, and he claims that they now own 80 per cent of the town- and city-centre hotels. From the early 1970s a significant number of South Asians went into this sector and in particular one group, the Gujaratis (whence the well-known expression in the United States of 'Motel-Patel' or 'Potel', in reference to the surname Patel, very common amongst Gujaratis, including Muslims). The image of the Gujarati motel proprietor, which was immortalized in the film *Mississippi Masala* by Mira Nair (1992), is not a mere myth: Gujaratis control nearly 85 per cent of all hotels and motels owned by Indians. Asian owners have formed an association, the Asian American Hotel Owners Association (AAHOA), in which Indians are in a large majority (more than 80 per cent). Estimates are that members of the association control 30 per cent of the total number of hotel rooms in the country and 50 per cent of the cheaper end of the market (owners swear that the quality is far higher than it is depicted in Mira Nair's film!).[44]

Indians had considerable financial difficulties in setting up these businesses, as banks did not consider them creditworthy and therefore refused them loans. They had to rely on their own resources and on family help. Since then, the remarkable success of Indians in this sector has allayed the fears of the banks .

As a final remark, it is worth noting that in the United States as a whole, a substantial number of South Asians manage and/or own businesses with a turnover as high as several million dollars. Most are Hindus, but some Muslims have also reached the top of this tree. Among them, Farooq Kathwari, a Kashmiri, who is the Chief Executive of the firm Ethan Allen, and Shakeel Nauman (who arrived recently, in 1991), Director of Downstate Clinical

Laboratory, and Ebrahim Lunat (who arrived in 1977), an Indian Muslim from Tanzania who is the director of an accountancy firm.

Keys to success

Two main reasons are advanced for the economic success of a number of South Asians in the United States: they are keen to succeed, which encourages them to work hard, and they have support from their family, both financially and psychologically. These reasons may be valid but are disputed by some as a myth perpetuated by white Americans who, they claim, are attempting to side-step their responsibility towards less successful immigrant groups, African–Americans in particular. South Asians are seen as a model minority group and this can also be a pretext not to help them with state benefits to which they are entitled (see Chapter 9). It is also often forgotten that many South Asians were already highly qualified when they arrived in the United States, so that they had an initial advantage over other ethnic minority groups.

Besides family support, fluency in English and a higher educational level, other factors have helped the South Asian community to economic success: their good understanding of the client–provider relationship, which encourages them to develop good relationships with those in positions of power and authority, and the importance of the concept of *izzat* (honour), which heavily depends on the image conveyed to the 'Other'. This has resulted in South Asians behaving in such ways that would earn them the regard of others, of the employer in particular. This same concept of *izzat* makes success a require-ment: it is unthinkable that the immigrant should have to return to his homeland and admit defeat to his family.[45]

The not-so-fortunate

Not all immigrants from the subcontinent are in an enviable economic posi-tion. Some, especially the recent arrivals, are often in lowly or poorly-paid jobs: taxi drivers, newspaper vendors, waiters, factory workers, washers-up (as the earlier description of Coney Island has already indicated).

In New York, even more than elsewhere, the labour market is segregated: thanks to an informal network of mutual help, immigrants from a particu-lar region develop a monopoly, together with their families, friends and clients, of specific niches in the labour market. Thus, in Manhattan, Indians (especially Gujaratis) have more or less cornered the newspaper-selling market, though they are gradually being replaced by the Pakistanis and Bangladeshis who work for them: the Pakistanis and Bangladeshis, the more recent arrivals in the sector, are often the actual vendors, in kiosks owned by the Gujaratis. I interviewed several of these vendors and the most interesting conversation was with 'Mansur', a Pakistani, and 'Mirza', a Bangladeshi. Their kiosk was in a smart building in Manhattan which was mostly accommodating offices.

'Mansur' and 'Mirza' work for a white owner. 'Mansur', who is about 40, and has been in the business for longer, behaves as if he were the boss of 'Mirza', who is ten years older than 'Mansur'. He does not hesitate to tell him off for errors in calculations, and when a client appears, 'Mansur' stays seated while 'Mirza' serves him.

'Mansur' says he arrived in the United States as a visitor five years previously (to the interview, so in 1990). His brothers, who are pharmacists, had him to stay. He lived in New Jersey with one of his cousins. His wife and three children stayed in Pakistan. He studied science in Lahore and gained a degree, and then looked after his father's business. Since his move to the United States, one of his brothers has taken over the business.

'Mirza' arrived in the United States three years before (in 1992), to escape from a difficult economic situation in Bangladesh. He lives with his wife and two children in a small apartment in Brooklyn, and has no other relatives in the United States. 'I wasn't expecting a menial job like this,' 'Mirza' complains. When I ask him what he was doing in Bangladesh, he does not reply directly but simply says 'it was better than here'.

I ask them why so many South Asians have chosen this kind of work. 'Mansur' replies:

> It's a job where you can be independent and earn money . . . Americans employ us because they know South Asians are ready to work more than eight hours a day [unlike Americans].

'Mirza' adds promptly: 'and because they [South Asians] accept low wages.'
'Mansur' is not cheerful but he seems happy with his lot:

> All South Asians are in the same situation. Those who have succeeded are few and far between.

This feeling is born of an observation limited to his own circle and could also be an attempt to seek reassurance or to avoid seeing his own difficulties by convincing himself that all immigrants of colour meet the same fate in America. 'Mirza' seems to be more bitter and upset than 'Mansur':

> My life is a daily struggle. We [my family and I] hardly ever go out, we have no friends. With 1200 dollars a month we barely make ends

meet. My son will soon have to start working, or we won't be able to pay all our bills. I don't know about our children, but my wife and I will certainly go home to our country.

'Mansur' will also, when he has made enough money, return home to Pakistan (or so he claims).

Another job that reflects the desire to work independently, but also demands long hours, attracts many immigrants from the Indian subcontinent: taxi driver. In 1992, 92 per cent of New York taxi drivers were immigrants, of whom 21.3 per cent were Pakistanis, 10.2 per cent were Bangladeshis and 10 per cent were Indians (mostly Sikhs), so altogether 40 per cent of the total number of immigrant taxi drivers in New York. *Taxi-vala*, a documentary on New York taxi drivers, made by Vivek Renjen Bald, examine the aspirations and disillusionments of immigrants for whom America was not the Promised Land they had dreamed of. Irfan says:

> We used to think that we go over there, we will make enough money. So we don't have to worry–we just need to go to America and then everything will be okay. We just work eight hours and every day we will get $100 or something like that. And we were happy that we're gonna make more and more money . . . [but] when I came here and it was a recession period–and it still is–many people were jobless, and I was also jobless. I had a lot of wishes that I will do this and that, but after three months I did nothing–I stayed at home or just roamed about. I couldn't get a job . . . Then I realized it's very hard to live in America.[46]

One Pakistani taxi driver whom I interviewed, says:

> I've been in the United States for three years. I did an accountancy degree in Lahore. When I have enough money, I might do a masters in accountancy. There is another driver who's doing a masters in Brooklyn. He drives his taxi twice or three times a week to pay for his studies. I need to work seven days a week. I have a wife and two children to feed . . . It's very hard, I hate this work. I have to wake at 3.30 in the morning and be at work at 5. I work until 5 p.m., I go home to Queens, eat, and then go to bed at 8.30 or 9. I have no family life even . . . And my customers aren't particularly nice. Sometimes they won't pay or get cross if they are late. It makes me nervous. At rush hour it is impossible to overtake in Manhattan. I can't fly, my taxi doesn't have wings. I just wonder how much longer I have to be in this.

The job is not only hard but also dangerous. In 1992, 45 taxi drivers were killed in New York (from all ethnic groups), and 35 the following year. Since 1993 (when a 27-year-old Pakistani driver was shot), South Asians have been regularly joining in the protests of drivers against the violence they are subjected to. The fear of South Asian drivers is such that some refuse to take customers into the neighbourhoods known to be dangerous (especially Harlem, which has been nicknamed the Khyber Pass by the drivers). A controversy has recently arisen between South Asian drivers and African–Americans (including well-known figures like the former mayor, David Dinkins, and Hollywood actors such as Danny Glover and Denzel Washington[47]), who complain that New York taxi drivers, and especially South Asians, deliberately avoid stopping for them.[48] This attitude is explained not only by the fear of having to go into 'dangerous' areas, but also by marked anti-black prejudice amongst South Asians (see Chapter 9).

This kind of work particularly attracts illegal immigrants, as it seems that given the shortage of taxi drivers in New York, the police generally do not enquire about the citizenship status of the drivers, even when they have broken the law.

The interviews recorded above also show that some recent arrivals who have had to take up low-status work had gained higher education qualifications (degree or masters level) in India, Pakistan or Bangladesh. But their qualifications have little or no value in the American workplace. In fact, most of the immigrants arriving in the United States from the Indian subcontinent, especially doctors, have to repeat at least a part of their studies. Doctors are prepared for this, and go along with it, especially as most of them arrive relatively young (though I did meet an Indian dentist who was repeating his studies at 47!). Other immigrants, who arrive as graduates in history or literary subjects at the age of 40 or more in the United States, are not necessarily prepared to start studying again, especially if they have arrived with a family to support. They are therefore constrained to take on work for which they are overqualified. This can lead to frustration and many of them become disappointed, bitter and introverted. This can lead to tensions in the community, as the earlier immigrants blame the more recent ones for being a burden on the community or, 'worse', that they give a bad impression of the community to American society at large. This tension between the different waves of immigrants, whose social status is also different, is not a feature of only South Asian immigrants. Nadine Gallery de la Tremblaye has studied the Armenians in California and she notes that the original community, who wished to portray to American society 'the image of hard-working, ambitious and committed Armenians' is now very critical of recent Armenian refugees 'who seem to them to be lazy, lacking in ambition, and out to milk an economic system to which they don't contribute.'[49]

Similar sentiments are to be heard in the South Asian community, who echo the opponents of the social security system and think the newer immigrants a burden not only on their own community but also on the host society.

In any case a certain number of immigrants do live in real poverty, and tend to become isolated from their own folk and from the rest of society. As an indication, the 1990 census shows that 8.2 per cent of Indian families were living below the poverty threshold, as compared to 10 per cent of all New York families (African–American families: 21.8 per cent; Hispanics: 28.5 per cent). Nationally, 34.3 per cent of individuals who had arrived from India between 1987 and 1990 were living in poverty, that is, a third of recent immigrants.

A prosperous community

Although poverty is tending to increase in the South Asian population, the average income of families is also growing significantly. According to the 1990 census, Asians (of all origins) are the wealthiest of the non-white American population. Within this Asian group, immigrants from the subcontinent seem to be in a particularly favourable position. For comparison, the average income of an American family in 1990 was 35,225 dollars[50] (39,741 dollars in New York[51]), for an Indian family it was 49,309 dollars (46,056 dollars in New York). Indian families receive higher incomes than white American families (43,072 dollars in New York) and are in second position behind the Japanese (63,653 dollars).

South Asian families where both partners work have a particularly high standard of living.

As a result, most live in the residential suburbs of the large cities. The few recently arrived South Asian immigrants who do not enjoy such a high standard of living tend to live near each other, though they do not form ethnic enclaves (except for Coney Island). They conform therefore to the American model,[52] which suggests that each new wave of immigrants settles at first in neighbourhoods near the city centre (in this case the south of Manhattan, the Bronx and Brooklyn); then, when their circumstances improve, they gradually move further and further away from the centre (in this case, Queens and then later Long Island). Their lifestyle shares many characteristics with that of middle-class America (nuclear families,[53] spacious homes and luxury cars, keen participation in sport and so on)[54] and their experience resembles that of other ethnic groups who have arrived in the United States with the principal aim of achieving economic success.

It is noticeable that South Asians set great store by saving and investing money, more so than many long-established American families. Most families make a point of sending a part of their budget as 'remittances' to those family members who have stayed in the subcontinent. The home family often put up the original cost of the trip to the United States, and this reward to them also underlines the importance of family links even after migration.

In his study of Sikhs in the United Kingdom, Arthur Helweg describes the various successive objectives of remittances: in the first place they improve the financial situation of the family; they then allow the family to move to a new level of ostentation as consumers, thus demonstrating a higher social status; finally, through investments, they enable the home country to grow richer.[55] If the immigrant stops sending money, this can be seen as failure. Helweg adds that as the length of stay in the United Kingdom increases the sums sent in remittances tend to fall, because the immigrant is now almost or completely settled and it seems much less likely that he will return to the Punjab. Helweg also points out three variables which seem to affect the immigrant's willingness to send money: interest rates in India will influence any decision to invest; his view of the future (whether or not he is planning to return to his home country); and how secure he feels in the host country (which explains why South Asians from Africa have heavily invested in India, as they felt in a precarious position).[56]

In the United States, there is a similar situation, at least for recent arrivals. However poor they are, they feel keenly a moral obligation to send money home and few fail to do so. Thus 'Mirza', the Bangladeshi newspaper vendor, whose monthly income of a few thousand dollars is barely enough to feed his family in the United States, regularly sends money to his parents. In the United States also, however, the sending of remittances seems to diminish as the stay grows longer.[57] According to my interviews, some immigrants who are from wealthy families indeed never send money home. Faroque Khan, the Kashmiri doctor, is one of these, and instead he has always given presents to his family when he has made visits home to the subcontinent.

As a final comment, it is worth noting that immigrants, as they stay longer, tend to save less and consume more (and get into more debt), in other words they adopt the traditional lifestyle of middle-class Americans.

Conclusion

The demographic profile of South Asian immigrants in the United States, or more exactly in New York, is showing rapid growth. The subcontinental population is on the whole young and is made up of nuclear families. South Asians emigrate in the hope of improving their social and economic situation. Few return to their home countries. Many have been educated to a high standard, and this has enabled them to achieve considerable prosperity, even if some have had to shift to a different sphere, which for many has been the world of business – a demonstration of their high level of adaptability. However, a growing number of immigrants find it hard to succeed, this indicating a potential transformation of the profile, in the future, of this so-called 'model-minority'.

PART 2

ADAPTING IN CONTEXT

3

RELIGIOUS PRACTICES
Transplanted or reinvented?

We saw in the introduction that Islam is a fundamental marker of identity in South Asia, both in countries with a Muslim majority, Pakistan and Bangladesh, and in the country where they are in the minority, India. The South Asians we are studying have now emigrated to a country, the United States, where civil religion, with its well-defined rites involving sacred scriptures, personalities and sacred objects and places, underpins the ethos of the nation.[1] Americans exhibit a higher level of religiosity than other Westerners, demonstrated by their membership of religious groups and their participation in, and financial commitment to, religious activities. Religion has, for most immigrants – whether newly arrived or well-established – been a major element in the creating and maintaining of their individual and group identity. Because of its very acceptance as an identity marker by American society, it has been in some way sacralized. Religion creates a sacred link to the past and helps to bridge the gap between generations.[2] Religion also acquires a cathartic function, in that it protects the immigrants from too brutal an acculturation and Americanization, which could become potential sources of psychological disorders. Even if religion does have this function, this does not mean that it may not be in some ways reshaped under diasporic conditions.

Observance and religiosity

Religious obligations: theoretical aspects

The practice of Islam can in principle be summed up in the observance of the so-called Five Pillars of Islam: the belief in the unicity of God and in his Prophet Muhammad; the five daily prayers (*fajr, zuhr, 'asr, maghrib* and *isha*, the prayers respectively at dawn, midday, afternoon, sunset and evening); the month-long Ramadan fast; the alms tax (*zakat*); and the pilgrimage to Mecca at least once in a lifetime for anyone who is able to do it. To these compulsory observances are added some prohibitions (non-*halal* meat, pork, alcohol, usury (*riba'*), illegal fornication) all recorded in the normative corpus, the *shar'iah*; and the obligation, should the need arise, to engage in 'holy war' (*jihad*) to propagate Islam or to defend Islam from danger. The practice of Islam does not therefore require a complicated institutional infrastructure; the lack of clergy emphasizes this. A faithful Muslim can carry out his canonical duties independently of any social or religious official body.[3] The Shi'a, in particular the Isma'ili and the Ahmadiyya are to a certain extent exceptions, as they acknowledge the leadership of a spiritual head.

It is, however, a problem to carry out these canonical duties in a non-Muslim country because Islam recognizes no distinction between the temporal and the spiritual.[4] Indian Muslims were already acquainted with this issue before emigration, unlike their co-religionists from Pakistan and Bangladesh. But the situation in India, where Islam is a part of the religious landscape of South Asia, is not at all comparable to that in a Western country such as the United States. In India, the Muslim community can come up against problems from time to time, but its members are not generally perceived as foreigners and their religious infrastructure (mosques and religious shrines) have been part of the landscape for a very long time. Things are very different in the United States, and one can well appreciate that it might not be easy to live day to day as a Muslim, in such a society, for all that it has been rather tolerant of religious particularisms.

Parameters to define religiosity

Let us not forget that the concept of religiosity is complex because it is ambiguous in its relation to observance: 'a weakening in practice (the behaviours exhibited) does not fatally signify (in a measurable way) a weakening of the sacred.'[5] It is also the case that religiosity is easily misrepresented in interviews, as the replies given by interviewees can be affected by matters other than religion, such as the religious pedigree of the interviewers and/or the confidence they inspire in their interviewee, or indeed how secure the immigrant feels more generally in his/her life as a whole.[6]

Another point worth noting is that for practical reasons, the majority of my interviews were carried out in mosques or in other religious centres and this can give an inflated impression of the religiosity of the South Asian immigrants in New York. In fact, according to other researchers who have examined this question[7] and from my calculations based on the interviews I conducted with leaders of the Muslim population, only about 20–30 per cent of South Asians are regular practising Muslims.

For a good many immigrants, a comparison with the religious practice in their country of origin suggests that the longer they stay, the more observant they become. This phenomenon is not directly to be imputed to the length of stay, but is more a result of the change of family status (see below) which follows on the decision to stay more permanently in the United States. Bear in mind also that religious observance traditionally increases with age, especially after 40, amongst Muslims generally.

There is also an important distinction to be drawn between the first wave (in the 1960s and 1970s) and the second (1980s and 1990s). Those arriving in the second wave may not, at the very beginning, have had much time to devote to religious activities (regular attendance at the mosque, especially) but they have often displayed some observance at an individual level from early on, for instance in keeping the fast and respecting the prohibitions on food (notably on *halal* meat). Some of the first-wave South Asians, in particular those who arrived as students, chose on the contrary to adopt an anti-dogmatic, even an atheistic attitude and, as a result, they almost or completely gave up religious observance. This behaviour changed as their stay grew longer and when they married, as they rediscovered their religious heritage. This disparity between the South Asian waves of immigrants can be in part explained by a growth in religious feeling across the world in the 1980s (including in South Asia); in addition, there are now far more mosques in the United States, and this availability encourages Muslims to be more observant. The first wave of immigrants did not have the benefit of this infrastructure when they arrived. In fact, New York is geographically very well placed to encourage religious practice, as there is an ever-growing number of mosques and Islamic centres in the area (see Chapter 5).

The relative lack of religiosity displayed at the start of their stay by the highly qualified students and immigrants of the 1960s and 1970s is in contrast to the fervent religious practice, from the start, of many of the 1980s and 1990s arrivals. Does this indicate a link between level of education and religious observance? Michèle Tribalat studied the migrants in France and she observes that those who did not have schooling as children are markedly more observant than the others.[8] The matter is not one of simple correlation, however. Grace Davie notes:

> It is just as true that higher social groups are on average more inclined to be believers and practitioners, as that a higher level of education (usually linked to a raising of social status) has a negative influence on religious belief.[9]

It is certainly true that many of the immigrants in the 1960s and 1970s were not very religious at a certain stage of their stay in the new land. But their level of education does not seem to be the only reason for this behaviour: there were

few structures in place for them and there were at the time strong Marxist influences which were another factor. It should be also underlined that South
Asians, unlike the early pioneers to America, do not usually emigrate for religious reasons, so that they do not see religion as a crucial marker in the
preservation of their ethnic identity.

The level of education attained is no longer a significant factor in the degree
of religious observance in most immigrants, whenever they arrived. Evidence
shows that there is a similar level of commitment and observance amongst doctors and engineers as amongst newspaper sellers and taxi drivers. However, it
is the case that immigrants of a higher social status participate more actively in
the life of mosques and other religious organizations, whereas the practice of
those of lower social status is, for pragmatic reasons, limited to mosque attendance on Fridays (their work hours are longer and less flexible).

Educational achievement can have an effect, though, on the interpretation
of Islam by an immigrant, in particular on his understanding of theological
issues such as the degree of choice given to individuals by God, a matter which
occupies the educated more than the uneducated.[10] The type of Islam practised (popular, mystical, or strict) can also vary according to the level of
education (this will be examined further on). In Chapter 6, we shall also see a
correlation in the South Asian populations between educational achievement
and allegiance to different movements within Islam. On the personal level,
however, and on the level of the family, education can influence individual
behaviour, for instance in the matter of the status of women. As a general rule,
an educated immigrant will not object to his wife having a job outside the
home, especially as she will often be educated also. Those with less education,
however, often invoke a narrow interpretation of Islam on the question of
'appropriate' behaviour of women, and they discourage their wives from taking
work outside the home, except when their financial situation makes this
unavoidable. It is true that the wives of these immigrants are likely to be less
educated themselves. They therefore cannot enter either medicine or teaching,
both of which are considered suitable employment by South Asian Muslims.
The jobs traditionally taken by South Asians of lower educational standard
(street selling, restaurant waiting, taxi driving) are not considered respectable
for a Muslim woman.

The marital and family status of an immigrant is probably the most significant variable in determining the religious behaviour he will exhibit. Religion
offers the married immigrant and his family a particularly attractive framework
for social activity outside the family itself. Religion takes on a fundamental role
in the lives of immigrants as they settle into the new country, and the structures
and practice of religion become a central part of the process as the individual
and the group adapt and maintain their identity. The presence and role of a

wife is often crucial. This is not only because she is often more religiously inclined than her husband – a phenomenon not only present in Islam[11] and one which continues through into immigration – but also because the wife influences the religious behaviour of her husband, making him keep more strictly and regularly to the prescribed practices.

The birth of children, and especially their maturation, is another major factor which contributes to the increase of religious practice within families over time. Fenton also points out that as over time children come into the family, religious activity ceases to appear to be a personal and family custom, but becomes instead a conscious and deliberate effort.[12]

Customs and laws of Islam: the family framework and the social space

The pillars of Islam

Whether it be a habit carried over from life in the subcontinent or a conscious choice, the South Asian immigrant population still gives considerable importance to religious practice.[13] There is a variation in the enthusiasm for different aspects of the prescribed behaviour. As in other parts of the world, the Ramadan fast is respected by a significant number of the Muslim immigrants: the explanation rests on the collective and the social dimension of the fast (even though fasting is above all an individual act). The fast besides creates a special feeling of celebration, especially within the family circle.

The canonical prayers, which are seen as a solitary act, are observed by only a small minority. Friday prayers, however, which have a collective dimension, attract a higher number of the faithful. The situation is similar in France.[14]

There is, however, a difference between Muslims in France and those in the United States in the observance of *zakat* and of the pilgrimage: Muslims in the United States give these two matters a higher priority. According to Jocelyne Cesari, French Muslims demonstrate a fairly high level of generosity when funds are needed for a prayer room or a mosque.[15] But South Asian Muslims in New York make financial contributions to projects beyond places of prayer. This is probably explained by the fact that they are one of the wealthiest minority groups in the United States. To pay the canonical alms is in some way a purification – exactly as the Qur'an describes it – or even a 'relief' to the conscience to those immigrants who are particularly well off. It is true that many came from prosperous backgrounds before their emigration to the United States, but since their arrival they have grown considerably wealthier, in absolute terms at any rate. Many therefore feel the need to give part of this wealth as a sign of gratitude to God (and maybe a

prayer that their prosperity will increase further). There is also a vague sense of
guilt in some, who feel that in some way they have given up on their former
homeland and/or their family. This probably explains why the South Asian
population (in all faith groups, in fact) becomes involved in a large number of
projects in India, Pakistan and Bangladesh to build orphanages, hospitals and
the like. In South Asia itself there is a long tradition of members of the bour-
geoisie, women especially, engaging in charitable social work amongst the
poorer classes. This habit, which is not truly enough a purely religious activity,
seems to continue beyond emigration: many South Asian families, especially
during Ramadan if they are Muslim (and at Thanksgiving, in imitation of the
Americans!), visit hospices and charitable institutions (not necessarily Muslim-
run ones) to make gifts (mainly of money, clothes and food). And a small
number of Muslims hope that in practising *zakat* they can carry out *da'wa*: as
they give aid to particularly disadvantaged groups, some African–American
groups for instance, they use the opportunity to preach on Islam in the hope of
gaining converts.

Where *zakat* is concerned, sectarian affiliation is a matter of some importance, since Isma'ili, both Bohra and Nizari, have to pay considerable sums to
their respective leaderships, to include not only the *zakat* itself but also other
extra taxes, *dashond*, etc., which provide the financial support needed by the
community's institutions.

The pilgrimage (which is as highly significant for French Muslims of all
generations and all levels of education)[16] is bound up for South Asians in the
United State with the life of the community and the sense of unity of Islam.

On the practical level, arrangements are made by agencies and Islamic associations, often run by South Asians, in New York, which book plane tickets, and
in some cases organize the whole journey. What is offered (favourable rates,
luxury hotels, trips to sites of interest, etc.) is reminiscent of commercial pack-
age holidays. Long-distance travel has vastly improved and the wealth of many
South Asians in the United States has grown, so that more and more young
couples are carrying out this religious duty, which has traditionally been ful-
filled in old age.

In addition to visiting Mecca, Twelver Shi'a and Isma'ili are to visit the
holy cities of Kerbala and Najaf. This is done by Shi'a dispersed in the diaspora with a show of fervour equalling that of Shi'a from the subcontinent. For
the Bohra the duty to notify their leadership of any foreign travel still applies
after emigration. One yellow-card-carrying Bohra[17], 'Abbas', complains:[18]

> I have just visited Kerbala. I had to ask permission [of the *Da'i*'s rep-
> resentative in New York]. I have been unemployed for four or five
> years, so I haven't been paying my dues [to the leadership]. To be

allowed to go to Kerbala, I had to pay what I owed . . . The Bohra
have guesthouses everywhere in the world.[19] In Kerbala too. But I was
not allowed to stay in it, because you have to have a green card.

The authority exercised by the Bohra leadership beyond emigration is a matter
to which we shall return; the point I wish to emphasize here is the importance
to Shi'a of the pilgrimage to Kerbala as a way of stressing their Shi'a identity.

'Abbas' then showed me, with considerable display of emotion, the photos he
took in Kerbala. He has a serious illness, which is why he is not working, and
he wanted to make the pilgrimage to thank God for keeping him alive and
enabling him to return to a reasonably normal life. This journey to Kerbala is
reminiscent of the pilgrimages South Asians make, whatever their sectarian
affiliation, to Sufi sanctuaries, to give thanks for a happy event or to plead for
help if they are in trouble of some sort. There are, for example, many Bohra
who regularly visit the sanctuary of Haji Ali in Bombay. There are no such
sanctuaries in New York, so when an event seems to call for such a pilgrimage,
it is necessary to travel a long way. The major pilgrimages to the holy places of
Shi'ism are of such significance, however, even for Shi'a in the Indian subcontinent, that they would not contemplate going instead to a local sanctuary.

Observance of the canonical rules can raise difficult questions when it comes
to public places, especially the workplace. The observant Muslim's life is bound
by laws regulating worship, in particular the daily prayers. And although individual practice is not severely hampered by moving to a new place, since the
believer does not need the assistance of any clergy, it is not easy for the believer
to meet all his obligations strictly in the United States.

A small minority do however perform their prayers at the workplace: I
shall describe two cases. One is Faroque Khan, the doctor, a chairman of
medicine with considerable responsibilities in the hospital where he works. He
is much respected by his staff. His high position in the hierarchy and his evident
westernization (witness his physical appearance and his manners, which are
those of a British Indian gentleman) seem to allow him to carry out his duties
as he wishes (in particular his prayers), without apparently arousing any hostility in those around him. He also has his own office, so he does not have to
pray in full view of his colleagues.

My other case is also a doctor, but the similarities end there. This person is a
woman, 'Sitara'[20] who does not enjoy such a high position in the medical hierarchy, and who looks very different (she wears the *hijab* and the *shalwar kameez*),
a fact which makes Americans immediately assume her to be a fundamentalist.[21]
Her experience at work is therefore different from that of Faroque Khan.[22] She
too carries out the daily prayers (in a small room), but has had to put up with
hostility from several colleagues for a long time. Then things improved a bit:

> They realized that they cannot talk to me when I am praying.
> Telephone messages are now taken for me. Some are still very hostile,
> but they no longer show it.

She tries to keep as close as she can to the requirements of Islam and says she
is not in the United States to seek economic or social success. This is demonstrated by her attitude to *riba'*, loans on interest which are forbidden in Islam;[23]
she never takes out bank loans and lives a very austere life. She does not, however, express any desire to return to Pakistan, her homeland, but rather speaks
very highly of the United States, which she sees as a free country *par excellence*.
She is not seeking social advancement and has little concern about what others
think of her.

These two cases are typical only of a small minority, as most immigrants
place their social and professional integration into society above any other
considerations including religious ones.

Unlike daily prayers, the prayers on Fridays and those required on the two
major religious festivals in the Muslim calendar Id ul-Fitr and Id ul-Azha
seem to pose few problems at work for most immigrants. These three prayers
are invested with all the more importance by most (in the Indian subcontinent
and in the United States) because they are often the only prayers that are
observed in the year. Friday prayers, which are to be said at the mosque, coincide with the lunch-hour, so most Muslims are granted permission to leave the
office. Some mosques (such as the Islamic Center of Long Island[24] or ICLI) give
out free sandwiches at the end of prayers. In addition, in order to avoid difficult negotiations with employers when the hour changes in the middle of the
year (2.30 p.m. in Summer Time), some mosques, such as ICLI, hold Friday
prayers at 1.30 p.m. all year round. This decision is not universally approved,
and most mosques observe the time change in summer.

Many self-employed workers (especially shopkeepers and taxi drivers) regularly
go to the mosque on Fridays. The impressive number of taxis parked during the
hour of Friday prayers outside the Madison Avenue mosque in Manhattan,[25] not
far from a South Asian taxi company in Lexington Avenue, might lead one to
suppose that all Muslim taxi drivers in Manhattan attend that mosque.

Shopkeepers who also are owners of their shops, such as 'Nadim', a
Bangladeshi grocer in Lexington Avenue, generally ask an employee to mind
the shop for them during the hour of Friday prayers. Given the growing
number of mosques in New York, there are fewer obstacles now to Muslims
being able to meet their obligations.

There has been a marked change in the attitude of Americans in their
readiness to grant their Muslim employees a day's holiday to celebrate the two
Ids. In the early 1980s, it was very difficult for a Muslim to have the day off for

the Id, as employers argued that the festivals were not on a fixed day in the Gregorian calendar; in the 1990s, the situation became easier for two reasons: many practising Muslims are willing (as are Jews) to work on Easter Day or Christmas Day (especially in hospitals) or to work on Saturdays and/or Sundays, in lieu of a day off for the Id; in addition, some mosques work out the date in advance, on the Saudi pattern and each month make calculations based on the first sighting of the moon. Muslims therefore have enough time to make requests to employers and schools. However, some mosques still wait, according to tradition, for the first sighting of the new moon to decide both when Ramadan starts and when it will end in celebrations: this means that the date of the festival is only sure on the previous evening. Since 1996 some states, including New York, have agreed to grant a day's holiday for the Id without deducting the day from an employee's annual holiday entitlement.

The food laws

There are three main items forbidden to Muslims: pork, meat from animals not slaughtered according to ritual, and alcohol. To these can be added blood, animals which have been consecrated to a pagan deity, and intoxicating substances other than alcohol (drugs for example).[26] We shall examine the first three.

As in Europe, a large majority of those I interviewed abstain from eating pork. Many reasons are given: besides respect for the Qur'an, some immigrants rationalize this prohibition by pointing to the medical dangers that can come from eating this animal, such as tapeworm, which occurs more frequently among those who eat pork than among those who never have. Habit is also a factor: some refuse to eat pork, not because they see any harm in it, either intellectually or morally, but because they did not eat it as children and psychologically they are not prepared to start as adults, especially as pigs are considered to be dirty animals. Incidentally, it is said that the percentage of Hindus who eat beef is higher than the percentage of Muslims who eat pork.[27] Is this just because Muslims tend to be more dogmatic than Hindus or is there maybe another reason (which incidentally would not contradict the first explanation)? Hindus and Muslims refrain from beef or pork, Hindus because the cow is sacred in their religion and Muslims because the pig, on the other hand, is reviled in Islam. Maybe it is psychologically easier to 'desacralize' a sacred animal (and eat it) than to elevate an animal considered vile into 'sacredness' sufficiently for it to be edible?

As far as *halal* (ritually slaughtered) meat is concerned, it was available in very few shops when South Asian immigrants began to arrive in New York in the 1960s and 1970s. At that time, most immigrants bought non-*halal* meat (except pork); some ate it as it was, and others washed it, recited over it the appropriate formula from the Qur'an (generally the *shahadah*) before eating it. Muslims who did not wish to eat non-*halal* products, but also not keen on a vegetarian diet, went to a farm, bought a cow, a lamb or a chicken, and then conducted the ritual slaughter themselves. 'Abid', a Kashmiri immigrant who is a doctor, tells me of the procedure he had to resort to in the 1970s:[28]

> I had a patient who was a butcher. I asked him if he would take a Muslim butcher's boy onto his staff, who would be able to slaughter some or all of his meat according to Muslim ritual. I promised him he would have many clients, as the Muslim population was growing fast. He accepted, and his business did very well.

For many immigrants, kosher products had become possible substitutes for *halal* food. But many, of all levels of education, did not know when they arrived of the existence of kosher food, and that it could be consumed by Muslims. This is no longer the case. Immigrants such as 'Nisar', who is from Pakistan, a businessman by profession, find other ways to respect, more or less, the food laws. 'Nisar' says:[29]

> One can eat any meat, provided only God's name has been pronounced when it was slaughtered. At work, before I eat my meat, I say *Bismillah* . . . I also eat kosher food.

The prohibition on alcohol is more often flouted (as it is by Muslims in Europe), but it is nevertheless respected by the majority of the Muslims I met. It is difficult to give a reliable figure, since many Muslims are secretive about the truth of their alcohol consumption, especially if the questioner is potentially an abstainer from alcohol.

Abstention from alcohol, and indeed any food restriction, is a problem when it comes to the issue of the socialization of immigrants in a society where it is a fundamental element of social interaction. Guy Rocher gives this explanation of the symbolism of alcoholic drink in a number of civilizations:

> To drink together is to remember ties that bind, shared feelings, events celebrated together. Family celebrations and ceremonies are watered with libations . . . A meeting with old friends calls for a glass. In many religions, an alcoholic drink symbolizes the communion of the believers.[30]

In Islam, however, the 'communion of the believers' is not achieved through an alcoholic drink. In the United States, alcohol is important not only in the social life of individuals, but often also in their professional lives. It then immediately becomes more difficult for Muslims to keep to this religious prohibition. So they, therefore, admit that for professional reasons, or even for social reasons, they do sometimes transgress, particularly businessmen and businesswomen, as they are unwilling to compromise their integration into American society.

Other Muslims, for whom abstention from alcohol is not a real problem professionally (doctors, for example), do not consider that the food restrictions (including pork and non-*halal* meat) are a social handicap. 'Nighat', an immigrant Pakistani doctor, exclaims:[31]

> I go every year to Christmas celebrations. I have fruit juice and vegetables. That way, I am part of the mainstream and I keep my religious identity!

'Hasina', an Indian immigrant, a computer programmer, is surprised at my question:[32]

> Why should socializing with Americans be a problem? It's fine if you don't drink alcohol and just eat salad and fish!

Not all are able to be as positive about their situation, although they live in the same social milieu. 'Saida', a Kashmiri immigrant, also a doctor, explains:[33]

> At first it was difficult to have American friends. When I went to parties and asked for orange juice, people would say 'Orange juice is for breakfast.' We had to limit our social circle to people who respected our differences. Now people drink less and there are more vegetarians. It's become more acceptable not to drink alcohol. In fact, I do sometimes sip a bit of champagne. But if anyone insists I have a drink, then I refuse.

Some Muslims, the more strict ones, voluntarily isolate themselves from social life by refusing to go anywhere where alcohol is served. They are a minority, however. Most are either happy to go along, at least to a certain extent, with American social customs, or – more frequently – to do without alcohol and pork, and to turn a blind eye to the issue of *halal* if they are invited to an American function.

As to the question of whether Muslims are allowed to eat with non-Muslims, this seems not to arise in the American context, all the more so since according to some interpretations Muslims are allowed to eat with People of the Book. Yvonne Haddad, however, says that of all Muslims in the United States, the South Asians are the most punctilious in their observance of forbidden foods and not eating with non-Muslims, because they have lived alongside the Hindus, who traditionally offer food to the gods, which is absolutely forbidden in Islam.[34] South Asians are therefore more inclined to avoid contact with other religious groups, even Christians. It is true that some Muslims from the Indian subcontinent are reluctant to accept invitations from non-Muslims, for fear of being served forbidden food. The more observant, not wishing their wives to be in the company of strange men, also avoid any dinners where mixed company is inevitable.

In all, it would appear that behaviour in the matter of food is a significant indicator of religious belief (the rules are followed in migration out of conviction), but it is also a very clear symbol of identity: 'Habits in relation to food disqualify [that is, show up] the Other.'[35] Whereas 'Medieval Christian Europe raised wine and pork into cultural symbols to stand against Islam,'[36] Muslims in the United States, a Christian country, have made the avoidance of pork and (to a lesser extent) alcohol into the ultimate symbol of their otherness.

Hijab and riba', two sources of controversy

The hijab: symbol of domination or instrument of liberation?

The question of the *hijab*, which is more of an issue for second-generation immigrants, will be again dealt with in Chapter 4. However, a number of first-generation women have also chosen to wear this distinctive sign, often used as a symbol of Muslim identity. The *hijab* has been, and still is, much debated. Is the veil compulsory for Muslim women? The Qur'an gives an answer in verses 24:31[37] and 33:59.[38] Interpretations differ but that does not concern us here. The position of South Asian women in New York on the question is our concern (and their position is illustrative of the variety of response usually given), together with the way the veil is worn by those who are immigrants, and especially when they are at work.

Women in the Indian subcontinent do not wear the *hijab* in the same way as Muslim women in Europe or the Middle East: they either cover their head with the end of their sari, or they wear a simple *dupatta* (a kind of long scarf, thrown over the shoulders or worn on the head, which does not completely cover the hair: it is usually the third coordinating element of the *shalwar kameez*); or they wear the *burqa* (Indian version of the *niqâb* and the *chador*), which covers them from head to toe (even the face and hands are completely hidden). In some areas of the Indian subcontinent the *burqa* is commonly worn, but it is tending to disappear in most of the urban centres from which hail the majority of

Muslim women now living in the United States (they belong to the westernized elite rather than to the traditional elite – the latter does prefer to maintain the traditional *purdah* system as a sign of respectability[39]). The *dupatta*, on the other hand, is still often worn.

In the United States, most women, and especially those who are working, are very conscious of their visibility if they wear traditional dress, so – notwithstanding a sentiment of schizophrenia – they tend to wear western dress for work and activities outside the home and keep their traditional garments for when they are with their families.

Women do nevertheless dress with a certain modesty, observing Islamic and South Asian standards. Outside home, saris and the *shalwar kameez* are worn for formal dinners and other celebrations. When meeting with other Muslim families, women will tend to wear the *dupatta* on the head rather than on the shoulders. The *burqa*, on the other hand, has more or less disappeared from the wardrobe of South Asian women.

The *hijab*, it is worth noting, transcends the sectarian divides, or nearly: in revoking the principle of *purdah*, the third Aga Khan made it unnecessary for women to wear the veil.[40] The Bohra leadership, on the other hand, demanded that its members wear a veil, the *rida*, even in the country to which they had emigrated: this is more like the Indian *dupatta* than the *hijab* as seen in the West. Any person infringing the regulations on clothing imposed by the spiritual leader and his representatives is liable to sanctions.[41]

The opinion of most Muslim women who practice their religion but refuse to go along with the 'physical' aspect of the *hijab* is illustrated in the following comments, both from women doctors. 'Zubaida' is from Pakistan:

> I wear western dress at work. I wear the *hijab* in my soul. I feel liberated from inside . . . But I don't hide my religion from either my patients or the staff [of the hospital where she is a paediatrician]. For the Id, I put henna on my hands. Before giving a child an injection, I murmur '*bismillah*'. My patients ask me what it means. When I explain, they are delighted . . . My husband works in a Catholic hospital. I told a nun at that hospital that I was soon going to go on pilgrimage. She asked me to greet my God from her. I said he was the same God, and that during the pilgrimage I would be dressed just as she was, all in white and with no make-up.

Behind the rather euphoric and apologetic tone of these words – it is a feature also found curiously enough amongst women who wear the veil – there is a desire for integration, mixed with a desire to portray Islam in a way that will be compatible with the expectations of American society.

The other woman who does not wear the veil, 'Rukshana', an Indian, says:[42]

> At work, I wear a frock or a skirt. As I am a doctor, I don't want my patients to feel embarrassed because I wear different clothes or I cover my head. I know some women who work in a sari, and that's not a problem. Everyone has their own view of things.

In contrast to these two women are two others, also doctors, who do choose to wear the *hijab*. As in the previous examples, one is Indian and one Pakistani. Neither wore the *burqa* before they emigrated. Now, they cover their hair with the *hijab*, a choice of head-covering which is not typical of South Asia, but is adopted throughout the world by all the supporters of a militant form of Islam. The term *hijab* then takes on a generic meaning: 'the item of covering clothing women use to accord with Islamic principles, independently of the ethnic or national origin of the wearer.'[43]

The first woman, 'Shabnam', from India, tells me her story and about the reactions she meets at work:[44]

> At first, I didn't wear the *hijab*. I found it embarrassing in front of my patients. Then I went on the pilgrimage, and when I came back, I was wearing the *hijab*. I felt I needed to show that I had come back changed by the pilgrimage. That's why I wear it. I've never taken it off since. It makes me feel confident and strong, and more powerful too . . . And it has never caused any trouble, not even from my patients. None of them are Muslim but some congratulate me that I am able to carry on with my job as a doctor and yet keep to my culture . . . My colleagues too were happy to accept my new appearance. Sometimes they joke but it's never mean. One nurse bet me that I wouldn't keep it on for long . . . The first three years after I emigrated, seventeen years ago, I wore trousers, and then I started wearing the *shalwar kameez* again, and I felt much better . . . Outside the hospital, people don't seem to care what I wear . . . But I know some young women who have been insulted by kids and called terrorists. But that was just after the attack on the World Trade Center [in 1993]. The biggest problem is ignorance. When you explain Islam to people, they are surprised: 'I didn't know your religion was like that.'

The second veiled woman, 'Sitara',[45] tells me:

> At first, people asked me stupid questions. 'It's hot. Why don't you take off your scarf?'; 'You're educated, so why do you wear a veil?'; 'Do

you have leprosy? Or are you afraid of catching it?'; 'You want to try to be a nun, but you'll never make it.' Now people in the hospital are used to it and they respect me more . . . I have no problems with my patients . . . Sometimes I am called 'Sister' and people say 'We need your conservative approach.' People like to confide in me: for example, one woman told me she was living with a married man. She asked me what she should do.

Once again, one can see a change over time in the reactions of others: an initial hostility is replaced, if not by acceptance, at least by tolerant neutrality. 'Shabnam' emphasizes that Muslims must educate Americans about Islam, and we shall see that this is something which is a concern for many Muslims in the United States, especially those who hold office in Muslim organizations.[46] In the case of 'Sitara', it seems, curiously, that the woman wearing the veil acquires a new function: she becomes a confidante or even a confessor – in spite of the paradoxical nature of this new role – because her 'uniform' is a reminder of a familiar profession. Does this point to an acceptance of Islam in American society? Or maybe to the fact that these immigrant women are trying to become integrated into American society, refusing to see a potential hostility and at the same time wanting to preserve, and indeed proclaim, their differences? We shall come back to this later and attempt to find an answer.

The issue here is to see what it is that makes these women, after they have emigrated, decide to start wearing the veil, an open signal of their religion which, if not actually a negative image, is at least a sign of being alien, and this at the same time as wishing to become absorbed into the host society. It is true that many people are more religious after they have made the pilgrimage to Mecca ('Shabnam'), but this alone does not explain the need they feel (expressed in an often vague way) to assert their Muslim identity so openly. In addition to the doctrinal reasons for doing so, wearing the veil after immigration suggests a strengthening of Islamic identity as a result of the process of migration itself. These women come to see migration as an important element in their understanding of Islam, and as the ultimate justification to wear the veil. In fact, many women (and men) are opposed to the mechanical, quasi-automatic, ways in which religion is observed in their homeland and they prefer to apprehend religion in a more rational mode in migration.

One more case, presented below, illustrates even more clearly the link between migration and the affirmation of identity. This is as yet a behaviour seen only in a small, extreme minority within the Muslim community. The declared objective of the small group of Muslim women to which this person[47] belongs is the construction of an identity clearly distinct from, or even in opposition to, the host society.

The woman in question, 'Faiza', is in her forties. She is from Lucknow, in Uttar Pradesh. She emigrated to the United States in 1970 in order to join her husband, an engineer. She has four children and is not very highly qualified; hence she has never been gainfully employed in New York. As she does not speak English very easily, she speaks to me in Urdu. Whenever she goes out, she puts on a *burqa* which covers her from head to toe, leaving only her eyes visible.

> In Lucknow, I didn't wear the *burqa*. I didn't even say the five prayers. Here, I wear the *burqa*. It's not because I necessarily want to look different, but I am bound to look different . . . I was here when I first read Mawdudi. My husband is very religious and he reads a lot. I read his books. But he didn't ask me to read them, I read them myself . . . After [I had read Mawdudi], I understood what Allah has given us to do. I understood that I have to wear the *burqa* . . . People look at me oddly but I can't help that . . . In India, children learn a few rituals, but nothing is explained to them.

This woman's more strict observance is indeed a consequence of migration, since she says of herself that she is more religious after emigration than she was before (and she acts differently as a result). She could certainly have 'discovered' Mawdudi in India, before or even without emigration, but this curiosity about him and the changes she has made to her life after reading him are related to her life as an immigrant woman: she is isolated in the home when all their children have gone to school, she is far from her family, and her isolation is aggravated by her poor level of English, which prevents her making contact with the host society.

There is another recurrent feature in conversations with Muslims in New York. Many South Asians make the point again and again that the process of migration has helped them better to understand their religion: they contrast their own interpretation of Islam in the land of migration with their previous understanding, or with that of those they have left behind and who, they think, have not moved on. This is a classic phenomenon, experienced by many immigrants to the United States and elsewhere. The most famous South Asian is none other than Mahatma Gandhi, who 'rediscovered' Hinduism when he spent some time in London.

'Zoya', an Indian immigrant from Hyderabad, and a secondary school teacher, says on this matter:[48]

> I did receive a religious education in India, reading the Qur'an and so on, but it was in the United States that I understood Islam and began to appreciate it. I found the answers to many questions I was wonder-

ing about when I was in India, and which the *Maulwi Saheb*[49] couldn't
answer. In India, I had the idea that Islam was terrifying, and it would
punish you and send you to hell for the smallest sin. It was when I got
here that I understood that Islam is peace-loving and compassionate.

South Asian Muslims perceive that they gain a better understanding of their religion when they have emigrated and this changes the image they have of Islam.

The matter of the veil is still controversial (less in the United States than in
France, however), even within the Muslim population of the United States: on
the whole, the majority do not object so much to the *hijab* as such, more to the
insistence that it be worn compulsorily by every woman who claims to be a
Muslim; they also object to the image in the Western (or, in this case, the
American) mind of the *hijab* as the ultimate symbol of male domination over
women. Defenders of the veil, especially those who wear it, see it more as
expressing a conscious choice to be identified as Muslim. Most of these
women, far from keeping a low profile, claim the right to be the main educators of their children, the Muslim adults of the future, whom they wish to see
educated in all the rules and precepts of Islam. Thus they construct a space
where they can assert their feminine identity. The formation of this identity is
not necessarily a result of conflict with the host society: unlike Muslims in
Europe, Muslims in the United States, especially South Asians, are not disadvantaged economically, nor are they in conflict either on political or cultural
grounds. This affirmation is more in the logic of a reappropriation of the
Islamic religion by women and this is true in Muslim countries also (notably in
Turkey and Iran – *chador* instead of *hijab*[50]). This is a 'claim to dignity', and an
attempt to enter some sectors of the social arena usually the preserve of men.[51]

The riba': a protest against the
atmosphere of materialism

The second issue which gives rise to a variety of interpretations within the
Muslim community in New York is the *riba'*,[52] interest received on a loan, and
usury, both prohibited in Islam. There are very few countries which respect this
prohibition, as it is hardly compatible with the functioning of a modern economy. Muslim immigrants around the world, and especially in the United States,
are very little concerned by this particular prohibition. Some, however, do
raise the matter on a theoretical level, though most will admit that it is impossible to apply this Qur'anic principle in contemporary societies. There are
various different justifications: some insist that Islam, and this prohibition in
particular, must be interpreted in the historical context. Thus, in the time of
the Prophet, interest rates could be extortionate, whereas this is no longer the

case today. Others argue that this law can only apply in a Muslim country. Some draw a distinction between loan at interest and usury, and say that this law should apply only at the personal level, so that loans with interest between individuals should not be allowed. The question of receiving interest on money placed at a bank is quickly dismissed by most with the following argument: 'Why should this money profit others? We might as well give it to the poor.'[53]

There is, however, a small minority within the Muslim population of the United States which is very keen to live strictly according to Qur'anic principles and which try to respect the rule in spite of the difficulties it causes. In practical terms, it means that these immigrants do not enter into any transaction involving interest, refuse the interest normally paid on their bank accounts, and do not buy anything on credit. Though very few in numbers, some Muslims do claim to abide by this law, and their spartan life-style suggests this is not fabrication.

'Faiza', the immigrant from Lucknow who wears the *burqa*, is one of these, as is 'Sitara', the woman doctor who performs her prayers at work. Both rent their homes, own an old car, avoid restaurants, luxury goods, and so on, and on the whole live an austere life. 'Faiza' sends her daughters to a university in New York where the fees are not very high, and her son is funding his own studies with a scholarship. 'Sitara' is comparatively better off, as she has a good job and is unmarried, but she nevertheless is similarly almost ascetic in her lifestyle. 'Nadim', the Bangladeshi grocer in Lexington Avenue, has chosen to rent his shop premises rather than buy with a mortgage. Apart from 'Nadim', all the people I met who keep the Qur'anic principle of *riba'* were persons holding office in Islamic organizations who wished to be seen as models in the Muslim community.

Of all sectarian groups, it is the Bohra who face this question of *riba'* with acuteness: in order to qualify for the famous green card, the *Da'i*'s disciples have to observe the prohibition of *riba'*.[54] This is one of the major sources of criticism of the *Da'i* by his followers. The prohibition, strictly speaking, is still valid for those who have emigrated, but it has in practice become 'disapproved'.[55] (It is still forbidden for Bohra to work in a bank, however.) As a compensation, the religious authorities have undertaken to lend any money needed to their followers, without interest. 'Salman',[56] a Bohra shopkeeper in New York who has a green card and is very keen to obey all the instructions of his spiritual leader, says he has not taken out any loans since he bought his house. If he needs money for his daughter's education, he will use help from his community. Bohra still have, however, the characteristic of a merchant community in migration, and in fact the Bohra leadership encourages its followers, if necessary with financial help, to engage in business and to run their own shops and businesses.

The Bohra, however, are a very small proportion of the South Asian Muslim community, and at present there is no indication that there is a growing number of Muslims who keep to this particular religious prohibition.

To meet the needs of this small minority, there are now measures in place: Islamic financial institutions have been set up, such as the MSI Finance Corporation (Muslim Saving and Investment) in Los Angeles, which opened in 1985.[57] It functions according to the system of 'shared ownership', with partners sharing in both profits and losses, so that risk is shared out, in this case between the MSI and any person who wishes, for example, to buy a house. The buyer pays 20 per cent of the cost of the house, and the balance is paid by the MSI. The buyer therefore only owns 20 per cent of the house, and must pay rent to the MSI for 15 years to buy back at market value the part of the house owned by the financial institution. As the market value is subject to variation, there is an element of risk for both parties.

Opponents to the Islamic bank voice at least two criticisms. The system, they say, does in effect use interest, but under another name. The way the system works is vulnerable to fraud, such as that which brought down the BCCI (Bank of Credit and Commerce International) in July 1991. Admittedly the BCCI was not an Islamic bank, but a number of Islamic banks held money in it, so many savers who had put money in these Islamic banks were ruined.[58]

At present, only Los Angeles and Houston (Texas) have Islamic financial institutions along these lines. It is difficult to predict the future for Islamic banks in the United States, because so far the vast majority of the Muslim population has chosen not to use them. Their survival depends on their being able to offer rewards similar to those offered by the mainstream financial institutions, while still allowing Muslims not to violate Islamic precepts.

The question of *riba'* also raises the issue of the financing of mosques. Is it right to borrow money from banks to build and run mosques and Islamic institutions? All the institutions I visited in New York answered in the negative, and assured me they had used other means to subsidize their activities (see Chapter 5).

Rites of passage[59]

Circumcision and other initiation rites

Circumcision does not call for much comment, except that it is a custom respected by almost all Muslims, all the more so as this practice in itself does not pose a problem in the United States, where three-quarters of babies in the total population are circumcised. The traditional celebrations on the occasion are on a smaller scale than in the Indian subcontinent (several dozen guests, sacrifice of a lamb, and so on). In fact, in New York, circumcision is carried out

in the hospital itself in the next few days after the baby's birth. In most families, it is a brief ceremony, or it is linked to the traditional ceremonies on the
occasion of a birth. In some families it is celebrated with *chhati*, the sixth day
ceremony, or more frequently with *aqiqa*, when the child's head is shaved; contrary to tradition, *aqiqa* in New York does not include however the sacrificing
of a sheep. Either the family asks their relatives back in the subcontinent to
sacrifice a sheep in their name, or they make a donation of money to the poor
(in New York itself, or they send the money to their relatives who make the gift
on their behalf), or to the local Islamic centre.

When the child reaches the age of four years, four months and four days, the
family organizes a ceremony to introduce the child to the Qur'an (*Bismillah*). In
the subcontinent, this ceremony is the occasion for a lavish feast, but in New
York the event is on a much smaller scale, and the family invites a few close relatives and friends. The imam of the closest mosque is invited to initiate the
child by making him recite the first revealed sura (*Iqra*), and this is followed by
a festive meal.

Burial: dying in America

Burial is a matter of more interest as it raises two crucial issues, the place of
burial and the accompanying rites.

In a novel entitled *Beyond the Walls, Amreeka*,[60] Tahira Naqvi tells the story of
a Pakistani woman, Sakina Bano, who comes to visit her son in the United
States, at his insistence. In the plane, she is seized with panic at the thought of
being buried outside Pakistan, should she happen to die while on her trip:

> Suppose she suffered a heart attack just this instant and died? Why,
> people often died quietly and without a fuss, didn't they? Would the
> airline transport her back to Pakistan? What if the plane had to
> make a landing in the country they were flying over when she died,
> and her body abandoned there among strangers? She knew Cairo
> was their first stop, but were they near Cairo? She couldn't be cer-
> tain. But the thought that Egypt might be the place where she was
> left for burial provided some comfort. At least she would be among
> Muslims.[61]

Once she has arrived in the United States, Sakina Bano hears a woman in a
mosque in Connecticut one Sunday telling of the death of an old Pakistani
woman: all the shops were shut, the family could not even buy a shroud for the
body, and had to beg for new white sheets from their acquaintance. Fear seizes
Sakina Bano again:

Sakina Bano's mouth became dry. She felt sweat rise like tiny thorns on her skin . . . Bedsheets! What an unfortunate woman. And what guarantee they were all cotton? Wash and wear is what they are making these days. And to be buried among strangers – such isolation. Poor woman, to be so far from home and die, to be wrapped in bedsheets which said, on small tags somewhere, 'Made in Amreeka'. Will the angels condescend to enter a grave where a body lay draped in a shroud made by Christians?[62]

Many elderly people visiting the United States experience similar fears, or almost. From my interviews,[63] however, it seems that most of the Muslim immigrants – like their co-religionists in the United Kingdom,[64] but unlike other Muslims in Europe who wish their body to be sent to their homeland[65] – are buried, or ask to be buried, in American soil. Immigrants who have no family in the United States are the exception. In the case of Pakistanis, a charitable organization, Edhi (founded by the eponymous Abdul Sattar Edhi), pays for the repatriation of the bodies of the poorest immigrants.[66]

It seems that the main reason for wishing to be buried in the United States is neither the Islamic law which says that a Muslim must be buried where he dies, nor the practical difficulties of the great distance, greater even than for Muslims in Europe, that separates them from their country of origin. The reason seems to be more that Muslims wish to be buried near their children, who are likely not ever to leave the United States to go back to the country of their ancestors. At a deeper level, whatever their level of social and cultural integration in the United States, Muslim immigrants have feelings of gratitude and a sense of belonging to their new country, all the more so if they have enjoyed financial success and benefited from the religious tolerance accorded to them. These sentiments are not so evident among European Muslim communities, which are economically less advantaged, do not necessarily enjoy the same level of religious freedom, and have not infrequently found themselves used as scapegoats in difficult times.

Though Muslims may choose to be buried in the United States, they still prefer to be buried according to the traditional Islamic rites.

It is not easy however to apply strictly the Islamic precepts relating to burial. In Islam, the burial must happen within 24 hours of death, and the body must face Mecca, which is difficult to achieve in the American context. Various mosques have for some years been setting up the structures necessary to satisfy the needs of their faithful. There are not yet Muslim cemeteries in New York, but the mosques have bought some tombs. As soon as someone dies, most often in hospital, once the death certificate has been obtained the family contacts one of the suitable mosques and the procedure starts. At the Islamic Center of

Long Island, these structures are not yet in place (there is no morgue in the mosque, for example), but ten or so people, men and women, have volunteered to carry out funeral rites. One of the women, 'Ismat', an unemployed Pakistani immigrant, describes the procedure:[67]

> As soon as the doctor announces that the patient has died, we tie his/her two big toes together, we close his/her mouth, and we remove all her jewellery if it's a woman. We wash the body and put it in a coffin. Of course, according to Islamic tradition, it is better to bury the body straight into the ground in its shroud, but that's not allowed here. The mosque gives us the shroud. We try to bury the body the same day, or the next day. It's not always easy because the cemeteries are closed at weekends and holidays. Sometimes the body is in Manhattan and it has to be brought here . . . The funeral undertaker is responsible for the body. I don't like that, especially if it's a woman, as she is on her own with him. In Pakistan, people watch by the body and read the Qur'an all night . . . You have to study specially for two years to be an undertaker. The [Long Island] mosque is trying to build a mortuary and to appoint a qualified Muslim. The other mosques, where they have mortuaries, are permitted to keep the body for one night . . . The men take the body to the cemetery, in a car, not on foot like they do in Pakistan. The women are not supposed to take part in the procession and go to the cemetery, but some go afterwards and recite *Fatihas*.[68] We [the Long Island mosque] have bought 40 tombs for 400 dollars each in the Washington Memorial Cemetery [on Long Island]. There are only 22 tombs left. Now our community is getting older. We want to buy 200 more with the financial help of members of the mosque . . . It's here that I've learnt how to care for the dead. I had never done it in Pakistan. The mother of one of my friends died. No one knew what to do. I thought, someone has to see to this, so I did it. But I'm still learning. There are a few women in the community who know what to do, and they are training us, me and others. One day, Doctor X brought a doll and demonstrated what we had to do. I'm not a very practicing person, but looking after the dead is gaining me *sawab*.[69]

This account shows the efforts of the Muslim population to respect the rites of Islam, in spite of the difficulties and the adjustments required (the burial is not necessarily on the day of death, the procession is in a hearse, not on foot, burial is in a coffin, not in bare earth). It also implies that people who previously had little qualification to carry out certain burial rites are asked to bear new responsibilities and duties in the new land. It also points to new departures in practice from the South Asian way, where women are not favourably viewed at the graveside. In New York, although women are not involved in the funeral itself, some do go to the cemetery for prayer and meditation.

A final note: Muslims do not share cemeteries across sectarian divides: each group has bought separate grounds. The Ahmadiyya have reserved 200 tombs in the Long Island cemetery. The ceremonies themselves are little different, apart from the prayers for the repose of the departed soul, as each minority includes in its liturgy an allusion to their respective spiritual leaders. Sectarian divisions notwithstanding, all Muslims express the same wish to be buried according to traditional rites.

In conclusion, it would appear that South Asian Muslims in New York, as also those in France,[70] are attached to the importance of keeping up the traditional rites of passage, even if the circumstances in which they now live dictate that the formalities have to undergo some modification.

The Islamic festivals: *Maulid*, the substitute for Christmas

The Islamic calendar has regular festivals, prominent among which are the Id ul-Fitr, the end of the Ramadan fast, and the Id ul-Azha, which commemorates the sacrifice of Abraham. These two festivals are the occasions of much feasting in the Indian subcontinent. What about in the United States?

Before I look at the two Ids, it is worth remembering that Ramadan – the holiest time of the year because the first revelation of the Qur'an is considered to have happened during this month – is an occasion for festivities every time the fast is broken. We have seen that many South Asian immigrants keep the fast after emigrating. For many, the breaking of the fast happens in the home, or alone, without much partying. Some Muslims, though, try to give a community feel to this holy month by gathering every evening, or at least at the weekend, to share the *iftar*, the meal that breaks the fast.

A number of New York mosques have made arrangements to enable their faithful to break the fast in their buildings. Volunteers prepare the meal, which is supposed to be lavish, for several dozens, or even hundreds of people.

The mosques and *jama'at khana* of New York Muslims offer these services, whatever their sectarian affiliation. The *tarawih* prayers are absent, however, from Shi'a mosques, because the tradition is considered to have been terminated and then reintroduced by the second caliph, Umar. This is why Shi'a praying in Sunni mosques retire after the *isha* prayer.

On the occasion of the Ids themselves, Muslims try to recreate the joyful atmosphere of the celebrations in the subcontinent. For some, though, to be far

away from home on this day of celebration is a particular sadness. The newly-
arrived immigrants, who are at the bottom of the social scale, often give vent
to their loneliness and boredom on this day of celebration.

'Mirza', the Bangladeshi newspaper vendor, sighs:

> For me, the Id isn't a celebration. On the contrary, it's the day I real-
> ize how alone we are here, my wife and I and the children.

For most, though, the Id festivals are a celebration and for many Muslims a day
on which to go to the mosque (the 'Id Muslims'[71]). Hundreds of people, resplen-
dent in traditional dress – some have bought new, according to tradition –
converge on the mosques. The traditional prayer for the day is sometimes
repeated for the benefit of latecomers or for those who could not get in at first
because of the large numbers. The faithful are encouraged, as *zakat*, to give
money to the mosque. Depending on where the mosque is (city centre or suburbs),
and on the season and the weather, a picnic is organized with the financial contribution and with the help of many volunteers, who help prepare dishes, etc.[72]

The Id ul-Azha traditionally involves the sacrifice of an animal (sheep usually). New York Muslims have two options: they can either ask their family in
the subcontinent to sacrifice an animal on their behalf or they can give to char-
ity the price of an animal. Immigrants who wish to carry out this rite
themselves go to specialized farms which supply *halal* meat to butchers. In a few
states there are abattoirs licensed by the local authorities for this purpose.

Apart from the two Ids, there are other times of celebration in the Muslim
community. The Shi'a gather in the month of Muharram and commemorate
the martyrdom of the imam Husain. This occasion also celebrates the model
Muslim family consisting of Muhammad, Ali, Fatima, Husain and Hasan.
The celebration takes the form of meetings (*majlis*) during the first ten days of
Muharram. They happen either in a private home or in the mosque. In the
meetings, the faithful beat their breasts (*matam*), chanting '*Ya Ali*', '*Ya Husain*',
while others, with great emotion, recite the tragic story of the events at
Kerbala. Flagellations do not frequently happen, according to the leader of the
Al-Qoei mosque (see Chapter 5), as Shi'a in the United States prefer instead to
give blood in the hospitals.

Iranians and South Asians do not usually share these meetings, not only
because of a relative lack of relationships between both communities (see
Chapter 5), but also because each group prefers to hear the story of Husain's
martyrdom in their own language.

> Iranians were invited to their [Pakistani] Ashura session, but that gen-
> erated mutual irritation . . . the Iranians found the Urdu recitations of

the Kerbala story outlandish and funny, rather than tragic. The deep emotional tones of mourning simply could not be produced for them in the up and down cadence of the Urdu language. And so in the midst of one of these sessions, when the Iranians retired to another room to do one of the namaz prayers, they were accused of being disrespectful to the martyr of Husain.[74]

But the very fact that the recitations are in Urdu in the South Asian *majlis* is an attraction for some Sunni, who welcome the chance to attend a ceremony in their mother tongue.

'Iqbal', an immigrant from Aligarh, who trained as an engineer, but now works as a consultant for a computing company, says:[75]

> I'm not a Shi'a. But I like going to their *majlis*. It's not very often I hear Urdu outside my home in this country.

In New York, on the tenth day of Muharram (*ashura*), when the celebrations reach their climax. Since 1996, the South Asians have been organizing a procession on Madison Avenue, between 42nd Street and 65th Street, where the Pakistan consulate is located. The expressions of grief at the martyrdom of Husain are kept at a low level as the faithful beat their breasts and carry replicas of the memorial stone from Husain's mausoleum. As there are not very many South Asian Shi'a in the United States, these processions do not draw big crowds.

The celebrations may be low key in the land of migration, but the Muharram festival is still a crucial element of Shi'a identity in the United States: it marks them out not only from the host society but also from the Sunni majority. For some, their participation in Shi'a rituals is limited to this occasion, this annual celebration is therefore all the more important to the community.[76]

In the Indian subcontinent, milestone events in Islamic history (such as Manlid, the birth of the Prophet Muhammad, or *Shab-i-Miraj*, the 'night journey' of the Prophet[77]) or in family life (the death of a relative, or *barsi*, the anniversary of a death) are the occasion, especially among the Barelwi,[78] for festivities which are not inspired so much by the Qur'an as by the prophetic tradition. These celebrations shaped in part by Hindu practices, or at least so their detractors claim – in particular offerings of food are made – are condemned in South Asia both by traditionalists and modernists.

These practices, which are more cultural than truly religious, are kept up by many South Asian families after emigration. I was present at one such commemorative ceremony in a family from South India. It was the day of *Shab-i-Barat*, the 'Night of Deliverance' on the 14th of the month of Shaban (8th lunar month). The family members present were 'Afsana' and 'Hasan', the parents, and 'Rafiq', their youngest son (the two older children did not wish to join in the ceremony), and they sat around the sitting-room table. The wife had prepared *nan* and *halva*, and lit some incense sticks. The couple recited some passages from the Qur'an – especially the *Fatiha* (first sura of the Qur'an) and the 112th sura – while moving their bodies backwards and forwards.[82] The young son had his head down and looked very bored. The parents asked their son to repeat after them *du'as* in the names of all the deceased members of the family. To finish with, everyone took a mouthful of *halva*.

This rather brief ceremony was attempting to reproduce as faithfully as possible the rites practised in the Indian subcontinent, and in so doing to preserve the religious and cultural identity of the family. Some elements of the rite were omitted but this was by force of circumstances rather than by choice. The bread used in this ceremony in the subcontinent is not simple *nan* but is specially prepared according to a recipe not necessarily available to those who have emigrated. The men visit the graves of relatives before the ceremony itself, and give out food to poor people living near the cemetery. In the United States, however, very few have relatives buried nearby. More importantly, this tradition is being re-enacted from memory, as it is not written down, so it is necessarily approximate. The reaction of the children suggests that they are indifferent to, or even reject, practices which they do not understand. They have become used to an education system which favours active understanding over passively accumulated knowledge. The rites and mechanically reproduced gestures do not develop the religiosity of the second generation.

It is not only the second generation which is casting doubt on the value of these practices, as we shall see when we examine how little impact the Barelwi have had on the South Asian immigrants (Chapter 6).

A final observation: the various sectarian groups, Nizari, Bohra and Ahmadiyya in particular, celebrate throughout the year the various anniversaries of the birth and death of their respective spiritual guides, thus demonstrating that they wish to preserve an identity that is not only religious, but also sectarian. They do not intend to become part of a big Islamic melting-pot.

'American' leisure: a careful selection

As a religion, Islam advocates a rather austere lifestyle. In this regard, it is in line with the puritan philosophy of some Protestant sects in the United States, but out of tune with the ambient hedonism in American society, or at least with its yearning for joy and fun. Joining in leisure activities is often the only way, outside the workplace, of coming into contact with Americans, and this can serve as an indicator of the level of social integration of an immigrant or of a community. There can be major differences in the form this takes, according to age and gender. The celebration of American festivals by South Asian Muslims is finally of a particular interest because for Americans some of these festivals have become symbols of adherence to the concept of civil religion. This is best exemplified by the sacred aura of Thanksgiving.

Most South Asian Muslims I interviewed were fully engaged in the leisure life offered by American society. Some activities which do not sit well in a Muslim ethic, however, give rise to disapproval in the community (in the first generation): swimming in mixed public pools; dancing at events where there is no way of avoiding mixed gender company, and so on. Apart from a few restrictions adopted by most of the immigrants, women in particular, the South Asians who lead an austere life are in fact few and far between, unless of course their financial situation imposes limitations they might not have chosen.

A small minority of people who have a strong desire to live according to strict Islamic law do keep to Muslim company exclusively. Some refuse to watch films or listen to music, and watch only the news on the television, which they view as the ultimate means of 'mental corruption'.

Of the American festivals, the South Asian Muslims only celebrate those which have no religious connotations. They are happy to observe Independence Day (4 July) and Memorial Day, and those which emphasize family links (Mothers' Day, Fathers' Day). The two which are the most enthusiastically supported by this Muslim community, however, are without doubt Halloween and Thanksgiving, the first because it is a festival for children, and the second because it transcends religious affiliations and is a sign of gratitude to God. To celebrate Thanksgiving also implies an endorsement of the American ideology as embodied in the concept of civil religion. 'Sikander', a young Bangladeshi student born in the United States, explains how his family celebrates Thanksgiving:[84]

> Last year for Thanksgiving, my parents invited about forty people. They were nearly all Bangladeshi. The food too was Bengali. It wasn't very different from the way Americans celebrate Thanksgiving, except that they say Grace before eating, and we say *bismillah*.

A number of immigrants also say they are regularly invited to the homes of Americans to celebrate Thanksgiving. Being involved in this nationally symbolic celebration is for the immigrants an expression of their wish to become integrated, this being compatible with the preservation of their religious identity. In New Jersey, for Thanksgiving in 1996, the American Muslim Alliance Social and Family Services (AMASES-NJ), a recently formed Muslim association, raised funds to buy 300 turkeys and send them to the Somerset County Food Bank Network in Bridgewater.[85]

Christmas is becoming more and more secular but most Muslims still see it as a religious festival and do not join in. Jesus is recognized as a prophet by Muslims and given due respect, but they reject the concept of divine incarnation. Some Muslims also draw attention to the pagan origins of the festival. Christmas trees and the exchange of presents are therefore forbidden in most Muslim homes. In contrast, many Sikhs and Hindus have embraced the celebration of Christmas (the Hindu family I stayed with in New Jersey have done so, for example) and celebrate as enthusiastically as the Christians. Muslim immigrants do, however, give cards and presents to their Christian friends and neighbours.

So that their children do not feel that they 'miss out' on Christmas, Muslim parents celebrate Manlid with presents; or else, in celebrating the Ids, they substitute presents for the Idi money, often a token amount, which is given to children in the Indian subcontinent. These presents are given in the American way: laid out on the sitting room table, with each child's name called out, and so on.

The New Year – which of course does not coincide with the beginning of the Islamic calendar year – is celebrated by most South Asian Muslims because of its secular and almost universal nature.

A small minority of Muslims do not join in with any 'American' festival at all, and prefer to celebrate only the Islamic festivals.

Conclusion

It is estimated that between 20 and 30 per cent of Muslims in the United States are regularly observant. The number tends to grow as the years go by, not only because of the reasons examined in this chapter, but also because of the relative degree of religious freedom enjoyed by all who live in the United States.

To apply the *shari'ah* law strictly in the matter of divorce, childcare, marriage, inheritance and adoption is to come into conflict with American law.[86] Problems do occasionally arise in questions of childcare (especially where there is a mixed marriage) but on the whole the vast majority of Muslims respect American legislation.

The food prohibitions could be seen as creating an obstacle to the socialization and to the integration of Muslims into American social life. Similarly, a strict interpretation of *riba* could call into question the very reason why so many chose to emigrate, that is to improve their standard of living. However, the religious freedom enjoyed by Muslims in the United States, and the social structures which so favour them in New York (ever-increasing numbers of mosques, of *halal* butchers and so on) have combined to enable Muslims to maintain their religious traditions without much difficulty, in spite of occasional displays of discrimination against them (see Chapter 8).

This maintaining of religious traditions is not a mere transplantation, but implies a reinvention caused by the process of migration (as testified by the wearing of the veil, food prohibitions, burials and the celebration of festivals).

It should also be said that the relatively high level of education of most South Asian Muslim immigrants is a major asset for them as they seek to maintain their religious life: Americans respect them for this reason, and therefore are inclined to show them more tolerance than they would to less advantaged population groups. The Muslims immigrants themselves are also likely to be more flexible in their attitudes to some Islamic laws, which many can see as needing to be understood in their historical context, and therefore as less easy to apply in a modern secular society: divorce by *talaq*,[87] polygamy, childcare automatically given to the father, and so on. Above all, as we shall see in Chapter 5, this high level of education is closely linked to high earnings levels, and this in no way hampers the degree to which immigrants are observant in their religious life – rather, it means that they are able to set up efficient organizations and the institutions needed for the practice of their faith.

4

THE SECOND GENERATION
A 'masala'[1] identity

The second generation is now getting to an age where it is composed of adolescents and young adults, and the process of maturing means that it needs to create its own identity. They belong to a social group which sets them somewhat apart from what Kepel describes as the 'new young proletariat'. The majority of young South Asians in the United States are in a distinct category, owing to their parents' economic success. Kepel writes about these young 'black-white-beurs':[2]

> In this last decade of the twentieth century, the workers' movements and the trades unions are no longer in a position to take responsibility for the demands and the future in society of this new young proletariat of black, white and 'beur' youths, who are on the margins of the job-market, and living in the run-down French suburbs or the Anglo-Saxon inner cities. They proclaim their allegiance to Islam – which they load with very diverse meanings. In doing so these young blacks in America, Indians and Pakistanis in the United Kingdom, and North Africans in France take on a new community identity. They deliberately cut themselves off from the culture around them and the dominant values of the nations of which, on the whole, they are citizens by right, claiming that the society is *de facto* excluding them.

Young South Asians in the United States do not, on the whole, suffer this kind of social exclusion. Do they therefore have a different sense of their identity? Or do they also see Islam as a significant identity marker? Is this Islam necessarily the expression of a reactive identity?[3]

Before attempting to answer these questions, we shall briefly look at their school and higher education paths, and at their professional ambitions. We shall then examine the issue of acculturation.

School life and social behaviour: a 'model minority'

American society tends to see the South Asian immigrants as a 'model minority'. This distinction is also awarded to their children, who shine in school and at university and are very little represented in the youth delinquency statistics.

There are many South Asians on American campuses, including all the best ones: Harvard, Princeton, Columbia and others on the East Coast; Berkeley, Stanford on the West Coast. Their success is due to the social background of these young people, who were mostly brought up in wealthy and educated families, by parents who gave full support to their schooling. In the Indian subcontinent, and especially in India itself, the atmosphere in schools and universities is highly competitive, and this is carried over into their country of adoption. South Asian first-generation immigrants are keen to see their children achieve the same, or indeed a higher educational level to their own; they put therefore considerable pressure on their offspring. Parental authority is strong, and characteristic not only of South Asians but of the whole Asian minority, in particular Chinese and Japanese; this helps to explain the almost total lack of delinquency in this population.

There are shadows in this scene, however. Some young people do indeed go along with their parents' ambitions and go into medicine or engineering, but others prefer subjects perceived by their parents as less noble, or riskier, in that they do not guarantee stable, well-paid and prestigious employment: law, politics, journalism, business, and so on. In fact, it is not unusual to find young South Asians who have embarked on a study of medicine (pre-med) to please their parents, only to switch a few months later, maybe through lack of commitment, to other areas of study – this kind of change of direction is easy to make in the United States, where specialization in a particular field of study only starts two or three years into higher education. This situation often provokes bitterness and disappointment in the parents, and can in some cases – admittedly not very often – lead to real conflict between generations.

In behaving like this, young people are merely following the example set by their peers of European extraction in the early twentieth century:

> In Europe, children on the whole obeyed their parents without any objections, and followed in their footsteps; in America, however, children soon began to behave very differently. They no longer wished to follow in their father's footsteps, but rather to overtake him.[4]

In the case of the young South Asians, however, though they may wish to 'behave very differently', they may find that overtaking their parents is not easy to achieve, particularly for those whose parents have already reached high social and financial positions. Such a situation leads to anxiety and uncertainty in some, as they are torn between their own ambitions and those of their parents, whom they are not wanting to disappoint.

At a conference organized by some young Indians (including non-Muslims) in Houston, some young people expressed their feelings on this matter:

> Another [second-generation Indian] said parental pressure also extended to careers, with the children's ambitions either ignored or overruled . . . And another said when he announced he wanted to take English literature as a major, 'my mother wept'. Another participant told about the son of a physician couple. He wanted a career as a teacher of history, she said, and 'his parents' first reaction was, 'You will earn very little money.' It is amazing how much of the American criterion for success we have incorporated into our lives – a big house, a big car – these seem to be the only indications of success. What actually matters is that you can look back 20 years from now and say, 'I did something that gave me satisfaction.'[5]

It could be argued that the first and the second generation both follow the pattern set by earlier immigrants to the United States in the nineteenth and early twentieth centuries, in the sense that the first generation aspires above all to social and economic success, whereas the second seeks primarily to find personal satisfaction. It is worth noticing also the American criterion of success described above, which finds expression notably in having a big house and a big car: though it does not actually symbolize Indian or Islamic values, it does however express the aspirations of South Asian immigrants wherever they are, whether in the United States or in Europe, and whatever their level of education. Thus, in France or in England, South Asian immigrants, whether they are grocers or doctors, can be seen driving Mercedes or BMWs. A similar type of behaviour, stimulated by the economic liberalization, can also be observed in South Asia.

Many second generation South Asians are indifferent to these ostentatious signs of wealth and success, and even deride them. One girl makes fun of her parents in front of me and calls them 'rich' in a way that gives the term a pejorative sense, saying that they live in a house that is too big for four people, that they go to the most expensive resorts for their holidays, and so on. Members of this generation are out of step, it appears, with their peers today in South Asia, who since the economic liberalization in India at least are in the grip of a frenzy of consumerism, and are behaving in a way very similar to the first generation of South Asian immigrants to the United States. This describes the reaction of a young South Asian woman born in Buffalo (New York) who decided to move to India:

Sitting on her bed in a modest third-floor, one-room apartment in south New Delhi, Munjal, a native of Buffalo, New York, says she hates the snobbishness of many nouveau riche upper and-middle-class kids whose obsession with expensive clothes and gadgets is reminiscent of Americans in the 1980s.[6]

However, not all young people from the second generation in the United States are critical of their parents' ostentatious lifestyle; rather, they see in this success an encouragement to succeed themselves and they hope to fulfil all their parents' expectations of them.

Such conflict as does exist between the ambitions of parents and their children presents interest in that it foreshadows possible future conflicts regarding this time the acculturation process of young South Asians.

There are very few indications showing a rise in the delinquent behaviour, in the form of violence or law-breaking, of young people from the subcontinent. However, the letter below, published in *India Abroad*, is interesting in that it shows how young South Asians are seen as a 'model minority' not only by the host society but also by their elders in their own community:

> . . . I was crossing the field, and it was about 8 p.m. Some Indian teenagers were walking slightly ahead of me. The moment I came near them, they started teasing me. They were using dirty and malicious words . . . One of them asked for my wallet. By that time, I realized that they were trying to rob me. *It was beyond my imagination that a group of Indian teenagers could perform such a vicious act.*[7]

Was this an isolated incident or is it a prelude to further events of this nature? Could this be because children of more recent immigrants are finding it more difficult to become integrated in society? Or because young people are frustrated at not being able to live up to their parents' expectations?[8] It is too early to say as yet, and for the moment the description of 'model minority' seems on the whole to be justified, judging by educational success and a peaceful social behaviour. The prejudices the letter betrays are 'positive', certainly, but they are defined on ethnic criteria. This letter seems to suggest that this kind of behaviour, though out of the ordinary in Indian children, would have been understandable in children from other ethnic groups; the tendency therefore to prejudice is latent and worth noticing.

This question must also include a look at whether there are any gender distinctions to be made here. I have no data on delinquency but educationally, are there differences on the careers of girls and boys in the South Asian community? Do parents value their daughters' education as highly as their sons'?

In the Indian subcontinent, but also in the United Kingdom,[9] there is occasionally a perceptible dichotomy between the education given to girls and boys, showing that parents are more concerned about their daughters' marriages than about any professional path they may follow. In the United States, things seem very different. Nearly all the families I met wanted their daughters to go on to higher education, in spite of the cost, financial or otherwise. This desire implies, however, a contradiction as seen in the opposition between higher education and the withdrawal on ancestral values.

The following case is a good illustration: 'Salma'[10] is 20 and is studying at a good American university. She was born in the United States and her family is originally from Hyderabad. She finds it difficult to conceal the bitterness she feels at her parents' conservative views. She also emphasizes their ambiguous attitude when the question of education arises:

> I had a very strict upbringing. My parents are very religious, very conservative . . . When I still lived at home, I was never allowed my say. . . . My parents want me to have an arranged marriage. But they think education is so important that they have agreed to sending me to study hundreds of miles away from home. They allowed me to live in a student residence. Of course, they are worried and want me to call them every day, but they have nevertheless made the sacrifice.

It is clear that the choice to educate daughters and to send them to college miles away from home, in order to give them the best possible chance of future success, is not one that is lightly made. Many parents face this dilemma: the longer a young person goes on studying, the more he/she may become accultured. Despite this fear, parents do not try to curb their children's, not even their daughters', education. They, spare no effort, however, to ensure the transmission of cultural and religious values to their offspring.

Parental expectations and efforts: how to curb Americanization

The inculcation of Indian and Islamic values starts at a very young age. In families where the mother works, efforts are made to secure the services of an Indian, Pakistani or Bangladeshi babysitter. The parents who failed to find one express their disappointment, especially those whose children do not speak the mother tongue. The presence of grandparents in the family cell is seen by the migrants as a major advantage in the process of transmitting traditional and cultural values. The grandparents in this case become the role models.

Some parents, in an effort to halt the Americanization of their children, send them to India, Pakistan or Bangladesh for a part, or indeed all, of their school career, often to the best schools available (such as the Dun School in Dehradun in India), or they emigrate without their children. This practice is, however, often disapproved of within the immigrant community: children who then come to the United States for higher education after a school career in India are faced with several difficulties as they try to adapt to the American system. They have in a way to live their parents' experience over again.

Many South Asians emigrated in the hope of giving their families a better life. Even though they may not like the *mahaul* (atmosphere) in the United States, to use the expression of the Bangladeshi newspaper vendor 'Mirza', they wish their children, including their daughters, to study in the United States and to improve their chances of finding a job commensurate with their expectations.

Most immigrants therefore keep their children with them and seek other ways in which to pass on to their offspring the values they hold dear. To this end, they exercise a strict control over their children's lives, over their acquaintances and any outings. They encourage them to make friends within their own community. Girls in particular are closely supervised and although there was no significant dichotomy in the matter of schooling, it is clear that there is one in that girls enjoy less freedom than boys.

Since the 1980s, immigrants, with the same ends in view, have instigated a system of Sunday schools in the mosques and Islamic centres. New York particularly has witnessed a dramatic increase in the number of such establishments.[11] Summer camps are also laid on during the school holidays. Nathan Glazer, in his analysis of the Jewish community in the United States, explains the function of these camps for instruction and the building of relationships within the ethnic and religious group. His analysis makes it clear that South Asian parents, like other ethnic minority groups, both now and in the past, lay great store by the family. In this, they follow the pattern of minorities migrating to the United States, worried about and resistant to the risks of Americanization.

> Such questions as "Why am I a Jew?" must now arise, and it is harder to answer them in the middle-class suburb where everyone looks alike than in the urban neighbourhood where the ethnic groups are marked by outer characteristics, as so many distinct species. The parents know no answers to these questions, either because they have had no Jewish education or because their Jewish education consisted of a certain degree of traditional observance and some Hebrew and Bible (perhaps even a great deal), which does not serve to answer questions. A new form of Jewish education thus becomes necessary, and the

modern Sunday school and weekday school, designed to adjust children, to teach them why they are Jews, is gratefully accepted. It takes
over from the parents a task they are incapable of handling.

For Muslims, of course, religion and ethnicity are not so intertwined, so the
question 'Why am I a Muslim?' is not such a keen issue as for Jews. The issue
tends to be rather 'How can I stay a Muslim?' There are nevertheless striking
similarities between the two communities, both in social origin and in the
matter of religion: many of the South Asian Muslim immigrants have
received little in the way of religious education – a few traditions, a little
Arabic and a very superficial knowledge of the Qur'an. Above all, both communities are facing the same problems with their second generation and are
looking at similar solutions. This acknowledges the crucial role of children in
the survival and renewal of a community, whatever that community might be,
in the land of migration. This is what Nathan Glazer says about the importance of children:

> . . . the Jewish culture of the suburban areas, after the Second World
> War, is child-centered. The problem of how to raise the children, how
> to educate them, where to live so that they will have suitable play-
> mates, and so on, makes up a good part of middle-class conversation.
> And among the Jews these concerns are undoubtedly more wide-
> spread, because the Jews are more family-centered than perhaps any
> other large group in the country. A higher proportion marry, a lower
> proportion get divorced, and in general, fewer adult Jews live outside of
> families than is the case among other Americans. *Judaism is in large
> measure being re-created for the children*, who play a surprisingly large role in
> the service of the suburban synagogue and for whom religious festivals
> are recast so as to emphasize the pleasant and attractive elements.

This extract calls for several remarks. First of all the importance of the family,
which is characteristic of both communities. Secondly, the way in which both
communities have drawn out the sense of fun in their religious celebrations,
which echoes what was seen in the last chapter (Manlid and Id, as it were substitutes for Christmas). This is crucially important in the life of the community:
for some children and for their parents, these are the only times when they
show their attachment and sentiment of belonging to the community.

The comparison with the Jewish community is also apposite in that the Jews
are seen by the South Asians as a 'model minority', not only in the earlier sense
of their character being exemplary, as the South Asians are themselves, but also
in the proper sense of the phrase, in other words that this community should

be a model to follow, and attempts should be made by South Asians to reach the same level of success.

Glazer emphasizes that family discussions are often about the children. The reputation of a family within the community rests in large part on the success and the behaviour of the children, that is on their readiness to maintain the cultural and religious heritage. In other words, the ideal child is one who respects his or her parents, speaks the mother tongue, is observant in his or her religion and accepts the idea of an arranged marriage. When I ask 'Ismat'[15], an immigrant Pakistani woman, about this last matter, she answers:

> I think my children's happiness is the most important thing, and I don't mind who they marry [non-Muslim, non-Pakistani]. The only problem is the community.

The scrutiny of the community seems to weigh less heavily in the United States than in the United Kingdom or in South Asia, but it is nevertheless there. It would seem, though, that it is easier in the United States than elsewhere for families who wish to escape the scrutiny of the community to keep their distance, in particular when they live in upper-middle class suburbs, with no ethnic concentration, and do not or hardly participate into community activities. In any case parental expectations and the readiness of the second generation to respond to them are a central concern for most families.

Young people's expectations and reactions: from conformism towards identity awakening

Externally, the second generation look very American. This can be observed in their speech, in their accent especially, which makes it difficult on occasion for even their own parents to understand them; but also in the way they express themselves forcefully, almost aggressively, or in the verbal expressions used, such as 'Jeez' (an abbreviation of 'Jesus') after sneezing, which they prefer to the more Islamic *alhamdulillah*, and even in their writing (the way letters are formed). Their clothes also are American, including quite paradoxically for girls who wear the *hijab* (which we shall come back to), as are their gestures and ways of moving, both of which betray that same forcefulness and aggressiveness. They also display a desire for independence and intimacy; this last is often expressed by locking themselves into their bedrooms, which leads to surprise, even dismay in their parents, who see this as a most unusual way to behave from a 'South Asian point of view'.

These external characteristics are certainly not a sufficient description of the second South Asian generation, however. There is, it would appear, a dichotomy in the behaviour of these young people and the importance they attach to cultural referents. The interest they show to one or the other cultural system changes over time, in most cases. In a short story, a (non-Muslim) member of this second generation, Anu Gupta, writes:

> I had 'started' as a child who hated herself for being different, who then tried to be like everyone else, and who now, after college, is proud of who she is.[16]

This description corroborates my own observations in the field. It seems that the period from childhood to adolescence (the school years) is a time for conformism. In the next period (at university), young people on the other hand wish to seek out their heritage, symptomatic of an identity quest.

The school years: wanting to conform

The life of second generation immigrant children seems to be modelled on their peers in the middle and upper classes: they seek out the good schools, take piano and tennis lessons at the weekend (between sessions in front of the television), they socialize with American children, mostly white, as they are in the schools praised by South Asians; they join in the celebrations, especially Halloween and Thanksgiving, and they prefer 'American' food, Hollywood films and American music (rock, rap, rhythm and blues, and so on). Arthur and Usha Helweg note that these children put pressure on their parents to go to the leisure parks (such as Disneyworld) or holiday resorts their American friends like.[17] Trips to the subcontinent are not often welcomed by the children, especially when they have to stay cloistered in the family home. Trips to the homeland and their own experiences there, even when very young, are crucial in determining the way the children perceive the part of the world from which their parents hail, and this in turn will influence how willing those children are to maintain their own ethnic heritage.

To come back to the wish to conform, South Asian children can be teased, sometimes in a discriminatory way, in the schools they attend, which tend to be mostly 'white'; this reinforces their wish to appear 'as normal as possible'.

'Kabir', a 19-year-old student of Pakistani origin, remembers his school years:[18]

> When we were at school, my brother and I, we were the only coloured kids. They called us 'niggers'. The others looked at us and made jokes about camels; they didn't even know we were Muslims. From the second grade onwards I was ashamed of being coloured. Later I realized that these kids weren't necessarily racist, just naughty. We

were better treated at high school and I had white friends. I wanted to be white like them.

'Fazilat', a 20-year-old Gujarati student from eastern Africa, adds:[19]

When I was little, I always said I was American. I hated it when people asked where I was from.

This concept of conformism is complex, because in younger children it is 'one-way', and describes a desire to fit in with the American peers, whereas in adolescents, it works on a second level also, as young people wish to fit in with both their peers and their family.

Parents do not seem to be unduly concerned at the Americanization of younger children. They are often still fully occupied in the early stages of their economic integration; they therefore do not have time for the 'cultural' education of their children. Moreover, as the parents are themselves trying to become integrated into the new society, they see their children's acculturation as a good sign for the future: accustomed from an early age to the American system, they will not face the same problems as their parents. Some parents express pride in the apparent ease of their children in the American environment. It is when children reach puberty, and the parents may have now achieved the economic success they were hoping for, that they devote more attention to cultural and religious matters, and begin to see the Americanization of their children, and especially of their daughters, as a potential threat to their cultural heritage and acknowledgement of their origins. In particular, they fear that excessive westernization will estrange young people from their families or encourage them to enter at some later stage into marriages (or other relationships) of which their parents might not approve.

The young people themselves compare their parents' behaviour with that of their friends, including their Asian friends (especially Chinese and Japanese), and see it as least liberal[20] of all, particularly when it comes to activities outside of school or family. In fact, although parents in the United States are generally more liberal than parents in South Asia, they have not always realized that society in their homeland has also changed, in India especially, where the urban middle classes at least have relaxed some of the restraints placed on their children. To spend the night in a friend's home, or to go to a dance-party, does not provoke the disapproval they once did in the big cities of the subcontinent.[21]

However, if we consider the level of conservatism of the parents, the propensity of the children to rebel remains relatively low, and for some this desire to please will mean that they will ultimately accept an arranged marriage. This low propensity for rebellion, which shows up in analyses of the relationship between the generations in a diasporic situation, shows that young South Asians accept without much reaction family authority, and the traditional role the family plays in shaping an individual's social life.

The second generation young are nevertheless torn between their wish to conform both to family and to peers. This can lead to a compartmentalization of their lives, which itself generates a kind of schizophrenic or 'schizoid'[22] behaviour. Ron Kelley gives us the thoughts of a convert to Islam:

> The kids [of immigrant Indo-Pakistanis] come into the house wearing Levi 501s . . . They take off their make-up and jackets. They put on their Indian clothes. They're kind of like pajamas. And then they eat Pakistani curry and their parents think everything's OK. They don't know that when their kids walk out of the house, they're totally American.[23]

Most young people, 'wanting to please everyone', as 'Kabir' emphasizes, admit that they conceal from their parents some of what they do outside the home, especially in the matter of relationships, intimate ones in particular, with members of the opposite sex. 'Sikander', the young man of Bangladeshi origin, says:

> My parents don't like most of my friends, and they really don't like me to go out with girls. Especially as none of my girlfriends up to now have been Bengali or Muslim: there have been Whites, Blacks, Hispanics . . . My parents don't like me to listen to rap either. So whatever they don't like I do behind their backs. Because I want them to be happy and proud of me.

But he expresses regret that there should be this barrier to communication with his parents, and adds:

> If my parents were more prepared to accept what I do, in some way they'd have more control over me, because I wouldn't go behind their backs.

It seems, then, that in childhood, most young South Asians are keen to adopt a conformist attitude towards the host society, and are reluctant to search into their own cultural heritage for any cultural referents. Most children, of any ethnic background, are conformist (they want to appear as 'normal' as possible), but in South Asian children this is also understandable as they are often isolated in residential areas, and go to schools where most of their friends are white. Discrimination at school makes them even more eager to model their lives on those of their white peers. Children and young adolescents, move between a total Americanization, or almost, and a compartmentalization of their lives.

The university years: 'seeking out roots'

Parents' realization that their children need to maintain their cultural heritage, which we have already observed during the high school years, and in some cases from birth, becomes stronger as the child matures. So when the child moves from adolescence to adulthood, the anxiety of parents increases dramatically. They make every effort to bring the child back within the orbit of family and tradition, encouraging them for instance to make frequent trips to the homeland, endlessly rehearsing the advantages of an arranged marriage, and exposing the dangers and problems of drug use, alcohol, single-parent families, and high levels of divorce as good reasons to avoid too much Americanization.

Young South Asians at university do indeed start to display a greater interest in their roots, but this seems to result less from parental pressure, and more from their new environment. School was largely a white environment and gave little opportunity for contact with other ethnic minorities, in particular other South Asians. University, on the other hand, offers endless opportunities to meet a wide variety of people from very diverse backgrounds. On many campuses, especially those in the large cities such as New York, students gather quite spontaneously along ethnic lines. These campuses thus become a sort of microcosm of American society and the South Asians tend to gather together.

'Arbaz', a student from an Indian family, studying at Queens College, confirms this trend from his own experience:[24]

> Here, everyone spontaneously joins their own ethnic group. The students, especially the new ones, feel more at ease that way. They can speak the same language, and they have the same culture. There are some Indians who keep to themselves and have their own friends, but there aren't many of them.

The second generation is moreover aware of a certain racism latent within the white population (and non-white, in fact) and no longer tries to become totally assimilated. This awareness creates the conditions for an identity assertion.

This assertion can manifest in various ways: in the choice of friends (of same national, ethnic or religious background); in acquiring a taste for the foods typical of the homeland, or even of the family's home region; in renewed efforts to master (or even acquire) the mother tongue; in reading South Asian authors; in learning from lectures on Indian or Islamic civilization, concerts, and exhibitions on India, Pakistan and Bangladesh; in taking part in conferences and debates on matters relating to South Asia. Students also wish to go and spend time in their country of origin. This is not only to visit the town or village from which their parents came and to meet relatives – with whom communication can be hampered by lack of language or indeed by accent – but they also wish to travel throughout the subcontinent, or even to spend some weeks and engage in voluntary work with humanitarian organizations. It is worth noting here that members of this second generation are not only taking hold of their roots, but they are also moved, as their parents were, by a sense of mission to help the homeland (see Chapter 3).

This search for roots and identity can take on a dynamic dimension, as traditions are reconstructed, reinvented. *Bhangra* music, for example, originally from the Punjab, has been mixed with reggae, rap or techno through the diaspora, and has become very popular among South Asian young people. We shall come back to this issue in Chapter 8.

The move to university is not a complete reversal of the Americanization of the second generation, however. Most would claim from then on to have a 'double' culture. The 'double' life they led in high school is not completely abandoned: they are still anxious to please their parents and since the latter continue to disapprove of some of their offspring's activities, so young people behave differently according to where they are. 'I only tell my parents what they need to know,' 'Fazilat' tells me, smiling.

For some South Asians, the claim to have two cultures and the schizophrenia caused by the compartmentalization of their lives can bring on doubts and questions about their own identity. In *Aavaaz*,[26] an 'ethnic' magazine, one young person's comment gives a good picture of this conflict of identities:

> Your historical identity is mixed up. Who are your heroes . . . George Washington and Abraham Lincoln or Akbar the Great and Mahatma Gandhi? Sitting in history class you identify with the American colonists fighting for independence in 1776. Then you realize that your ancestors had nothing to do with it. Which nation's past is your own? You don't know.[27]

Trips to South Asia can reinforce this identity malaise in that young people no longer feel they really belong in either world. Some feel or are treated as Indians, Pakistanis and Bangladeshis in the United States, and yet as Americans in India, Pakistan and Bangladesh. Others are able to feel that belonging to two places at once is an enriching experience.

The second generation has coined various phrases to express this malaise, one of which is the famous ABCD: *American Born Confused Desi*.[28] This acrostic has recently been extended to include the whole alphabet: *American Born*

Confused Desi, Emigrated From Gujarat, Housed In Jersey, Keeping Lotsa Motels, Named Omkarnath Patel, Quickly Reached Success Through Underhanded Vicious Ways, Xenophobic Yet Zestful!

ABCDs are contrasted to the newly arrived FOBs (*Fresh Off the Boat*). East Asians are sometimes described by the image of a banana (yellow on the outside and white on the inside), Blacks by an *oreo* (a chocolate biscuit with a vanilla filling) and South Asians have ironically taken on the description used by Hispanics – a coconut, which is brown on the outside and white on the inside – as a way to describe a *Western Mind in an Asian Body*,[29] or the cultural hybrids they feel themselves to be.

It can only serve to increase the unease of young South Asians that their parents are themselves confused as to the best way to bring up their children: too strictly and they are provoked to rebel; too liberally and westernization gallops out of control. The young people see themselves as an experimental generation – Priya Agarwal uses the expression 'guinea pigs'.[30]

Young people frequently complain to me about their parents' inability to understand the conflicting pressures they face and the difficulties this causes. 'Sikander', the young man of Bangladeshi origin, puts it like this:

> I'm always embarrassed if I think I'm going to have to discuss my problems with my parents, my father especially. I always think he won't understand, especially if I'm depressed. He's very strong, and he thinks my problems are nothing compared to what he had to live through when he was my age.

This comparative lack of communication with parents further nurtures the identity confusion of their children.

It is not so much the absence of bearings which puts these young people into turmoil but rather the difficulty to choose between a plethora of points of reference. A study of the influence of religion in this regard will help to identify some to these points of reference and how they weigh on the young people. We shall also look at the problems for young Muslims of living in a society seen as permissive by 'traditional bodies', which in this case means parents, but also imams in the mosques and the teachers in the Islamic schools.[31]

Islam, a pillar of identity

Religious education: a variety of agents

To begin with, let us look at the religious practices of young people. In the first generation, as we have seen, religiosity tends to increase with the birth of children and, especially, as they start to grow up. Parents see the practice of Islam as the most effective way of transmitting traditional values and limiting the westernization of their children. Religion is tasked with inculcating not only values but also bearings so as to avoid the 'disintegration' within American society.

When immigration started, there were few institutions teaching Islam, and parents therefore were the main religious educators. Since then, although parents are still the main teachers, Islamic schools have now been endorsed with an increasing role. A growing number of Muslim children go on Sundays to these schools to learn the Qur'an and the rudiments of Arabic (see Chapter 5). The proportion of Muslim parents who prefer Islamic schools to the state schools is still very small, however: most do not wish to sacrifice the economic and professional future of their children, nor to compromise their social integration into American society. Full-time Islamic schools might encourage the youths to develop an isolationalist behaviour; most parents therefore prefer to look after their children's religious education themselves. Others choose to use a system of private lessons at home, calling on the services of an imam, for example. This option, it should be underlined, is modelled on the religious experiences of the parents in the subcontinent; in the United States, however, it is a practice fairly unusual, as there are few imams able to take on this role, but also because the Sunday schools offer a unique opportunity to meet with other members from the community.

The children now in their twenties learnt their religion at home, taught by their parents, whereas those who are younger will from an earlier age have been given more academic teaching. As the latter are mostly still quite young, it is difficult to evaluate the impact of this teaching on their religiosity and identify construction, in other words to know whether this identity will be significantly different from that of their peers a few years older.

Altogether, in spite of the growth in Islamic schools, the parents' role in transmitting on to their children Islamic values and a sense of a distinct identity remains a crucial one. The part played by Islamic schools should not be underestimated, however. As well as building up the community, they offer a religious education which is perceived by children as more rational than religious life at home, which does not extend beyond a few mechanical rituals. Those rituals are, in addition, resented sometimes by children, not only because they may interrupt their favourite television programmes but also because they fail to make much sense for children who are used to the American system of education that promotes reflection.

Religiosity and observance: a variety of practices

Second generation youths present similarities to their parents in their religious observance, their behaviour varying according to the requirements of their religion. Few observe the daily prayers, but they do attach more importance to the fast, and in general to the month of Ramadan. A study of the attendance at university prayer rooms was revealing.[32] In the week, only a handful use them for daily prayers but the Friday prayers draw quite a number of young South Asians because of its collective dimension. It is, however, during the month of Ramadan that the number of students performing their prayers increases noticeably. It appears that young people continue to attach the same importance to this month as did their parents' generation.

Qur'anic prescriptions on food are on the whole observed by this second generation. As do their parents and their peers in France,[33] they respect the ban on pork. Some follow this rule not only for the reasons given by the first generation, but also out of respect for their parents.

The importance of the food regulations in identity formation is explained by 'Rafiq', who is eleven years old and of Indian origin:[34]

> Before, I used to feel Muslim first, because of food, and because that's the first thing you know about: at school, there would be sausages for lunch and I couldn't eat them, or I'd be invited to my white friends' houses and their parents would say 'It's pork chops for dinner,' and I'd be very embarrassed. Now, at school, it's a cafeteria system, and you can choose what to eat. And now my friends know I don't eat pork, so they offer me something else. Now that I don't need to think about what I eat, I feel American first.

The insistence on *halal* food is more often flouted, however. The prohibition on alcohol is also often ignored, in a way that recalls both the first generation and young Muslims in Europe. The consumption of alcohol is often seen as a rite of passage by adolescents in Western societies, and this makes it into a particular difficulty for young people wishing both to respect the traditional prescriptions and prohibitions of their religion, and to become integrated into the host society. But the avoidance of alcohol can also become a means for young Muslims to mark their distinct identity. 'Zoya', a teacher from Hyderabad, rejoicing that her son does not drink, exclaims, 'My son is known by his friends as the *Arizona Iced Tea Kid*.'[35]

Some young people, however, do not choose to assert a distinct religious identity quite so obvious, and this can lead to difficulties since the way of life of young Americans may appear incompatible with the austerity demanded by

Islam. Beyond alcohol, such is the case with sports, especially those requiring clothing that does not fit in with the Islamic norms, with dances and with modern Western music, which not only runs counter to Muslim ideology but also, say the traditionalists, is sexually arousing.[36] Proms, the ritual celebration to mark the end of high school life, which require that one have a partner of the opposite sex, are equally condemned by the traditionalists. The response of both parents and children to these contradictory pressures reveals a tendency to compromise. Hence, parents rarely prevent their children from taking part in sporting activities, which they know to be highly valued in the American education system, because they are very keen to see their children succeed academically and professionally. Fearful that their children will rebel, they try to rationalize their own reaction by stressing the full confidence they place in their children, thus justifying themselves in their own eyes and in those of the community for their 'permissiveness'. The young, for their part, usually unwilling to forego their involvement in American society, but also anxious to please their parents, once again compartmentalize their lives to resolve the tensions.

Young people compartmentalize also in their religious life: they do drink alcohol and go to dances from time to time, but they do not for all that reject their religious heritage or their Muslim identity.

This Muslim identity comes in two forms. It can be passive, some young people practising religion as their parents have taught them, mechanically and without any genuine interest in it. This is, however, mostly the case in younger children. As they grow older, they tend either to completely reject their religious heritage, or they seek to discover it anew and to perpetuate it in the land of migration.

'Sadat', an immigrant from Pakistan, an accountant, says:[37]

> Here, young people can often be better Muslims than in Pakistan because it's something they have chosen, and because it's not forced on them by society as it is in Pakistan. In Pakistan, people fast because of family and social pressure. Here, if you fast, it's because you want to . . . My son, who was born here, spends a lot more time praying than I do, for example.

This more marked religiosity indicates a more intellectually owned identity, and points to a carefully thought-out process of self-definition. This means that young people will want to know about religion, but not necessarily in the way their parents taught them. There are also some young South Asians who are drawn by the spiritual rather than the dogmatic side of religion and they merely observe on a minimal level (they may respect the prohibitions, especially of food, and occasionally keep the fast).

The teaching given by parents does remain of fundamental importance, as it is often a predictor of the religious behaviour of the second generation. Transmitting knowledge from one generation to another can have complex repercussions, however. MK Hermansen tells us that Muslims who practise Islam and add in cultural traditions (as do the Barelwis and the Shi'a) have a greater chance of successfully passing on their religion to their children. It seems, therefore, that the way in which religion and its rituals are transmitted determines their survival in migration: if the transmission is done through cultural events and memorable rituals, the impact on the religiosity of the second generation will be assured.

This hypothesis seems to be demonstrated in the Shi'a community: the *majlis* especially, family celebrations, fulfil this role through the feelings of devotion and emotion they arouse in the participants. Children are part of these celebrations from their earliest years, and hence absorb the value attached to the model Muslim family, the *ahl al-bayt* ('the house of the Prophet'). This devotion is a requirement by the history of the Shi'a movement, even in a non-Muslim environment.[38] Shi'a parents teach their children the close link between obedience to the laws of religion and the love of the *ahl al-bayt* who gave their lives to ensure the survival of Islam.[39] The effect of the *majlis* on the family, and in particular on parents, also has an influence on the children's behaviour:

> As one Canadian Shi'a told me [Vernon Schubel], when he was very young, he would attend the majlis and watch his father cry. When he became a bit older, he would pretend to cry so as to emulate his father. Now he cries automatically upon hearing the gham. It has become a response that is beyond his control, compelling evidence of the power of the Shi'i religion.[41]

Shi'a rituals, by being able to hold the attention of the young people of the minority sect, seem to have an assured future. The Barelwi rituals, on the other hand, do not enjoy the same power of attraction and seem less secure. In fact, it would be more accurate to say that these rituals are of Barelwi inspiration, since those who practise them do not necessarily all claim to be Barelwis themselves – there are officially very few of these in the United States. The Barelwi traditions are indeed very visual and concrete, so that they are easily reproduced by the younger generation once they have seen them carried out in the family space. But in reality, the second generation has a limited interest in the rituals, or is indeed uninterested, and in some cases voice clear criticism of the rites, of which they understand neither the import nor the meaning: they are tuned into rationalism and put little value on perpetuating religion by means of social and cultural traditions inherited from their country of origin.

This kind of attitude leads to a distinct view of Islam and creates not only a gulf between the generations in their respective perceptions of religion, but also the conditions in which a redefined Islam can emerge. This redefinition process, in very few cases, may attract young people to a way of life similar to that advocated by fundamentalist groups throughout the world, while for some others it can lead them to engage in reasserting the value of Islam.

A handful of budding Islamists

Many young Muslims wish to affirm their Islamic identity, but on the whole this is expressed in behaviours and practices restricted to the private sphere. There are a few, however, who have been won over to a rigorist view of Islam and prefer to proclaim their Islam-ness more openly, both physically (through their clothing) and in their bearing towards the host society, where in particular they see themselves as charged with a mission to practice *da'wa*. I shall come back to this last point. I will here deal with the questions of the *hijab* (the veil) and *riba'* (interest and usury), and seek to define the motives behind the choices made on these questions. The issue of the veil, as far as young South Asian Muslim women are concerned, must be seen in the light not only of the Indian–American context across the generations, but also in that of their own generation in the wider Muslim world, across ethnic origins. In other words, we shall try to understand the choice made by the young Muslim women in New York in relation both to the first generation of their own community and to the young Muslims in Europe.

Let us first examine a few real cases of young Muslims who have chosen to live a life which is as true as they can make it to Islamic ideals. Only one girl I met was wearing the veil against her parents' wishes. All the others I interviewed, girls wearing the veil, and boys wearing flowing trousers and beards, have at least one very religious parent. In France, young people in North African families suffer because their parents are not able to pass on to them a sense of identity that links them to their past or to their country of origin,[42] but these young South Asians are learning on home ground the points of reference which will help them to establish their own identity. However, this very explicit religiosity cannot be explained only in terms of continuing family traditions.

The wearing of the veil in the United States does not raise hackles in the way it does in France, and even less so in New York. There are isolated objections here and there, especially in schools, but there is no national debate on the matter. If there is a disagreement, it is usually resolved in favour of the person wearing the veil. 'Asghari', whose family comes from Hyderabad, and who is 20 years old and now studying at university, tells about how her old school reacted to the religious behaviour of Muslim girls attending:[43]

> I went to a Catholic girls' school. One day, I started wearing the *hijab*. They said nothing. Then I and some other Muslim girls asked if we could have a prayer room and they let us have one. But one day, because we were wearing skirts that were longer than the school uniform, the head teacher asked us to make our skirts shorter. My mother came to the school and said she would contact the media, so the school backed down.

It is worth noting that many girls from particularly observant families go to Catholic schools, so that they are not forced into a mixed environment, and yet have the best possible chances in their educational and professional lives in the United States. Indeed, most of these children (and this applies also to boys) are in no way taken out of the economic system and they go on to universities, including to the best ones.

Yet young Muslims in New York and their peers in the French suburbs should not be systematically contrasted. They all share the experience of a confused identity, although for young South Asians this is not as poignant. For both groups, their heightened interest in religion is an extreme expression of their identity crisis, and is also part of a re-emergence of Islam worldwide. It is also worth noting that although South Asians are less subjected to discrimination on a personal level, what they perceive as a more general hostility to Islam in the United States does influence their identity construction.

Their concern for rationality also encourages young people to explore religion not just through the rituals they have learned through their South Asian heritage, but also through studying the scriptures (the Qur'an and the Hadis in particular), which they (re)interpret according to their needs. Some take these studies to a deep level and carry the logic of their search for meaning and rationality to its height, opting to follow a way of life which they interpret as true to Islam. In young people on both sides of the Atlantic one finds 'a desire to renew an inner purity, defined according to an Islamic tradition, which their parents, though Muslims also, are not considered worthy of.'[44] This concept of purity has two aspects: it refers not only to a desire for internal purification, but also to a 'pure' practise of religion, as 'Asghari' describes:

> What I love in the United States is that you can practise Islam in the purest way possible, without all the cultural stuff of our parents' generation.

However, we saw in the last chapter that some members of the first generation – noticeable especially amongst women who wear the veil – seem also to wish to come to a more intellectual understanding of their religion in the land of migration, and to leave behind them the more mechanical ways of practising Islam that they knew in their home country. These individuals are a small minority, but they bear witness to one outcome of the process of migration, and they show one way in which members of successive generations can have experiences in common. Girls who choose to wear the veil do so in the spirit we noted in the first generation of immigrants and re-assume this outward sign of Islam for two reasons. By doing so, they firstly reassure parents that they are protected from the nefarious emancipation they might otherwise be led to in American society. Secondly, they do it for themselves: under the 'protection' of the veil, these girls, who are often highly educated, feel they can enter professional areas which were traditionally the preserve of men, without fear of offending Islamic law. Wearing the veil also gives them a sense of interior pride, which can sometimes turn into a sense of superiority over other, non-veiled, Muslim girls, who they feel are in danger of losing their integrity in the host society.

I witnessed in a car a conversation between a Pakistani mother, 'Ghazala', a dentist who wears a *dupatta* to hide her hair, and her two daughters, 'Wahida' and 'Maliha', who both wear the *hijab*.[45] The mother was asking questions on Islam, using Western clichés to test her daughters' ability to explain Islam rationally. 'Ghazala' turned to me afterwards and explained this conversation:

> I purposely ask my daughters these questions because Muslims must be able to give an rational answer to the challenge of the West.

'Wahida', the eldest, added:

> Here, people don't know anything about Islam. It's a challenge for us to practise our religion.

These comments show a desire not only to have a deeper intellectual understanding of Islam for oneself, but also to be able to present it to others in a rational way.

The open display of Islam-ness, whether it be through clothing or in some other way, does not always, however, seem to stem from a careful examination of religion or from a spiritual quest. It may betray intense identity crises, young Muslims wishing to display their otherness, indeed their opposition to the host society. The example of 'Zohra', who was born in the United States and was 18 when I interviewed her,[46] is a case in point. She was wearing a scarf when I first met her. Two weeks later I caught sight of her at a lecture on Islam in a university in New York, covered from head to toe by a *burqa* which left only her eyes showing; she was taking notes without removing her gloves. The incoherence of what she said, and her aggressiveness, made it very difficult to maintain any kind of discussion with her. She told me, however, that she was studying medicine, but that she had no intention of actually practising, as she would rely on her husband to provide for her (she was not yet married when we spoke). When I expressed surprise that she had chosen such a lengthy and difficult course of study, she replied that the Muslim community needed women doctors, and if her husband were to die, she would not want to be left destitute; she also said she wanted to learn more. During the course of our discussion, in which she maintained an austerely rigid stance, she repeatedly emphasized that Islam leaves no room for compromise or adaptation. She also explained her wearing of the *burqa* by saying that God had guided her to do so. She said her family supported her in this choice. Her general demeanour betrayed a wish to make herself as different as she could. 'Sadida', the immigrant from Lucknow, had also chosen the *burqa*, but she stood out by her gentleness and the coherence of her discourse. 'Zohra', on the other hand, seemed to me to be an adolescent, in the grip of a typical rebellion, in the midst of a strong identity crisis. It would be interesting to meet her again in a few years' time. It would not be surprising to find her very much changed, and this would corroborate the analysis of Khosrokhavar, who says that Islam 'is often merely a stage, one of many individual experiences which give meaning to the different experiences of life.'[47] One can also wonder whether the desire to study medicine, without intending necessarily to practise in the future, might not be another sign of the high status of education amongst the South Asian population in the United States.

Although most young Muslim women, whether or not they wear the veil, are not in this rather exceptional category, the particular case of 'Zohra', although it is extreme, shows that these behaviours are related to the sense of identity, and it underlines the importance of religion as an expression of difference.

The *hijab* is quite often worn with jeans, indicating not only that these young women are becoming Americanized, but also that clothing might be the first stage of marking out a homogenizing process among Muslim girls. The combination of *hijab* and jeans, or *hijab* and a long skirt, which is difficult to imagine in the South Asian context, seems to be becoming the uniform of a section of young women who share an uncertainty in the face of a materialistic and individualistic society. This uniform is an outward sign of their search for identity and it also serves to create bonds between them by standardizing their physical appearance and breaking down the barriers which were erected by their immigrant Muslim parents between the different ethnic groups. I noticed that it was difficult to tell young women wearing the *hijab* apart from their faces alone, especially Egyptians from South Asians, as their skins are very similar colours. It was also worth emphasizing that there is nothing in the manner of these young women which suggests that they feel in submission to any kind of authority; they are deliberate, challenging even. In the subcontinent, a person's behaviour, and especially a woman's, is often dictated by the way in which they are seen by society around them. In the United States this awareness of how they are perceived seems to vanish, at any rate with girls who wear the veil. They appear to disregard how they are seen by those around them, and in this show of independence they paradoxically find themselves in the mainstream of a certain American concept of freedom of spirit. The girls described here are those, and they are the majority, who chose to wear the veil themselves, rather than those who wear it only because of parental pressure. One could argue that this indifference to the opinion of the host society could show that these girls feel they do not belong in the society. In fact, my interviews demonstrated that most of them think that the United States is the ideal country in which to live and practise Islam, because of the freedom available; I also noticed that the opinion of their community, which on the whole does not necessarily approve of the wearing of 'ostentatious'[48] religious symbols, was not acknowledged as a significant influence on these veiled girls.

Up to now, I have mostly examined the female population with reference to the wearing of the *hijab*. The young men present many similarities, both in their behaviour and in their reasons for wishing to rediscover the 'true' Islam. Their search for a sense of identity is provoked and sustained by the ambient hostility, or so they feel it to be, against Islam in American society, and it is fuelled by their education which has encouraged them to question themselves and the world around them. Above all, their quest for Islam is an attempt to supply what they feel secular ideologies have failed to provide.

Young Muslims face similar choices as their elders in choosing appropriate 'Islamic' behaviour. The issue of *riba'* is one which comes up again. 'Farida' is twenty-one, of Bangladeshi extraction, and this is how she explains the difficulties she has to go through in trying to fund her studies:[49]

> Should I borrow from the bank, or should I stop studying? I can't decide. I tried calling on the solidarity of my [Muslim] brothers and sisters, but that didn't help much, except that I understood that there isn't much sense of unity in the community.

Another young man, 'Arshad', of Pakistani extraction, and 23 years old, assert that he sticks to the prescriptions of *riba'* :[50]

> It is possible to live in the United States without taking out loans. Of course I was lucky – I got a scholarship for my studies. And I know I'll

have to do without a car and that I won't be able to buy a house, but I don't mind. I think the way people in my [Pakistani] community are so taken up with consumerism is ridiculous. You can live just as well without owning a car or a house.

The religious behaviours described above are those of a very small minority. However, although religion is often practised in private, it remains of great importance to young people in the construction of their own identity and in their desire either to perpetuate their own heritage, or on the other hand to blend into the dominant culture. The importance of religion is thrown into yet sharper focus when it comes to the issue of marriage.

Marriage: the stakes don't get any higher

Heaven is where you have:
an American salary
a British home
Chinese food
and an Indian wife

Hell is where you have:
an American wife
British food
a Chinese home
and an Indian salary

Does this joke, found on the Internet, reflect the South Asian ideas of marriage?

What is certain is that the issue of marriage is central because it is not only the ultimate sign of the degree of assimilation of a community into the host society, but it is also one of the main preoccupations – the marriage of daughters in particular – of both first and second generations. It also allows us to evaluate the survival and strength of links to religion, ethnic group, sect and caste. We shall also examine whether the tradition of arranged marriage, still very common in the subcontinent, persists after emigration. In other words, does the second generation keep to – or does it wish to keep to, since not all young South Asians are yet of marriageable age – the tradition of marriages arranged and endogamous, as their parents and their peers in the subcontinent experience them? It is worth noting here that although arranged marriages are almost exclusively endogamous, it does not follow that love-matches are necessarily exagamous.

The worries and expectations of the parents

The following dialogue, between 'Safia', a well-to-do Pakistani Sunni immigrant, mother of three (one girl and two boys), and myself sums up quite well, I think, the South Asian expectations of marriage:

Q: Who would you like your children to marry?

A: Anyone, as long as they make my children happy.

Q: Even non-Muslims?

A: Oh no! They must be Muslim. In fact that's my only requirement.

Q: Even if they weren't from South Asia?

A: Yes. Though frankly, I'd prefer someone from Pakistan. It makes things easier. But I've changed over time. If they are at least Muslim, then I'll be happy.

Q: Even if they were African–American?

A: Oh no! In fact, for our children to be happy, it would be better if they weren't too different from us. . .well, from them, I mean. And anyway, African–Americans are converts.

Q: So you're saying any Muslim apart from an African–American. Even a Shi'a?

A: [hesitates] I'd rather not, but I'd prefer a Shi'a to an Isma'ili or a Ahmadi.

Q: How about a poor Sunni Muslim Pakistani?

A: Who would want a poor husband or wife for their child? I'd rather they were of the same economic status as us.

We hence observe a discontinuity between the ideal (marriage to a Muslim, whatever his/her ethnic, social or economic status, or less importantly, his/her sectarian affiliation) of what one hears said officially and in groups (in the mosques especially) and the actual hopes which individual immigrants will (or might not) admit to in private. In fact, the vast majority of South Asian parents want their offspring to marry within their own community.

The conversation recorded above shows the preferences that most immigrant parents have on the matter of their children's marriage, but it also suggests that the children themselves have a major say in choosing their spouse. In reality, there is another discontinuity, this time relating to the behaviour of parents and the way they express their marriage hopes for their sons and daughters: the daughters are far more likely to be pressured into accepting an arranged marriage.

Regula Qureshi has analysed the ways in which Muslim girls in Canada are introduced to social life as they mature, and the ways in which this is designed to bring them round to the idea of an arranged marriage. I shall summarize her study, which my observations confirmed. Traditionally, marriages are arranged between families without consulting the children. Children are accustomed early to the idea that marriage will be arranged for them, and that social intercourse between the sexes is contrary to South Asian Muslim values. When families emigrate to North America, they continue to bring their children up with these values, especially the girls. The girls are encouraged to behave in modest ways (such as in their manners and their choice of clothes). Their social contacts are limited to school and family. At home their activities are restricted to homework and housework. If they go out, they usually go with the family, and the outings are to the shops, or to visit family or friends. Girls are encouraged not to have any kind of intimate acquaintance with members of the opposite sex. As Farhad Khrosrokhavar emphasizes, a woman preserves the honour of her family by safeguarding her virginity.[51] If she fails to observe this precept, she runs the risk that no 'suitable boy' from her community will want to marry her.

In a few rare cases, to avoid any danger of a marriage against their wishes, parents send their daughters to live in their home country, or they arrange to marry them very early. On rare occasions, an entire family returns to India, Pakistan or Bangladesh. Most parents, though, wish their daughters to finish their education, so these cases are exceptional.

Boys are also supposed to marry according to the traditional expectations of the South Asian Muslim community, but their marriages are not necessarily arranged, and above all they are able to live much freer lives than their sisters. The taboos on friendship with the opposite sex are not quite as strict, though any signs of deep attachment are frowned upon.[52]

Some of the more liberal families do not see arranged marriages as very relevant in the diasporic context, though where they occur they raise the social status of a family.[53] The great majority of families, however, still attach much importance to fully endogamous or at least partly endogamous (within the Muslim community) marriages.

The issue of marriage and the debates it raises are not confined to within the family, but have been much aired in recent years in the public sphere of the mosques and Islamic associations. These associations are keen to encourage Muslims to cross the ethnic divides, and to insist only on marriage within the wider Muslim community. Arguments against mixed marriages (with non-Muslims) are periodically rehearsed both in sermons or meetings and in Islamic magazines. I attended a meeting on the subject at the Long Island Islamic Center. A variety of arguments were deployed: the increased risk of moving away from religion; the higher percentage of broken mixed marriages; the difficulties of passing on the Muslim faith to the children. The marriage of men to 'Women of the Book', Christians or Jews, is permitted in Islam, but it is increasingly discouraged in the United States. This is because it is the woman usually who teaches religious values, so that children are more likely to follow her religion; such marriages also reduce the chances for a Muslim woman of finding a husband who will share her faith. This problem is in fact becoming acute and has raised the concern of Muslim families. Choosing a husband for a girl is becoming more and more difficult, not only because more boys are marrying out but also because boys are prepared to go back to their country of origin to find a spouse, and girls far less so, for reasons that are explained below. Social segregation also makes the situation difficult: men and women are separated in the mosques and in Islamic organizations, so that social meetings within the community are not easily achieved. We may wonder whether the South Asian Muslims are moving towards the situation of the Parsis[54] in London and Karachi, where the number of unmarried women is growing, because women are unwilling to marry outside their community, but there just are not enough 'suitable boys'[55] available within their own community. Members of the Muslim population have over the last few years been realizing that their daughters might find themselves in a difficult position if they are not offered more opportunities to meet people within the Muslim community. We shall come back to this point later.

Reactions and expectations of young people

There are no official statistics on mixed marriages in the United States. My own interviews suggest that many young South Asians do not necessarily object to arranged marriages (hence to endogamous marriages). One young man of 22, 'Aslam', of Indian extraction, says:[56]

> I've not had a girlfriend yet. My parents wouldn't like it, and I don't want to upset them. I've not really thought yet about marriage. If I don't find anyone, my parents will look for someone for me . . . Arranged marriages have been working for a long time in India, so they can't be that bad.

An interesting point of reference is a poll, carried out on the fiftieth anniversary of the founding of Pakistan, in which 87 per cent of Pakistanis said they were in favour of arranged marriages.

Young people do however expect their parents to show some flexibility. They want their parents to allow them to exchange telephone conversations and letters with the chosen spouse and even to meet him/her before the marriage. The most favoured scenario is one in which the spouse is chosen from among a number of suitors introduced by the parents. For the latter, what matters is the principle of endogamy, a reflection of their resistance to assimilation. As is the case in the United Kingdom,[57] most young South Asians I interviewed said they wanted to marry a Muslim, but they did not insist on the issue of ethnic origin. My observation is that South Asian Muslims rarely do in fact marry outside their own ethnic group. If they do, it is usually outside the faith as well, and usually to white Americans. Some of these white spouses convert, but not systematically.[58]

The issue of marriage suggests that young South Asians are usually not rebellious, and are quite keen to please their parents. The high failure rate of (love) marriages in the United States encourages them to accept endogamous marriages, indeed arranged marriages. Some even praise arranged marriages, both to convince others (in this case the host society) and no doubt also to convince themselves that they were right in their choice.

The marriage question also betrays a trend in the community to slow down the process of assimilation into the host society. Young people who express a wish to marry a Muslim are not necessarily particularly religious or strictly observant. They are nonetheless attached to their ethnic and religious heritage.

Sectarian affiliation does not seem to affect whether young people marry within the community. The smaller communities, be they Twelver Shi'a, Bohra or Ahmadiyya, do perhaps show a tendency to exert more pressure to 'marry in', in order to ensure the group's survival. An analysis of the marriage advertisements in *India Abroad* from January to December 1996 demonstrates that sectarian affiliation is still an important issue, whereas geographical origin is not so important and language even less so.

This conversation with 'Shabana', a Bohra girl who was born in the United States, confirms this analysis:[59]

Q: Do you go out with boys?
A: No; there aren't many Bohra here.
Q: Do you only want to go out with Bohra?
A: Yes.
Q: Do you think you will have an arranged marriage?
A: No. But I want to marry a Bohra. Because we'd have more in common. We'd get on better.
Q: Are you very religious?
A: No, but I might be later. That's why I'd rather marry a Bohra. . . Children should grow up with just one religion. . . If I don't find a Bohra here, I'll go to Toronto or London, but not to India or Kenya, because I feel Western now.

This last sentence shows that young South Asians in the United States see their peers in the subcontinent or in East Africa as more conservative than they are themselves. In East Africa, South Asians have tended to live in strictly segregated communities, faithfully reproducing the way of life they knew in South Asia. 'Shabana' identifies herself with other Bohra of the diaspora, apart from those in Africa. It reinforces the idea that even the second generation can have a preference for endogamous marriages whatever their sectarian affiliation. Young people, however, tend to prefer to be allowed to choose their spouse.

Choice of spouse: return to the homeland?

We have seen that many young people accept without much objection their parents' marriage plans for them. Many, in particular, accept to marry someone from the same religious and ethnic background.

Arranged and semi-arranged marriages are changing both in terms of time and space, and these changes affect the choice of partner as well as the place they are chosen from. Differences according to gender are also noticeable in the way a partner is selected.

At first, because of the small number of South Asian families in the United States, parents nearly all went back to the homeland to seek out their child's bride or groom. These marriages, between one person who had lived all his/her life in the United States and one who has spent all his/her existence in South Asia, tended, and still tend, to create tensions between the couple. 'Rukshana', who is from Aligarh, tells of her daughter's experience (atypical however, in that the daughter chose her husband):[60]

> When she was nineteen, my daughter was fascinated by India, and by Bollywood. She fell in love, or thought she did, with my sister's son. They married and her husband came here. But he couldn't adapt. He found America society too liberal, and he was very controlling of my daughter. In the end they divorced.

Aside from difficulties stemming from intellectual and cultural compatibility, the relationship of the couple is weakened by an inbuilt imbalance. If the husband is the immigrant, he will feel doubly disadvantaged: not only will he have to learn from his wife all about the American way of life, but he will also have to live with her family, whereas tradition advocates the reverse. If it is the wife who has come to the United States, she will be at the mercy of her husband and her in-laws, whom she may hardly know, in a country which is also totally foreign to her.[61] In South Asia itself, it used to be considered a great advantage to marry one's child to an emigrated Indian, Pakistani or Bangladeshi. Over the last few years, though, certain negative stereotypes have come to light: young women of the diaspora are accused of being too westernized and of putting their careers before their family life. Horrible stories do the rounds, telling of men who married women from the subcontinent only to take their dowry and jewels, and then abandon them. Such stories, and the many cases of men who have claimed to have important jobs in the United States, when it subsequently emerged that they were garage attendants or grocers, have made South Asian families more cautious about finding a spouse for their offspring in the diaspora. These marriages, besides, are not a cheap undertaking for a family (travel, visas and so on) and couples have to wait two or three years to obtain a visa, even after the marriage has been celebrated.

Marriages across the continents do still happen, but it seems that they are mostly of men from the United States to women from the subcontinent. Men feel that the women in the United States are too westernized and they prefer to marry someone who they feel will have more respect for tradition. Regula Qureshi has clearly shown that education and social status are often more important to a man than marriage, as a man can generally more easily find ways to express himself as an individual without stepping outside traditional family norms.[62] This tendency of men to seek a bride in the subcontinent of course makes it more difficult for women to find a partner within their own community. The male point of view is that South Asian women in the United States are 'paranoid' in their refusal to enter with them into any kind of intimate relation which might lead to marriage. The following dialogue, taken from a novel, illustrates this. A young (non-Muslim) Indian doctor from New York, who has recently married an Indian girl, goes to the airport to collect his bride, who has arrived to join him. On the way, he talks with his Indian taxi driver:

> 'Could you not meet an Indian woman living in the US?', asked Vyshna as he turned into the airport.
> 'I've dated a few, but it just didn't work out. They had the attitude that I was going to take away their rights. We had a difference of opinion regarding the definition of the word 'independence', I guess.[63]

Women more frequently marry outside the community, as they are convinced that South Asian men are more likely than most to keep a tight control over their wives. If they do accept an arranged marriage, or to marry within the community, they show a clear preference for a husband chosen (by their parents or by themselves) from among the South Asian community in the United States rather than the subcontinent. They hope that a husband brought up in the United States will allow them a greater freedom than one newly arrived from the subcontinent. Remember the words of the young Bohra woman, who very much wanted to marry within her community, but someone from the diaspora in the West.

This is the reason why the South Asian community is now trying to restructure its social life, and to allow greater opportunity for young people of the same religious, even ethnic or sectarian group to meet each other. Professionals in particular, are addressing this issue. Associations such as the IMANA (Islamic Medical Association of North America), for example, were formerly designed specifically for Muslims who shared a profession to meet but they now invite young people to attend their annual conferences. This kind of association has the advantage, from the parents' point of view, that it limits the social contacts their children will make to the Muslim community, and indeed to a milieu which is often not only exclusively South Asian, but also compatible socially. 'Ansar', a Kashmiri immigrant, and a member of IMANA, was delighted that his son, also a doctor, married a young Pakistani woman doctor whom he had met through the activities of the association.[64] For many parents, who wish to see their children marry Muslims, but do not wish to impose an arranged marriage on them, this method of finding a partner is the ideal solution.

The marriage ceremony: a replica of the South Asian formula?

To end this chapter, I shall describe a marriage ceremony I attended in December 1995. It was not necessarily a typical ceremony for the Muslim South Asian population in the United States, but it had a number of significant features which are characteristic of the community.

The bride, 'Zainab', was 27 at the time I spoke to her, and had lived in New York since she was eight. Her family was from Hyderabad, and had come to the United States in 1976. Her parents were both teachers and on a modest income. 'Zainab' had done very well in school and at Princeton, thanks to a scholarship, and was at the time studying for a doctorate in communication science at the famous university of Pennsylvania. She was marrying her cousin (her mother's brother's son), an engineer from Hyderabad (an FOB, I was told by one of the bride's friends). 'Zainab' had decided three years earlier to enter into this marriage, but her husband had suffered delays in obtaining a visa. The marriage was suggested to 'Zainab' by her parents, who left the final decision to her. There was no betrothal ceremony beforehand. This wedding is fairly unusual in that often the religious ceremony for an intercontinental marriage happens in the Indian subcontinent, because a larger family gathering is possible. But the bride's family chose to hold the ceremony in the United States, as their expenses (mainly air fares) would be kept down. The groom, 'Anwar', was admitted to the United States on the basis of his professional qualifications.

The marriage ceremony lasted for two days, but was fairly low-key in comparison to ceremonies in the subcontinent. On the first day (in the evening, in fact) there was the ceremony called *mehndi* or henna ceremony (henna is a substance which is applied to the hands and feet of the bride) in the bride's small family home in the Bronx. Only the women attend this ceremony. American friends were invited (some South Asian, some white American, one African–American and one Chinese). Altogether 15 women were present. Spread out on the table were the bride's wedding 'gown' (a multicoloured *ghagra*[65]) and some jewellery given by the groom's family to 'Zainab'. The evening began with a dinner – a subtle mix of Indian and American food – and continued with some rather syncretistic dancing (in which Indian and American dance styles were synthesized); the bride, who was not very familiar with Indian dances, laughed as she danced, 'I'm learning not to be an ABCD!' A few young women who wore the veil were present, but they stayed away from the festivities. The henna ceremony itself then began. 'Zainab' asked her mother if she should say the *isha* prayer before it started. Her mother said she could leave it until later. 'With henna on my hands?' 'Zainab' asked, and she went to pray in the room next door. The entire marriage ceremony was in fact interspersed by the daily prayer, mostly at the request of the bride herself. Her religious observance was also betrayed by her ways of speech: she frequently said *insha'allah* ('if God wills it') and alhamdulillah ('praise God'), in an accent that sounded more Arab-American than Indian. When I asked her if she was worried by the idea of marrying someone who had never lived in the United States, she said she had given the matter much thought and that as both she and her future husband were both faithful followers of Allah, their marriage should be a success, although she realized that it would not be an easy ride. The henna ceremony began under the lights for the video camera (the whole ceremony was filmed by members of the family) and the photo flashes. Two veiled young women applied the henna.

The religious ceremony itself, the *nikah*, took place on the following day. It happened in the home of friends of the bride's family: they were better off and had a house large enough to accommodate about one hundred people. The house was decorated for the occasion. The settee on which the couple were to sit had been curiously arranged: it was covered in a red and black velvet fabric, so that it looked like the chairs provided for wedding couples in grand hotels on the subcontinent. Above the settee a white canopy had been hung, decorated with paper roses and a golden garland, reminiscent of the train of a Western bride. Behind the settee there was an Islamic inscription.

The groom, 'Anwar', and his family (seven people altogether), were about an hour late, true to South Asian form (admittedly there was a snowstorm that day). They had arrived in the United States that same morning. In the corner of the lounge, wearing her *ghagra*, 'Zainab' was reciting the *asr* prayer. Most of the women were wearing the *shalwar kameez*; the groom was wearing a Western suit, but also a turban (*pagri*). The *nikah* ceremony began: the bride's brother recited some verses from the Qur'an in Arabic with an American accent, and then read out the English translation. Men and women sat in two adjoining rooms, separated by a *purdah* made of garlands. The women watched on a television screen the ceremony that was being celebrated on the men's side. The bride's brother introduced the groom. Then the bride's sister introduced her, followed by her friends. This tradition is not from the subcontinent, but is borrowed from American culture, and is associated with the speeches and toasts to the bride and groom.

After these introductions, the bride's brother gave the *azan* (the call to prayer) and some of those present, including the wedding couple, recited the *maghrib* prayer. The ceremony then resumed. The witnesses came over to 'Zainab', asked her, in Urdu, if she was willing to marry 'Anwar', and gave her a *mehr* (a dower, which would remain hers if the couple were to divorce) of gold bracelets. 'Zainab' acknowledged them in silence and signed a register. The witnesses then translated to the women what had just been said. Then it was the turn of the *qazi* (or judge) to ask 'Anwar' if he was willing to marry 'Zainab'. The young man repeated three times in a loud voice *qubul hai, qubul hai, qubul hai* (I am willing). There was then a recitation from the Qur'an, followed by the translation into English. Then followed a sermon on marriage in Urdu from the *qazi*, which was also translated for those present. The groom then went over to 'Zainab' and joined her on the settee and, somewhat embarrassed, the couple allowed the many amateurs present to take photographs.

Then came a festive meal. The food had been prepared entirely by the women of the bride's family. The food was laid out on the dining room table in the way of grand Indian restaurants or hotels. The men ate in the main living room and the women went down into the basement. Long tablecloths were spread out on the floor. The women sat down cross-legged and relished their meal.

The bride's friends gave her some lingerie (not really in accordance to the norm of Islamic modesty).

The young couple were to spend the night in a hotel. They would register their marriage with the American authorities the next day. They would not go on honeymoon straight away for financial reasons.[66]

This marriage demonstrates the desire to maintain religious and cultural traditions, but it also suggests that changes are being made, not radical but significant in some ways. In the first place, this marriage shows the lack of correlation between the level of education and the propensity to enter into an arranged marriage. From a very early age, children absorb the rules that govern marriage and sexuality, so that there is rarely much opposition to parents' wishes in the matter. The strong tendency towards compromise, already mentioned, is here corroborated. In this case, the parents did not impose their decision on their daughter but let her take her own decision. Most immigrant families and especially young people may accept endogamous marriages but not as much arranged marriages. However, on occasion, the only way of staying in the community is to have an arranged marriage. It is worth noting that despite the marriage described above, marriages between cousins are less frequent in the United States than in South Asia, or even in the United Kingdom.

In the ceremony itself, a certain number of aspects show how cultural and religious traditions are being maintained: the henna ceremony, the segregation of men and women, the kind of food served at the main ceremony, the meal around a cloth on the floor, the clothing worn by the women and especially by the bride, and the video recording of the entire ceremony (though not by a professional, as it would generally have been in the subcontinent). There was one major difference in comparison to middle-class weddings in the subcontinent, where the amount of money spent on the occasion is often huge (ceremony in a large hotel, with several hundred guests, and so on), which can be financially crippling for the family. Many weddings in the United States are also lavish affairs, especially as South Asians living abroad are often given to ostentatious spending as a sign of social prestige.[67] The wedding I was invited to, on the other hand, was modest. No dowry was asked of the bride's family by her in-laws, although the custom is widespread in the subcontinent. There were probably three reasons for this: when cousins marry, a dowry is far less frequently required; the girl had American citizenship, which is often considered to be an adequate substitute; and religious families often avoid this custom, which is perceived to be one take from Hinduism – in Islam, the man pays the bride price, rather than the other way around. And a *mehr* of gold bracelets was indeed given to the young woman. The dowry system however has not been abandoned in diaspora – except in very religious families – especially when the groom goes to the subcontinent to seek out a bride. The dowry can then reach monumental proportions, especially if the groom is very well qualified. When the marriage takes place between two young South Asians born in the United States, and if the marriage is an arranged one, the question of the dowry is also raised frequently.[68]

Another feature which would have been very unusual in a marriage ceremony in the subcontinent were the interruptions, by the bride herself, for the recitation of the daily prayer, in the very room where the marriage was being celebrated. Such a phenomenon demonstrates the increased and more extrovert Islamization of Muslims in the diaspora, even when the family, as in the present case, would not claim allegiance to any fundamentalist group. And on the subject of Islamization, a new type of segregation was evident at this wedding: it was not only the men and women who stayed apart, but women also, since during both ceremonies the girls who chose to wear the veil stayed together, a distance away from the other women.

The question of Islamization leads us to discuss the location of the main ceremony, in this case a private home. In South Asia, most weddings are still celebrated in homes, in hotels, or in community halls designed for such occasions. However, amongst fundamentalist groups in particular, there is a detectable move towards celebrating weddings at the mosque, in imitation of a tradition which goes back to the time of the Prophet. This tradition is not hallowed by scripture, since marriage in Islam is a contract rather than a religious act. In the United States, weddings celebrated in the mosque are on the increase, not so much because of the influence of fundamentalist groups, but maybe in imitation of American weddings, which are celebrated in a church, hence in a consecrated space. The mosque in the United States is in fact not only a religious space, but also a community resource. Rooms are reserved in them for various kinds of celebrations, including weddings, a fact which can give rise to controversy. Strictly orthodox Muslims consider that the mosque is exclusively a sacred building, and that it should not be profaned by hosting activities which are frivolous or even anti-Islamic (in case music or dancing are included). They oppose the use of the mosque for celebrations. In fact, in mosques belonging to South Asian groups, marriages are only celebrated in a way that strictly conforms to the requirements of Islam, and any ensuing festivities take place in a hotel or a private home. In the Arab community, on the other hand, it would appear that rooms in some mosques are kept both for religious celebrations and also for more festive occasions.[69]

To return to the marriage of 'Zainab', some of the external features, such as the decorations used, were borrowed from both South Asian and American traditions. A particularly remarkable feature was the introduction of the couple by their family and their friends, the only truly Americanized trait of this wedding, apart from the translation into English of the Urdu phrases and the readings in Arabic from the Qur'an. This last practice, which is rarely done in the subcontinent where few people understand Arabic and not all the guests would necessarily understand Urdu, corroborates our earlier hypothesis that immigrants wish to have a greater rational understanding of their faith.

Conclusion

Young South Asian Muslims are on the whole highly educated, thanks largely to their parents' efforts to make this come about, even if their offspring do not always choose the career path they might have preferred. The young are therefore, as their parents were, structurally integrated into American society. They are hence different from many of their peers in the United Kingdom, and from the African–Americans in the United States and the North Africans in France. They are nevertheless still strongly attached to traditional values, as testified by the high value they place on the family, which is still the central point of reference.

Islam is a strong component in the sense of identity of young South Asian Muslims. However, this often seems to be a response to a search for meaning in a highly materialistic society, rather than a strike back at the host society, leading to confrontation, as seems to have happened to many of their peers in the United Kingdom and the North Africans in France. Discrimination does affect some young South Asians in the United States, and may reinforce their sense of identity, but it does not seem to be the principal factor. There is also a distinction to be made: on the one hand are young people for whom Islam is an important part of their identity, but they do not carry this sentiment into a visible or rigorous practice of Islam; on the other hand a small minority not only questions the traditional teachings, but in fact pursues the study of Islam to the point of living as strict a Muslim lifestyle as is possible in a non-Islamic country. The process of migration and the style of American education have combined to cause quite a few young people – more than among their peers left behind in the homeland – to refuse to take part in rituals in which they cannot see any meaning, and to expect rational explanations. The youths do not try so much to rationalize religion itself but tend to apprehend Islam on a more rational mode in migration, as the mechanical way of practising religion which is still current in South Asia is not satisfying.

The conciliatory attitude of young people to their families and the importance they still attach to Islam in the construction of their identity combine to make them still open to the tradition of endogamous marriages, and even to arranged marriages, though their format may be less rigid than they have been in the subcontinent.

There are still internal conflicts for these immigrants' children, it must however be said. Their parents often do not understand the contradictory pressures assailing them from family and American society. These contradictions can lead to schizophrenic behaviour and a compartmentalization of their lives in a more marked fashion than in the first generation, especially among adolescents. Some (not many) of the young rebel against parental authority, either by breaking away altogether, or by taking up a strong Islamic stance (they wear the veil against their parents' wishes, or express dissatisfaction with the mechanical rites they see them practising). In some other cases, this uneasy sense of identity can open up the doors of creativity, as young people seek to define themselves – this has led in particular to a flood of novels and short stories by young South Asians, women especially: at least three anthologies have already been published of short stories, poetry, essays and extracts of novels.

There is still the question of attitude towards American society. The preceding analysis suggests a close link between the society and the way young South Asians are seeking to define themselves. They express their 'otherness' in response and in reaction to the society around them, but it has been the process of their migration – or rather, their parents' migration – to this particular country, the United States, which has enabled a certain line of thought leading to a particular construction of their identity and the establishment of the cultural and/or religious organizations which help define them.

PART 3

REDEFINING ISLAM

5

ISLAMIC INSTITUTIONS
Proliferation and plurality

The expansion in mosques and Islamic centres

Mosques and Islamic centres were first set up in the United States in the first half of the twentieth century. The oldest mosque – still there today, but now a site of historic interest – was built by Arab Muslims in Iowa in 1934.[1]

In the following years, mosques and Islamic centres were built across the United States. From the 1960s and '70s onwards, when large numbers of qualified immigrants arrived, South Asians especially, Islamic institutions multiplied. In 1992 it was estimated that more than 2,300 mosques, schools, Islamic centres, Islamic publishing houses and so on had been set up in the United States.[2]

Establishing an exact number of mosques and Islamic centres is not easy, though, as not all are officially registered. New ones are regularly opened, and others move or close down.

Since 1992, the American Muslim Support Group, based in Missouri, has undertaken to list Islamic institutions in the United States in the *Resource Directory of Islam in America*, edited by Sheila Musaji. This directory shows that in 1994 there were 953 mosques and Islamic centres. New York state, with 124 mosques, was behind California (158), and ahead of Illinois (67). Only four states had no mosques: Hawaii, Maine, Vermont and Wyoming.

In New York itself, there were more than 70 mosques in 1993 – twice as many as in the previous decade[3] – of which half were built by immigrants.[4] There were twelve on Long Island in 1995.[5]

Towards American mosques?

As the number of Islamic institutions has grown, their role also has changed. Before the 1960s, mosques were built to meet personal needs (maintaining faith and culture[6]) and for the here and now (the need for a Muslim cemetery, for children to receive a religious education and so on[7]). Since the 1960s, the religious education of the second generation has remained one of the chief functions of the mosques, but they have also expanded their activities into other areas. Islam is apprehended in a more dynamic mode, as immigrants seek to think through the ways Muslims should live and behave in a non-Muslim society. The role of the mosque is now extending beyond simply meeting the needs of the community: it is becoming the sacred space in which the ideal Muslim community may come to life. It can be gauged from the multiple functions of the mosque. To the usual religious roles (place of prayer, of religious instruction and of celebration for Islamic festivals) are now added both social functions (wedding celebrations, the organization of funerals and so on) and a political function, the mosque becoming the focal point for the development of group solidarity. This last dimension is particularly significant, as the United States gathers Muslims from widely varying cultures around the globe. The mosque is becoming the hub of a community which is built across ethnic divides. Mosques serving specific ethnic groups are, however, also established given that the Islamic community in the United States is growing considerably in size as the years go by.

Mosques, the Islamic space par excellence, serve to signal to Americans the presence of a Muslim population. They symbolize the institutionalization of Islam in a non-Muslim country, hence legitimizing the Islamic religion in the American context, particularly vis-à-vis Jews and Christians. As an indirect consequence, the mosques are also becoming the strategic points from which missionary activity, or *da'wa*, is organized, this being one of the main preoccupations of the current Muslim leadership in the United States. Proselytes for a long time aimed their preaching at the Muslim population, urging them to practise their faith in a more rigorous way; they are now turning towards the non-Muslim population as well. Two approaches are used: direct proselytizing, and a more indirect approach, in which proselytes hope that non-Muslims will be attracted to the exemplary lifestyle of pious Muslims.[8] Islamic organizations have been set up with missionary activity as their principal aim and we shall further examine this issue at a later stage. The mosques themselves are also, to a greater or lesser extent, engaged in converting people to Islam.[9]

This coalition in role of the mosques in the United States can be explained in a number of ways. It has first to do with a change in the social and economic profile of Muslim immigrants: in the first half of the twentieth century, Muslims were few in number and were on the whole not highly educated, and keen to merge quickly into the host society. From the 1960s onwards they were joined by large numbers of Muslims, mainly from the professional and intellectual classes.

The 1960s were moreover characterized by worldwide Islamic revival.

Students were influenced in large numbers by the fundamentalist thinkers of the twentieth century such as the Pakistani Maulana Mawdudi (see Chapter 1), and the Egyptian Sayyid Qutb (1906–66),[10] who took up the concept of community based on the idea of the *umma*. In the context of an immigrant group within a host society, it led to a growth in the sense of being a distinct community. Inevitable tensions opposed the earlier immigrants to the newer arrivals: the former did benefit from the religious teaching of the latter, but some continued to maintain that immigrants should seek to become assimilated into the host culture.[11]

The ethnic composition of these new arrivals also played a part in the transformation of Islam in the United States. The South Asians, who arrived in the 1960s and '70s, were particularly energetic in setting up community structures: the Pakistanis because Islam is the *raison d'être* of their home country, and the Indian Muslims because they are used to negotiate a space and legitimacy in a non-Muslim environment.

From the 1970s onwards, Muslim countries, in particular Saudi Arabia and the Gulf countries, donated large amounts of money to help set up durable organizations and institutions in the Muslim community. This assistance, however, also earned these countries the right to exert their influence on these organizations.

The American context must also be taken into account as we look at the growth of Islamic institutions. Freedom in the United States permits these religious groups to practise their religion, as religious organizations are protected by the constitution. This does not, in practice, prevent discrimination against Muslims (see Chapter 8), urging the latter to reinforce their efforts at organization, as a defence against hostility.

The ways in which these institutions are built up are in large part borrowed from American society: the mosque tends to function along the same lines as a synagogue or a church. In addition to the new functions of the mosque, outlined above, a new tradition emerged in migration: 'services' on a Sunday. The 'Lord's Day' is the only official day off in the United States, when Muslims can gather at the mosque and participate in various activities: meetings, discussions – or even official conferences with Muslim or non-Muslim guest speakers – taking different themes each week, and often focusing on the needs of Muslim communities in a non-Muslim context. Classes are also conducted for children (study of the Qur'an, lessons in Arabic). We saw elsewhere that a growing number of marriages are being celebrated in mosques (see Chapter 4).

Although Muslims are using their mosques in a similar way to a church or a synagogue, they are anxious to mark out their differences from the other two religions of the Book. They are very keen that the mosque should be clearly defined as Islamic, in the hope that this will help to make Islam a permanent and recognized feature of the American cultural landscape. The outside appearance of the mosque is therefore most important, and Muslims seek to give this sacred space a distinct and visible Islamic flavour.[12]

As the role of the mosque has changed, so also has that of the imam, which is now more akin to that of a pastor or a rabbi. His traditional tasks of leading prayers and preaching have been joined by others: in many mosques, the imam gives advice on matters of belief and religious practice; he is part of the administrative team at the mosque; he teaches the Qur'an and Arabic to children; he visits the sick in hospital.[13] If he speaks good English, he can also become the spokesman of the Muslim community and inform Americans about Islam, speaking in churches, synagogues and schools.[14]

The imam's role has indeed changed but the absence of clergy as such and of a supreme religious authority still remains a challenge. When the first mosques were built in the United States, the function of the imam was frequently taken on by novices who then imposed their own views, although these were not invariably in conformity with Muslim orthodoxy. When large numbers of Muslim immigrants arrived in the 1960s, they came with 'imported' imams, who had been trained in seminaries in Muslim countries, or at least countries with a large Muslim minority population, such as India. These imams have received a traditional religious training and are more orthodox than their predecessors. They were, however, less well able to understand American society, and are therefore ill equipped to meet the needs of immigrants. Hence, they are more likely to drive them, and their children especially, away from religion. Some of these imams are also funded by governments abroad and tend therefore to preach in a way that would serve the interests of their funders. And they are prey to the temptation of any community leader to abuse their position for their own ends, relegating the interest of the community in second place.

To counter this kind of difficulty, the American Islamic College was set up in 1983 in Chicago, on the initiative of Ahmad Sakr, Lebanese by extraction, who had been a representative of the Muslim World League to the United Nations. This body exists to educate imams, or at least a Muslim elite within American society. It is accredited by the Illinois Board of Higher Education to grant Bachelor of Arts degrees in Islamic studies and Arabic. It offers four-year courses in 'secular' subjects (history, political sciences, social sciences, computer science and so on) and in religious subjects (study of the Qur'an, of the Hadis, of the *fiqh* – Islamic jurisprudence – of Muslim thought and ethics, and so on). The institution is open to non-Muslims as well and welcomes students from all corners of the globe (especially the Middle East, Asia and Africa). Students are offered a Muslim environment and courses taught by specialists. The AIC is currently the only institution of its kind in the United States.

During my research in New York, I did not meet a single imam who had been educated there. Indeed most mosques in the United States are still having to employ 'imported' imams. The 1990 immigration laws made it easier for imams to come to the United States, however; it says that a mosque, or any other religious establishment, can cause a 'religious professional' to come, as long as he is qualified to degree level at least, and has a minimum of two years' professional experience.[16]

The move to America has changed other roles besides the imam's. Women have also been affected by the developments in mosque life in the United States. In the subcontinent, women were rarely involved in the activities of the mosque. Ashraf 'Ali Thanawi, in *Behishti Zewar* ('Ornaments of Paradise'), one of the reference manuals used by Muslims in South Asia, recommended that women should pray at home.[17] In the last few years, a group of Sunni women in Kerala, and some Shi'a women in Lucknow, who wanted to be allowed to pray in the mosque, provoked a defensive reaction from fundamentalists.[18] In the United Kingdom, in Bradford in particular, few mosques make space available for women to pray.[19] In the United States, on the other hand, women are in some places an important part of the life of a mosque. They do not often attend Friday prayers – South Asian women come to these even less frequently than other Muslim women – but they sometimes turn up in large numbers on Sundays or to perform the *tarawih* prayers during Ramadan. In New York, even the Tablighi Jama'at mosque has a room reserved for women (see below). In more progressive mosques women hold positions of responsibility in the administration. Leading prayers is still however a male prerogative, while women pray in the room next to the men, the prayers being relayed over a loud-speaker.

In fact, the religious observance of women has changed greatly in the United States. Their needs were traditionally met by the Sufi shrines and in their absence, women have created organizations and new forms of worship. More than one hundred Muslim women's organizations have been created.[20]

It appears that the mosque develops its own characteristics in diaspora. A sacred space *par excellence*, it also takes on social and political functions on a dynamic mode. Far from being the mere transplantation of an existing institution, it has taken on new and essential roles to serve a Muslim community anxious to ensure the survival of its religious heritage. Relationships with the host society are also negotiated within it.

A few cases are presented below, to explore the complex structure of American mosques. It is worth bearing in mind that only 20 to 30 per cent of Muslims regularly attend the mosque; the remainder are concentrating on becoming integrated into American society.

Case studies

I have chosen as my case studies four Sunni mosques, each individual in its way, and I shall show how they were set up and how they function. None of them is affiliated to a particular Islamic movement. All four are officially open to all Muslims, regardless of ethnic group.

I will then study two other Sunni mosques. They do not officially present themselves as Bangladeshi, but they are typical of mosques that cater for a specific ethnic group.

Lastly, I shall look at the mosques and *jama'at khana* of the sectarian minorities: the Shi'a, the Isma'ili Nizari, the Bohra and the Ahmadiyya.

Sunni mosques and Islamic centres

It seems that the white American journalist who converted to Islam, Alexander Russell Webb (1847–1916) was the first to set up an Islamic institution in New York, in 1893. The Ahmadi sect claim to have converted him (see Chapter 1),[21] but a number of other sources suggest that he converted in 1891 when he was Consul in Manila, following a correspondence with a member of the Bombay town council, a certain Budruddin Abdullah Kur. The following year Webb went to India, where he collected funds from rich and influential Bombay businessmen, and then to Turkey. He returned to New York in 1893 and established the American Moslem Brotherhood. He was nicknamed the 'Torch Bearer of Islam'. He also founded the Moslem World Publishing Company, which published two journals, the *Voice of Islam* and *Moslem World*. Webb was accused of embezzlement, however, by the Nawab of Baroda amongst others, and his reputation and projects were brought to ruin.[23]

At the beginning of the twentieth century, Muslim immigrants from Poland and Russia founded, in 1907, the American Mahommedan Society, the first institution in New York to be organized around a mosque. The mosque has been extended and changed over the years, but it is still in existence.[24]

In 1928 a second 'proper' mosque was established by a Moroccan called Sheik Daoud Ahmed Faisal: the Islamic Mission of America for the Propagation of Islam and Defense of the Faith and the Faithful. He also founded an Islamic school in 1950, the Institute of Islam. The Islamic Mission of America was situated in Brooklyn and up to the 1960s it drew mainly diplomats, businessmen and students. From the 1970s, however, they were replaced by factory workers. Faisal was helped by another Moroccan, a certain Mohamed Kabbaj, who took over leadership of the mosque when Faisal died in 1980. The principal achievement of the Islamic Mission of America was to bring Muslim immigrants and African–Americans closer together. The

African–Americans were offered an alternative to the rather unorthodox Islam of Elijah Muhammad's Nation of Islam,[25] which was based in Chicago and had opened a branch in Harlem in 1946. Malcolm X became imam there in 1954. From the 1950s onwards, black Islam thus became a significant feature of the New York scene.[26]

In 1952, the United Nations moved to New York and brought into the city a large number of Muslim diplomats and dignitaries. They played a founding part in the building of the Great Mosque of New York.

The 'big mosque' of New York

The largest mosque in New York, and the oldest in Manhattan, is between 96th Street and Third Avenue, hence on the edge of the posh downtown and the south-east of Harlem (Map 7). This mosque is known as the Islamic Cultural Center of New York (ICCNY), and according to the leadership it is the first stage of a huge project which will include a school, a library with a reading room, and a museum.

The idea of the mosque first arose in the 1950s, in response to the needs of Muslim staff at the United Nations. The project only really gathered pace in 1966, when the governments of Kuwait, Saudi Arabia and Libya gave 745,394 dollars for the construction of the mosque. The government of Malaysia gave another 10,000 dollars. Land (about 3,000 square metres) was acquired in North Manhattan for 308,000 dollars. Egypt undertook to appoint imams trained at Al-Azhar.[28] A board of manangement was set up, and construction work started, over the remains of an old building.[29]

It was not until 1991 that the mosque was ready for inauguration. Between 1967 and 1989, the completion of the building was announced four times, but the project was delayed by a number of legal proceedings. One particular accusation was that the leadership of the mosque had been abusive when dismissing an Iranian contractor because he had taken on Jewish technical consultants. Conflicts also opposed the progressive and the traditional factions in the board of management on matters of architectural design. On the basis of a compromise, Skidmore, Owings and Merrill,[30] a particularly well-known firm of architects, drew up the final plans.

The official inauguration of the project took place on 16 May 1987 in the presence of the Mayor of New York, the diplomatic corps of the Muslim countries, and of the Muslim community. From 1988, the Id ul-Fitr and Id ul-Adha prayers were said in the basement of the mosque, before the building works were finished. Three thousand people came to each. The mosque itself was officially inaugurated on 25 September 1991 during a ceremony at which the Emir of Kuwait, Sheikh Jaber al-Ahmad al-Jaber, was present. His government had given half of the 17 million dollars needed to erect the mosque.

The building is impressive, its external architecture resolutely modern. The interior is luxuriously appointed: the floor is covered by a deep almond-green carpet with marble around the edges. The calligraphy is in the *kufi* style. The choice between *kufi* or *nasta'liq* is significant, as it shows which ethnic group is the dominant one in the mosque. The *kufi* style is preferred by Arabs, the *farsi* or *nasta'liq* style by Iranians and South Asians. The first is straight and angular, the second rounded and cursive.

After initial apprehension, people in the neighbourhood now seem to have accepted the presence of such a symbolic building. It is only at the time of the Id festivals that they show irritation, as the festivities attract thousands and increase traffic.

Since the Islamic Cultural Center was established eight men have held the presidency of the board of management, of whom there was only one Pakistani, Amjad Ali, the others having been mostly Kuwaitis.

Two Egyptians are working as imams, one of whom is Dr Abdel-Rahman Osman, who is also the Director of the mosque. *Resalah*, the official bulletin of the centre, shows that the role of the imam is very varied, and this corroborates our earlier observation on the multiple functions of the imam. According to *Resalah*, the imam leads prayers, and answers questions on religion asked by individuals or groups, Muslims and non-Muslim alike. The questions may arrive by post – from the United States and from abroad – or can be asked over telephone, or through personal meetings. They can come from governments, prison authorities, political personalities, the media or from lawyers, *Resalah* explains. The imam is also expected to welcome visitors from different religious or educational institutions. He has to reply to invitations to conferences from schools, churches and syna-gogues, and take part in ecumenical meetings and discussion groups. Sometimes he is a teacher, giving religious instruction at the weekend to interested parties, and at other times he is a marriage counsellor helping the faithful to solve their mat-rimonial problems; finally, he is in charge of running funeral ceremonies.

This impressive list of duties was confirmed to me by Abdel-Rahman Osman himself, who had been trained at Al-Azhar. In Muslim countries the imam does not have as many responsibilities, as a number of the tasks can be carried out by the *qazi*, the *mufti*,[31] and so on; the diasporic context and the resultant lack of resources explain this phenomenon. This demanding list pre-supposes that the imam will be a figure of consensus, well respected, of moderate views, able to rely on the support of a majority of his faithful, and not likely to arouse hostility from the host society. Being 'catapulted' from a for-eign country is not a guarantee of survival, especially when he comes into the position of imam in the prominent Islamic Center of New York.

In fact, Abdel-Rahman Osman is a most affable and dignified man, and he seems well able to meet the challenges. He preaches on Fridays in *Arablish* (English with a strong Arab accent) and his sermons are both moderate and show his desire to call Muslims to unity. But it is difficult to forget that he has only recently arrived in the United States and may not always be able to live up to the expectations of the immigrant population. His position on many issues is conservative. When I express surprise that so little space was reserved for women, when the mosque is designed to take 3,000 worshippers, he replies that it is easier for men to come to the mosque, as women are busy with their household duties; they might be pregnant, be bringing up young children, or be menstruating. This kind of statement is unlikely to appeal to the younger generation.

Women are indeed not much in evidence in the mosque, when many come to worship on a Friday. I went one Friday in November 1995, when about 2,000 people had responded to the call to prayer. There were only about 50 women, in the same room but on a mezzanine, at the back. No South Asian women were present, although there were many South Asian men among the American, Arab, Indonesian (for example the *muezzin*[32]) and other Muslims. The absence of the South Asian women can be explained by the fact that (apart from the Shi'a) women in the subcontinent attend the mosque even less than do women in other Muslim (or non-Muslim) countries. The issue of location is also significant: only a very small number of South Asian Muslim women live nearby, whereas most South Asian men frequenting the mosque usually work not far away.

As to ethnic origin, people attending this mosque come from varied backgrounds. Its diversity seems to be a microcosm of the Muslim population of the United States. When prayers end, however, people seem to gather spontaneously on ethnic lines. This backs up what a Pakistani leader once said 'We pray together, and then the Pakistanis go back to their curries, and the Arabs to their kebabs.'[33] After a few hurried conversations, most go back to work.

On the day I went to this mosque, I saw a small group who stayed behind to chat; some were crowding around the imam, asking him questions. Then a small group took shape around him and a young African–American woman. She had just announced that she wished to convert to Islam. The imam made her recite the *shahadah*, reminded her about the Five Pillars of Islam, and about the principal prohibitions. The group then shouted out *Allahu Akbar* ('God is great'). The following moments were intensely emotional. A man asked the girl what her first name was. She replied 'Patricia', and he replied, 'From now on, you will be Latifa.' Several people congratulated her and encouraged her. Conversion had happened. A few moments later, another African–American group gathered. Most were Christians who wanted to know more about Islam. The imam spoke with them for a few moments.

Unlike other mosques, the 'big mosque' does not engage in missionary activity, the imam told me. People come to convert on their own initiative.

Although the imam does not act as a missionary to non-Muslims, he is responsible for teaching young Muslims on Saturdays, when they come to learn Arabic and to read the Qur'an, so as to make sure that they will preserve their religious heritage. The Sunday classes are taught by volunteers. The classrooms are in the mosque basement, as are the imam's office, the hall used for social events, and a small Islamic bookshop. The bookshop stocks various books on the Muslim religion, in English and in Arabic. There are also books, mostly published in the United States, which explain how to live according to Islam – they are support materials for the classes given at the mosque – and the place of women in Islam; there are Arabic dictionaries, children's books, prayer beads, prayer mats, calendars, as well as stickers, bookmarks and mugs with Qur'anic inscriptions, or even typically American catch-phrases such as 'I love Islam'.

The Islamic Cultural Center of New York, in its monthly bulletin *Resalah*, regularly reminds readers about the meaning and practice of the Five Pillars of Islam, and recounts the history of Arabs at the height of Muslim civilization. There are also a few pages for replies to readers' questions on respecting Islamic requirements. As with many Islamic centres, marriages are a part of the activities at the big mosque of New York. In some cases, the whole ceremony happens in the mosque itself; in others, only the religious part takes place there, while the rest is organized elsewhere.

The Islamic Cultural Center of New York, the principal mosque of Manhattan, seems to be very well organized. It occupies a very particular position from the ethnic point of view: it attracts mostly immigrants at present, but its location not far from Harlem could be a key fact in drawing closer immigrants and African–Americans, following the lead of the Islamic Mission of America set up by Faisal in Brooklyn.

The taxi drivers' mosque

All mosques in New York are far from being as organized as the Islamic Cultural Center in Manhattan. Some could hardly be called mosques at all, not only because of their appearance (no dome or minaret), but also because they do not fulfil all the functions normally taken on by the mosques in the land of migration.

Nevertheless, these basement prayer rooms are an essential part of the lives of the immigrants who wish to observe the prescriptions of Islam. On Fridays especially, at the time for noon prayers, these mosques play a role similar to that of the larger, more organized mosques. They welcome many faithful who will have chosen the mosque because of where it is located. Depending on the neighbourhood, the social profile of the attenders will vary. In the south of Manhattan, the Ar-Rahman Foundation Inc. Masjid, on Madison Avenue and 28th Street (Map 7) appears to welcome nearly all the Muslim taxi drivers. Many of these are South Asian. Their main agency is nearby in 26th Street. At the time of Friday prayers, passers-by can hardly fail to be struck by the line of taxis parked in front of the building, which gives no external sign of being a mosque, and simply blends into the buildings next to it.

In the following brief description of this mosque, I hope to bring out both how it is different from the Islamic Cultural Center in the specific needs it meets, and also the similarities it shows with the 'big mosque'.

The director of the mosque, Firoz Shaikh, is an Indian Muslim. He is originally from Bombay but has lived in Hong Kong – his father had moved there – before emigrating to the United States in 1977. He is the manager of an accountancy firm in Manhattan and lives in a residential suburb on Long Island. He chose to take on this role to follow a family tradition as his grandfather was an administrator in a mosque in India and his father in a Hong Kong mosque.[34]

The Madison mosque was set up in May 1991 to meet the religious needs of Muslims living and working in the neighbourhood. It consists in an entrance hall, where worshippers leave their shoes, and a basement room which is used for prayers. Behind is the director's office. Only a tiny space is reserved for women, as this mosque mainly serves the needs of men wishing to pray during the working day.

The building belongs to an Iranian Jew. The rent is paid from the donations of worshippers. The director assures me that no bank or government has made any contribution. During Friday prayers money is collected from the faithful, who come from a variety of ethnic backgrounds, though South Asians are in the majority. The sermon, however, is given in Arabic and in English, but never in any language from the subcontinent. The imam is not full-time: there is a rota, drawn up by the director, and each week a different person, from a different ethnic background, leads the prayers. Hence the imam and the director are not the same person, and indeed the mosque takes measures to ensure it will not be seen as the place of prayer of a particular ethnic group. The only label the director will admit to is that of a Sunni mosque, but he adds that Shi'a 'brothers' occasionally join in the prayers.

About 75 to 100 worshippers frequent the mosque each day. Friday prayers draws about 800, which is far more than the room can hold. Some have to pray outside, which provokes mixed reactions from the neighbours. The call to prayer is given from the doorway of the building, and can therefore be heard by the neighbours. The director, however, is keen not to create resentment, and has forbidden the use of loud-speakers. A separate entrance has also been built, in order not to disturb other occupants of the building. A larger space is currently being sought to meet the growing need, and worshippers are asked to finish their prayers as expeditiously as possible.

This mosque strictly limits its activities to prayer, especially on Fridays, and it truly seems to represent the space of the 'workers', regardless of their ethnic origin.

The Muslim Center of New York: the South Asian mosque

The Muslim Center of New York (MCNY) is, in contrast, the perfect example of an ethnic mosque. The leadership is not keen to admit it, but it can be described as the South Asian sacred space, specifically that of the Pakistani and Indian population. The Bangladeshis have built their own mosques (see below). The MCNY is in Flushing, in Queens (Map 7), in an area of New York where there are large numbers of South Asians.

The MCNY was opened in June 1975 when there was no other mosque in Queens. It was registered in 1977 as a non-profit making organization, not liable to tax. A flat was rented on 41st Avenue in Flushing, and then in 1979 a house was bought for cash – 75,000 dollars – at 137-64 Geranium Avenue; finally in 1987 an adjacent house was purchased, again for cash – this time for 350,000 dollars.

Two years later, the two houses were demolished, and construction was started on a mosque and community centre. The project was inaugurated on 21 May 1989 in the presence of the then Mayor of New York, Edward Koch, and official representatives from Queens.[36]

When I visited in December 1995, the mosque was not yet finished. It was officially opened on 22 September 1996, in the presence of the imam Shaikh Saleh Abdullah Bin Humaid from the Al-Haram mosque in Mecca, and of the consuls of Saudi Arabia and Indonesia and others. Nearly 2,000 people came to the ceremony.[37] With its dome and minaret – from the plans I saw – there can be little doubt as to the nature of the building: a mosque in the heart of Queens.

According to the vice-president of the mosque, Muhammad Tariq Sherwani, the neighbourhood reacted with indifference. A handful of individuals expressed misgivings, but without displaying any outright hostility. One apparently said, 'The problem with these people is that they pray five times a day.' It is only during Friday prayers, however, that large numbers of people (about 200) come to the mosque; during the rest of the week there is little 'dis-turbance'.

The total cost of the project was 3.5 million dollars. The centre was undoubtedly helped to raise the necessary finance by its affiliation to the ISNA (Islamic Society of North America), of which more later, and its adherence to the Council of Masajid, an organization founded in 1978 and based in New Jersey; its vice-president Dawud Assad, is the United States representative of the Muslim World League. The government of Saudi Arabia also helped financially.[38] The total cost has not yet been met, however, and the centre is appealing to the Muslims of New York, of the United States, and indeed of the whole world, to raise the 400,000 dollars needed to pay back the loans (without interest!) and to finish the interior decoration.[39]

The centre is about 1,600 square metres on three floors, linked by a lift. Space is available for over 550 regular worshippers at prayers, and 1,600 on special occasions such as the Id. Separate staircases lead to the women's area. Other facilities are provided in addition to the prayer rooms: eight classrooms, a library containing nearly 3,000 volumes in English, Arabic, Urdu and Turkish, with a reading room, a kitchen, a funeral parlour, a flat for the care-taker and two flats for rent, and an underground car park so as to avoid any negative reactions from the neighbourhood which could be triggered if large numbers of cars were parked near the centre.

When I visited the construction site, the calligraphy had not yet been pre-pared or inlaid. Sherwani told me it would be in the *nasta'liq* style, because, he assured me, Pakistanis cannot read *kufi* calligraphy. The choice of *nasta'liq* does indeed point to a South Asian majority, Pakistani in particular: the 200 families who are members of the centre are more than 90 per cent South Asian, Sherwani says. At first, there was a Shi'a family involved in the mosque's activities, but now all members are Sunni.

The imam is Pakistani and was trained in Pakistan. He was appointed after he had responded to an advertisement placed by the centre in a Pakistani newspaper. He preaches in English and in Arabic, however. Sometimes in Urdu for the women, Sherwani adds.

The president's post is held by a South Asian from Tanzania, Ebrahim Lunat. He is an accountant by profession and one of the wealthiest South Asian Muslims in New York. He shares the running of the mosque with the democratically elected members of the executive committee and the board of management.

The centre serves three crucial functions. Firstly, it has a religious role. Its second role is social: it offers services to the community which have become the customary preserve of the mosque in migration – funerals, marriages, and so on. The centre employs *qazi* licensed by New York city to officiate at marriages, though they have no power to grant divorces. Some of the marriages take place between South Asians and Americans and in these cases the Americans convert shortly before the ceremony. The third role is educational (religious instruction for children). The teaching happens both in daily classes and in classes on Sundays. The daily classes are taught by the imam; the Sunday ones are more comprehensive and are run by about ten volunteers, with 153 students attending. The daily classes are simply in reading the Qur'an, whereas the Sunday classes also include the study of the *sunna*, the *fiqh*, the fundamental principles of Islam and the history of Islam.

The MCNY has chosen as its principal aim to meet the needs of South Asian families. It does not pursue links with other bodies: the press, churches, or political organizations or representatives. In this sense it offers a prime example of an ethnic mosque.

The Islamic Center of Long Island: the mosque of the future?

The Islamic Center of Long Island (ICLI) is in many ways different from the mosques I have described above. Because of its exceptional level of organization, I shall give a detailed study of the ICLI.[40]

The mosque is located on Brush Hollow Road in Westbury, a residential suburb of Long Island (Map 7). The only clue to the building's identity is its green dome surmounted by a crescent.

Of the 12 mosques in Long Island, the ICLI was the first centre to be built as such, whereas the others were set up in renovated buildings.

At first, five or six families met in the basement of a church. They searched the telephone directory to find Muslim names and then went door-to-door collecting money for the construction of a mosque. Fourteen families put together 10,000 dollars each thanks to which land was bought in 1984. The construction project was given to an American company, the Global Construction Company, which was, however, unable to meet its clients' demands. A public works engineer of Kashmiri origin, Nazir Mir, was then engaged and entrusted with the entire responsibility for the building of the mosque. The initial construction phase was completed in February 1993 just before the beginning of Ramadan. The leadership are hoping to enlarge the mosque in the next few years.

Funding has been entirely ensured by the local Muslim community, who regularly organize dinners to collect funds (following the typically American method of fund-raising). The total cost of the mosque is estimated at two million dollars. The centre has raised this sum in a remarkably short time, a fact which demonstrates not only the growing numbers of the Muslim population –

between 20,000 and 30,000 on Long Island according to some estimates – but also their religious fervour and their wealth. Long Island is indeed home to a large number South Asian Muslim families with a very high standard of living.

The funding of the activities of the ICLI follow the same pattern. Social events are regularly organized in the evenings to raise money. During the annual dinner, couples are expected to pay up to 5,000 dollars to attend. Members also regularly pay a part of their salary to the ICLI. This system means they can avoid taking out loans from any bank – and thus violate Islamic law – nor do they need to borrow from foreign governments, which might expose them to external influence.

The mosque is not yet finished and looks at the moment quite austere. There are no internal decorations. According to Nazir Mir, various plans are in store to decorate, for instance covering the walls or the ceiling with wood, which he says will give a Kashmiri touch. Apparently, an artist from Afghanistan will do the calligraphy, probably a mixture of *kufi* and *nasta'liq*, a first sign that the ICLI is seeking to break down ethnic divides. The long-term objective is to represent a variety of cultures inside the mosque.

Many worshippers crowd in for Friday prayers (300 to 500 people). The women (of whom there are only about 15) do not pray completely separately from the men. The front space, which can take about 250 people, is reserved for the men. A corridor divides the room into two. The space at the back is officially reserved for women; however, men, who come in far larger numbers than women to the mosque, encroach on the women's space, especially on Fridays, and may be then praying almost next to the women. The sermon is always preached in English.

Two-thirds of those who come to this mosque are of South Asian origin; the others are mainly Arabs (about 15 per cent), Afghans, and Central Asian Muslims. African–American Muslims represent only five per cent. This number is low both because mosques tend to cater for specific ethnic groups, and because relatively few African–Americans live in the posh suburbs. In fact, most of the worshippers at the ICLI belong to the more affluent classes of the population, whether American or immigrant.

The large South Asian majority in this mosque is made clear in the composition of the board of management. The board and the executive committee both have an overwhelming majority of South Asians. When I visited in 1995 and 1996, the president of the executive committee was Qamar Zaman, a Punjabi doctor who had migrated from East Africa. The vice-president, who in this mosque is always a woman, was Farida Khan, a woman doctor from Aligarh. The president of the board of management was a Punjabi doctor from Lahore, as was the imam himself. The spokesman for the mosque was Faroque Khan, the Kashmiri doctor we have already met. Only the

administrative secretary and the director, who is responsible for interfaith dialogue and communications, were not from South Asia. The secretary was a
Tartar from China and the director an Arab from Syria. Apart from the massive numbers of South Asians, the visitor is also struck by the number of
medical physicians: amongst 28 members of the board of management and
the executive committee in 1995–96, 18 were doctors.

The ICLI has a democratic constitution: every two years the executive committee is re-elected, together with three members of the board of management.
With the 'big mosque' it is one of New York's best organized Islamic centres.
But in contrast to the big mosque, it has been careful not to allow power to be
concentrated in the hands of the imam. The imam of the ICLI, Hafiz
Mohammad Ahmad, who was trained at Medina and Al-Azhar, was
'imported' from Pakistan. As opposed to some other imams, his functions are
limited to being the imam and the 'guardian of the temple'. He lives with his
wife and children in a small house within the perimeter of the Islamic centre,
and he acts as caretaker.

Committees of all kinds have been set up by the board of management.
Each is chaired by a different person, man or woman, who are all members of
the centre, and are in the main highly educated. Most of these committees exist
to help immigrants with various problems: religious instruction for children,
arrangements for breaking the fast (every year during Ramadan, evening meals
are available for about 300 people), funeral arrangements, marital relationships, dealing with domestic violence, help with looking for work and so on.
Other committees look after the financing and upkeep of the mosque. Some
exist for public relations: contacts with other mosques, or with churches and
synagogues for interfaith dialogues, and so on. A new committee has been set
up to establish relationships with non-Sunni Muslims, Shi'a and Isma'ili, but
also with the Ahmadiyya, which, as one member of the centre told me, had
caused hostility in some ICLI quarters. Other committees have political roles
(meetings with American politicians, lobbying the American government to
help Muslim countries, especially Bosnia, and so on). The ICLI publishes a regular bulletin, the *ICLI Newsletter*.

A special committee has been set up for relationships with the press. The
imam, who does not speak much English, does not fulfil this role either. The
spokesman is Ghazi Khankan, a Syrian. When a major event affecting
Muslims in the United States occurs, the Long Island media posse, and sometimes the New York media posse, make a bee-line for the ICLI. Khankan
replies to questions from journalists (especially for the *Westbury Times* and
Newsday two local newspapers) and radio and television (WABC and WNYC in
particular). After the attack in Oklahoma City, since Muslims were immediately
suspected, Khankan was interviewed. The same happened after Yitzhak Rabin

was assassinated. The press is also invited to report the Id ul-Fitr celebrations, for two reasons. Muslims are residents in the United States or even American citizens, but they are still relatively unknown by the American public; they would like to receive the kind of media coverage given to the Christians and the Jews. The ICLI also hopes that the publicity will help in raising funds for the running of the mosque. In 1993, the ICLI was chosen by an American television company for a programme on Islam in the United States. Khankan also represents Muslims in a television programme called *Father Tom and Religious Leaders*. In this programme, which is put out by cable company 25, TeLIcare, in New York, Father Tom Hartman chairs a gathering of Christians, Jews and Muslims. Another religious programme on the same channel, *The Women's Forum*, is put together by a group of women, and an Egyptian member of the ICLI, Sanaa Nadim, is on the team. Although the ICLI is dominated by South Asians in terms of numbers, it is in fact Arabs who mainly manage the external relations. This may be a second indication that the mosque is seeking to overcome ethnic divisions.

Beyond prayers and the activities described above, the ICLI organizes topical discussions on Sundays. People from outside the centre are invited, Muslims and non-Muslims.

I attended a number of these meetings and I have chosen to describe one particular session in detail. It was a lecture on women in Islam, given by a certain Kaukab Siddique, held at the ICLI in November 1995. Siddique is of Pakistani origin and teaches English at the University of Lincoln in Pennsylvania. He is well known in the United States for his progressive views on Islam, in particular on the place of women in Islam.

On that day, many people were present, nearly a hundred. The men sat on the left, and the women on the right. The women were wearing a *dupatta* (they were mostly women of the first generation); very few were wearing the *hijab*. One woman, a member of the ICLI, explained to me why men and women were sitting separately and why the women were wearing the *dupatta*:

> There are a few fundamentalist members of the centre who insisted that we should sit separately, with our heads covered. We [the progressive members, including the men] gave in because it didn't seem to us to be crucially important. Some things are much more important, such as contact with non-Muslims and non-Sunni.

Most of those present were South Asians. The theme chosen ensured that as many women as men attended, which was not usual. Some of the young people looked very American, wearing basketball caps back to front. A few girls were wearing jeans and *dupatta*.

Kaukab Siddique gave his lecture in English. He laid stress on the importance of women within Islam: nothing in the religion, he said, obliged them to submit to men. He emphasized that to exclude half of the population denied the meaning of the notion of the *umma*. He recognized that within the Qur'an there are contradictions on the question of women and he insisted that only the later *sura*, which are gentler towards women, should be taken seriously. He drew a parallel with the prohibition on wine, which also evolved, and he made it clear that one should understand the Qur'an within its historical context. Siddique then went on to criticize all kinds of fundamentalism and was particularly harsh about the government of Saudi Arabia. Throughout his lecture, he referred constantly to the Indian subcontinent. At the beginning of the lecture, he said he was speaking in the light of Hanafi jurisprudence; he contrasted Arabs and non-Arabs, and said clearly that Arabs did not have a monopoly on Islam. He quoted the Shah Bano[41] affair, which only the South Asians would have known about, and also the affairs concerning Rushdie and Taslima Nasreen, two writers from the subcontinent who have been 'manipulated' by the Western media in order to 'weaken Islam'. In effect he was accusing the American media of being responsible for anti-Islamic prejudice. He referred to Christianity, in which woman is held responsible for the fall of Adam.

The lecture was followed by a debate. A small number of the men present expressed doubts about Siddique's arguments on the status of women in Islam. One man said he was surprised that no woman was prominent in the time of the Prophet. 'Surely that proves the inferior status of women?' he said. One woman murmured, 'I don't think he understood anything. He must have been asleep. Unless he is a male chauvinist.'

The lecture was interesting not only in the contradictory reactions it provoked, but in other ways also. First the way the issue of women was addressed. According to the director, the ICLI is probably one of very few Islamic centres to express such opinions on women. My own observations confirm this statement. Women have been essential to the immigrant population as guarantors of the religious heritage but they are not yet, by a long way, considered to have equal status with men.

Siddique's thoughts belong in a modernist logic, because he is opposed to an understanding of Islam, which leaves out the historical context, whereas the fundamentalists insist that the message of the Qur'an is unchangeable in time and space. Interestingly enough, Siddique's audience did not react strongly to this interpretation.

The lecture was in English, although the speaker and most of his audience understand and speak Urdu fluently. The centre advocates Islamic unity across ethnic divisions, and is keen to appear as promoting such unity. The speaker, however, was constantly referring to one specific tradition, and to personalities and events known only by the South Asians – an apparent contradiction. It is true that Siddique is not a member of the ICLI and that he knew he was addressing a mainly South Asian audience.

A final observation on this lecture: Siddique's references to Christianity and his criticisms of the American media are both characteristic of Muslim discourse in the United States, a point to which we shall return.

As in many other mosques, the religious education of children is a central activity at the ICLI. As we have seen, the idea of establishing Islamic centres in many cases came about in reaction to the risk of extreme Americanization of children. At the ICLI, the task of educating children was one of the earliest the centre faced. At first eight children came on Sundays to study in an old building. All the teachers were volunteers. Now the Sunday school has 325 students, who are taught in six graded levels. The teaching is on both social and religious matters: reading of the Qur'an, Arabic, the life of the Prophet, the practise of Islam in daily life, the social laws of Islam, discussion of contemporary issues (abortion, welfare state and so on), and the history of Islam.

The way in which teachers are chosen by the management at the ICLI shows that they consider religion to be more important than culture: the education committee has a South Asian woman as its president, but most of the teachers are converted Americans or Arabs (out of twelve, only two are South Asian). Arabs are best qualified to teach the sacred language and the reading of the Qur'an. In this particular setting it is more difficult to teach a culture-based syllabus, since both teachers and students come from very varied cultural origins. American teachers are also chosen for very specific reasons. At first the teaching methods were largely inspired by those used in the subcontinent. But the children found the classes boring and repetitive. The ICLI management changed the policy and, as I saw for myself, the teaching is now according to American principles, encouraging thoughtfulness and participation by the children. The teachers are American Muslims, mostly converts, who are more used to American teaching methods. Some are professionals employed by the centre, others are volunteers who teach in their spare time. The ICLI also organizes extra-curricular activities for children, excursions and summer camps, for example, where religious instruction and sporting activities are combined.

I went to some of the Sunday classes at the ICLI. One was called 'Islam, the natural way'. It was aimed at children aged from about seven to twelve. The teacher was an American convert, of Cuban extraction, who qualified at the University of New York in education science. The children love his way of teaching, like a black preacher giving a sermon. The subject that day was Islam and industry. The teacher gave many concrete examples to awaken the children's interest. He explained to me afterwards that he teaches the children about everyday things so that they can understand how Islamic behaviour fits into daily life. And indeed, on that day, the children asked many questions: is share-dealing Islamic? Is it Islamic to play the lottery? (the teacher gave negative answers to both of these), and so on.

Young second-generation members of the ICLI have started their own club, the Muslim Youth of Long Island. They meet every Saturday from 11 until the prayer of *zuhr*. They have set up a study group with a particular syllabus for the year: recitation and memorization of the Qur'an, explanations of the verses, study of the life of the Prophet and analysis of rules of behaviour appropriate to everyday life, and to other areas of life; in their Media Watch programme, every week they carefully examine the local newspapers and other sources of information to pick out all the articles about Muslims or of interest to Muslims. During their meetings, they discuss very specific areas of interest: Islam and democracy, the welfare system in Islam, the economic system in Islam, Islamic identity, and so on. Like the adults, the young people are ideologically divided between modernists and fundamentalists; the question of the *hijab* in particular is a live one and, more generally, equality between men and women.

In November 1995 the adults opened their own education forum. They meet on Sunday afternoons to discuss a particular theme, sometimes to continue the lecture or conference of that morning. The main objective of these meetings is to encourage the faithful to listen and understand each other, as I was told by one of the instigators of these sessions.

Beside the religious and social functions, the mosque also has a political function. Each week at the ICLI, after Friday prayers and after the Sunday conference, worshippers are invited to sign petitions and write letters about Muslims who are suffering discrimination or violence in the United States or in the rest of the world (for example letters about a Muslim prisoner who wanted to organize prayers in an Indiana prison and was put in solitary confinement; letters about the Moros in the Philippines, the Muslims in Kashmir and so on). These petitions and letters are sent either to the person guilty of discrimination against Muslims in the United States or to the State Department when the issue is in another country. The State Department usually replies, even if it is just to send a report on the situation of Muslims in the difficult area of the world which has been targeted. American politicians of all parties are also often invited to give their opinion on a particular subject. These invitations show that the ICLI is keen to promote itself, and to make contact with influential American personalities, especially in the world of politics.

As the titles of the various committees suggest, the external contacts of the ICLI go beyond the political sphere into the religious sphere. Rather than work in isolation, the centre seeks to link up with other mosques and Islamic centres. This can extend beyond simply coordinating with other mosques in a spirit of 'brotherhood'. The relationships can become competitive, with each institution trying to demonstrate that it is better built, better organized, more visible to the media, more successful in teaching religion to its children. The competition, however, between mosques at the ideological and territorial levels does not seem to be as widespread in the United States as it is in the United Kingdom. The leaders at the ICLI and the other mosques are therefore sure that this competition will not necessarily have a negative impact on the Muslim community. Competition can in fact be helpful: rather than undermining the unity of Muslims, it encourages each establishment to improve its welcome, its organization, the quality of its religious instruction, and so on.

The ICLI has also extended its contacts with non-Muslims. Interfaith dialogue with Christians and Jews, say the leaders, is the best way to integrate into and be accepted by American society. Relationships are being built up in particular with members of the Jewish community, who live in large numbers in the residential suburbs of Long Island. Faroque Khan, the Kashmiri doctor, and Ghazi Khankan are the principal architects of this initiative. Since 1992, members of the ICLI have been meeting regularly with the Beth El synagogue at Great Neck. Together they have founded an association called American Muslims and Jews in Dialogue (AMJD). Discussions are held on the two religions, and the two centres run student exchanges and seek to develop welfare services together.[42] These contacts between religions aim at helping integration but they can also have a hidden missionary purpose.

The ICLI is very active in welfare services, for the same reason. A *zakat* committee has been created for this purpose. It urges members to concentrate their financial efforts at home (in the United States) rather than abroad, to help Muslims suffering from poverty. Some members of the ICLI take this one step further, and recommend that help should be provided not only to Muslims but also to non-Muslims, notably in the hope that a raised profile and public gratitude will encourage conversions. The ICLI does not engage in direct, aggressive missionary activity. Conversions do happen fairly regularly in the mosque, but it is through their exemplary behaviour that members hope to attract new converts to Islam.

Altogether, the ICLI appears to be a modern and original Islamic centre: its level of organization (though the reception facilities are not as efficient yet as at the ICCNY or the MCNY), its fund-raising methods (which ensure financial independence, largely, of course, because most of its members are comfortably well-off), its democratic system (regular renewal of leadership and delegation of roles), its efforts to transcend ethnic barriers (by offering responsible posts to people not from the subcontinent, by employing converts as teachers), the importance it gives to women and its campaign to make its mark on the

American landscape all contribute to this image. The ICLI is conscious of its assets, and would like to be seen as a coordinating force among the New York mosques, or at least an exemplary Islamic institution.

The Bangladeshi community: a clear-cut identity

There are ten Bangladeshi mosques in New York: one in Manhattan, one in the Bronx, six in Queens and two in Brooklyn. The description 'Bangladeshi mosque' officially implies a place of prayer where the imam is of Bangladeshi origin. But this goes beyond the mere ethnic belonging of the imam; Bangladeshi mosques, perhaps more than other South Asian mosques, are distinctively ethnic.[43]

In January 1996, I interviewed the leaders of two mosques, the Madina mosque in Manhattan, the largest in size, and the Masjid ul-Aman in Brooklyn (Map 7). All the Bangladeshi mosques in New York seem to work on the same pattern.

The building housing the Madina mosque, on 11th Street and First Avenue, was acquired in 1979 with financial help from the Bangladeshi government (25,000 dollars), which was led at the time by Zia ur-Rehman (1975–81), from the Kuwaiti government (10,000 dollars) and from a few other Arab countries. Originally, the mosque was under the control of the Tablighi Jama'at, which was expelled in the 1980s. They moved to a mosque in Queens.[44] Now, the Madina mosque is controlled entirely by Bangladeshis and does not follow any particular Islamic movement. The very ethnic nature of the mosque is clear from the membership of the board of management (all members are Bangladeshi), from the ethnic origin of the imam ('imported' from Bangladesh he does not speak English, but is reasonably fluent in Urdu), and from the language of the sermon (it is delivered in three languages: Arabic, English and Bengali). Even the *khutbah* is given in Arabic, and the talk which follows it in English and in Bengali. The nature of the building is evident from the minaret and the notice which gives the name of the mosque.

Friday prayers draw about 1,500 people, other prayers about 150. Most of the worshippers are Bangladeshi, reflecting the strong presence of this population in this neighbourhood. Other worshippers are mainly South Asian and Arab, with a few African–Americans. All social classes are represented.

As with all Bangladeshi mosques in New York, no place is reserved for women at Madina. According to the director, there is not enough space for the men during Friday prayers. If they had to provide space for women as well . . . But it seems that the women are not satisfied with the situation, and they are currently exerting pressure on the mosque authorities to provide them with a room for prayer.

Children, on the other hand are, as elsewhere, very well looked after by the mosque authorities. During school terms Saturday classes are organized for them, and in school holidays classes meet six days out of seven. The teaching is by the imam and the muezzin. Two or three extra teachers are employed during holidays.

This mosque has few links with American society. It does, however, encourage relationships with other Muslims, and is represented, for example, when Muslim scholars from the subcontinent come to visit.

In essence, therefore this mosque is above all a religious institution. Social life, especially since women are not much involved, is not an important feature: at most it is a meeting place for Muslims of the same ethnic origin.

The Brooklyn mosque (Map 7) is very similar to the Madina mosque in the way it works. However, it is much smaller. It is a private home which has been converted into a mosque, so there are no external signs of its nature, except for the notice in Arabic, English and Bengali giving its name.

As at the Madina, the mosque is led by Bangladeshis, and they are also in the majority among the attenders (nearly 500 during Friday prayers). The sermon is preached in English, Arabic and Bengali. There is no room for women, who therefore are not allowed to attend. However, the imam told me that another house has recently been purchased, in which a room should be made available for women. The two houses have been bought from members' donations. At the weekend and during holidays, there are lessons on the Qur'an. At first the neighbours were hostile (stones were thrown at the mosque) but now things have improved, and the leaders of the mosque did not complain of any further acts of vandalism or overt hostility.

The personality of the imam is the important difference between this mosque and Madina. As well as Bengali, he speaks perfect English, Arabic and Urdu. He was formerly a Professor of Islamic Studies at the University of Dacca. Of all the imams I met in New York, he seemed to be one of the most highly educated. His house was overflowing with books. This high level of education explains why he has taken on so many roles (teacher, marriage counsellor, spokesman for the mosque), and indeed he effectively coordinates all the Bangladeshi mosques in New York.

On the whole, however, the Brooklyn mosque meets needs similar to those met by Madina and all other Bangladeshi mosques; the religious function is the most important.

'Our mosques are very conservative,' a Bangladeshi leader told me. This particular characteristic of Bangladeshi mosques is explained by a number of factors. The Bangladeshi community in the United States is even more divided than other South Asian groups, into different waves of immigration. On the whole, the first wave of immigrants were very highly educated, whereas the more recent waves are far more likely to be of rather low social standing. This dichotomy has had a strong impact on cultural and religious institutions: the first immigrants were heavily imbued by the secular ideology prevalent in Bangladesh in the 1960s and 1970s, and they tended on arrival to cooperate with Bengali Hindus in running and setting up secular cultural organizations. Fairly soon, however, they set up their own institutions. The more recent immigrants, on the other hand, are less educated and much more religious. From the first, they have put effort into setting up mosques and Islamic centres. There are complex reasons for this change. The mere fact of the different levels of education cannot explain the greater religiosity of the more recent immigrants. Quite a few of them did go to university in Bangladesh, even if the qualification they hold is not good enough for the job they had hoped to get in the United States. In the context of the United States, there seems to be often in fact little correlation between the levels of education and of religious observance in an individual: the Pakistani and Indian Muslims in the United States are of all Muslims both the most educated and the most active in Islamic institutions. The increased religiosity of the more recent Bangladeshi immigrants might rather be a reflection of changes in Bangladesh itself. They left the country at the very moment when fundamentalism acquired a much higher political profile.

The refusal to allow women into Bangladeshi mosques could well be explained by the relatively lower educational standard of recent immigrants. Let us not forget that it is also a very new community. Traditionally, South Asian immigrants in the first instance set up institutions for men. Later on, as the community grows, and family members join them, women are included. Many Bangladeshis are still at the first stage of this process.

A final observation: the higher level of religious observance among new Bangladeshi immigrants does not weaken their ethnic allegiance. The Bengali language in particular, which is almost the *raison d'être* of Bangladesh, may not be used systematically within the family circle; it is however maintained in the religious institutions where it is the language of the sermon. However, Bengali is not taught to children in Bangladeshi mosques.

Conclusion: a few thoughts on Sunni mosques

The preceding case studies seem to me to illustrate how diverse the Sunni mosques of New York are in the way they are run, in their architecture, in the ways they are financed, in their objectives and in their leadership. The place of women and ethnic affiliation are also important distinguishing features.

Some of these mosques meet the needs of busy workers who wish simply to fulfil their religious obligations. Others meet the needs of families who are trying to establish a social life outside work and to slow down the Americanization of their children.

Some mosques are financed from abroad. Others are keen to maintain their independence and seek, therefore, to finance their activities 'autonomously'. All avoid borrowing money from a bank, and thus respect the Islamic law which forbids loans on interest. Financial help from foreign countries, in particular Saudi Arabia, can raise questions about the influence governments have on mosques in the United States. This influence is difficult to quantify. One could perhaps say that a mosque that seeks to practise not only a rigorist but also a 'purified' Islam, and in particular is hostile to the cult of saints, might be said to be under Saudi influence. It should, however, be pointed out that this kind of Islam can also be found in self-financing mosques.

Architecture varies from one mosque to another; some are clearly identifiable, while others blend in. The inside may in some cases be richly decorated, but the outside is usually austere and geometrical. Muslims are keen to see their mosques 'incorporated' into the American landscape. However, the mosques are still distinctively Islamic.

As to the leadership, wide variations can be observed in the level of education (type and place of education) and in the variety of tasks undertaken (some had many jobs, while others were able to delegate a lot). Apart from the imam, who is a *hafiz* (he has memorized the entire Qur'an – a minimum qualification for an imam), remaining mosque leaders have not, on the whole, had specific Islamic education, apart from what they learnt at school or in their family. There is another interesting feature of mosque leadership: many directors of the mosques or Islamic organizations which are largely South Asian are twice-migrants. The presidents of both the ICLI and the MCNY, Qamar Zaman and Ebrahim Lunat, are both from East Africa, and the director of the Madison mosque, Firoz Shaikh, was born in Hong Kong.

Looking ahead a little bit, this phenomenon also exists amongst the sectarian minorities: the director of the Ahmadi mosque in New York, Nazir Ayaz, lived in East Africa and in the United Kingdom before emigrating to United States. The leadership of the Isma'ili community, both Nizari and Bohra, is also made up of people who emigrated from African countries. Even at the great Shi'a mosque in New York, the Iraqi imam's principal assistant, who looks after external relations, is a young South Asian woman from East Africa.

Two main reasons can explain this trend: immigrants who moved (or whose ancestors moved) some time ago to former Western colonies, in East Africa in particular, tended to maintain ancient traditions, perhaps more so than their peers in the subcontinent. Many often lived confined within their own communities, and were not exposed to many external influences. They arrived in the United States with their culture, and especially their religion, relatively ossified and much prized, perhaps to a greater extent than with other immigrants.[45] Also, their experience has taught the twice-migrants that they will stay in the United States. For them there is no myth of return. They are therefore particularly energetic in setting up religious institutions.[46] At the same time, however, they are keen to smooth over ethnic divisions. It was the fact that they were Indian, rather than Muslim, which moved Africans to adopt repressive policies.

Breaking down ethnic divisions is indeed a growing preoccupation amongst Muslim leaders. Many mosques catering largely for South Asians are still clearly ethnic, and although mosques are still being built for specific ethnic groups, many efforts are being made to transcend these differences. The ethnic origin of the imam, however, and of the members of the board of management, the style of dressing, of women in particular, can all indicate in any given mosque that ethnic affiliation continues to be an important factor.

A perceptible linguistic evolution is to be noted, symbolized by the language of the sermon. Apart from the Bangladeshi mosques, all the others have chosen to have the sermon in English. This not only breaks down ethnic barriers, but also places emphasis on the content rather than the form of the message. Proselytes recommend that English should be used rather than the vernacular. Linda Walbridge, who has studied the Lebanese Shi'a in Dearborn, observes that there is a difference in the content of the sermon according to whether it is given in Arabic or in English. When preached in Arabic, the aim of the sermon is to remind the faithful of fundamental principles of Shi'a Islam, rather than to speak of the role of Islam in America, and to explore reasons for adaptations to the new environment. Sermons in English tend to be more missionary in character.[47]

Among the South Asians, Arabic is given a higher importance than the languages of the subcontinent, including Urdu, even though Urdu is one of the main components of Muslim identity in South Asia. In many mosques dominated by South Asians, there is little or no emphasis on transmitting language and even culture. The situation is fairly different in the United Kingdom, where mosques are much used for the teaching of Urdu.[48] In the United States, the emphasis on religion is such that religion seems to supplant culture: only Arabic is taught because it has close links with religion. It is interesting to note that Lebanese Christians in the United States no longer use Arabic as it does not have religious significance for them, and use English instead.[49]

There is another interesting linguistic feature in mosques in the United States.[50] Muslims who attend mosques regularly call each other 'brother' and 'sister'. This strikes one as very unusual for South Asians. In the subcontinent, this expression is usually employed as a mark of respect to a slightly older person. But in the United States, the expression also works in the opposite direction: it is used to address someone younger. When there is a big age difference between two people, the younger will call the older one 'Uncle' or 'Aunt' in the subcontinent, certainly not 'brother' or 'sister'. In the United States, it would seem, relationships are becoming in a way more democratic as the hierarchy of age is disappearing, and the notion of brotherly relationships is taking over.

The expressions 'brother' and 'sister' are now firmly established in the vocabulary of the Muslims who often go to the mosque. This emphasis on family links between men and women seems to be also helping to bridge the traditional gulf between the sexes. It would seem that the words 'man' and 'woman' are disappearing within the mosque environment.

In a more general way, in the immigrant community, the fact that worshippers at the mosque and members of Islamic organizations are calling each other 'brother' and 'sister' suggests that they are finding there a substitute wider family.

This terminology also echoes the Christian tradition. In fact, many aspects of the organization of Islamic centres in the United States have features taken from Christianity: meetings on Sundays, weddings at the mosque, a more active role for women, and so on. Although they may not be run in the same way as the churches and synagogues set up by Christian and Jewish immigrants when they first arrived in the United States, mosques also go beyond the religious role, and fulfil a similar function as a privileged social space for the community.

The issue of vocabulary calls for another comment: South Asian Muslims who often attend the mosque tend to abandon words of Persian origin, which have traditionally been employed in the subcontinent, and replace them with words of Arabic origin.[51] Thus *salat* (prayer in Arabic) has replaced *namaz* (Persian equivalent); *Assalam alaikum* or *Wassalam alaikum*, and, less frequently, *Allah hafiz*, are all used instead of *Khuda hafiz* (*Khuda* is the Persian word for 'God') as a way of taking leave. In the subcontinent, the Arab words given above are mostly used only by fundamentalists, linked to the Jama'at-i-Islami and the Tablighi Jama'at, and amongst workers who have come back from the Gulf countries. In the United States, these Arabic words have become part of the vocabulary of most Muslims actively engaged in the life of their mosque (including mosques which are not linked to any particular ideological movement) even if they have never lived in an Arab country. The main reason may be that they have increased contact with Arabs in United States: since the Iranian revolution Arabs have more actively tried to encourage Muslims around the world to become more Arabized. The increased use of Arabic can also be seen as symbolizing attempts to transcend ethnic divisions by means of a common religious vocabulary. Persian was for a long time the language of culture of Indian Muslims,[52] but it is now dying away, and in the United States it is being pushed aside by Arabic for any word with religious connotations.

In conclusion, the mosques by meeting many needs and fulfilling a variety of functions are developing their own characteristics in the American context, quite different from what they were in the subcontinent.

This analysis will now continue with an examination of the organization of institutions amongst the sectarian minorities.

The Islamic institutions of the minority sects

The Twelver Shi'a: a clearly separate identity

The Muslim Foundation, based in Bloomfield (New Jersey), was set up in 1980 to meet the needs of the Indian and Pakistani Shi'a community in the three states of New York, New Jersey and Connecticut. In 1994, this organization published a directory which listed 381 Shi'a families from the subcontinent, so about 2000 people in the United States.[53]

When they first arrived, the Shi'a usually joined the religious institutions of the Sunni. As the Muslim community grew, they were encouraged to set up their own institutions. They still occasionally take part in Sunni activities. According to the *Nationwide Muslim Directory*, in 1994 there were 14 Twelver Shi'a centres in New York State, of which 11 were in New York itself (three in Manhattan, three in Brooklyn and five in Queens). There are two in Long Island and one in the small town of Medina (!), northeast of New York.

In December 1995 I visited the biggest of these Islamic centres, located in Jamaica, in Queens, at 89 Van Wyck Expressway (Map 7). It is called the Imam Al-Khoei Foundation, after the Ayatollah of Najaf, Sayyid Abul Qasim al-Khoei, who was one of the major religious leaders of the Shi'a when he was alive. His followers are estimated to reach 150 million throughout the world. The Foundation's headquarters are in London. Imam Al-Khoei and his son Sayyid Muhammad Taqi al-Khoei have now both died, and the Ayatollah Sheikh Mehdi Shamsuddin has been appointed by Ayatollah Sayyid Ali al-Husaini Al-Seestani to lead the Foundation..

The Al-Khoei Foundation enabled the construction of the largest Shi'a Islamic centre in New York, over the ruins of an abandoned factory. It was opened in 1989. An interesting feature is that the centre is led by an Arab, who is also the imam, Fadhel al-Sahlani, who was invited to come from Iraq, even though most of the faithful are South Asian. Various other members of staff at the mosque are also South Asian: the imam's personal assistant, the librarian, who is a Muhajir from Karachi, and so on.[54] Most Arab Shi'a are concentrated in the Detroit area, and only a few live in New York.

At first, a number of Iranians came to this mosque, but they soon preferred to set up their own organization. According to Georges Sabagh and Mehdi Bozorgmehr, the religious observance of Iranians in the United States is strongly marked by their observance in their own country. In other immigrant groups, in particular amongst South Asians, there is a perceptible increase in religiosity after immigration.[55] The most observant Iranians feel close to Ayatollah Khomeini, a rival in terms of religious leadership of Ayatollah Al-Khoei. It is not surprising therefore that they would rather have their own establishment. Many other Iranians are secular, or even atheist. The Iranian community in the United States has probably the highest number of non-religious, indeed atheist Muslims. For many Iranians, religion was the reason they lost their properties and privileges. These Iranians prefer to celebrate, in addition to the Muslim religious festivals, or exclusively sometimes, pre-Islamic festivals, such as *No Ruz*,[56] this being another reason for creating their own separate organizations. Language has also been a significant factor here: the Iranians attach enormous importance to their own language, Persian. In a mosque such as Al-Khoei, where the imam is Iraqi and most worshippers are South Asian, the sermon is necessarily in English. As already noted, the Iranians also feel out of place during the Muharram *majlis*, which the South Asians recite in Urdu.

The sectarian minorities do not escape ethnic divisions. Shi'ism alone cannot weld the community together. In New York, however, Iraqi and South Asian Shi'a pray together in a number of mosques.

Architecturally, the outside of the Al-Khoei mosque looks like a renovated building on which a dome and a green and gold minaret have been placed. The inside is very richly decorated. The prayer room can hold about 2000 people. For Friday prayers, nearly 200 people come to the mosque. For the great religious festivals, nearly 3000 people jostle to get into the mosque. A huge folding screen separates men and women. In one corner there is a magnificent replica in miniature of the sanctuary of Husain at Kerbala. One of the walls of the prayer room displays a photograph of Imam Al-Khoei.

The highest point of the year for this mosque is the commemoration of Husain's martyrdom.

The mosque is run along similar lines to a Sunni mosque, in particular the big mosque in Manhattan. Al-Sahlani combines the functions of imam, mosque director, and *qazi*, giving judgment in matters relating to professional and marital conflict, and so on. The mosque itself has a variety of functions – religious, social and so on. It houses a full-time Islamic school, Al-Aman (see below) and religious teaching is also offered at the weekends and during school holidays.

Al-Khoei has established contact with other mosques, including Sunni mosques. Joint seminars are held, especially on the position of Muslims in the United States. Relations with non-Muslim bodies are, however, less prominent: it is exceptional with other religious institutions and occasional with the media.

The Al-Khoei Foundation is at the heart of the activities of South Asian Shi'a in New York. In its running it resembles the Sunni big mosque of Manhattan; in 1997, however, it was already of a more advanced stage in its formal organization (for instance in having an Islamic School).

The Nizari Isma'ili: a model of integration?

Isma'ili have been living in North America since the beginning of the 1970s, when governments changed in East Africa. In 1996 their numbers reached 20,000 in the United States, of whom 3,000 to 4,000 lived in New York.

A number of detailed studies on the Nizari community have been already published.[58] I shall therefore be fairly brief about this minority group. Besides, it may be well-known for its openness to the modern world but it is very reluctant to communicate any information on its internal running to strangers. Only followers of the Aga Khan are allowed into the *jama'at khana*. The following remarks are gleaned from published literature and from telephone conversations with some leaders and followers of the movement. There are about 75 *jama'at khana* in the United States, it is estimated.[59] Of these 75, 55 were officially listed in the *Isma'ili Directory USA* in 1985. The other 20 were private homes, motels, or university rooms.[60] Five of these 55 were in New York State. The others were spread out across America, with some concentration in California (nine), Texas (seven) and Florida (six).

The *jama'at khana* are attended by people of all ethnic origins: South Asians, Arabs, Afghans, Iranians and Muslims from Central Asia. However, the South Asians form the overwhelming majority of the Aga Khan's followers, and many of these have emigrated from East Africa. The influence of South Asians is evident in that the main languages used are English and Gujarati. Arabic is used for ritual prayer and English for the sermon, but Gujarati is used for the *ginan* still regularly chanted in the *jama'at khana*. Contact with Nizari from places other than the subcontinent does have an impact on the South Asian majority: they are realizing that Isma'ilism extends beyond narrow Gujarati culture.[61] So it would appear that the Nizari are succeeding, at least in terms of organization, in overcoming ethnic divides.

In terms of formal organization, the *jama'at khana* continue to fulfil traditional roles. Individual meditation and prayers (*du'a*) before the ritual dawn prayer are maintained in the United States, a few *jama'at khana* opening at three in the morning. However, American life is such that most Nizarian are unable to keep to this particular tradition, which in any case is not compulsory. Most are content to say these prayers home, at weekends, and to say the dawn prayers at the *jama'at khana* only on major festivals in the Islamic and Nizari calendar. The tradition of offering food to the Aga Khan has also survived. The offerings are distributed afterwards amongst members of congregation, mainly students and bachelors.

The Nizarian continue to pay their taxes and voluntary contributions, under the direction of the imam. The money is used principally for the benefit of the community in the United States.

The *jama'at khana* are mainly run by the *mukhi* and the *kamadia* (literally, the chiefs), the *mukhi* being highest in rank. As the representative of the Aga Khan, the *mukhi* has a role similar to that of a Sunni imam: he presides at religious and social events (weddings, burials and so on), is available to his followers who face problems (though he does not give his personal religious interpretations), visits the sick and so on. The women's side of the *jama'at khana* is run by the *mukhiyani*, though she does not lead religious celebrations.

Within western societies, and especially in the United States, the role of the *mukhi* has changed. The Nizari leadership is particularly conscious that the community has new needs in this new environment. Young community leaders, all volunteers and professionally educated, have been therefore appointed in the United States, so as to meet the needs of their community, both in organizing its life and in solving social or emotional problems. These new leaders have ensured the economic and social success of this minority well-integrated in the Unites States.

The Isma'ili community in the United States wrote a constitution in 1977, which lays down a system of committees to manage the different *jama'at khana*. Whereas the Nizari community as a whole is under the leadership of the supreme Council, located in Nairobi, four communities have been set up in the United States, each responsible for running one particular region. The Eastern regional committee is in New York, as are the headquarters of the Isma'ili National Committee. This committee included ten members, and aims at drawing up objectives and strategies over five-year periods. The principal objectives are to promote the religious education of children and adults, to develop networks providing financial help and help in finding work, to safeguard the unity of the community (the leaders, wherever they are in the United States, maintain permanent contact with each other), to encourage integration into American society (without compromising the community's own religious heritage) and to maintain local committees attuned to the needs of the *jama'at khana*.

The task of preserving specific religious traditions is devolved to local Isma'ili groups. These groups provide training to volunteers who can teach in the *jama'at khana* after the daily prayers.[62]

In terms of their relationship with the host society, the leadership encourage Nizari members to become integrated into the local community, wherever they are. As a symbol of this, each Nizari is asked to pray daily for the world and for his host society. At the Christian new year, an extra prayer is said for the leader of the country where they live, in this case for the President of the United States (even if they do not approve of his politics).

To sum up, the organizational structures put in place by the leadership have enabled the Nizarian to combine social integration with preserving their religious traditions.

The Da'udi Bohra: voices of dissidents

According to the nephew of the current *da'i*, Moin Muhiuddin (the son of Muhammad Burhanuddin's elder sister), who is himself a resident of Pennsylvania, about 4,000 Bohra live in the United States. About 500 families have settled in the tri-state area (New York, New Jersey, Connecticut).[63] As with the Nizari, many Bohra emigrated from East Africa.

The Bohra have set up elaborate institutions in both India and Eastern Africa, but in the United States their level of organization is still at a preliminary stage. There is only one *jama'at khana* in the United States, in Detroit. Four others are being built in Chicago, Los Angeles, Houston and Dallas. Community centres (*markaz*) are, however, scattered throughout the United States. The Centre which covers the New York area is located in New Jersey[64] because of a higher concentration of Bohra in this state: about 90 per cent of those living in this region are New Jersey residents. The authorities of the New Jersey centre refused to allow me to interview them. I was therefore unable to visit the the community's centre. I interviewed a few followers of the *da'i*, who were mostly dissidents, and was thus able to know a little more about this community.

The New Jersey Centre, as with other Bohra centres, is administered by a committee, led by a president, the *amil*, or chief, who is directly nominated by the *da'i*. As the unique representative of the *da'i*, the *amil* holds in his hands almost every power: he alone can allow ceremonies, in particular marriages, and he himself celebrates them. Pilgrimages only happen with his agreement. And it is he who collects the taxes owned by the community. Crucially, it is his prerogative to distribute the green, yellow or red cards to members of the community. Such power can quickly lead to despotic behaviour. Such is precisely the case in the New Jersey centre, according to the Bohra dissidents, who are very critical of his authoritarianism. 'Riyaz Paanwala',[65] for example, who is openly dissident, complains about the harrassment he suffered from when his son got married, although his son is less of a dissident than he is. The son was even marrying a woman whose father was submissive to the leadership of the *amil*. The *amil*, however, refused to celebrate the marriage. 'Paanwala' was hassled by his son's father-in-law to rejoin the community. According to 'Paanwala', the leadership's difficulty in collecting enough money to build a mosque in New Jersey could be explained by the community's reluctance to pay their taxes, precisely because of their leader's despotism. Fear rather than conscience seems to be the reason why the majority of the Da'udi pay their taxes.

The dissidents are particularly bitter because their Bohra leaders in the United States have not received any specialized religious training. They take on the role as volunteers and keep on a secular occupation at the same time.

Most of the Bohra, however, comply with the leadership's requirements, because they fear to be ostracized: this can be particularly painful in migration, especially in a country where group solidarity tends to be negotiated within the community, notably in the case of recent minorities. The Bohra, or at least those who accept to obey all the rules, are easily recognized by their appearance and their clothes: men shape their beards after a certain fashion and women wear a long garment which covers the whole body.

The Bohra in the United States, in particular the dissidents, observe that the community has, however, evolved in comparison not only to India and Pakistan, but also to East Africa, and even the United Kingdom. Behaviours which would have caused excommunication in the subcontinent or in East Africa are tolerated in United States. One Bohra, for example, made a mixed marriage (with a Nizari woman) and he is not meeting all his obligations as defined by the leadership (in particular he does not pay the compulsory taxes), and yet he has escaped excommunication.

The denunciations 'Paanwala' makes against the leadership, and they are strong, would put his life in danger in India, and yet in the United States he is relatively free. He not only accuses the local leaders of failing to render accounts to the community for the money they collect, but also denounces the authoritarianism of the supreme leadership. His meeting with the Indian sociologist Asghar Ali Engineer, who has been outlawed by the community, was seen as another provocation by the leadership – 'Paanwala' was put on the red list – but it also demonstrates the freedom he enjoys in the United States. This relative freedom can be explained by the vast geographical distance from the leadership in India, and by the scattering of the Bohra in the United States, unlike some areas in East Africa.

'Paanwala' does feel quite isolated in his community. Though it is too early to be sure, but the United States may well become in future a base for dissidents to set up a coherent opposition to the Bohra leadership. It is also possible that some might abandon da'udism in favour of Twelver Shi'ism, or even Sunni Islam; this would not be a new development in the history of the Bohra. 'Paanwala' told me that if he had a choice, he would choose to stay Muslim but not Da'udi Bohra. His emotional attachment to his community is strong, however, so he still is hesitant.

For the moment, 'Paanwala' told me, the immediate change is that most members of his community are becoming more 'Bohra', for fear of reprisals. The community remains very self-contained, as shown in that the Bohra, officially in any case, exclude themselves from any Muslim activity outside their own group, and indeed from social activity in the host society. The Bohra have integrated structurally, but the leadership strongly discourages social integration and obviously assimilation as well.

The Ahmadiyya, frenetic proselytizers

Although the number of Ahmadiyya is only 3,000 or 4,000 (including converts, who are mostly African–Americans), there were in 1994 26 mosques and Ahmadi centres, spread across 17 states, with some concentration in the North East of the country.[66] The headquarters of this community are located at Silver Spring, Maryland. In 1993 Mirza Muzzafar Ahmad, the *amir* (head) of the Ahmadi community in the United States, opened a large mosque, Bait-ur-Rahman (House of Mercy), at 15 000 Good Hope Road.

New York State has two Ahmadi centres, one in Holliswood in Queens, at 86–71 Palo Alto Street, and the other in Rochester, at 564 Merchants Road.

I visited the Holliswood centre, Bait-ul-Zafar (Map 7), one Sunday when a huge blizzard hit New York. The centre director, Nazir Ayaz,[67] was keen to point out the enthusiasm of the followers of Mirza Ghulam Ahmad, who in spite of the weather, as they did every Sunday, were indeed coming in fairly large numbers (except for the women) to the centre's activities.

The Ahmadi centre in Queens, located in a residential neighbourhood with a high Jewish population, was inaugurated in 1985. It was financed by donations from the community, who are obliged to give to the movement one sixteenth of their salary. If this money is not enough, the leaders make an appeal for larger financial contributions.

In the absence of a dome or a minaret, only the large Arabic inscription of the *shahadah* on the left of the entrance door reveals from outside the nature of the building.

Inside, the ground floor is reserved for men and the first floor for women. On the ground floor are the director's office and the men's prayer room, and there is a separate prayer room for women on the first floor, and a kitchen. The library, where I interviewed Nazir Ayaz, is also on the first floor. Since women are not allowed to lead the prayers,[68] a loudspeaker relays the reciting of prayers and the imam's sermon. Unlike the Shi'a, and to a certain extent the Isma'ili, who sometimes pray in Shi'a mosques, the Ahmadiyya must exclusively pray in a mosque whose imam has sworn allegiance to Mirza Ghulam Ahmad.

The sermon is only ever given in English because orders have been given by the leadership that the Ahmadiyya are to prove their loyalty to their new country. We have noted previously that mosques where preaching happens in English tend to be keener on proselytizing than the mosques were the sermon is in the vernacular language. The Ahmadi movement is indeed characterized by aggressive proselytizing. The director is not shy about this. He confirms that the movement's main aim is to propagate Islam. To emphasize this, he shows me a display of Qur'ans translated into 50 languages. Like the followers of other proselytizing movements, the disciples of Ghulam Ahmad are keen to denounce ethnic divisions. The director is proud to say that his centre welcomes Muslims from all ethnic backgrounds. In actual fact, most Ahmadiyya are Pakistanis. The rest are mainly African–Americans.

The Ahmadi centre organizes activities similar to those in other Islamic centres. There is a women's section, a youth section, and a section for elderly people. Fridays and Sundays are the important days of the week. On Fridays usually about 100 worshippers come to the centre. On Sundays, men and women gather separately and discuss a particular theme. The children are taught, often by women who are volunteers. In addition to the traditional teaching given in other Islamic centres on Sundays, the children study the Ahmadi precepts as taught by Ghulam Ahmad, the history of the Ahmadi movement, and a comparative study of other religions. Most of the books used are imported from the major Ahmadi publishing house, Islam International Publications, in the United Kingdom. However, no languages are studied, not even Arabic. This again is in allegiance to the host society. Paradoxically, some women teach Urdu (but not Arabic) to some of the younger members of the community in groups, rather than classes, as an optional 'extra-curricular' activity, as are martial arts.

Women represent a very important element in the Ahmadi community. Among the whole Muslim population, they enjoy a particularly high level of education. According to Ayaz, they are 100 per cent literate. This does not, however, mean that all the women active in the movement seek gainful employment. Their education is for the benefit of the community. They take part in the activities of the mosque and the Ahmadi centre, and teach, but they also devote themselves zealously to proselytism: they put on discussion groups, distribute Ahmadi literature, and so on.

Internally, the Holliswood centre is run along fairly similar lines to those of

other sectarian minorities, in particular the Isma'ili centres. There is no electoral system *per se*. The national *amir* makes a recommendation to the London
leadership for the appointment of the director to a local Ahmadi centre and
London gives a decision. The leadership team is appointed for three years. All
active members of the centre work as volunteers and are also in paid employment elsewhere. Reports on the centre's activities are regularly sent to the
supreme head of the community, Hazrat Mirza Tahir Ahmad.

The job of imam devolves to the 'missionary', who is also the representative
of the supreme leader, the Khalifat ul-Masih. Each of the six major regions of
the United States has its own missionary. In the North East region, the missionary in charge is Mukhtar Ahmad Cheema, who has under his care a
variety of Ahmadi centres. When he is not at Holliswood, prayers are led on a
rota basis by people judged to be competent. When he is present, he not only
leads prayers but also preaches the sermon and answers questions on Muslim
law. He can also be asked to teach new converts.

Cheema[69] who was born in Sialkot in Pakistan, was from 1984 to 1989 the missionary in Ghana. He returned briefly to Pakistan, and in 1990 he was 'posted' to
the United States. In Pakistan, he trained for four years at the Missionary Training
College at Rabwa, where future missionaries are imbued with a passion for
preaching, and taught intensive Arabic and English courses, as their proselytizing
will be more effective if they completely master these languages.[70]

Cheema's main task, he told me, is to serve the community. He is also to
maintain a regular dialogue with representatives of other faiths by inviting
them regularly to discussions, whether they are non-Ahmadi Muslims (though
these are usually reluctant to respond to his invitations), Jews, Christians or
Hindus. The intention of these discussions is to correct any wrong ideas about
Ahmadi Islam. They also represent a vehicle for proselytism.

And proselytism is indeed the second facet of his role, as the name 'missionary' suggests. The meaning that the Ahmadiyya give to the concept of *jihad*
calls here for comment. They are often criticized by other Muslims in that they
do not see the jihad as a 'holy war'.[71] In reply to Sunni criticism, the
Ahmadiyya insist that in the United States they do believe in *jihad*, but in the
sense of a personal struggle to avoid disobedience to God. They also feel that
this theory enables them to present themselves to non-Muslims as a tolerant
and peaceful sect, and that the Ahmadi interpretation of *jihad* is a tool for
proselytism. In the United States, the concept of *jihad* as a holy war against
non-Muslims is in any case not current amongst non-Ahmadi South Asian
mosques and Islamic associations, as Muslims are in such a small minority. A
handful of very committed activists are however engaged in *da'wa*, both
Ahmadiyya and non-Ahmadiyya.

The Ahmadiyya, borrowing from Christian models of missionary activity, use a fourfold method: proselytizing 'in the field' (discussions with individuals or with groups, going to meet them or inviting them to debates); publishing vast amounts of literature which is given out freely to Muslims and non-Muslims; voluntary social work; and discrediting of other religions, for which all the missionaries have been trained. They emphasize the defects and the alleged doctrinal inferiority of these religions. In Christian countries, Christianity is obviously the main target. In the United States, though the Ahmadiyya continue to criticize Christianity, they also argue that it was mis-represented after the death of Jesus. They are then able to present Islam as the true Christianity.

Is this frenetic proselytizing bearing fruit? It would seem not, for in New York, the Ahmadiyya have only converted about two people per year in the last few years. There are facing fierce competition from more orthodox groups also proselytizing. Tony Poon-Chiang Chi adds that their isolation from the rest of the Muslim community also accounts for their lack of suc-cess:[72] the Ahmadiyya have been declared heretical by other Muslims and they have in a sense little choice in this isolation. It is also voluntary, however, because the Ahmadiyya insist that they can only pray under the guidance of one of their own imams, and that they can only marry within their own community.

To sum up, the Ahmadiyya are very much a minority amongst Muslims, but they are nevertheless very organized. The Ahmadi centres are run along very similar lines to those of other Muslim groups, especially the Sunni. They are, it seems, the Muslim movement most actively engaged in proselytizing, leaving aside the Tablighi Jama'at and the Jama'at-i-Islami, whom we shall examine in a moment. Because of their minority status and the attacks regularly directed against them, the Ahmadiyya seem to consider that proselytizing is their only means of survival.

Conclusion: a few thoughts on minority sectarian institutions

Our study of the minority sects has shown that in the activities offered to their followers they have the same aims as the majority Sunni community. The principal differences in the minority sects are linked to their leadership: apart from the Twelver Shi'a (not all the Shi'a mosques follow the same pattern as the Al-Khoei Foundation), all these leaders owe allegiance to leaders outside the United States. These sects are merely the American part of a vast network which covers the whole world. This has implications for the appointment and training of these leaders, and for the financing of the movement. In fact, the money travels in two directions: the Ahmadiyya, the Nizarian and the Bohra pay a part of their income to the leadership; in exchange, if they need it, they receive help to fund their activities. Each one of the supreme leaders, the Aga Khan, the *da'i* and the Khalifatul Masih, has visited his followers in New York during the last few years. The fact that they obey a supreme leadership outside the United States does not seem to hamper the integration of these minority sects. To a certain extent, in particular in the case of the Ahmadiyya and the Nizarian, the strong framework in fact helps their integration. Most importantly, the Ahmadiyya and the Nizarian are bound to swear allegiance to the host country and the leadership strongly encourages them to disregard any ethnic divisions, in order to concentrate their efforts on maintaining their religious identity, and on proselytism in the case of the Ahmadiyya. This encouragement to become integrated is strengthened by the fact that many of the leaders of these communities are twice-migrants, proportionately more than in the Sunni community, and this is particularly marked in the Nizari community.

Islamic schools: a viable alternative?

A small minority of South Asian parents, considering that the teaching available on Sundays is not sufficient, have chosen full-time Islamic schools for their children. To counter the argument that the schools can promote isolationism, these immigrants say that even if only one per cent of Muslim children attend the schools, then at least Muslim leadership in the United States in the years ahead is assured. They cannot accept their children growing up in an environment which runs counter to Islamic values, and advocate separate education for girls and boys.[73]

In 1994, 104 Islamic schools had been set up in the United States, across 29 states, and of all sectarian affiliations. There are ten in New York State, of which the majority (six) are in the city itself and Long Island.[74] The schools outside the city of New York are at Aurora (Dar Ul Uloom), Rochester (Sister Clara Muslim School or SCMS) and Westvalley (Islamic Academy). Those in the city of New York and Long Island have been set up in Manhattan (SCMS), in the Bronx (SCMS), in Brooklyn (Islamic Institute and Ikhwanul Tawheed), Queens (SCMS in Corona; Al-Iman in Jamaica) and Westbury (Crescent School).

The schools are all private, and they are financed from donations and from fees. They give both standard American and Islamic education. Timetables are built around the daily prayer.

I visited two of the schools in New York, Crescent and Al-Iman. Both are housed by an existing Islamic Centre, respectively the ICLI and the Al-Khoei Foundation. They opened simultaneously in September 1991, but are quite different in character. The first difference is in sectarian affiliations: one is

Sunni, one is Shi'a. But, Sunni and Shi'a children may go to one or the other according to where their parents live. Al-Iman is totally integrated to the Islamic centre, and it depends on the centre in terms of premises and finance. The principal of the school is the imam Fadhel Al-Sahlani himself. The Crescent school, on the other hand, simply uses rooms in the ICLI during the week, and many members of the centre would like them to move elsewhere as soon as possible. With two exceptions, the membership of the management boards of the school and the ICLI are completely separate. The conflict between the two is one between modernists and fundamentalists. The school feels that members of the ICLI who send their children to public or private American schools are bad Muslims. The ICLI, on the other hand, feels that the school is too isolationist, even fundamentalist, in its attitude to American society. As a result, the finances are much more difficult at Crescent than at Al-Iman.

A third difference can be observed in the standard of the premises they use. The students at the Crescent school are in fairly modest accommodation, to the extent that the American authorities at first hesitated to allow the school to function, as they were not sure conditions were adequate in terms of safety and comfort (for example heating), and so on. The children at Al-Iman, on the other hand, are in modern, even luxurious accommodation. Their 6,750 square metres include air-conditioned, spacious classrooms, a high-tech science laboratory, a library, a canteen, a meeting and conference room and a gymnasium.

Another difference lies in the ethnic origin of the children attending. Al-Iman welcomes children from all ethnic backgrounds, including African Americans and Hispanics. At the Crescent school, on the other hand, the vast majority of the children are South Asian. The reason for this is that Al-Iman is in Queens, a New York borough were the residents have a very varied standard of living; the close link with the Al-Khoei Foundation enables the fees to be kept at a reasonable level (950 dollars per year), which makes the school accessible to disadvantaged ethnic groups. The Crescent school, on the other hand, is in a residential area where there are few African–Americans or Hispanics. It relies on fees to keep functioning, as the donations of the community are not sufficient; the fees vary between 2,000 dollars and 4,500 dollars per year as the children move from kindergarten to secondary. As a result, there is a dichotomy in the number of children attending; there are nearly 250 at Al-Iman (there were 85 when the school opened, so it has tripled in four years) and only 70 at the Crescent school (but there were only 10 when it opened). The Crescent school will take children at any time during the year, whereas Al-Iman takes only 20 students in each class, and will not take any one after the school year has started.

Both schools are however run along similar lines, and offer similar activities. Both are strictly disciplined. In the older classes the sexes are separated. Uniform is compulsory. The Crescent uniform, white and blue, is reminiscent of English and Indian schools. The girls wear a white *hijab*. The girls at Al-Iman wear a tartan (!) skirt and a navy blue *hijab*.

The teachers at Al-Iman are from varied ethnic backgrounds, but most (five out of seven) at the Crescent school are South Asian. They were trained either in the United States or in their home country, but not all have been trained in education, nor in the subjects they teach (particularly if they teach one of the Islamic subjects). All are more or less well qualified, nevertheless. At the Crescent school, the teaching implies a true commitment to Islam, as teachers work full-time on low salaries, or part-time as volunteers.

The Board of Education of New York City has validated the teaching of these two schools from kindergarten to 11th grade at Al-Iman (up to 12th grade from September 1997), and from kindergarten to 8th grade at the Crescent school (the Crescent school is currently trying to extend to high school level). This recognition by the American authorities means that students can move to any public American school and qualify for university. Both these schools claim to offer at least as good an education as a good American school. They support this claim by pointing to particularly brilliant children from the Al-Iman and Crescent schools who have moved on to the major American high schools. These children do well in national exams and enter American universities. At the Crescent school in particular, most of the children are from families where the father, and often the mother, are highly educated, and are in jobs matching their qualifications. One can assume that these parents would not have sent their children to a mediocre school.

Both schools offer a standard American curriculum and also an Islamic education. The students learn: maths (with occasional reference to the historical role of the Arabs in the development of maths) and other exact sciences, English, social sciences (with particular emphasis on Islamic history), a foreign language (Arabic, and sometimes a second language, usually European), Islamic studies (study of the Qur'an and the Hadis, of the life of Prophet, study of the *fiqh* – though not in any great detail – and basic Islamic concepts), gymnastics.

The two schools make different choices in terms of schoolbooks. For the compulsory subjects, both schools use the most common books studied in American schools. For Islamic studies, Al-Ima uses books published in Muslim countries (Iran, Iraq and Pakistan in particular). The Crescent school, on the other hand, uses books on Islam which have been published in the United States by IQRA, the International Educational Foundation, by the Chicago Foundation for Islamic Knowledge, by Message Publications in New York and so on. In the free atmosphere of the United States, all kinds of publishing houses have been set up. These books are often well presented and they are certainly more attractive to children than those published in the subcontinent, for example.

The teaching methods used in both schools, as in the Sunday schools, are very much modelled on American methods. Children are encouraged to develop a critical mind, and above all to participate actively in class. They are also offered extra-curricular activities, such as writing articles in a school magazine and visiting museums and other places where they can extend their learning. The Crescent school hopes soon to create a 'Young Alims (*sic*) Club' for young people who wish to study the *fiqh*, the *shari'ah*, the Hadis or the Qur'an in greater depth.[75]

Despite initial financial difficulties, either because the American authorities were hesitant to license schools (mainly for safety reasons), or because most Muslim parents were reluctant to send their children to an Islamic school, these schools have in fact, since the early 1990s, begun to flourish in the United States, and particularly in New York.

The two case studies above show the complexity of the issues involved and the wide variety of situations in which this kind of school has been set up by the immigrant Muslim community. Most have similar objectives, especially when the South Asian community is in the majority; they wish to give girls and boys alike a sufficient level of education in the compulsory subjects to put them on a par with the good American schools, and at the same time an Islamic education. However, the Islamic teaching is not particularly sophisticated, and the teachers have not necessarily had specialist training in religious sciences. The main aim of these schools is not to create future Muslim scholars but to counteract an environment seen as permissive. However the thought of creating a future Muslim elite is also a major concern: any encouragement to better Islamic education, including what is offered in extra-curricular activities (clubs and so on), is probably best understood in this light.

In the United Kingdom, apart from the private Al-Karam school at Eaton (Nottinghamshire), most Muslim schools offer a very traditional Pakistani education which is not very attractive to young British Muslims.[76] Schools such as the Crescent school in United States, even when they are overwhelmingly South Asian, are distinctly modernist in their approach: English is the working language for religious topics, rather than the Urdu used in England (in the Deobandi schools); the teaching methods are stimulating to the children; audio-visual methods are often used; and the education offered enables young people to fulfil their ambitions and move into secular professions later on.

These Islamic schools do indeed qualify young people to enter university, but they nevertheless encourage isolationism. The vast majority of Muslim parents are very aware of the risk, and as they consider the social integration of their children to be their highest priority, they look for schooling elsewhere.

6

ISLAMIC MOVEMENTS
A transnational dynamic

The mobilization of South Asian Muslim immigrants in the United States to set up Islamic institutions has resulted in the creation not only of mosques but also of Islamic organizations. In many cases, they are offshoots of organizations which already existed in the subcontinent, such as the Jama'at-i-Islami, the Tablighi Jama'at and the Ahl-e-Sunnat (the Barelwi movement). Some have kept close ties with the parent organization, while others have distanced themselves. In this chapter, we shall examine how these organizations have developed in America, and what influence they have on South Asian Muslims.

The Muslim Student Association (MSA) – leading the way

From the early 1960s, South Asian Muslim students became involved in Islamic student groups. As these groups were not well organized, South Asian students, together with Muslims from other countries – Arabs, Turks, Iranians – held a national conference at Urbana, Illinois, and founded, on 1 January 1963, the Muslim Student Association. Nearly 75 students from 10 American campuses were present.[1]

The MSA set up networks, and extended its activities to all major American campuses. The organization was working under the umbrella of an executive committee, elected once a year at the annual conference, when matters of policy were also decided. The MSA had multiple objectives: to help students in their daily commitment to and practice of Islam, to inform non-Muslims about Islam, so as to counteract prejudice, and to engage more or a less directly into proselytizing activities.[2] By promoting unity between Muslim students, regardless of nationality, the MSA was not only playing a crucial role in creating a Muslim identity in the United States, but it was also setting foundations for a pan-Islamic organization.

The increasing numbers of students involved in the MSA, and financial help from abroad, made it possible to set up in 1971 a permanent secretariat at Gary, Indiana. In 1973 a full-time director was appointed. In September 1975, at Toledo, Ohio, the General Assembly passed amendments to the constitutional structure which enabled full-time staff to be appointed. A vast property (500,000 square metres) was bought for 500,000 dollars at Plainfield, Indiana. Departments for education, publications, training, public relations, finance and administration were set up, led by scholars and activists.[3]

The MSA is still active on American campuses. Of the 239 Muslim student associations listed in the *American Muslim Resource Directory* in 1994, 189 were branches of the MSA. These associations, MSA and others, were spread through 40 different states, including Hawaii and Wyoming. There were 21 in New York State (of which 18 were MSA), nine in New York City (six of which were MSA) and three on Long Island (all three MSA).[4]

In New York I visited two universities with MSA branches, Columbia and Queens College. Both had been given rooms by the university authorities for their activities. The Columbia MSA, which was set up in 1956 and is the oldest branch in New York, is in room 102 in Earl Hall, where student associations are housed. The religious associations are in the basement. In the room next to the MSA is the Jewish organization, and Catholics and Protestants are opposite. In Queens college, the MSA also has a room in the Students' Union, on the first floor, not far from the room used by the homosexuals' association. On the door a notice proclaims 'Say No to Alcohol and Gambling'. Inside, the two rooms are similar: they are small, and serve as both office and library; several carpets cover the floor.

The major difference between the MSA groups in Queens and Colombia lies in the number of students. Since there is no official membership, it is difficult to give precise figures, but at Columbia, because the university is much larger, there are far more students involved in the association. Also, most of the Columbia students are newly arrived in the United States, whereas nearly all the Queens students are second generation. For the Columbia students, the MSA helps them to maintain their religious traditions, whereas the Queens students see the MSA as a place to (re)discover their religious heritage. The ethnic differentiation is also striking: The Columbia students have very diverse backgrounds (Indonesia, Turkey, Yemen, Malaysia, South Asia and so on), where as the Queens students are mostly Pakistani, Guyanese of South Asian origin, African–Americans and Hispanics. At the time of my visits, the MSA president at Columbia was a student from Yemen, and the Queens president a Hispanic recently converted to Islam.

The two associations also offer different types of activities. At both, it is true, Friday prayers are the main activity. At Columbia about 50 students attend, but at Queens only about 10. During Ramadan, Columbia has an official meal to break the fast each evening, whereas Queens only does this occasionally. Most of the Muslim students at Columbia live a long way away from their families, and they like to break the fast together. The students in Queens, being second generation, tend to break the fast with their family.

In January 1996, I went to one of these fast-breaking evenings at Columbia. The event happened at five o'clock, in the basement of the university chapel (!). About 20 students, all male, lined up to pray behind a Yemeni student. One was praying with his baseball cap back to front on his head. A few girls, some with, but most without the veil, came to join the group. There were soon about fifty young people in the room. A groaning table awaited them. Even the traditional dates had not been forgotten. Every year during Ramadan, a Muslim restaurant offers free food for 20 people to the Columbia MSA. The remaining dishes are prepared by the students themselves. Boys and girls sat down separately. Once the meal was over, the atmosphere became more informal, and girls and boys chatted together. At about half past six, the students cleared up and went back to their work.

Apart from organizing the daily prayer and the breaking of the fast, the Columbia MSA invites students to weekly discussions on a variety of themes: living out Islam in the West, the place of Islam in the world, a study of a sura in the Koran, and so on. Political matters are discussed, but students are rarely mobilized for a particular political cause. The main objective of the association is to create a place to meet for students who share a religion and wish to preserve their religious heritage. The association is fairly self-contained, and has little contact with other religious or cultural groups. Some of the activist students belong to the Jama'at-i-Islami and advocate strict observance: for example, they criticize young Muslim women who do not wear the veil. This does not endear them to other Muslim students. Of the South Asian students, some occasionally say Friday prayers in the MSA room, out of a feeling of guilt, they say, but most prefer to go to other associations, such as the Zamana club, which offers cultural activities to people of all religious affiliations.

The Columbia MSA does not, officially and directly, engage in *da'wa*. If there is proselytizing, it is very indirect in that it seeks to convert people because of exemplary behaviour by Muslims.

This is the key difference between the Queens MSA and the Columbia MSA. At Queens, every two months, the MSA organizes meetings with students, and the main objective is proselytism. This often takes the form of a stand on campus, and sometimes outside the campus. The activists draw students and passers-by into discussions. Once a term, a more elaborate proselyte event is laid on, when the MSA members invite students, both Muslim and non-Muslim, to join them. There is a carrot to draw them: a free lunch.

In November 1995 I went to one of these meetings, which was entitled 'The Muslim Student Association Presents Islam'. The MSA students had booked a room and carefully prepared the lunch, offering a variety of dishes. White cloths were spread out on the classroom tables. At the entrance to the room, were placed several free copies of Hammudah Abdalati's book, *Islam in Focus*, which is well-known in North America. A few dozen non-Muslim Americans had responded to the invitation (only in one sense of the word![6]). Boys and girls were sitting next to each other, and the atmosphere was a merry one. Some student members of the Pakistani club were also present. Once everyone had eaten, the 'serious' talk began.

'Zakir', a young man of Pakistani origin, bearded, wearing a kind of white djellaba and a white skullcap, gave an openly proselyte talk. He started by saying that he would use the name Allah, and not 'God', to avoid any confusion with Christ, Buddha or Gandhi. He then spoke insistently about the very specific claims in the Qur'an and Islam that there is clear division between the Creator and his Creation; he emphasized that the Creator did not rest on the seventh day and that Creation is not divine. After this introduction, he affirmed that Islam was the only true religion, and insisted that this religion must be understood in its totality. To illustrate this last point, he used a rather unspiritual comparison: 'If company A offers a contract to company B, and company B refuses the contract, it is the whole of company A which is rejected. If only one point in the contract is rejected, then the whole contract is cancelled or unworkable.' To close, he made allusion to the solar system and the galactic city quoted in the Qur'an, as a proof that the Muslim sacred book has scientific validity.

This talk did not provoke much reaction. There were two questions from non-Muslim Americans students. One asked 'Zakir' whether he had read the Bible. He retorted, 'Which Bible? There are multiple versions, but there is only one version of the Qur'an.' Another student wanted to know if he believed in the separation of church and state. He replied in the negative, saying that Islam covers all aspects of life.

A short while later, the room emptied as students returned to their work. I then interviewed 'Zakir'. He was born in the United States, of Punjabi parents, and was 24 years old. His family was very religious, and at the age of 17 he became even more committed after an accident killed one of his best friends. He has learned Arabic, and says he knows it better than Urdu or Punjabi, but not well enough to read the Qur'an without translation. Ideologically, he claims to belong to the Salafi movement. This reformist movement appeared at the end of the nineteenth century, inspired by Jamaluddin al-Afghani (c. 1839–97) and Muhammad Abduh (1849–1905). Its name comes from 'Salaf', meaning 'the pious ancestors', and implies a desire to restored Islam to its original form. However, this movement had been shaped to a certain extent by modernism (a desire to unify the four schools of jurisprudence, and to re-establish *ijtihad*), and even by rationalism (it calls on scientific arguments to justify religious beliefs).[7] Although it was founded to combat Western imperialism, the social and political measures the movement put forward were modelled on western ideas, and took account of modern scientific progress, though without rejecting fundamental Islamic principles. The talk 'Zakir' gave was not modernist or rationalist to any great extent; he was advocating a return to a traditional and rigorist faith, and his main objective seemed to be the struggle against political and social systems inspired by the West.

The Salafi movement in the United States has grown considerably since the late 1980s. Its main recruits come from Arabs from the Gulf, and white and African–American converts. There are few South Asians involved, it would seem. As the movement is still at an early stage of its life, it was not really possible for me to study its organization in America. According to Steve Johnson, the two main Salafi centres in North America are in New Jersey (Al-Hijra Society) and in Canada.[8]

During the interview, the ideas 'Zakir' expresses, especially on women, tended towards the traditionalist literal interpretation of the Qur'an. 'Zakir' says that he lives in the United States, a secular country, because there is no true Islamic state anywhere. The only place in the world where there is something approaching an Islamic state is the region of Mecca and Medina – but not Saudi Arabia, 'a country sold out to the West' – and ideally he would have liked to live there. His duty to his family prevents him from leaving the United States, however. He does say that he enjoys the freedom the United States offers to everyone. He is able to preach openly, without any fear. He compares himself to the Jehovah's Witnesses, with whom he sometimes talks, each side trying to convince the other that its own religion is superior. He speaks in a very calm way, and seems to think himself charged with a mission.

A Hispanic convert is officially the president of Queens MSA, but 'Zakir' is the real leading light. He is a computer science student at a university in Manhattan, and comes regularly to Queens to give classes on Islam twice a week, and in Arabic once a week. The two Islamic classes I went to were very similar (he declared that Islam was superior to all other religions, and criticized Christianity and Judaism). Jews and Christians are described in the Qur'an as 'People of the Book' (*Ahl-e-Kitab*), but 'Zakir' calls them *kafir*. In fact, among traditionalists, the word *kafir* applies to any non-Muslim. The occasional references 'Zakir' makes to Hinduism point to his South Asian origins, and seems to be an echo of the historic rivalry between Hinduism and Islam, and between India and Pakistan, reverberating as far as a classroom in Queens College. The *tawhid* (unity of God) and its immediate corollary, a virulent criticism of *shirk* (associationism), are fundamental elements of Islam, and 'Zakir's' heavy insistence on this is characteristic of the Salafi movement.[9]

There were very few students at this class, which happened during the lunch hour, about seven or eight, half of whom were recent converts.

'Zakir's' main proselyte strategies are diatribe and the belittling of other religions: principally Christianity, because he is in a Christian country, and Hinduism, because he is originally from the subcontinent. As we have already seen, the same methods are used by the Ahmadiyya. Here, the methods used are reminiscent of those of Ahmad Deedat, the famous South African preacher (originally from Gujarat). In 1958 he was the founder of the Islamic Propagation Center, an organization which exists to combat Christian proselytizing, and Deedat's own technique is to point to Christianity as the main enemy of Islam. He travels regularly throughout the West, in England and in the United States, and knows how to draw crowds.[10] There are some who like to emulate his virulent style, but he has also antagonized many Muslims in the United States. 'Zakir' does not launch into violent diatribes against Christianity or the West, but his basic inspiration seems to be derived from Deedat.

To return to the MSA itself, one last facet of its activities is the organization of large-scale evening meetings, with a dinner and invited Muslim personalities. In December 1995, a meeting entitled 'Islam in Focus'[11] was held in its university premises for nearly one hundred students, mostly Muslim, but not all studying at Queens College. Three Muslim personalities had been invited, one of whom was the charismatic African –American imam, Siraj Wahhaj, from the Al-Taqwa mosque in Brooklyn, which became famous through its campaign against drugs. The subjects discussed were the classic ones often discussed at this kind of meeting: 'Jesus as a prophet of Islam', 'Islam and the media', 'Muslim involvement in American politics'.

The MSA at Queens appears to be very well organized, but there is only a small handful of Muslim students regularly involved in its activities. There are many South Asians at Queens, but they only occasionally take part, mostly during the month of Ramadan, as they prefer other ethnic organizations. The hard core of the MSA, which is only about ten students, keeps its distance from other organizations, both ethnic and religious.

Because the MSA was designed to meet the needs of students, towards the end of the 1970s there emerged the idea of an Islamic association which would cater not only for students but more generally for immigrants. At the 1981 annual conference, the principle of an umbrella organization was adopted, and the Islamic Society of North America (ISNA) was officially founded. It moved into the MSA offices at Plainfield. In October 1981, thanks to financial help from Muslim countries, construction work finished on the building, which until then had housed only the MSA. The total cost had been 3.4 million dollars.[12] All MSA associations were formally affiliated to the ISNA. A Pakistani, Ilyas Ba-Yunus, was elected as the first president. Proselytizing and education are presented as the main objectives of the association.

The ISNA embraces quite a number of organizations. In addition to the MSA it includes other bodies, such as the North American Islamic Trust (NAIT), a financial institution which assists in the building of mosques and Islamic centres, and the Islamic Teaching Center (ITC), the principal task of which is to propagate Islam (through training programmes and the distribution of literature on the subject), especially in prisons. Some organizations are more specialized, and are aimed at one particular group. The ISNA includes three professional associations; the Islamic Medical Association (IMA), founded in 1981, the American Muslim Scientists and Engineers (AMSE), created in 1969, and the American Muslim Social Scientists (AMSS), established in 1972. These three associations mainly exist to provide a place where Muslims in similar professions can meet and exchange ideas, and they also help those who have recently qualified to find work. The IMA (Islamic Medical Association) and the AMSE also invite Muslim doctors and engineers to the United States, so that they can receive further training before going back to to their own countries. When there are natural disasters in Muslim countries, the IMA sends doctors to help the Red Crescent. The AMSS, which was founded on the initiative of the Palestinian scholar-cum-activist Ismail Al-Faruqi (1921–86),[13] exists to encourage its members to engage in social science research and to study contemporary issues in the light of Islam. Its objectives also include the promotion of research projects on Islamic societies, setting up institutions to study social and political issues, and cooperating in research projects with institutions already set up in the United States and in Muslim countries.[14]

Young people are also catered for. An organization for young people (12 to 18 years old), the Muslim Youth of North America (MYNA), is affiliated to the ISNA. Its main activities include organizing conferences (the first annual conference happened in December 1985) and camps where young people come to receive Islamic teaching and to meet other young Muslims. Through these meetings they develop a sense of common identity. The ultimate objective is to train up future leadership in the United States.[15]

I will not describe the activities of the ISNA and its different branches in any further detail, as it was the subject of a thesis in 1989.[16] The headquarters, furthermore, are in Indiana and not New York.

The Islamic Circle of North America (ICNA): the official branch of the Jama'at-i-Islami?

Another group for immigrant Muslims was born as an extension of the activities of the MSA,[17] the Islamic Circle of North America (ICNA). Its membership is mostly South Asian and its headquarters are in New York. It has not so far been studied, except in a lecture by Usha Sanyal in 1993 at the University of Colombia.[18]

The origins of ICNA go back to 1968, when a group of Pakistani students were inspired to create an Islamic movement in North America which would help Muslims to live according to Islam. The organization (originally a study circle – *halaqa*) was formally set up in 1971. Until 1976, the organization claimed affiliation to Islamic movements imported from Muslim countries, in particular the Jama'at-i-Islami. It was largely dominated by South Asians; the working language was Urdu, which was used for discussions also. In 1976, the organization discussed the question of its identity: would it remain merely the American branch of Islamic movements outside the United States, or should it become an independent American Islamic organization? The majority voted for the second option. The following year, the ICNA became an autonomous association with its own constitution. From then on, English was the only language used in sermons, discussions, and so on. In 1983, the ICNA bought a small building at 166–26 89th Street at Jamaica (Queens), where it now has its headquarters, Al-Markaz[19] (Map 7). According to Zahid Bukhari, the president of the North East branch of the ICNA, the organization now has about 50 branches in North America.

Until 1994, joining the ICNA was a long and demanding procedure: during a probation period, which could last for five years, the religious observance and the moral character of a candidate was carefully examined before he or she could be accepted as a member of the ICNA. These strictures meant that very few people joined. A few voices started to advocate a more open policy, though some of the older members expressed their opposition. In 1994, the procedure was finally simplified. A new constitution was drawn up. Now, an aspiring member simply needs to fill in the form to say that he accepts the *aqida* (doctrine), the objectives, the working practices and the programme of the ICNA; he has to promise to cooperate with the organization in its struggle, and commits himself to faithful Islamic practice day by day. The *aqida* of the organization is the profession of faith, belief in a unique God and in his Prophet.[20]

Thanks to this new policy, the number of members has grown: according to Zahid Bukhari, in 1996 there were about 15,000 in the entire continent of North America, including Canada.[21] He estimated that there were in addition about 5,000 sympathizers. This organization, therefore attracts some 20,000 Muslims across the American continent.[22] This high number suggests that it has moved on from the Jama'at-i-Islami, which traditionally functions with only few followers.[23] The numbers attending the annual conferences of the ICNA has grown over the years: in 1989, 1,400 Muslims took part, in 1990 there were 2,000, and in 1996 there were more than 5,000.[24]

In 1989, Zahid Bukhari carried out a research on the delegates attending the annual convention. 290 people were interviewed. The results showed that most were young (48 per cent were under 34 years old) men (83 per cent) who were well-educated (87 per cent had been to university). 80 per cent of the delegates were from the east coast of the United States, of whom 66 per cent came from the tri-state area (New York, New Jersey, Connecticut). South Asians represented more than two-thirds of the participants (71 per cent); the others were Americans, Canadians (9 per cent) or Arabs (6 per cent). 62 per cent said that Urdu was their mother tongue, 12 per cent said English, 6 per cent said Arabic and 5 per cent said Bengali.[25]

Since then, the profile of delegates has somewhat changed: at the 1996 conference, half of those present were women. This sudden growth in the number of women in the 1990s coincide with the second generation reaching maturity. There are two consequences: women who have no job outside the home now have time to spare, and as children grow towards adolescence and adulthood, parents start fearing increasingly that their offspring might become accultured. Hence the desire to join in the activities of organizations who claim as a major objective to hold back the Americanization of the younger generation. Most of these women are the wives of members of the ICNA.

South Asians are still in the majority in the organization, but according to Zahid Bukhari, there is a growing number of members from countries outside the subcontinent. This was confirmed at the 1996 conference, when Muslims from many ethnic groups attended.[26]

However, when I visited the headquarters of the ICNA in 1996, South Asians were in the main leadership positions. The director was a Punjabi from Lahore (Zahid Bukhari), the general secretary, an Indian from Hyderabad (Sheikh Obaid, who was replaced in 1997 by Tariqur Rahman, probably a Bangladeshi) and the imam was an Indian from Lucknow (Maulana Naseem). Most of the members were chatting in Urdu. However, African–Americans, a few white converts and a Bosnian were among the active members of the organization. The women's section, on the other hand, is still almost entirely dominated by South Asians who converse, hold their debates, and listen to lectures in Urdu.

In terms of leadership and internal structure, the central organization has a general assembly, a president (*amir*), a *Majlis ash-Shura* (consultative committee), an executive committee, a general secretary, and heads for the central departments.

The general assembly is the final authority for any decision about the ICNA. Any new member to the general assembly is submitted to very strict conditions: in particular, members are bound to observe the compulsory laws of *shari'ah* and to abstain from any 'major sins'. They are not allowed to earn their living in any way which goes against Muslim precepts. They also have to introduce *da'wa* into the lives of the family, their friends and their acquaintances, to try to bring up the children according to Islamic tenets, and if necessary to 'reform' the lifestyle of their spouse, if he or she is engaged in activities which goes against Islamic norms. Finally, they are not simply to preach to those around them, they are to undertake to spend a significant amount of time propagating Islam more widely to American society. Failure to keep to these rules can mean temporary suspension, or even expulsion. All members of the assembly have to keep reports on their activities and on their personal devotional life, and if requested submit these reports to the leadership. This system means that the quality and devotion of each member can be evaluated.

The *amir* of the ICNA is elected by secret ballot for two years (renewable for one term) by the general assembly. He is responsible for the organization and for ensuring that ICNA policies are carried out. Members are taken onto the general assembly or expelled from it only with his agreement.

The *Majlis ash-Shura*, or consultative committee, is the political arm of the organization which helps and advises the president. The executive committee aids, counsels and facilitates the president's work as he applies the policy decisions which the *Majlis ash-Shura* implements. It has five members chosen from among the consultative committee. The heads of the central departments are appointed according to the same procedure. Their responsibilities are defined by the president himself.

In order to strengthen and extend its impact on the American continent, the ICNA has divided North America into six regions, five in the United States and one in Canada. This division is temporary and can be modified if the president so decides. The functions of the regional organizations are also very clearly defined, and each one has, at a local level, a role similar to that of the central organization.

The organization's finances are controlled by the *Baitul Maal* (Treasury). Members of the ICNA contribute through a system of compulsory taxes and sympathizers also make donations. Any donations with conditions attached, or from governments or other organizations, are automatically turned away.[27]

The ICNA would appear, therefore, to operate autonomously. The organizational structure, however, is lifted from the Jama'at-i-Islami in Pakistan, which, like the ICNA, is run along clearly defined hierarchical and bureaucratic lines. This ICNA structural network covers most of the United States.

Ideologically also, the ICNA continues to defend the ideals defined by Mawdudi. The leadership itself consists of members who were nearly all affiliated, among the South Asians at least, to the Jama'at-i-Islami before emigrating to the United States. This is true of Zahid Bukhari, who has been in the United States since 1983 and holds a doctorate in political sciences from an American university, and also of Maulana Naseem.[28] Naseem, an older man, went to the Aligarh Muslim University to study psychology and philosophy, then to the Nadwa't-ul Ulama,[29] where he learned Arabic. After his studies, he returned to his family's business. During the state of emergency in India (1975–77), he was thrown into prison because of his affiliation to the Jama'at-i-Islami (he had joined in 1946); at the same time he lost his business. In 1980, he went to the United States as a guest of MSA students. They advised him to stay, since he had little in the way of the future in India, either economically or politically. Since then, Maulana Naseem has become a highly respected person in the Muslim community. He is often invited to preach in mosques and he looks after issues related to marriage (he celebrates marriages, and more especially gives advice to help settle marital conflicts), and after the religious education of children.

Members of the ICNA who were card-holding Jama'at-i-Islami members before they emigrated have generally kept their card; they are now, therefore, in possession of two cards, as the Pakistani Jama'at-i-Islami allows (and probably even encourages) its diaspora members to keep their cards. However, any person who definitively leaves the United States is not allowed to keep his/her ICNA card.

Major figures in the Jama'at-i-Islami organization, such as Khurram Murad (1932–97), a former vice-president of the Jama'at-i-Islami in Pakistan, are regularly invited to speak at the ICNA conventions or in *The Message* (see below).

The anti-Rushdie campaign organized by the ICNA in New York (see Chapter 7) also shows the ICNA's links with official branches of the Jama'at-i-Islami, notably with the Islamic Foundation of Leicester in the United Kingdom.

The ideological debt owed by the ICNA to the Jama'at-i-Islami, both in its organization and in its philosophy, is still very much in evidence, though the political dimension has gone. Any political ambition to transform the State is very much on the back burner, or indeed written out of the ICNA objectives. To turn the United States into an Islamic state is not on the agenda, even though such an idea may not be completely absent from the thoughts of some activist members. The idea however is still emphasized that Islam should regulate every aspect of one's life, even in a secular society, and that only the defined law should rule the behaviour of Muslims. Since the ICNA advocates a return to Scripture and to a literal interpretation of the Qur'an and the Sunna, and insists on a rejection of Western society, in this case American, it has as an organization good fundamentalist credentials. Though no hostile aggression is expressed towards the United States – members undertake to act within the legal and democratic framework – American society is still denounced for the 'social evils' it promotes, listed in *The Message*: 'AIDS, poverty, alcoholism, crime, adultery, discrimination, suicide, ill-treatment of children, stress, pornography, drugs, homosexuality, abortion.'[30] This list might well have been drawn up by fundamentalist Christians, who are also very active in the United States. The organization therefore has a double objective: to Islamize Muslims in the United States (that is, to turn virtual or nominal Muslims into practising Muslims), paying particular attention to the second generation; and to propagate Islam in American society.

This lack of a political programme and the emphasis on proselytizing, both within the Muslim population and outside it (which seems to imply that it is greater observance by individuals which is a necessary basis for establishing an Islamic state, whereas the Jama'at-i-Islami would usually advocate the opposite process) would seem to bring the ICNA closer to the Tablighi Jama'at. A similar picture emerges in India and in other countries where Muslims are in the minority.[31] The ICNA, however, denies that it is similar to its fundamentalist rival. It emphasizes that its structures are different from those (apparently much more loose) of the Tablighi Jama'at and that it uses much more modern methods in activities. Other points of difference, in the subcontinent and elsewhere in the world, include religious behaviour (Muhammad Ilyas's movement insists more on individual faith) and political behaviour (see Chapter 7).

The ICNA puts much effort into using modern technology in its activities, the media and information technology in particular. These are many and they are aimed at different groups within the population, with particular emphasis on young people. Various types of media are used. The ICNA publishes a magazine in English, *The Message International*. At first, this publication was called *Tehrik* ('Movement') and it first appeared in 1977. Originally in Urdu, it was published termly in Canada. In 1986 an English edition was added. The following year, the magazine changed its name to *The Message*. Since July 1989, it has been a monthly review, published in New York under its new name of *The Message International*.[33] At the ICNA annual convention in July 1996, it was announced that in the following October a bi-monthly Spanish edition, *El Mesaje*, would begin to appear.

The Message International had 6,250 subscribers in the United States in January 1996.[34] Since it was first published in July 1989, the presentation has become progressively more attractive, the style more lively, and the editors have not shied away from such things as eye-catching puns (*Olé to Allah*, for example, as the title of an edition on Hispanics[35]). The ethnic origin of the editors has also become more diverse. At first they were mostly South Asian, but now there are also Arabs and quite a number of white and African–American converts. The subject-matter of articles has also evolved. At first, *The Message* dealt on the whole with Muslims in the Indian subcontinent, and with the ideals of the Jama'at-i-Islami. It then extended its interests to include problems which face Muslims in the United States. Its scope these days is very wide: the value and significance of practices and prohibitions in Islam (Ramadan, pilgrimage, *da'wa*, *riba*); the position of Muslims in the world (Bosnia, Iraq, Algeria, India, Palestine, Sudan, and so on); the position of Muslims in the United States (discrimination, family issues, the education of the young, the status of women); black Islam (Malcolm X, Warith Deen Muhammad); current affairs (cloning – which it favours, because 'there is nothing in the Qur'an or in the Hadis against it' – AIDS in the Muslim community, the elderly and the duty of each Muslim to look after them); in-depth articles on background issues (fundamentalism, multiculturalism, immigration) and articles on different Christian sects (with the aim of showing that they are inferior to Islam). Some controversial themes are the subject of discussion in its pages: whether to emigrate to a non-Muslim society, whether or not to consider the United States as 'home', whether or not to take part in American politics. Women and the young are also invited to contribute articles. The articles on women are presented as modernist: families are encouraged to educate their daughters, to allow them to practise sport (in a girls-only environment) and to choose their own husbands (provided, of course, that the girl chooses a Muslim man). Most of these articles adopt a defensive tone and aim to demonstrate that women are treated fairly in Islam. There are often interviews with Muslim intellectuals, members of the Jama'at-i-Islami or sympathizers. These have included Mumtaz Ahmad (a professor of Pakistani origin who teaches at Hampton University in Virginia, and is well known for his study of the Jama'at-i-Islami and the Tablighi Jama'at), Sayyid Hossein Nasr (a professor of Iranian origin who teaches at Washington University and has written many articles on Islam) and Khurram Murad. 'Islamic' quizzes and poems lighten the tone of the magazine. There is a section for questions from readers: is it Islamic to sell water? are Muslims allowed to eat with knives and forks? and so on. Occasionally matrimonial advertisements appear in some issues (though never more than two per issue). The magazine is a resolute campaigner against the persistence of ethnic barriers within the Muslim community, and yet these advertisements mention the ethnic origin of the 'candidates' (generally Indian or Pakistani).

Apart from this magazine, the ICNA also regularly publishes an impressive quantity of brochures, tracts, and other prospectuses on matters relating to

Islam: an introduction to Islam, a hagiography of the Prophet, the status of women, a hagiography of Malcolm X, and so on. This literature is widely distributed, about 500,000 items per year on average.

One of the departments of the ICNA, called Sound Vision, specializes in producing computer, audio and video material, and distributes 'Islamic' audio and video cassettes. These are, for example, documentary programmes explaining the principles of Islam, interviews with converts, talks given by activists or by famous preachers, such as the imam Siraj Wahhaj, and recitations of the Qur'an by specialists. Sound Vision has also developed software programs, for example to help users learn to recite the Qur'an in Arabic with the help of a computer. One program gives a translation of all the Bukhari Hadis (HadisBase); others enable a search by key word or key theme for any extract from the Qur'an (QuranBase, TafseerBase), in three languages (Arabic, English – the translation by Yusuf 'Ali – and French – the translation by Muhammad Hamidullah), thanks to an indexing system and a structure using hypertext. Learning the Qur'an and Arabic becomes fun, thanks to tests and quizzes which help the learner to monitor his or her progress.[36]

There is a separate department of the ICNA dedicated to children, called the *Youth Section*, as children are also specifically targeted by Sound Vision, which has created for them a video programme called *Adam's World*. This programme draws its inspiration from American puppet shows such as *Sesame Street*, and represents Sound Vision's best-selling product. With the help of this programme, children – and converts – learn how to pray and how to accomplish ritual washing by following the example of a puppet(!), and how to write *bismillah* in Arabic. Muslim values, such as respect for parents, are also taught through this mode of communication. The cassettes take viewers to the holy places of Islam, to Muslim countries, to the most beautiful mosques in the world and so on. Songs also feature: 'Allah, there's only one God', based on a popular song by Yusuf Islam, 'Ka'aba' . . . although in theory the more conservative of Muslims prohibit music.[37]

Another example of the way in which the ICNA uses modern technology is the 24-hour telephone helpline ('toll-free *da'wa* hotline'), which answers calls from people wanting to find out about Islam. On average, this line receives ten calls per day. According to Zahid Bukhari, 12 people have converted because of the line during the last few years. There is another telephone line for American journalists to make inquiries, and since September 1996, the ICNA has had its own website.

By making plentiful and instrumental use of modern technology, the ICNA aligns itself with the fundamentalist groups who accept 'science, as long as it does not invade the territory of faith and dogma'.[38]

The remaining activities of the ICNA are very similar to those of mosques and Islamic centres in New York: there is a Sunday school, wedding services are offered, and so on. A welfare committee, ICNA Relief, has also been created. It aims to help disadvantaged Muslims in the United States and throughout the world. In January 1996, ICNA Relief absorbed a charitable organization, UMMAH (United Muslim Movement Against Homelessness), which was founded in 1992 by Khatib Akbar Jihad. The ICNA also helps needy non-Muslims in the United States. For example, when there were floods in the Midwest in May 1997, the organization appealed for funds from Muslims to help the victims. The MSI (Muslim Savings and Investments), based in Texas and mentioned in Chapter 3, is also a branch of the ICNA.

The main focus of the ICNA, however, is proselytizing and the organization deploys a number of means to this end. It prints and distributes a large amount of literature and, as we have seen, it has established the toll-free *da'wa* hotline. *Da'wa* Field Trips have been set up, and a system of 'NeighborNets', groups of up to eight people who meet weekly to study together, to develop close relationships, and to proselytize (for example by inviting individuals to meetings or to seminars on Islam). These pietistic methods are undergirded by the ideas of Khurram Murad, considered to be one of the foremost thinkers on proselytizing in the West since his book *Da'wa Among Non-Muslims in the West*[39] was published. According to him, proselytizing is not to invite someone to change their religion, or to transfer their allegiance to a rival religion. He does not think of Islam as a new religion, but rather as a return to the one true religion. Judaism and Christianity, in their original forms, are therefore the same as Islam is today.[40] This train of thought is reminiscent of the Ahmadiyya way of thinking.

There is a separate section for women, who are also very active within the ICNA. For the men, the organization is as important for its social function as for its religious function, as it provides a place of meeting; for women, the social aspect is even more important. In the absence of the wider family, the ICNA is a substitute network of social relationships – between women, since segregation is the order of the day; for women who are not in paid employment (and they are in the majority in the ICNA) the organization offers opportunities to take responsibility. The reader will recall 'Faiza', the woman wearing the *burqa* from Lucknow (see Chapter 3) – she is the president of the women's section of the ICNA. Under her leadership, about 20 women of the first generation, all from South Asia, meet regularly. All their discussions take place in Urdu. They discuss a wide variety of subjects, ranging from the importance of maintaining one's Islamic identity to contemporary political problems.

Segregation between men and women, although it is not enforced at the large conventions, does give to the women a certain amount of freedom, as they are able to run their own affairs. The most active women within the

ICNA travel quite regularly, mostly in groups of two or three, to visit branches of the organization across the whole of North America.

We shall now examine the impact of the ICNA, which not only is imbued with the ideals of the Jama'at-i-Islami, but also defines itself in opposition to the host society, on the Muslim community. As Francis Robinson has pointed out, fundamentalist movements tend to flourish in societies which are in a state of transition, or are becoming more urbanized and developed, such as in South Asia, or within populations which are in a state of transition, such as immigrant groups.[41] In the United States, the South Asian Muslims are immigrants and therefore in a state of transition, and come from urban and educated populations. The development of an Islamic state which could seem to most immigrants to be incongruous in the American context, is no longer a priority for this organization, for all that it was born of the Jama'at-i-Islami. The ICNA, moreover, deploys a variety of strategies to ensure that the younger generation remain under the fold of their parents and preserve their religious traditions, a matter very dear to many Muslim parents. It would seem, therefore, that the ICNA is well placed to exert a certain influence on the Muslim population in the United States.

In fact, my interviews with immigrants suggest that this organization is viewed with a certain ambiguity. The name of the Jama'at-i-Islami tends to throw up defences. The movement is branded as fundamentalist, and so not to be associated with. But the ICNA itself does not appear to have an entirely negative image in the community, unlike its British equivalent, the UK Islamic Mission in Leicester. The ICNA is seen as an Islamic organization like any other, wishing to promote Islam in the United States. Even the Barelwis, who are firmly opposed to the Jama'at-i-Islami in Pakistani and in England, though they still condemn the latter as a fundamentalist political party, view the ICNA, in the words of the Barelwi mosque director in Woodside, as a 'good organization'. Maulana Naseem, a prominent figure in the ICNA, is often invited by members of the community to resolve marital conflicts or to teach children. As one immigrant told me, he is not considered by the community to be a party man. Among the immigrants who are subscribed to the official ICNA magazine, *The Message*, can be found a number who advocate the integration of Muslims into American society, and reject isolationism. It would therefore appear that the ICNA has been able to transform its image from being the United States branch of the Jama'at-i-Islami to being an autonomous and respectable organization, carrying an acceptable message.

The fact that the ICNA is relatively autonomous can be traced back to the nature of the Jama'at-i-Islami in South Asia, which takes on a different form according to the country in which operates. It is above all a religious movement in India, but a political party in Pakistan. Each branch of the Jama'at-i-Islami works relatively independently, though links between the different groups are maintained. This was shown when the Jama'at-i-Islami in Pakistan gave support to Iraq during the Gulf war, whereas the Jama'at-i-Islami in India and Bangladesh supported the other side. The political nature of the Jama'at-i-Islami, and indeed the fact that it wishes to take power, in both Pakistan and Bangladesh, means that it has to conform to the norms of each country: it becomes a Pakistani organization in Pakistan and a Bangladeshi organization in Bangladesh. In the United States, the ICNA is first and foremost a religious organization (as it is in India), and aims at being considered as such, and at meeting the needs of Muslims in the United States. It does not cater only for South Asians, but addresses itself also to other Muslims, particularly since South Asians are not (unlike in the United Kingdom) the only Muslim group in the United States.

The ICNA may be relatively autonomous from the Jama'at-i-Islami, but it does not for all that have significant impact on the Muslim community as a whole. The majority of immigrants prefer to go to 'independent' mosques. In the main, they are concerned above all to become economically and socially integrated, and they do not feel invested with a particular mission. The ICNA demands from its members a large time commitment. It does remain, however, that a number of student associations, Islamic research centres and religious centres are under the control of the Jama'at-i-Islami and its avatars. But above all, by seeing the ICNA as one Islamic organization among others immigrants legitimizes not only its existence but perhaps also its ambition to represent Muslims in the United States. As the ICNA is not particularly ostracized by the Muslim community, it has been able to establish links with other Islamic organizations, and to mobilize with them (in support of the Bosnians for example).

Although the message of the ICNA is antimodernist, the methods used to draw Muslims and non-Muslims alike are forward-looking and adapted to American society. Members are encouraged to use English in discussions, at least in the men's section, and technological possibilities are fully exploited, though it should be pointed out that this is not only true of the ICNA: the Jama'at-i-Islami in Pakistan and in the United Kingdom also use very modern methods in their propaganda. American tools such as puppets and songs are also used. The ICNA continues to recruit its leadership mainly from the first generation of South Asians, but efforts are being made to include Muslims not originally from the subcontinent in all activities of the organization, even in leadership positions (African–Americans and Bosnians for example). It so happens that the ICNA leaders were for the most part affiliated to the Jama'at-i-Islami in Pakistan before they emigrated to the United States, but the organization does not rely on a system of 'imported' leaders specifically from

Pakistan. Moreover, the ICNA offers women a non-negligible space. An increasing number of women are taking part in the activities of the association (the Jama'at-i-Islami in Pakistan, in fact, also has a women's section), and they are using *The Message International* as a forum in which to express themselves, as nearly all its articles about women are written by women. The place of women in society is not seen only through conservative eyes: they are often encouraged to go to university, to choose their own husbands, and so on.

The relationship of the ICNA to its host society is very complex. This complexity is reminiscent of the vacillations of Mawdudi in the 1930s, when he was wondering whether it was preferable for Muslims to be isolationist in India, or whether they should rather throw themselves into political and social action.[42] In the United States, the individual and collective identity of the ICNA is very clearly defined in opposition to the host society, but that very society is admired for the freedom it offers and for its democratic and pluralist traditions. This attitude of the ICNA is similar to that taken by the Jama'at-i-Islami in Pakistan and in India. In Pakistan, the Jama'at-i-Islami is so anxious to have its existence and its right to expression guaranteed, that it has proclaimed itself to be in favour of democracy under military regimes, in particular under General Ayub Khan (1958–69).[43] In India, the Jama'at-i-Islami defends democracy as much as secularism, both of which are necessary to its existence. There is evidently a certain amount of self-interest in this position. The same situation can be observed in the United States, where religious movements, whether fundamentalist or not, rejoice, almost frantically, over the freedom they are given.

We should lastly point out that the ICNA operates legally within structures defined by the state, and seeks to co-operate with the state as well as with society. It meets with American journalists, and encourages participation in American elections, even if this latter issue raises controversy (see Chapter 7). It gives financial help to needy non-Muslims (almost certainly with a view to proselytizing). It would seem, therefore, that the ICNA might well have a higher profile among Muslims in the future.

The Tablighi Jama'at – one link in an international network

The presence of the Tablighi Jama'at in the United States dates back to 1952.[44] It moved to New York the following year. Today, the movement has its headquarters at the Al-Falah mosque, at 42–12 National Street in Corona (Queens)[45] (Map 7). The Islamic association of Corona was founded in 1976 by Pakistanis, many of them of humble social standing, who did not claim to belong to the Tablighi Jama'at or to any other religious movement. They erected the first building to be specifically designed as a mosque in New York.

The construction was finished in 1983. The Islamic Centre of Corona there-fore has not always been the home of the Tablighi Jama'at. It was in 1990 that Muhammad Ilyas's movement set up its headquarters there. The reader will recall that the Tablighi Jama'at, until it was expelled, had for a time operated out of the large Bangladeshi mosque in Manhattan.

The mosque is in a popular commercial neighbourhood, where Puerto Ricans and Colombians are in the majority, and is next door to the Jehovah's Witnesses' building . . . The 'cohabitation' is peaceful, it would seem. The mosque is two storeys high and is surrounded by a dome and a minaret. From the street, one can hear the muezzin's voice, though in accordance with American law he does not use a loudspeaker.

The mosque can hold about 200 people. A small room, which is completely separate, is reserved for women. Access to this room is through a separate entrance door at the back of the mosque. Instructions in English and Urdu on the door ask women to cover their heads correctly. Friday prayers are attended by about 50 people from different ethnic groups, but the majority are South Asians. The affiliation of most al-Falah faithful to the Tablighi-Jama'at is betrayed by their external appearance: whatever their ethnic origin, they all sport a beard without a moustache, and wear short pants and a long white robe. The sermon is usually in English and in Arabic, except when Tablighi preachers come from the Indian subcontinent, in which case the sermon is in Urdu. The board of management is largely dominated by Pakistanis, Indians (especially Gujaratis) and a few Bangladeshis.[46] The mosque has a funeral parlour, and on occasion celebrates weddings. Every evening, between five and seven o'clock, Islamic classes for children are offered by the imam himself (who teaches the boys) and his wife (who teaches the girls). Girls and boys are therefore segregated from their earliest youth in this mosque. All the books used for study come from Pakistan. During the winter of 1995, the mosque was col-lecting funds to open a full-time Islamic school, the madrasah Al-Falah Islamia.

Apparently, there are about 1,000 Tablighi Jama'at militants in New York (10,000 to 15,000 altogether in the United States). Nearly 60 per cent of these are South Asians, the others being mostly Arabs and converts. The Tablighis, in the United States as elsewhere in the world, are committed to active *da'wa*, both among Muslims and non-Muslims. Their numerical success is difficult to quantify.

What is well known is that the Tablighi Jama'at organizes regular large gatherings, though not annually as the ICNA does. In 1988, for example, a convention in Chicago drew more than 6,000 people; at the time it was one of the largest gatherings of Muslims.[47] When a subsequent convention hap-pened in Toronto, in July 1997, it drew between 3,000 and 4,000 people (remarkably, only about half the number at the previous convention). As with the ICNA, the border between the United States and Canada is often crossed, and the Tablighi Jama'at organizations in the two countries are in constant contact.

In New York, the Tablighi Jama'at is currently recruiting converts in the neighbourhood of Al-Falah, which explains the fairly remarkable presence of Colombians and Puerto Ricans among recent converts. But they are also moving into other neighbourhoods. To communicate their message, the Tablighi Jama'at prefers to go from door to door in groups. They do not publish any literature, or at least none that is available to outsiders, and do not use modern technology. The Tablighi Jama'at is as archaic in its philosophy and teaching, as it is in its preaching. The ideology of the Tablighi Jama'at does not seem to have been changed by its new American context. The followers of Muhammad Ilyas continue to adhere to a strict and conservative interpretation of the Qur'an and the Hadis, whether they are in the United States or anywhere else in the world.

The Tablighi Jama'at have maintained close links with their peers in the Indian subcontinent. The mosque in Corona is often visited by Tablighi Jama'at missionaries and preachers both from the subcontinent and also from other countries. Al-Falah is also in frequent contact with other mosques within the movement throughout North America (of which there are more than one hundred, according to the imam).

As far as women are concerned, as in the subcontinent,[48] they are allowed to go to the mosque. But this seems to be true only of New York, as elsewhere in the United States (in Los Angeles[49] and San Diego[50] especially), they are forbidden to go in. In these areas, the strict rules of *purdah* still apply.

In other areas of the social life of this group, neither the behaviour of the Tablighi Jama'at at Corona, nor any opinions offered by other Muslims about the movement suggest that it has tried to interpret religion in the light of modern society. In diaspora, the Tablighi Jama'at by taking in hand followers, almost as a sect[51] would, act as a substitute for the wider family. Total isolationism is advocated: if the necessities of economic life did not make daily contact with *kafir* necessary at the workplace, and if their proselyte activities did not force them into contact with non-Muslims, Tablighis would happily live completely separately from their host society. Though they have not been able to create a 'Utopian Medina'[52] either geographically or socially, they have taken refuge for the time being in a mental ghetto.

It is therefore not surprising that the Tablighis have made very little impact on the South Asian population in the United States. They are, as a group, still mainly South Asian, but they have very little influence on the community as a whole. Immigrants I interviewed were ambiguous in their attitudes towards the ICNA, but when it came to the Tablighi Jama'at,

anyone not belonging to the movement was definite about both the movement and its followers: the almost universal view, even among those who
were committed to mosques of other affiliations, was that they were narrow-
minded and obscurantist. So it would seem that the situation in the United
States differs from that in both Canada and England, where there are large
South Asian communities.[53] The Tablighi Jama'at does gather in large numbers in the United States and in Canada, with many travelling from one
country to the other. In addition, there are probably more numerous in the
United States than in Canada. But while in the 1980s the Tablighi Jama'at
was a major force in Muslim life in the West, this does not seem to be true
in the United States, where the Jama'at-i-Islami, wearing some new feathers,
seems in some ways to be having a greater impact on the South Asian immigrant population. Many student associations, Islamic research centres and
religious organizations are run by offshoots of the Jama'at-i-Islami. There is
as yet no Islamic School in New York under the control of the Tablighi
Jama'at. This situation can probably be explained by the high level of education of most immigrants from the subcontinent to the United States,
whereas the South Asian population in England and Canada is less well educated. The Tablighi Jama'at tends to recruit successfully mostly (but not
exclusively) from the lower social classes, among factory workers and the
unemployed especially. Besides, a growing number of Muslim immigrants
are wanting to be actively involved in American society, so they are unlikely
to warm to the movement's isolationism.

The Ahl-e-Sunnat wa-Jama'at or Barelwi:
a low representation

Although there are not many Muslims in the Indian subcontinent who would
formally admit to belonging to the school of the Barelwis, there are nevertheless many who practice a 'popular' version of Islam which largely owes to the
Ahl-e-Sunnat tradition. The most visible element of this is the worship of
saints. It is mainly rural and poorly-educated population groups which are
influenced by the Barelwi movement.[55]

Most immigrants to United States do not fit this description, however. The
high level of education among South Asians has prevented the Tablighi
Jama'at from having any great impact, it also militates against the growth of
the Barelwi movement in the United States. Some immigrants do bring with
them some forms of popular Islam. But these practices (especially *Fatiha*) usually remain confined within the home, and no efforts have been made to
institutionalize them by setting up places of worship. In addition to the social
origin of the immigrants, the fact that there is no *dargah* (a shrine of a saint) in

New York has also been a major obstruction to the growth of the Barelwi movement. In addition, it is immigrants committed to the Jama'at-i-Islami ideology who have played a major part in establishing religious institutions in the United States (bodies such as the ICNA and the ISNA, and the Islamic schools in particular).

Although the Ahl-e-Sunnat have not had a great impact on the immigrant population, this does not mean that there is no distinct organized Barelwi group in New York. After much searching, I found one Barelwi mosque, the Idara Tableeghul-Islam at Woodside, in a popular neighbourhood in Queens, at 32–13 57th Street (Map 7).

In fact, the mosque is a flat on the first floor of a block next to a garage of rather dubious appearance. The flat was turned into a place of prayer in November 1994, and is in a fairly poor state. There are three rooms and a kitchen. Carpets cover the floor, tinsel garlands and coloured lightbulbs hang on the walls. One of the rooms, the smallest one, is reserved for women. A loudspeaker conveys the recitations and preaching of the imam to them. However, I was the only woman present when I went there one Friday at the time for prayer. About one hundred men had come to carry out their Friday religious duty. Because of the lack of space, some of them had to pray in the kitchen. The vast majority were South Asian. Of all the mosques I visited, the Idara Tableeghul-Islam was the only one where the sermon was preached only in Urdu (which is also taught to children, together with Arabic and the Qur'an, at classes in the evening). The sermon was followed by a *zikr*,[56] during which the name of God was repeated, and a *na't*[57] was sung in Urdu in praise of the Prophet. These rites, and the way in which the flat was decorated (the tinsel garlands and coloured lightbulbs) were both characteristic of the Barelwis (also the sermon, followed by a *zikr* and a *na't*) and of their practices both in Pakistan and in England.[58] Some worshippers left the mosque after the prayer: it was hard to know if this was because they had to return to work, or whether they were only visiting this mosque because it was near their place of work, and not for any ideological reasons. Both explanations probably applied.

The board outside the mosque also indicates its Barelwi affiliation: *Ya Allah* is written in the top right-hand corner, and *Ya Rasul Allah* in the top left-hand corner. All Barelwi mosques carry these two inscriptions, either on the facade of the mosque, or at least above the *minbar*.[59] The board also announces the group's affiliation to the Hanafi school of jurisprudence. Most South Asians in fact claim to belong to the Hanafi school, but the other mosques I visited in New York, even those with a majority of South Asian members, did not emphasize the allegiance of their members to one or another school of jurisprudence. The director,[60] a separate person from the imam (who himself has been 'imported' from Rawalpindi), is a manager in a private company,[61] and he confirmed to me that the mosque belonged to the Hanafi school: he said to me that the mosque did not attach importance to any differences in ideological opinion, provided everyone followed Abu Hanifa. This emphasis on the Hanafi school is no doubt because of the high profile of Ahmad Riza Khan, himself a follower of this school of jurisprudence, who used it to justify his *fatwa*. Among the Barelwis, he is a venerated figure.

Another factor illustrated the importance the Barelwis attach to the teachings of their founder. Ahmad Riza condemned[63] the combining of two of the ritual prayers (*maghrib* and *asr*, for example). During the sermon, the imam, using the words of the Prophet to support what he was saying, recommended that the worshippers should not combine their prayers, and wherever possible should say each prayer at the mosque. Of course, one could also see this as an encouragement to be involved in a community activity.

Aside from Friday prayers, other group activities are peculiar to the Barelwi tradition. *Maulid* (the main festival in the Barelwi calendar, though it is also celebrated by a number of other Muslims), *urs* (especially that of Mu'inu'd-Din Chishti, and that of the *Pir* Mehr 'Ali Shah, a Qadiri at Golra Sharif near Rawalpindi,[64] to whom the director avows particular allegiance), *gyarhawin* (which commemorates, on the eleventh day of each month, the death of Abd-al Qadir al-Jilani [1077–1166][65]). As the mosque director pointed out, these celebrations are limited, given the few Barelwi who live in New York. As they cannot organize large processions, such as happen in Pakistan and in England, the New York Barelwis gather in the mosque in Woodside where they light incense sticks, recite the Qur'an, in particular the *Fatiha*, listen to lectures, practise the *zikr*, chant some *na't*, and eat some *halva* together. On occasion, they are joined by people who enjoy the family atmosphere, although they do not formally belong to the Barelwi movement. More than other groups, the Barelwis seek to reproduce as faithfully as possible the rituals they inherited from the subcontinent, and to recreate an atmosphere as 'ethnic' as possible, so for other South Asians their celebrations have a nostalgic appeal. The Woodside Barelwis also organize *qawwali* and *sama*[66] sessions during the *urs*, though this is not orthodox Barelwi practice. Ahmad Riza, who was influenced by the orthodox Sufis of the Barkatiyya Sayyid tradition of Marahra, did not specifically forbid music as a part of religious festivities (*urs* in particular), but he was not very much in favour.[67] The Woodside mosque is supposed to be committed 'one hundred per cent' to the teachings of Ahmad Riza, but according to the director it is also affiliated to the Chishtiyya brotherhood,[68] who do include music in their rituals. The organizing of *qawwali* and *sama'* does not provoke any controversy at the mosque. The director gives similar reasons for justifying participation of women in the New York *urs*, in spite of the fact that Ahmed Riza advocated that they should not be involved.[69] This involvement of women in mosque activities, in particular in the *urs*, should also be apprehended in its American context. In New York, the mosques fill the void created by the absence of Sufi sanctuaries. The women who are particularly longing to perpetuate some forms of popular Islam find a form of compensation at the Woodside mosque.

Although some teachings of Ahmad Riza have been abandoned, the Barelwi identity is still preserved. This particularly owes to the strong links which are maintained with Pakistan, which sends Barelwi leaders to give lectures in New York. The New York Barelwi are also visited by leaders from England. As yet, they are not organized enough to be able to send their own leaders to England or elsewhere.

Because of the lack of well-established institutions, for some major festivals, especially those as important to them as *Maulid*, the Barelwi attend the Shi'a mosques, notably Al-Khoei. Ahmad Riza was very critical of the Shi'a in his writings (he apparently even forbade his followers from wearing black and green during the month of Muharram[70]), but the Barelwi and the Shi'a nevertheless have much in common in their veneration of the Prophet and of his descendants.[71]

As far as their relationship with other Muslims is concerned, the Barelwi are famous for their rivalry with the Deobandi, both in the Indian subcontinent and in England, but their numbers in the United States are so limited that they cannot take on their traditional rivals, or if they do it does not hit any headlines. Most of the Sunni-led South Asian mosques may be ideologically close to the Deobandi (who aim to safeguard a fairly traditional version of Islam, and oppose popular Islam), but do not officially claim allegiance. Among all the mosques I visited, only two actually said they were close to the Deobandi, though they did say that they were not officially affiliated to the movement: the Muslim Center of New York in Queens, and the Masjid-ul-Aman (Bangladeshi) in Brooklyn. The ICNA and the Tablighi Jama'at are traditionally both very hostile to the Barelwi ideology. The ICNA however does not reckon them to be worth fighting, given the small influence they have in the United States. As to the Tablighi Jama'at, its followers are not supposed to engage in religious controversy.

Altogether, it would seem that the Barelwi in the United States are typical among new religious groups, in that they are still strongly attached to the traditions which they have brought with them from the Indian subcontinent. Many features proclaim that they are keen to appear distinctive: the interior appearance of their mosque, the ethnic homogeneity of the worshippers, the language used, and the type of sermon preached all confirm this; their place of worship is only recently acquired and will probably prove temporary; they are emphatically affiliated to one particular school of jurisprudence; they celebrate

specific festivals of their own in addition to the great festivals in the Muslim calendar. Contacts with other Muslims are still very limited, though the Barelwis
are planning to develop these in future. For the time being, there are no contacts with non-Muslims. The leaders of the Barelwis movement do not
specifically advocate isolationism, but their followers, many of whom are not
very educated, seem to live in the margins of society, and keep themselves to
the company of their own kind.

Since the 1980s, immigrants with less education than their forebears in the
1960s and 1970s have been arriving in higher numbers. This could cause a corresponding rise in the number of Barelwis in the United States. As a result, the
followers of Ahmad Riza Khan may become better organized, but rivalries
may also appear with other Muslim groups. It might also happen however that
those to whom the Barelwis ideology had previously appealed might come
under the influence of a 'purer' Islam as they settle in the United States. Only
time will tell. In Canada, the first hypothesis has proved true, and the Barelwis
are now becoming better established.[72]

Sufi Islam: not many takers

We have seen that the Barelwis have until now had little impact on immigrants
in New York. The version of Islam which they advocate is a popular one,
much influenced by Sufism. They are not however the only Sufi influence in the
United States. Various Sufi brotherhoods are becoming established in North
America, and among these the Naqshbandi[73] seem to be the most influential.

South Asian immigrants, in their search for religious meaning and structures,
prefer to adopt a more 'orthodox', even rigoristic, version of Islam, for the
same reasons which also explain the relatively small impact of the Barelwis: the
absence of Sufi shrines in New York; the role played by immigrants in the
1960s and 1970s, who were more or less influenced by the Jama'at-i-Islami, in
setting up religious institutions. Islam, on the other hand, tends to be more
attractive to American converts, whatever their ethnic origin (a similar phenomenon is apparent in Europe).

In December 1995, I had the privilege of attending a meeting of Sufis
which confirmed these facts. The meeting happened in the basement of a
clothing manufacturer in Manhattan on 39th Street, between Eighth Avenue
and Ninth Avenue. The disciples meet every Friday evening under the leadership of a Turkish *Shaikh* (spiritual master) of the Naqshbandiyya brotherhood.
The supreme *Shaikh*, who lives in Turkey, is a certain Nazim Aqqani, hence the
name the 'Aqqani Naqshbandi'. This order apparently has 35 centres in North
America, and its headquarters is located in New York. According to the *Shaikh*,
the order has some 10,000 disciples in the United States, of whom about

1,000 live in New York. On this Friday evening, at any rate, there were just about 50 people present, mostly American converts, Arabs and Turks, but not a single South Asian.

I should record briefly that there is a Sufi sanctuary in Pennsylvania. It was established by a Sufi *Pir* from Sri Lanka, Bawa Muhaiyaddeen, of the Qadiriyya brotherhood.[74] Bawa apparently arrived in the United States in 1971, at the invitation of an Asian student at the University of Pennsylvania who had heard talk of him, and invited him to America. He stayed until his death in 1986. He used to preach in Tamil (Americans and Sri Lankans translated his words simultaneously), in English or in Arabic. His sermons are now available on video cassettes. In 1984, a mosque was built at his request by his followers, on the pattern of one he had built himself in Jaffna. It has very modern technical equipment and provides all the services offered by the best organized mosques in the United States. Bawa also asked his followers to buy some land which could serve both as a cemetery and as a place to set up a farm. So they bought land at Coatsville in Pennsylvania, and built a sanctuary there following the traditional Islamic design. Bawa's body was buried there, and people visit on pilgrimage. During the month of Rabi'us-Sani, an *urs* is organized each year to commemorate the death of the master.

The Bawa Muhaiyaddeen Fellowship has about 1,000 disciples. They are very varied in the ethnic origin (including a few Sri Lankans). Bawa had not named a successor, so two imams run the mosque between them. Since the 1970s, about ten branches of this movement have been set up across the United States (there is one in New York), in Canada, in England, in Sri Lanka and in Nigeria. Each of these branches has between seven and eighteen members. The disciples have tried recently to overcome their isolation by establishing contact with other Muslim groups. They have met up with imams from mosques in Philadelphia, and welcome visitors from Muslim countries and educational establishments interested in finding out how the Bawa Muhaiyaddeen Fellowship operates.

I have heard of another Sufi sanctuary in the United States but I have no further details. There are, at any rate, still very few of these sanctuaries, and a Sufi Islam is not engaging the interest of South Asians. It tends rather to attract the 'indigenous' population groups.

Conclusion

The movements and associations I have described above, all of which are transnational, have very varied degrees of organization and activism. The Sufi movements and their avatars are still very limited in their appeal. The more rigoristic organizations, on the other hand, are meeting with more success. In general, the South Asian population is well-educated, and its members are therefore more likely to belong to, or at least tolerate, an organization such as the ICNA; the Tablighi Jama'at, on the other hand, is not so favoured, as it persists in being obscurantist, even in America. Though the ICNA has not changed at a fundamental level, the distance it has taken from the Jama'at-i-Islami has to a certain extent legitimized the organization in the eyes of Muslim immigrants and community leaders (including the Barelwis) so that they almost forget its ideology. However, the ICNA and the Tablighi Jama'at have one common ground, proselytism: they engage in *da'wa* towards other Muslims, and to a lesser extent towards non-Muslims. The international network built by the missionaries of these two very different groups has therefore now spread also to America.

PART 4

RELATIONSHIPS WITH OTHERS

7

THE EMERGENCE OF A 'UTOPIAN *UMMA*'?

The United States holds a real microcosm of the Muslim worldwide community. The constellation of nationalities and cultures which are to be found in America are not replicated anywhere except at Mecca during the pilgrimage. Within America, about 60 countries and about 100 subgroups are represented, as are most Islamic sects and schools of thought within Islam. The fragmentation is on many levels: cultural, national, regional, linguistic, sectarian, legal. But there is also ideological fragmentation (orthodox, revivalist, modernist, secularist). Haddad and Smith also note that the Muslim population is divided into its waves of immigration, into generations, by social classes, between immigrants and indigenous Muslims, between immigrants and students, between town dwellers and country dwellers.[1] Whether one identifies this as division or as diversity, the fact is that there are many fault lines. Here, we shall explore two in particular: sectarian divisions and national divisions (relationships with non-South-Asian Muslims, in particular with Arabs and African–Americans). In looking at these divisions, we shall try to establish whether existing sectarian divisions are reproduced, and whether contact with other Muslim population groups encourages South Asians to deepen these divisions, or even to create new ones, or whether on the other hand this contact with other groups is an opportunity for a new awareness of the universality of Islam, and any corollary efforts to create a new unity.

The fault lines

Looking across the sectarian divide: 'orthodox' versus 'heterodox'

Our study of mosques and Islamic associations gave us a first glimpse of relationships between Muslims: mosques are created along sectarian lines and, to a lesser extent, along national and ethnic lines. It is rare as yet to come across an Islamic centre which tries to transcend these divisions. However, apart from the Barelwi mosque, the division according to schools of jurisprudence seems to have lost its importance. 'We tolerate Muslims from other schools but not from other cultures,' one community leader told me.

The clearest fault line, in terms of organizational structures, is between the sectarian groups, as each group has established its institutions according to the norms of the sect to which it is affiliated. Although the Shi'a went at first to Sunni mosques, as soon as the community grew large enough they created their own organizations. The Isma'ili and the Ahmadiyya, on the other hand, did not wait for their communities to grow larger, but immediately set up their own separate organizations.

This parallel structure, however, does not completely preclude relationships or cooperation between the sectarian groups. It is also worth examining whether the prejudices of one group about another, especially those of the Sunni majority with regard to the minority sects, have been modified by the fact of immigration. The reader will remember that relationships between Sunni and Shi'a groups in Pakistan and in some regions of India, especially in Lucknow (see Chapter 1), are at times very tense. In Bangladesh, fundamentalists have even demanded that Shi'a should be declared non-Muslim.[2]

The Ismai'ili, whether Nizari or Bohra, and both groups are very small, have a rather neutral relationship with the Sunni, although some Sunni claim that Ismai'ilis should not belong to the *umma*. In Pakistan, the Isma'ili are tolerated because the third Aga Khan was active in the creation of the country, but the Ahmadiyya, on the other hand, were officially declared non-Muslim in 1974 (although some very high placed members of the government of Pakistan belonged to the Ahmadi sect) and they are now ostracized. In Bangladesh, pressure is being exerted on the government by fundamentalists to have the Ahmadiyya also declared non-Muslim.[3]

In New York, the situation is similar in some ways and different in others. On the whole, relationships between Shi'a and Sunni are free of conflict, and are indeed cordial. Sunni immigrants and community leaders I interviewed were more or less unanimously favourable towards Shi'a. The only proviso was that Shi'a should not be too politicized, in other words, that they should not be openly in favour of the current Iranian regime. This attitude of the Sunni I spoke to is probably more to do with a fear of American suspicion, rather than a deep hostility towards the Iranian regime. Shi'a mosques, Al-Khoei in particular, have also stopped the practice of the *tabarru*, the vituperative recitation against the first three caliphs. On an official level, the two groups issue mutual invitations to certain activities (meetings, conferences on Sundays, and so on).

On the individual level, Muslims seem to pray equally willingly in either a Sunni or a Shi'a mosque, which they are more likely to choose to attend because of its proximity to their home or to their place of work. As we have seen, some Sunni are keen to take part in religious ceremonies in their own mother tongue, and therefore are willing to take part in the Shi'a *majlis*. Marriages between Sunni and Shi'a are still fairly unusual, but a number of Sunni parents told me they would rather their children married a South Asian Shi'a than a Muslim from another sectarian group, or than a Sunni who was not South Asian.

This situation shows that tensions between Sunni and Shi'a in the subcontinent are more political than religious. In the United States, people are more anxious to identify themselves as Muslims in a non-Muslim society, rather than either Sunni or Shi'a. It should be pointed out, however, that the Shi'a are still keen to proclaim their identity as a group.

Relationships between Sunni and Isma'ili or Ahmadiyya as are not as good. The Sunni are in fact divided in their opinion of Isma'ili. Some consider them to be little different from the Shi'a, and to be 'full members' of the *umma*, whereas others, the traditionalists and the fundamentalists, would not grant them this 'privilege'. In particular, they condemn the veneration shown by the Isma'ili towards the Aga Khan and the *Da'i*, and condemn the Nizarian for being too westernized. However, they are less condemning of the Bohra, who are more traditional in their way of life. The Shi'a hold very similar views to the Sunni as far as the Isma'ili are concerned, although they are in fact closer to the Isma'ili in many ways.

The Nizari are aware that the Sunni are fairly hostile towards them, but the leaders tell me that they are trying to close the gap by inviting all Muslims to work together, since all are facing the same challenges within American society. This is clear from the names of the programmes in which they hope to involve the Sunni: the Aga Khan Trust for Culture, the Aga Khan Program for Islamic Architecture, the Aga Khan Development Network, and so on.[4] Nizari also invite Muslims from other sects to celebrate some of the Islamic festivals with them. In Los Angeles, in December 1995, for example, *Maulid* was celebrated jointly.[5] This festival, it should however be noted, is the subject of some controversy within the Muslim community, as the most strict observers are opposed to its celebration. And in fact, these strict observers are the most virulently opposed to the Nizari. The Nizari at any rate continue to operate in a fairly closed world, and the efforts to draw closer to other groups have not so far been very successful, except in international affairs (see below). As for the Bohra, whose leaders have forbidden them to go into any place of worship other than their own, they do not mix much with other Muslims.

As for the relationships between the Nizari and the Bohra, one Nizari leader[6] told me that there were few differences between the disciples of the Aga Khan and the Bohra. The *da'i*'s own nephew,[7] however, thinks that his community is spiritually much closer to the Sunni and the Twelver Shi'a than to the Nizarian, who, according to him, are not sufficiently obedient to Islamic precepts (they reduce their rituals to a minimum, for example).

As far as the Ahmadiyya are concerned, Sunni opinion is almost unanimous – in particular among the community leaders – in condemning them from a theological point of view. Shi'a share the same views, while the Isma'ili, who know that they too are considered in a dubious light by most of the Muslim community, prefer not to stand in judgment over the Ahmadiyya. The traditionalist and fundamentalist Sunni support Pakistan's decision to declare them non-Muslim. Other Sunni, although they disapprove of their belief in Ghulam Ahmad, feel that the Ahmadiyya are treated unfairly in Pakistan. Kashmiris, in particular, are mindful that the Ahmadiyya have always been accepted in their home region. In fact, I noticed that quite a few of those I interviewed, Indian Muslims and Bangladeshis in particular, claimed they did not know what difference there was between the Ahmadiyya and other Muslims. Pakistanis, on the other hand, are usually more familiar with the Ahmadi issue, for obvious political reasons.

As we have seen, some mosques, such as the Islamic Center of Long Island, try to include the Ahmadiyya in some of their activities, but this can meet with opposition from within.

The leadership of the Ahmadi community[8] complains about the ostracism it suffers from even in diaspora. It should be pointed out, however, that the obligation on the Ahmadiyya only to pray under an imam of their own sect, and to marry only within the followers of Ghulam Ahmad, combine to hamper any rapprochement with other sects, and in fact reinforce their isolation.

The hostility which persists towards Isma'ili and Ahmadiyya would seem to show that it is religious rather than political differences which separate them from the Sunni majority in the United States, even if the proscription on the Ahmadiyya in Pakistan is mainly political.

As a whole, it would appear that, though the more progressive factions are trying to establish mutual relationships, the gap separating these sectarian groups is only partly bridged in diaspora.

Relationships between ethnic groups[9]

In this section we shall examine in particular the relationships between South Asians and on the one hand Arabs, on the other hand African–Americans.

South Asians and Arabs: competition for leadership

Relationships with the Arabs are rather complex. Each group tries, even now, to set up its institutions within its own ethnic group, and these limit relationships with others. However, although culture and language separate the two groups, they are not completely isolated one from another. South Asians and Arabs who often go to the mosque are thrown together, both socially and through working together in the administration tasks at the mosque.

Each group perceives the other as being more conservative, or even fundamentalist. The Arabs argue that South Asians, and in particular Pakistanis, are more attached to rituals than the Arabs are because Arabic is not their mother tongue. For the Arabs, Islam is a total historical and cultural experience. They claim, therefore, to live more lightly towards their religion, and that their more direct contact with their religious roots enables them to be more flexible in their interpretation of religion than the South Asians.[10] South Asians, on the other hand, not only think that Arabs are more dogmatic than they are, but criticize them for acting as if they had a monopoly on the interpretation of Islam. 'Sadat', the Pakistani immigrant who is an accountant, complains that 'they won't call you brother if you're not an Arab.'

'Zoya', a woman teacher from Hyderabad, adds:

> They [the Arabs] think that Muslims from the subcontinent don't know much about Islam. They say we borrow from Hindu culture and are surprised that we don't wear the veil. Some [South Asian Muslims] have become more traditionalist under their influence.

However conservative one or the other group might be (and it is a relative concept, of course) in the context of New York the two groups do influence each other. In the United Kingdom, Islam as practised by Pakistanis is the dominant influence,[11] but in the United States, no one immigrant group seems to be imposing its own version of Islam than any other, even if there is some competition to be the leading group.

I did not meet many members of the Arab Muslim community, so it was difficult for me to measure the reciprocal impact of Arabs and South Asians on each other in the United States. According to Haddad, when South Asian Muslims arrived in America, at a later time than the Arab Muslims, divisions arose within the mosques, which had until then been dominated by Arabs, between those who preferred a cultural form of Islam (for example, they tolerated use of music in the mosque) and those who, under the influence of the South Asian Muslims,[12] advocated a stricter form of Islam.

South Asian mosques are also moving towards a simpler, and less ornate form of Islam, with fewer borrowings from vernacular traditions. An 'Arabized' Islam, one might say, which would tend to make immigrants from the subcontinent into more 'authentic' Muslims. In most of the mosques with a South Asian majority, for example, the sermon is preached only in English and in Arabic; children in these institutions are usually taught only Arabic. This phenomenon cannot be explained simply through the influence of the ideology of the Jama'at-i-Islami or of the other fundamentalist movements. Contact with Arabs and other ethnic groups has certainly played an important part.

South Asians and African–Americans: musulman hain, phir bhi . . .[13]

Relationships with African–Americans are even more complex, because cultural and linguistic differences are overlaid by the 'traditional' racism of South Asians towards black people. This quasi-hate of the colour black is so deep-seated that within their own community, South Asians discriminate between people of paler or darker skin tone. The main criterion for beauty in women is skin colour, which is supposed to be as fair as possible. The few African students who go to study in India are blatantly ostracized. Yet, there have been African population groups in the subcontinent since the beginning of the Muslim period (at least since the thirteenth century): the 'Habshi' (as they are universally called in India, whether or not they come from Abyssinia[14]) came as slaves but in many areas they progressed to positions of power and high social status (particularly in Bengal, in Gujarat and in the Deccan). In Bengal they even founded their own dynasty (1487–93). Nowadays, the word 'Habshi' is often used in a pejorative sense to describe an Indian with dark skin.[15]

In New York, of course, South Asians find themselves living alongside a large black community. Seeing so many African–Americans is often the first thing that surprises them, and their surprise is often tinged with irritation or disappointment:

> [He] had thought of going to the country of whites but there it proved not to be such. Wherever you turned only blacks and blacks: black porters, black checkers, black taxi drivers. In the streets most people were also black, meaning that *Amrika* and *Afrika* differed only in mere *m* and *f*.[16]

'Mirza', the Bangladeshi newspaper vendor, a recent immigrant to the United States, said this to me about them:

> Black people are fierce. They are illiterate and dangerous. I don't like the way they talk and walk.

As time goes on, South Asian immigrants become less inclined to express these thoughts so openly, but the prejudices are deep-seated, the heritage of colonization and of the myth of white supremacy.

Islam has only met with very partial success in overcoming these prejudices, especially as the immigrants do not often associate African–Americans with the Muslim religion. However, there are two sections of the South Asian population who fight against the racism expressed towards African–Americans, and they do it for different reasons: the second generation and the most religious among the Muslims. The tolerance of the second generation – however religious they may or may not be – owes much to their social environment, in the sense that they have internalized the official discourse in the United States which 'will not tolerate any established open racism,'[17] to quote the expression of Gary Marx.

The most religious amongst the immigrant Muslims are tolerant towards African–Americans as they wish to put forward the egalitarian ideal of Islam. Many of them recognize that the black Muslims are dedicated in their practice of religion. However, his tolerance is often only extended to black Muslims, and not to the black population as a whole. And with black Muslims, the admiration felt for the religious fervour is mixed, whether consciously or not, with a certain paternalism. As we have seen, even the most religious of parents do not wish their children to marry black Muslims.

However, when the South Asians started to emigrate to the United States and to set up their own religious institutions, they were bound to make contact with the African–Americans. Williams remarks that each group drew benefit from meeting with the other. The immigrants, whatever their ethnic origin, were able to model orthodox Islam to the 'Bilalians' (the name given to black Americans, which refers to Bilal Ibn Rabah, an Ethiopian slave who converted to Islam at the time of the Prophet Muhammad). African–Americans, for their part, were able to provide for the immigrants the initial religious infrastructure, and indeed an example of religious fervour. The propagation of Islam in prisons, in which many immigrants are very active, owes much to the initial influence of the African–Americans.[18]

However, the interaction between Muslim immigrants and indigenous Muslims is still very limited, for various reasons. The immigrants have their own cultural life and have racist tendencies; moreover, the social and economic differences between immigrants and indigenous Muslims are such that they stand in the way of closer interaction. In spatial terms, these differences also mean that the groups attend different mosques. Also, the African–Americans resent the superiority with which the immigrants treat them, and mind that they are not treated as full Muslims. 'Abdul', the Cuban teacher, says:

Our situation is rather like that of the Hindu untouchables who have converted to Islam. They cannot leave their origins behind. The arrogance and feeling of superiority of the other Muslims are still there. We are treated in the same way.

Quite a few of the immigrants find the zealousness of the African–Americans, characteristic of converts, but perceived as excessive, to be rather embarrassing.

It is also worth remembering that there are two main trends to black American Islam. On the one hand is the Nation of Islam, under the leadership of Louis Farrakhan, which is heterodox (Wali Fard is raised to the level of a God, and Elijah Muhammad is called a messenger of Allah), anti-white and anti-Semitic (because of the competition to be called the most oppressed people in history[19]). On the other hand is the American Muslim Mission, under the leadership of Warith Deen Muhammad, which is more orthodox and less racist.[20] Most immigrants condemn the Nation of Islam because of its heterodoxy and its racism, but they are more willing to relate to other black Muslims. Many of these, however, have suffered much from discrimination in the United States, and tend to be virulent in their denunciations of the evils of American society, and to insist on their differences with the white population. This denunciation of American society may find sympathy with the most militant among the immigrants, but most South Asians and other immigrants are above all keen to become integrated, and rather than underline the differences between themselves and the Americans, they prefer to focus on similarities between themselves and Judaism or Christianity. They therefore differentiate themselves from the African–Americans, and all the more willingly as African–Americans are stigmatized by the rest of the American population. Moreover, on the political front, African–Americans lay stress on their social and economic problems, whereas immigrants are on the whole more interested in matters of foreign policy.

In the long term, however, it may well be that immigrant Muslims and indigenous Muslims will get on better. According to Lawrence H Mamiya, the socio-economic level of black Muslims belonging to the American Muslim Mission has risen: it recruits mostly from the black middle classes, who are more receptive to the movement of Warith Deen Muhammad since it has become more orthodox. At the same time, the increased involvement of the black middle classes in his movement has encouraged Warith Dean Muhammad to pull back from his inflamed and heterodox speeches.[21] Over time, the converts have become more comfortable in their new religion (they feel less pressure to prove their Muslim credentials) and are therefore moderating their former excessive zeal. The immigrants, on the other hand, are becoming more involved in local issues, the longer they live in the United States.

Indeed, the Muslims who are most committed to the lives of the mosques are worried by any divisions within the Muslim community. An article in *The Message International* compared ethnicity (meaning here ethnic particularisms) to a social illness.[22]

Beyond the theoretical considerations, however, two main factors have emphasized to Muslims the need for greater unity. On the one hand, discrimination, to which we shall return. On the other hand, events abroad, which have, in various ways, contributed to the beginnings of pan-Islamic feeling in the United States: the Rushdie affair, the Gulf war and especially the war in Bosnia.

Events abroad: turning-points in the construction of a potential pan-Islamism

The Rushdie affair: a relative mobilization

The mobilization of opinion against Salman Rushdie, and against the Gulf war, was not as major an event in the United States as in France, and especially in the United Kingdom. However, the Rushdie affair did provoke a reaction in New York, the first of its kind in the history of Muslims in the United States. Between 10,000 and 12,000 people took part in the event; the figure was 15,000 according to the *New York Times* organizers.[23] The mobilization was orchestrated entirely, or almost entirely, by the ICNA: there was a succession of press conferences, of demonstrations in front of bookshops, and of letters of protest, and even of threatening letters (written mainly by individuals), sent to bookshops and publishers who were distributing *The Satanic Verses*. The demonstrators, however, unlike their peers in Europe and in South Asia, did not burn any books.

Apart from the mobilization itself,[24] the affair was interesting in at least two other respects. Firstly, in the ways in which information was propagated: as Emilie René has noted, it threw into sharp focus the globalization of communication in networks as a tool for mobilization. The Islamic Foundation in Leicester (which represents the Jama'at-i-Islami in England), having learnt from the Jama'at-i-Islami in Madras that the book was about to be banned in India, and that it was about be published in the United Kingdom, sent the controversial passages to the ICNA. The ICNA immediately launched its campaign and kept Leicester informed by regular faxes. The controversial passages were published in *Impact International*, a review close to the Islamic Foundation and distributed worldwide. They then appeared in various Islamic publications in the United Kingdom, in India and in the United States, and were also sent to all the embassies of the states in the Organization of the

Islamic Conference in London.[25] The Jama'at-i-Islami and its avatars showed, in this affair, not only that they are transnational, but also that the new technology would play a crucial part in the growth of a pan-Islamic movement. It is worth noting, however, that although the Jama'at-i-Islami launched the Rushdie affair in the United Kingdom, it was the Barelwis who organized the biggest demonstrations,[26] and gave the affair the huge prominence it eventually achieved. In New York, given the much smaller size of the Barelwi population, the ICNA launched the affair, made information available, and was also the driving force behind the demonstrations.

The second interesting aspect of the Rushdie affair is the way in which it brought to prominence, in the mind of many Muslims in the United States and elsewhere, the importance of fighting against anti-Islamic prejudices common in the West.

The Rushdie affair was indeed traumatic for the Muslim community, which felt that its reactions, as a group, were being tested[27] through the media hype. Rushdie himself became the traitor incarnate. The people I interviewed, however, almost all condemned Ayatollah Khomeini's *fatwa*. Some were opposed on principle to any *fatwa*, and others (who were in the minority) argued that it could not apply, given that there was no true Islamic state in the world. One community leader, however, did not think that the reward promised by the Iranian authorities to any person who found and killed Rushdie was in itself wrong. He compared it to the rewards promised by the FBI for evidence leading to the capture of a criminal, alive or dead . . .

The second generation was very young still, at the time of the affair, and so did not express many opinions. Interviewed now, most of the young people admit that they have not read the book, or that they have started it out of curiosity, but have not managed to finish it, and so they preferred not to give any opinion. Almost unanimously, however, they condemn Khomeini's *fatwa* for the same reasons as their parents do, though the older generation puts even more emphasis on the matter of principle as opposed to the practicalities. Some of the young people say they understand how the book can have aroused such fury, if indeed it does contain the passages that are supposed to be so offensive. However, they say that they value freedom of expression, and most of them are not in favour of banning the book.

The Rushdie affair did have some impact in the United States, then, and no doubt provoked an identity reaction among the immigrants, and helped to build up an 'imagined community' on the strength of the shared experience of being a minority under siege. In England,[28] however, the affair played a major role in the politicizing of apolitical Muslims, and this did not happen in the United States, for two reasons. In the United States, the South Asian Muslims are only a fraction of the whole Muslim population, whereas in England they are the majority Muslim group. The Rushdie book offended Muslims across the world, but feelings were most extreme in the subcontinent and in England. Also, South Asian immigrants in the United States are better integrated and better educated than their peers in the United Kingdom, and as they were keen to maintain this image, they chose to act with greater reserve, for fear of being compared to the fanatics burning books in the heart of Bradford.

The Gulf war – low profile

One year after the Rushdie affair, a second event took place provoking again uneasiness in the Muslim community: the Gulf war. Muslims in the United States were in a particularly awkward situation, since their host country was leading the coalition against Iraq. Some Muslims in the United Kingdom demonstrated vigorously against American intervention, but for Muslims in the United States to do this would have put them in a very delicate position. Some community leaders whose mosques depended financially on governments in the Gulf were also reluctant to speak out publicly against the American military action. As Gilles Kepel has noted, Warith Deen Muhammad, for example, although he was in close contact with Saudi leaders, officially gave his approval to the coalition's action against Iraq.[30] The principal Muslim lobby in the United States, the American Muslim Council (see below) also gave its support to the United States.

Most Muslim immigrants kept a low profile during the war, but some did take part in meetings and demonstrations for peace organized by non-Muslim activists. Others denounced the American intervention in their respective magazines. *The Message International*, for example, was clearly critical of American policy.[31] The ICNA (before the war) made the following statement:

> We do not support Iraq's invasion of Kuwait, or any other country's illegal invasion of any country for that matter. We strongly protest the involvement of US forces into Saudi Arabia which is caretaker of Holy Lands for the Muslims of the world. We condemn the Saudi government's invitation of US forces to Holy and Sacred places for over one billion Muslims and wish to remind the kingdom of Saudi Arabia that they must consult international Muslim community before taking any decision related to Holy Lands. We urge the US President George Bush to withdraw the forces from the Holy Lands immediately.[32]

This declaration summarizes fairly well the feelings of Muslims towards this crisis. When I ask them today about these events, they generally respond that they have not approved of Saddam Hussain's invasion of Kuwait, but in even greater numbers they condemn the invasion of Muslim holy sites by American troops, and the military intervention of the United States and allied armies, which in their opinion was done only to defend American economic interests, and not the territorial integrity of Kuwait.

This understanding of the conflict is based on the logic also adopted by non-Muslim opponents to the war (that economic and strategic issues were more important than moral ones, and that the given reason of a respect for laws governing international human rights was merely a cover for this). Muslims in the United States also felt empathy, not for Saddam Hussain (those I interviewed did not think much of him, and criticized his dictatorial behaviour), but rather for a Muslim country which they saw as a victim of what they saw as unjustified international aggression. Muslims outside the United States also felt this kind of empathy, born of their common faith – a sign of emerging pan-Islamism, at least at a strictly emotional level. Many Muslims condemned the occupation of holy sites, and felt that the conflict should have been resolved privately between Muslim states; they were also inclined to compare the situation to what was happening elsewhere in the world, in Kashmir or in Palestine, where the rights of countries and of peoples are also being flouted.

The second generation, however, apart from a small minority which is vocal in its support of Islam, have far more ambivalent reactions. Younger members were frankly puzzled by scenes of hostility to Americans on their TV screens. 'Mujib', a Pakistani immigrant, an engineer, and sympathetic to the Jama'at-i-Islami, says:[33]

> My son, who was 12 during the [Gulf] war, exclaimed, 'Why are the Muslims burning the American flag, our flag?' My son calls himself an Muslim American [different from American Muslim].

There is less confusion among older members of the second generation,[34] who express sympathy for the Iraqi people, tend to disapprove of the war itself, but they are so critical of dictatorial regimes such as that in Iraq, and of ultra-conservative regimes such as that in Kuwait, that they are not anxious to identify with fellow Muslims in those situations. 'Zeenat', a student of Pakistani origin born in the United States, says:[35]

> I don't see why we should support Saddam just because he's a Muslim. He was wrong to invade Kuwait.

'Salma', the student of Indian extraction, adds:

I know the Americans have been hypocritical. But I don't have any sympathy for Saddam or for Kuwait. Saddam is a tyrant. In Kuwait, social differences are enormous. Women have no rights. Women who go there from the Third World are badly treated and raped.

Even if one does not take account of the views of the second generation, the Gulf war did not in itself have sufficient rallying force in the United States to bring Muslims together from their different ethnic and social groups. As we have seen, one of the most influential Muslim community leaders, Warith Deen Muhammad, openly defended the American position. However, the two events together, the Rushdie affair and the Gulf war, happening as they did in fairly close succession, provoked a feeling among Muslims that it was becoming necessary to mobilize themselves in an effort to combat anti-Islamic stereotypes and to make Islam more familiar to Americans. The war in Bosnia, a third important event, then became the catalyst.

The war in the former Yugoslavia: the real catalyst

The war in Bosnia does seem to have been a decisive event in bringing together Muslims across divides both ethnic (South Asians, Arabs and African–Americans united in these efforts) and sectarian (the Nizarian, for example, joined the Sunni in raising funds). A Bosnia Task Force USA was set up, made up of ten Islamic organizations.[37] There were huge demonstrations, attended by tens of thousands of people, notably in Washington and New York, in 1994 and 1995. The demonstrators asked that the arms embargo be lifted, and for an end to the genocide of Bosnian Muslims.[38] Many immigrants who took part in these demonstrations or watched them on television still speak of the events with emotion, for to them they were the first clear symbol of a political awakening and unity among Muslims.

Some members of the second generation expressed to me that they had felt that Bosnians were like their brothers, while acknowledging at the same time that they might have been conditioned to this by their roots (by which they meant their family and their religion). These feelings of solidarity seemed to be for them a given, unavoidable, almost hereditary pan-Islamic feeling, even if they had not followed events in the former Yugoslavia particularly closely. Other young people went beyond this purely emotional feeling, and took an active part by demonstrating and asking for the lifting of the arms embargo. So it would appear that there is a dichotomy in the reactions of this second generation to these two wars, which both aroused Muslim feeling around the world – indeed the Gulf war probably more even so than the Bosnian war, because of the strength of international reaction and the weight of the forces

deployed. I can think of three reasons for this. Firstly, the age of this generation: the Bosnian war happened just as they were reaching maturity, when they
were in any case exploring their own identity and rediscovering their ethnic
and religious heritage, so that they were more open to sympathy for fellow
Muslims who were under threat. Secondly, the American role in the two wars
was rather different: in the Gulf war they were leading the coalition against
Iraq, whereas they fluctuated during the Bosnian war between a position of
neutrality and openly intervening to help Muslims; young South Asians, in
spite of the growing sense of their own identity, tend on the whole to identify
with the United States, even if this may be expressed in different ways by different people, or even differently by the same people at different stages of their
lives. Thirdly and lastly, and in conjunction with the second reason, the
American media protrayed the two conflicts in different lights: the Gulf war
was a fight against the Iraqi 'baddies', whereas the Bosnian war was a defence
of the poor Bosnian Muslims (to give a gross over-simplification). It is reasonable to assume that young South Asians were influenced by what they saw in
the media.

This concatenation of various factors, both internal to the community (ideological reasons) and external, pushed Muslims in the United States towards a
coordination of efforts and a unity of purpose. The Bosnian war was the principal catalyst. The interaction of the various organizations within the Bosnia
Task Force USA gave rise, in 1993, to the creation of the National Islamic
Shura Council (the national Islamic consultative committee), the first proper
move to create a national pan-Islamic organization.

Towards an Islamic melting-pot?

A pan-Islamic organization:
limitations and contradictions

The National Islamic Shura Council is a kind of umbrella organization, which
includes the presidents of the four most important Islamic organizations in the
United States: two represent Muslim immigrants and the other two the 'indigenous' Muslims. The first two are the ISNA and the ICNA, the second two the
AMM, and the Council of Imams of Atlanta of Jamil Abdullah al-Amin (Rap
Brown), formerly minister for justice in the Black Panther movement. The
creation of this organization, though not yet the final goal, was a symbolic step
towards a real sense of pan-Islamic identity, even though its functions are not
yet very extensive (the main one so far is an agreed date for the start of
Ramadan).

The National Shura Council does embody the initial will to work together and forge real and meaningful contacts between Islamic groups, across ethnic divides; and yet the limitations and contradictions inherent in such an ambition are already surfacing. The very limited functions, and indeed the very existence of the organization, are not well known by Muslims across the United States. One can also question how representative the organization is, given that its member organizations are conservative by inclination (Warith Deen Muhammad has close links with Saudi leaders, the ICNA with the Jama'at-i-Islami). It is true that Muslims in the United States, immigrants in particular, are not only made up of liberals. However, some Islamic organizations, such as the Islamic Center of Long Island or the Islamic Center of Southern California, though they are local associations, do attempt to reconcile tradition and modernity. None of these are represented.

The National Shura itself brings together the presidents of associations who themselves have widely diverging views on a number of matters. For example, we saw that Warith Deen Muhammad defended American intervention in the Gulf, whereas the ICNA and the ISNA made statements condemning the coalition's attack on Iraq. If, in future, there is another conflict in which Saudi Arabia took up a position against other Muslim countries, there could be dissension on highly sensitive points within the National Shura. Even the question of whether Muslims should take part in political life creates differences. Jamil Abdullah al-Amin from Atlanta advocates isolationism, but the ISNA and the ICNA on the whole (though not unanimously) are in favour of participation. These latter two organizations recognize that there are theological difficulties (the difficulty, for instance, of reconciling submission to Allah with acknowledging the legitimacy of the American government), but they tend towards the view that the advantages outweigh the inconveniences (the ability to exert pressure to protect civil and religious rights; the possibility that Muslims will exert moral (*sic*) influence on American political life; the opportunity to present Islam to non-Muslims, so to gain a platform for missionary activity).[39]

The National Shura, it would seem, has the potential to develop several fault lines.

Muslim parade in New York: an ethnic demonstration

The Muslim World Day Parade, which the Muslim Foundation of America has been organizing every year since 1985, is a second symbol of the efforts made by Muslims to promote pan-Islamism. The main aim of the parade, according to one of its organizers, the Afghan Habibullah Mayar, is to demonstrate the solidarity between Muslims.[40]

But the parade being modelled on the large New York ethnic parades started by the Irish (their famous Saint Patrick's Day Parade, which has become a bank holiday in the United States), it must appear to New Yorkers, as Susan Slymovics has pointed out, to be more akin to a demonstration of ethnic pride than to a religious demonstration, especially since so many South Asians take part in the procession. In addition, though there has been a Sikh parade for the past few years (which can be traced to the separatist movement in the Punjab), there is no formal Catholic or Jewish parade, even though Catholics and Jews respectively attend the Saint Patrick's Day Parade and the Israel Day Parade.[41]

The Muslim World Day Parade happens each third Sunday in September along one of the great New York avenues (originally Lexington, but now Madison; Fifth Avenue, the more prestigious avenue, is reserved for the longer-established ethnic groups), between 41st St. and 23rd St. The avenue becomes a vast open-air mosque while worshippers perform the *zuhr* prayer which opens the festivities. After praying, the crowd walk down the avenue chanting *Allahu Akbar*. This pious expression is normally used as a refrain during ritual prayers, but in the American (and more generally in the Western) imagination it has been associated since the Iranian revolution with Muslim fanaticism; its appropriateness in a New York parade was therefore carefully discussed.[42] The organizers decided in the end to keep it, but to chant it in such a way as not to alarm the American population or to cause hostility. Bands (in particular the Edgewater Park Fife and Drum Corps, an Irish band) march with the participants, who wave the flags of various Muslim countries. They also brandish streamers with verses from the Qur'an (and their English translation), and the names of different Muslim organizations. There are carriages bearing cardboard or papier mâché models of the local mosques (for example, the mosque of the Muslim Center of New York), of the great mosques in Muslim countries (for example, the mosque of the Dome of the Rock in Jerusalem and the Al-Haram mosque in Medina) and of the Ka'aba. The parade finishes with a large rally in Madison Square, where speeches are given by various personalities; street stalls sell food and books to the marchers.

The procession is mainly of men, and lacks the family atmosphere of the ethnic parades, the Indian and Pakistani ones, for instance.

The organization of the procession (for example, the building of the carriages) is quite expensive (one carriage can cost up to 25,000 dollars).[43] As with the building of religious institutions, the parade is funded through donations and through organized fund-raising dinners. There are no special budget allocations for the event.

Since this kind of public demonstration does tend to worry the local authorities, the mounted police are usually present to escort the parade. The police often have a fairly easy task, though, and they do not need to take any action, given the 'abstinence' of the participants who do not drink alcohol. According to Mayar, the parade often ends with the participants shaking hands with the police.

The city mayor, American politicians, and representatives of the Catholic church and the Jewish Rabbinate are also invited to take part in the parade, and their presence gives the parade an ecumenical character.

Although the organization is fairly careful and thorough, the numbers attending drop year by year. At first, about 60,000 Muslims joined the parade. In 1995 there were only 20,000. Mayar attributes this to the lack of entertainment:

> If Indian actors, he said, had been invited [as they are to the Indian parade on 15 August], people would be more willing to come out. But our parade is very sober. They aren't interested.

The desire to demonstrate Islamic solidarity does not suffice therefore to mobilize Muslims. The parade does, however, offer opportunities to meet other immigrants who share the same religion. But first and foremost, it enables Muslims to make their mark on the American landscape. In order to achieve this, the organizers do not hesitate to borrow from American methods, by using the carriages, the Irish band, and by providing the English translation of the Qur'an verses.

To return to the idea of pan-Islamism, we may add a third element we touched on in the previous chapter: methods of communication, and in particular the Internet.

Pan-Islamism and the new technologies: the Internet at the service of Islam

The huge developments in the field of technology which have occurred at the end of the twentieth century are said to have brought down frontiers and enabled all kinds of new contacts. These technologies have enabled Muslims, and especially students, easily to establish relations not only within the United States, but also with European countries, with Australia, and so on. We first met this phenomenon when looking at the Rushdie affair. At that time, fax proved an invaluable tool for the instigators of the anti-Rushdie movement to exchange information rapidly. Since then, the Internet has revolutionized worldwide communications. Nearly 100 Muslim organizations in the United States now have web sites. Most of these are student associations (they have given themselves the nickname *cybermuslims*). In the last few years, the major immigrant Muslim organizations (the Islamic Circle of North America, the Islamic Society of North America, the American Muslim Council, the American Muslim Association, the Council on American–Islamic Affairs) also have their own web sites. The sectarian minorities (the Nizari, the Ahmadiyya and others) have not been left behind, and they too have developed their own information networks. Via the Internet, Islamic organizations make available to everyone a description of how they function, of their objectives and of their activities, information about forthcoming meetings and conferences, call for online donations, and matrimonial advertisements (this last is particularly true of the organizations with mostly South Asian membership), and so on.

More general topics are also discussed: events in the Muslim world (the situation in former Yugoslavia has for the moment [2000] eclipsed the Palestinian situation); a subject of great interest is discrimination against Muslims in Western countries (cf. the Nike shoes affair in Chapter 8); the preservation and perpetuating of the Islamic heritage is also a major issue. People deemed to be competent are called on to answer questions from the faithful on different rituals, and on what attitude or behaviour should be adopted in a given situation to ensure that one remains a 'good' Muslim. Non-Muslims can also surf the web and discover the most beautiful mosques in the world, the Pillars of Islam, and so on. Chat groups have been set up linking Muslim students interested in theology, or who simply want to know more about the religion of their parents.

In fact, the Internet has become a most exploited tool for the propagation of Islam, not so much to non-Muslims as to Muslims themselves, and in particular the young. The work of proselytes travels much more effectively in cyberspace than on the ground, door-to-door, it costs far less, and it works not only on a national scale, but internationally. An example of this new role of the Internet as a tool for proselytizing was the meeting sponsored by the ICNA, in Silicon Valley in May 1999, of Muslim computer experts from all over North America. One of their discussions focused on the importance of using the Internet to expand proselytism.[44]

There has recently also been a growth in the use of chain letters, almost certainly a related phenomenon. These are modelled on the anonymous letters that are sent to people's homes, that seem to come from a *marabout* or some other guru, threatening the direst of consequences if one does not forward the letter immediately to 20, 30, or 50 other people. This kind of letter also circulates on the Internet. I received one myself. It came from Australia, but had emanated originally from Saudi Arabia, and claimed to be addressed to all Muslims in the world. It purported to carry the words of the caretaker of the Prophet's mausoleum. Apparently the Prophet had appeared to the caretaker in a dream and had told him that, of the 6,000 Muslims who had died that day, not one had gone to paradise. The first reason for this was that women no longer obeyed their husbands; other reasons were a greed for riches, lack of regularity in performing ritual prayers, and so on. The message told the recipient to forward the letter immediately to 20 other Muslims. To those who would comply was promised the earth. The letter cited the example of one person who obeyed its injunctions and was 'rewarded' (by promotion to a better job a few days later), and of another person who destroyed the letter and died a short while later. A few days later, I found the same letter in my morning post, translated into French, probably by Africans, since 'Ahmad' had become 'Amadou'. A little later again, I received a very similar letter, in English, this time apparently emanating from the disciples of Sai Baba, the Hindu guru. Most intriguingly, the letter made exactly the same threats and promises. Unfortunately, I was not able to trace either of these letters back to their original senders, as their defining characteristic is their anonymity.

Some scorn these letters (students in particular), but others are alarmed by them and religiously follow the instructions to send them on . . . thereby colluding, deliberately or not, in the scheme of people who claim to be official representatives of Islam (or of another religion), and take advantage of others' credulity.

This rather extreme example aside, the Internet is a tool, which is symptomatic of the globalization of communications and the melting away of traditional frontiers.

Conclusion

The Muslim population of the United States is above all characterized by its extreme diversity, in which the South Asians are only one community among many. The South Asians themselves are divided into many smaller groups. However, some recent events in the United States and elsewhere have brought the beginnings of a pan-Islamic movement to a hesitant birth. 'Traditional' methods to achieve this have been of doubtful value so far. 'American' methods have been adopted, such as the New York parade where an ethnicized Islam appears as the preliminary condition for its acceptance in the American landscape, and the Internet. These two moves have been more effective than traditional methods, and may herald the development of a new form of pan-Islamism.

8

IDENTITY AND ETHNICITY

Muslims and Hindus in the United States: *mleccha*[1] vs *kafir*?

We have just been looking at the issue of religious affiliation as it transcends national identity. We now need to look at the question from the other side, that is, ethnic affiliations.

An English (or rather anglo-Indian) word, *communalism*, is specifically used to describe confrontations between Hindus and Muslims in India.[2] Most researchers, including Asghar Ali Engineer[3] and Paul Brass,[4] insist on the economic and political dimensions of the conflict (the instrumental analysis), rather than on an inability inherent to Islam and Hinduism which would prevent the two communities from getting on together (the culturalist analysis[5]). Others, such as Sudhir Kakar, emphasize that an instrumentalist view of conflicts should not hide their social and psychological aspects, modernization and globalization appearing as serious threats to cultural identities.[6]

In contemporary India the Hindu nationalists represented by the Bharatiya Janata Party (BJP) have had considerable political success in the last few years, but Muslims and Hindus have nevertheless continued to live in relative harmony.

This would tend to suggest that these two communities, and indeed the Pakistanis and Bangladeshis also, should be able to co-exist reasonably happily in diaspora. The instrumentalist view would suggest that the motives (especially economic and political) for tension between Muslims and Hindus would have no *raison d'être* after emigration, or at least they would not be so in the United States, where South Asians are quite widely scattered. These communities are all living in an environment which is both culturally and religiously foreign to them. So even if the psychological dimension is taken into account, one might think that the shared experience of a common cultural heritage – which often transcends any religious divides – and a shared, or similar, language (especially Punjabi, Urdu/Hindi, Gujarati, Bengali) might together create the spirit of a regional minority.

In reality, however, things are very different. Hindus and Muslims do not confront each other in bloody riots on the streets of New York, but the very lack of communication between the two communities is striking.

The impact of the Hindu nationalists and the hindutva[8]

Hindus in the United States who are very keen to preserve their religious and cultural heritage are, if anything, more assiduous in going to the temple than they were in India (at least concerning urban and educated population groups).[9] As the mosques for the Muslims, the temples are the principal space of socialization for Hindu immigrants. The lack of a common space of worship is therefore a first reason for the relative lack of social contact between Hindus and Muslims.

Najma Sultana, who comes from Hyderabad and is the president of the New York branch of the AFMI (American Federation of Muslims from India),[10] a secular association of Indian Muslims, gives her view:

> Hindus and Muslims get on far better in India than in the United States. In India, at least you couldn't avoid coming across each other. Here, nothing makes us meet.

This situation does not however totally explain the polarization, which seems to be growing, between the two communities. We have already seen the important role played by immigrants influenced by the ideology of the Jama'at-i-Islami in Islamic organizations in the United States. His Hindu equivalent, the Vishva Hindu Parishad (VHP),[11] has also established itself firmly in the United States: VHP-America was founded in 1971 – only seven years after the parent organization in India – by a certain Mahesh Mehta, and it now boasts nearly 36 branches in the United States. It has an important role in the setting up of religious institutions in America. Its network includes the Overseas Friends of the BJP and the Hindu Swayam Sevak Sangh (HSS), the American equivalent of the RSS (Rashtriya Swayam Sevak Sangh).[13] The HSS is similar in its scope to the RSS: it runs training camps and promotes physical exercise, yoga and martial arts alongside discussions on Hinduism.[14] There is also the Hindu Student Council, started in 1990 and present in 13 universities in the United States.[15] It targets young people particularly. These organizations have a near monopoly on holiday camps catering for the second generation. Taking advantage of the vulnerabiltiy of immigrants, very keen to preserve their cultural heritage but faced with a dearth of alternatives, the US Sangh Parivar[16] has managed to become a major authority in meeting the needs of Hindu immigrants. The official discourse in the temples and the holiday camps may not be systematically political, but the groups do exert a significant influence on Hindus in the United States.

The BJP and the VHP have established themselves in most areas of the world where significant numbers of Indians have settled. However, as Hindus in the United States have a particularly high level of economic and social success, they are a prime target. Indeed, the Indian diaspora in the United States is a major contributor to the financing of the BJP and its associated organizations in India. According to *Sanskriti*, an Indian paper published in New York, at least 12.5 million rupees were sent to India between January 1992 and December 1993.[17]

The impact of events in the subcontinent: the Ayodhya crisis

Events in the subcontinent also contribute to this polarization between Muslims and Hindus in diaspora. The destruction of the Ayodhya mosque and the subsequent reactions are most revealing. Hindu nationalists claim that Ayodhya, a town in Uttar Pradesh, is the birthplace of the god Ram, and that the mosque, built by the first Moghul emperor, Babur (1526–30), was erected over the ruins of a temple dedicated to Ram. From 1989 onwards the Hindu nationalists led a vigorous campaign to reclaim the site and on 6 December 1992 the mosque was destroyed.

It is a well-documented fact that the worldwide Hindu diaspora took part in this campaign from its inception. Some of the bricks from the *Ramshila* ('Ram's bricks') that were carried as symbols in a procession in Ayodhya early in the movement, had been sent to India from the United States, from Canada, from the Carribbean and from South Africa.[18] After the mosque was destroyed, many Hindus outside India, in the United States in particular, were rather ambiguous in their reaction, hesitating to condemn the destruction of the mosque, and even indulging into the apology of the Hindu nationalists. There was interesting correspondence in the pages of *India Abroad*:

> . . . Ayodhya, a holy city (like Mecca for Muslims and Jerusalem for Christians and Jews) is believed to be the birthplace of Ram, our Hindu god. For over 60 years, Hindus have demanded the restoration of this Hindu mandir, but it has been of no avail.
>
> No Muslim religious services has been performed there for over 50 years. Just to get the votes of the Muslim bloc, the political parties have been appeasing these Muslims.
>
> So what is wrong in reaffirming the due place in the 85 per cent Hindu nation of our root culture?[19]

India Abroad also made it clear that a number of Hindu community organizations were ambivalent in their reaction to events in Ayodhya, and indeed some gave wholehearted support to the BJP.[20]

In August 1993 the VHP organized a large gathering (*hindutva mela*[21]) of Hindu community organizations in Washington, called Global Vision 2000, on the occasion of the centenary of Vivekananda's visit to Chicago and his address to the Parliament of the World's Religions. This drew a crowd of sufficient size to demonstrate the significant impact the VHP has on Hindu immigrants in the United States (about 4,000 people, of whom half were students invited by the Hindu Student Council). Murli Manohar Joshi, a former president of the BJP and now [2000] the minister for education, told the assembly that 6 December 1992 was the most memorable day of his life.

This conference was an unmistakable show of strength by the BJP and the VHP, and aroused much controversy. It was criticized by Indians in India and in the United States, where about 50 representatives of 12 organizations opposed to the communalist conflict in India demonstrated in front of the hotel hosting the conference.[22] It is also worth noting that most of the young people who attended were unaware of the discussions provoked in India by the event. Few knew of the role played by the VHP in the destruction of the mosque and the ensuing violence.[23] This shows how effectively the VHP has promoted itself to young people as the leading Hindu organization. It also demonstrates that young people give their support to the organization not for political reasons but because it meets their cultural and religious needs, and helps them in their quest for identity.

The Ayodhya crisis also affected relationships at an individual level. A number of Muslims I spoke to expressed disappointment at the reaction, which they perceived as ambivalent, of their Hindu friends to the destruction of the mosque. 'Rukhsana', the doctor who had emigrated from Aligarh,[24] gives her view:

> When I arrived in the United States, I was sure there were no problems between Muslims and Hindus, and I carried on thinking that for quite a while. But after the mosque was destroyed, people supported the BJP, even those from whom I would have expected a different reaction. Since then, I'm not quite so sure about the Hindus. Maybe they are not sure about us any more either.

The widening of the gap between the two communities has caused Indian Muslims to be more pessimistic about the situation of their coreligionists in India. This pessimism often exaggerated well beyond reality is not only the direct result of the Ayodhya affair, but is also a consequence of a reinforced ethno-religious feeling exacerbated by the diasporic condition: those who have migrated become hypersensitive in their perception of the vulnerability of the minority community they left behind. Expressions such as 'Muslim genocide' can thus be heard. It could be argued that the Hindu nationalists in India wish to commit cultural ethnocide against Muslims, but the human rights of minorities in India are sufficiently protected to preclude any genocide in its real sense, and certainly as an official policy of the government. Muslims have often been accused of causing Partition, and they have tended to keep a low profile in independent India, but they no longer feel the need to do this after emigrating, and they are likely to become more vociferous in their defence of the rights of minorities in India, regardless of the actual size of the problem on the ground.

Other South Asian groups in diaspora, especially Pakistanis, when they observe the Ayodhya crisis, the position of Muslims in India, and indeed the Hindus themselves, have their own point of view. Pakistanis have been reinforced in their belief in a 'hundred-year-old hostility' between Muslims and Hindus, and therefore in the justification of Partition, which is still a fresh memory for many. 'Safia', an immigrant from Pakistan, says:[26]

> I feel very anti-Hindu. My family fought for the creation of Pakistan. Two of my cousins are widows because their husbands died in the Bangladesh war. I never watch any Hindi films, and I never go into Hindu shops.

M A Kalam comments on the reaction of Pakistanis in England to the destruction of the mosque:

> While the sympathy expressed by the Pakistanis is genuine no doubt, it is hard to listen to such lamentations over and over again. The concern they have for their religious brethren makes them believe that anyone who is not a Muslim is a Muslim basher; every single non-Muslim in India is capable of committing mayhem and organizing a pogrom vis-à-vis Muslims! They think every Hindu belongs to the BJP, RSS, VHP or the Bajrang Dal – political parties or 'religious'/'cultural' organizations that had a hand in some way or the other with the demolition of the Babri mosque.[27]

These comments could also be applied to Pakistanis in the United States, who reacted in a similar way.

It would appear that prejudices and conflicts, rather than disappearing in migration land, seem to increase. This has led to a polarization between communities and the establishment of parallel organizations.

Separate organizations but labyrinthine associations

At the beginning of the migration process, people from the same area of the world tend to keep together, and then, as numbers grow, to split up into smaller groups. Organizations then arise defined by national, regional, linguistic and religious allegiances.

A similar phenomenon can be observed in the South Asian community, especially among Indians: Hindus, Sikhs, Muslims and Christians used at first (in the 1960s and 1970s) to belong to the same organizations. These, however, were typically dominated by Hindus, who at any rate are in the majority, so gradually the minority groups left these original organizations to set up their own (from the 1980s onwards).[28] The Sikhs left mainly for political reasons (Hindu expatriates were largely in support of the Indian government's repression of Sikh separatists, whereas many Sikhs of the diaspora were in favour of an independent state in the Punjab). Muslims and Christians left rather for religious reasons, since Hinduism is often an important feature of the life of Indian cultural associations (where sessions and events may start with a *puja*, for example). The impact of the BJP and the VHP on Hindu expatriates has reinforced this trend, urging non-Hindus to leave organizations labelled 'Indian'. Even pan-Indian organizations such as the Federation of Indian Associations (FIA), which is supposed to co-ordinate the celebration of Indian national festivals, is almost entirely dominated by Hindus.

Indian Muslims therefore decided to set up their own organizations, or to join with Pakistani cultural associations. Those who framed the notion of a partitioned territory were thinking of a country where all Muslims in the subcontinent would live together. The reality turned out very differently, and a third of Indian Muslims stayed on in India. Eastern Pakistan seceded only after a quarter of a century. The Muhajirs are nowadays seen as foreign by many Pakistanis, and they are engaged in constant conflicts with groups defending ethnic nationalism. One could begin to wonder whether a move to a 'neutral' land might finally succeed in bringing together population groups who have a common religion and geographical origin.

In fact, it has become clear in the United States that religion alone is far from being a sufficient factor to bring people together: other factors, language in particular, are equally important. Just as Hindus have built up organizations according to ethnic and linguistic allegiance, South Asian Muslims have followed suit, setting up associations along religious *and* linguistic lines.

This has resulted in Pakistanis and Muslims from North India tending to gather together, whereas North Indian Muslims and South Indian Muslims (in particular non-Urdu-speaking Muslims) maintain fewer relationships, and do not belong to the same organizations. Some Muslims from South India, Tamil and

Malayalam speakers especially – admittedly only present in small numbers in the United States – do take part in religious activities and identify with Islamic causes, but they join more willingly in the cultural events of Hindus, who share the same linguistic heritage, rather than in the events organized by Muslims from North India or Pakistan, with whom they tend to associate only at Sunday meetings at the mosque (if they are practising Muslims) or at major festivals. Such behaviour is further enhanced by the fact that South Indian Muslims, who are not Urdu speakers, are on the whole better integrated into Indian society than other Muslims, although they are no more or less religious.[29] An additional factor is that South Indian Muslims often complain of being ostracized by Muslims from North India and Pakistan.

'Bashir', a practising Muslim from Kerala (he was fasting on the day I interviewed) gives his thoughts on this:[30]

> I used to go to meetings of North Indian and Pakistani Muslims. But I felt completely excluded because I don't speak Urdu. They spoke Urdu together and made no effort to switch to English. So now I'd rather go to meetings of the Malayali Hindus. At least I feel comfortable there.

Speakers of Urdu considering it to be the language, if not of the elite, then at least the language of culture of Muslims in India, therefore feel themselves to be superior. It would seem that they have brought this sentiment with them into their land of migration, and the associated controversy with speakers of other Indian languages . . .

For Pakistanis, the issue with Urdu is different. Most of the Pakistani immigrants are either Muhajirs, whose mother tongue is usually Urdu, or Punjabis, who preserve their mother tongue but are happy to speak Urdu (they even seem to favour it as a sign of cultural refinement). However, Iftekhar Malik, in his study of Pakistanis living in Chicago, notices that those whose mother tongue is Urdu are very 'language-conscious' and keep themselves separate from other Pakistanis, including the Punjabi speakers.[31] This polarization of cultural forces, even within the same national community, can be explained by the fact that the population group is growing in numbers and so splitting into smaller ethnic groups, each seeing itself as superior to other groups. In this case, the Muhajirs are traditionally perceived as more refined, and therefore as 'superior' to the Punjabis and other Pakistani groups.

As with the Muhajirs from Pakistan, the Hyderabadis from India prefer to have their own associations, especially as they are present in large numbers in the United States, mainly in the Chicago area. In India this population group has a peculiar status as an Urdu-speaking enclave within a Telugu-speaking area, and they opposed the inclusion of the state of Hyderabad into the Indian Federation in 1948.

Urdu-speaking South Indian Muslims (apart from the Hyderabadis), if they wish to participate in the activities of North Indian Muslims, often have to change the rather unstructured (from a grammatical point of view) way in which they speak their mother tongue in order to fit in with the more orthodox, 'standard' ways of speaking of Muslims from the North, so as to escape criticism and mockery. Their own language therefore is changed through contact with population groups who speak it in a more 'orthodox' or literary fashion: it becomes grammatically more correct and loses the borrowings from other languages, such as Tamil. The difficulties of living in this shifting linguistic landscape have led some to give up on speaking Urdu outside their immediate family. 'Sultan', a young immigrant from Madras, now only speaks Urdu with his wife, and speaks English with other South Asians in New York.[32] Language therefore in some cases brings people together across frontiers, and in other cases is a cause of division even among people of the same national origin.

The prejudices felt by North Indians towards South Indians, and vice versa, die hard even in the migration land. North Indians consider South Indians to be 'ugly' and 'Hindu-ized', whereas the South Indians think the North Indians (and the Pakistanis) are 'stupid' and 'narrow-minded', or even 'fanatical'. These stereotypes are also part of the relationship between Pakistanis and North Indians of all areas. Paradoxically, Indian Muslims think Pakistanis are too westernized and complain that they are too showy, whereas Pakistanis think that Indian Muslims (from both North and South) are too Hindu-ized. The 'Pakistanness' as displayed by the concerned immigrants – symptomatic of the nationalism of individuals who have come from a newly-created country, pioneering in its ideology but not particularly well loved – irritates Muslims from India who prefer to keep a lower profile. The sympathy shown by Pakistanis after the Ayodhya affair, for example, touched some but exasperated more than a few. Partition and its repercussions are still an obsession for some: Indian Muslims blame Pakistanis, and the Muhajirs, in particular, for the present sufferings of Muslims in India, now that they are deprived of the Muslim elite who moved to Pakistan en masse. They also sharply criticize the lot of Muhajirs in Pakistan, who are often the victims of discrimination. Pakistanis, on the other hand, are paternalistic towards Muslims in India, but at the same time they cast doubt on their Islamness. However, one should not place too great an emphasis on these aspects, since on the whole Pakistanis and Indian Muslims (those from the North especially) get on reasonably well. As immigrants become less inclined to seek marriage partners from the homeland, and instead search within the Muslim population already living in the United

States, which the second generation are keen to do, the number of marriages linking the two communities will probably increase in future.

The issue of Bangladeshis has already been mentioned (see Chapter 5). Bangladeshis who emigrated in the 1960s and 1970s are generally more secular and tend to join in the activities of Bengali Hindu organizations, and only meet up with other South Asian Muslims at religious festivals. Their community behaviour therefore recalls that of Muslims from South India. More recent Bangladeshi arrivals, on the other hand, tend to be more religious than their predecessors (for reasons explained above), and they prefer to set up their own organizations – and/or to attend their own mosques – thus demonstrating the crucial importance of both language and religion. As for the relationships of Bangladeshis with other South Asians, they tend to be tinged with mistrust, as their own partition is still relatively recent history.

'Ghafar', a restaurant waiter of about 50 recently arrived from Bangladesh, a fervent Muslim and a good speaker of Urdu – as are many Bangladeshis of his age – says:[33]

> I don't think there should ever have been Partition, not in 1947 or in 1971. It has weakened the subcontinent . . . But I also think Pakistanis should have made the effort to learn Bengali. They never tried. What's more, they still think it's a Hindu language!

Religion and a (vague) sense of belonging to a geographical entity would not seem, then, to be enough to ensure a group's cohesion. Other factors, in particular language, play a major role.

The rather particular position of the so-called twice-migrants is worth noting here. Immigrants who have come to the United States via eastern or southern Africa generally get on well with those who have come directly from the subcontinent, but those who came via the Caribbean (especially Trinidad) or from Latin America (especially from Guyana and Surinam) have their own separate organizations. Emigration to these different areas of the world were of a very different nature. Indians from Africa mostly included professionals and traders, whereas emigrants to the West Indies and Latin America were usually indentured labourers. South Asians from the subcontinent tend to differentiate between both groups and are more inclined to feel akin to those who came via Africa. They even question the 'Indianness' and/or 'Islamness' of immigrants from Trinidad and Guyana as these population groups are more likely to have become mixed and 'creolized'.[34] Immigrants from Trinidad and Guyana, also because they are generally third or fourth generation, construct a different identity in reaction to this situation, claiming to belong to a particular ethnic group (for example Gujarati) and religious group (Hindu or Muslim), but they answer the question 'Are you South Asian?' in the negative. Some immigrants from Africa also express little attachment to the subcontinent as a geographical entity, but choose rather to emphasize their allegiance to a particular ethnic and religious group, regardless of time and space. Some seem to have a rather ossified picture of India: 'Abbas', the Bohra immigrant who is out of work, confessed to me that he didn't know that Hyderabad was a city rather than a state. It would appear, then, that the recent geographical origin of an immigrant is also very important in helping that person to describe him- or herself, and that language and religion are not sufficient of themselves to help to forge a unity within a group.

Lastly, it would seem that members of any particular group, be they Indians, Pakistanis, Bangladeshis or Guyanese, do not like to be confused with members of other groups. Pakistanis do not like being asked if they are Indian, Bangladeshis if they are Pakistani, Guyanese if they are South Asian, and so on and vice versa. There is a pride in coming from a particular country, but to that one should add, for example in the case of an Indian Muslim taken for a Pakistani, the desire to avoid being confused with a group which carries a rather negative image in the host society. This is an issue to which we shall return.

Constructing a South Asian 'pan-ethnicity'[35]?

We have just examined the first two stages of the formation of a community: when there are few members of a given community, they tend to stay together. Then, as the community grows, it starts to break up. The third stage is an awareness of these divisions that might be a threat to the community, so that it is becoming necessary to impose unity again. It would seem that the South Asian community is still in the second stage of this development, but efforts have nonetheless been undertaken to transcend the existing cleavages.

Since the destruction of the Ayodhya mosque, the gulf between the Muslim and Hindu communities has seemed to grow, but there have been attempts to invite reflection on the community tensions in India and to promote greater 'unity' between South Asians, or at least between Indians, in diaspora.

Until now, this rapprochement has taken the form of occasional meetings between community leaders, and there have been no major moves forward. In May 1993, a leader of the American Federation of Muslims from India (AFMI) (see above), Abdur Rehman Nakadar, invited to his home in Detroit about 50 Indian activists, among them representatives of the VHP, of the Indian League of America (ILA), of the Bharatiya Temple of Troy, of the Association of Indian Muslims (AIM), of the Bharatiya Family Services, of the Indian-American Forum for Political Education (IAFPE), of the Council of

Associations of Indians in Michigan, and of the Catholics from Kerala. The meeting reached a consensus that, whatever differences might divide Indians both within and outside India, the interests of India should be uppermost.[36] This kind of meeting, however, is still merely symbolic, and so far it has not led to the development of any effective umbrella organization.

The cultural interactions between South Asians of different ethnic and religious allegiances, on the other hand, are more significant. So far, we have seen language to be mainly a dividing factor, but it can also be the means for better cooperation, and a help to overcoming religious barriers. Sikhs, Hindus and Muslims can share their love of Urdu and take part in the same *musha'ira*, *ghazal*, and *qawwali* sessions, forgetting their differences for the space of an evening.

On 14 August 1993, I went to an open-air *qawwali* concert in Central Park, given by the world-famous Pakistani star Nusrat Fateh Ali Khan (who died in 1997) to celebrate Pakistan's independence day. Sikhs, and probably Hindus (they are less easily spotted), were just as enthusiastic members of the audience as the Pakistanis. The most interesting aspect of Nusrat Fateh Ali Khan lies not only in his capacity to attract large crowds from across religious groups, but also in the transformation he carried out at the musical level. This singer-composer grafted onto traditional religious music elements of foreign music, so that it lost its specific sacred character. He was strongly criticized for this by the purists, but he transformed himself into a star who was part-*qawwal*, part-pop, and more accessible to non-Muslims, as his success in India shortly before his death showed.[37] But as Philip Lewis has noted it, *qawwali* can also be a more effective way of retaining the interest of young Muslims than the more austere face of Islamism.[38]

Another 'art' form transcends even more remarkably the ethnic, religious and national divisions: Bollywood (the cinema of Bombay). In India itself, Bollywood is hailed as one of the best vehicles promoting communal harmony. This is true of the industry itself, and of the appeal of the films, which are viewed with the same enthusiasm in Pakistan as in India.

The same scenario is to be observed in the immigrant community. Whenever Bollywood stars visit the United States, they draw considerable crowds. 'Mansur', the newpaper vendor, says:

> There are more Pakistanis [at this kind of event] than at the Muslim World Day Parade. I shouldn't wonder if there were more Pakistanis than Indians coming to see the Indian stars. But there aren't so many Indians at Pakistani cultural events.

In fact, Pakistanis even attend the India Day Parades on 15 August which commemorate Indian independence, because each year an Indian actor is invited to lead the parade as the Grand Marshal. In 1997, for instance, on the fiftieth anniversary of Indian independence, the very famous actor Amitabh Bachchan himself was invited to carry out this duty. His presence ensured an even larger crowd, and it was not made up only of Indians.

These parades are an opportunity for South Asians to demonstrate their 'unity'. But they also enable minority groups to markedly put distance between themselves and on the one hand the community as a whole, and on the other hand their country of origin. I went to the India Day Parade in 1993. About 20 Christians walked past carrying a banner. Sikhs and Muslims, as distinct groups within the Indian community, were noticeable by their absence from the ceremony. The Sikhs as a community did not take part in the parade because of the hostility they have felt towards the Indian government since the events in the Punjab, and the Muslims were reacting to the destruction of the mosque in Ayodhya. As individuals, there were however Sikhs and Muslims among the crowd. That year, an incident occurred towards the end of the procession between Indians and a group of Pakistanis who were waving banners and shouting pro-Pakistan slogans. One of the Pakistanis started to harass a group of girls. A Sikh intervened, and the Pakistani, who was carrying a revolver, shot him three times and wounded him badly. The next day, a group of prominent BJP members went to see the young man in hospital to assure him of their good wishes. This pattern familiar from the subcontinent, where processions often end in violent confrontations, and where isolated incidents are hijacked by politicians, seems to have carried over into the land of migration. This incident, as it happens, also fits with the traditional image Sikhs had of themselves before independence as the defenders of the 'weak' Hindus from Muslim 'aggressors'.[39]

The parade, however, changes from year to year. In 1994 about 50 Muslims followed the banner of the American Federation of Muslims from India.[40] In 1996 in Chicago, Pakistanis were warmly invited to take part in the India Day Parade. Some were brandishing posters calling for the burying of the past and invoking a radiant future.[41]

The second generation: overcoming differences?

The Queens College clubs: a microcosm of relationships between South Asians?

The visitor to Queens College cannot fail to be struck by the number of South Asian clubs: the India Club, the Pakistan Club, the Bangladesh Club, the Sikh Youth Club, the Guyanese Club . . . As if these different clubs were a microcosm of the relationships between South Asians in New York. Yet, Sikhs and Bangladeshis share the same room, and when I asked how many members the different clubs had, they all replied between 60 and 70. But this in fact includes the total number of members of all the South Asian clubs (except the Guyanese Club). The clubs meet together frequently and invite each other to different activities and celebrations, so that the clubs in effect fail to distinguish between their respective adherents. They also cooperate financially, sharing out the costs of cultural activities.

Of all the clubs, the Pakistani Club seems most keen to establish its distinctiveness, or so the decorations of their room would suggest: there is a huge Pakistani flag on the window, and photos of Jinnah and Iqbal in the room. The Indian Club, on the other hand, has huge posters of Bollywood stars on its walls. When I went for the first time to the Pakistani Club, it was empty and closed. I then went to the Indian club and I realized that a number of members of the Pakistani Club, not least among them the vice-president and the general secretary, were sitting in the comfortable armchairs of the Indian Club. Some students are evidently members of several clubs at once.

The tensions of the subcontinent are not, however, completely absent. 'Vikram', a student at the Indian Club, remembered that someone once stuck a sticker with the inscription 'Khalistan' (name of the territory claimed by the Sikhs) on the door. On the whole, however, the young people seem to have left behind their ethnic and religious divisions, even though the very existence of the different clubs appear to give the contrary message.

'Arbaz' says:[42]

> At first, young people are sensitive to the differences between Indians and Pakistanis, between Hindus and Muslims, and so on, because they are under their parents' influence. But at university they meet other South Asians, and then they have no more . . . or rather they have fewer prejudices towards each other.

The emergence of a South Asian identity?

If divisions are being overcome, this might suggest the creation of a *South Asian* identity. There is, however, a problem here, which we must examine both semantically and terminologically. This English usage, 'South Asian', which is not well-known in France, is curiously enough also little known by those very people it describes in the United States, as I discovered during my interviews. When I introduced myself, saying that I was working on South Asian Muslims, I was asked many times, 'Ah, are you working on South Indian Muslims?' or 'You are working on South-East Asian Muslims?' This ignorance of the concept of South Asia and its constituent regions is particularly characteristic of the second generation, as was pointed out to me by Madhulika Khandelwal, a historian at the

Asian-America Center at Queens College.[43] And yet, as we shall see, once they are familiar with the concept, it is this second generation which expresses an interest in setting up 'South Asian' organizations.

This concept is not only terminologically difficult – a number of organizations have in fact used the phrase to define themselves – but it is also semantically difficult. It is inherently ambiguous, since the organizations which use it to describe themselves are often dominated by Indians. This very domination can prejudice the participation of other South Asians, who are not keen to see a recreation of the 'Big Brother' scenario so familiar in India's relationships with its neighbours in the subcontinent.

The matter is further complicated by those, some of them Indians, who are not willing to be described as 'South Asian': they do not wish to be associated with Pakistanis and Bangladeshis, fearing that if these population groups are associated with Islam in the mind of the Americans, this might confer a bad reputation which could in turn rub off onto them. A similar situation can be observed in the United Kingdom, where some Indians prefer to be labelled 'Hindu' rather than 'Asian'. In the United Kingdom this is exacerbated, since many Pakistanis and Bangladeshis have low social status, far more so than the Indian population, and they are drawn into conflict with the British authorities more often than other South Asians (the reader will recall in particular the Rushdie affair).[44] In London, for example, in February 1993, immediately after the Ayodhya incident and the violent riots that bathed India in blood (there were a few incidents in Bradford also), a group of Hindus demonstrated against the label 'Asians', and declared that they preferred to be known as 'Hindus', since the name 'Asians' was harmful to their reputation.[45]

In the United States, at all events, some progressive groups have come together, mostly thanks to initiatives by members of the second generation, to promote the concept of 'South Asian' as a unifying symbol. These organizations, which include Sakhi (a feminist organization), YAR (Youth Against Racism), CSA (Concerned South Asians), SALGA (South Asian Lesbian and Gay Association), SAAA (South Asian Aids Action), IPSG (Indian Progressive Study Group), the SAMAR (South Asian Magazine for Action and Reflection) team, LCD (Licensed Drivers Coalition), SAYA (South Asian Youth Action) and so on, may still be dominated numerically by Indians, but an increasing number of non-Indians are joining them, or at least are being encouraged to do so. These groups have a special mission to bridge the divides between South Asian communities.

The concept 'South Asian' may still be new and may be a trifle vague in the mind of many immigrants from the subcontinent, and yet in diaspora it takes on a particular significance. In the subcontinent, it is a geographical definition, and only that. In diaspora, it takes on a community dimension, implying the erasure of the borders erected at Partition.

Neo-bhangra, *the musical expression of a South Asian identity*

Beyond the confines of traditional organizations, one particular style of music has emerged as an effective tool to mobilize members of communities from across the usual divides: *bhangra* music. This musical style originated in the Punjab, but in diaspora it has mutated to such an extent that its present hybrid nature appeals to all sides of the South Asian community, and even to those outside it. This metamorphosis happened in the United Kingdom, where young South Asians introduced rap and reggae music into *bhangra*. This collaboration with African-American music came about not only because of the mutual influence of working class South Asians and Jamaicans, but also because the rhythm patterns of the two types of music were compatible, it seems (this would not have been true of rock or disco music, for instance). This 'neo-*bhangra*', a very creative form of music, has crossed the Atlantic and met with nearly as much success as it had in England. The hybrid character of neo-*bhangra* (which is not unlike the 'pop-raï' of North Africans, both in content and form) is due to the mixture not only of the South Asian and African–American genres, but also of languages (English, Hindi/Urdu, Punjabi). In terms of its impact, it transcends all barriers: ethnic (*bhangra* music is played also at Bengali and Tamil celebrations, for example), religious (both musicians and their audiences are Hindus, Sikhs, Muslims, . . .) and even social (it originated in the working classes, but is gaining in popularity among the middle classes). The popularity of neo-*bhangra* can also be explained by the ideas carried in the lyrics, which are sometimes compared to those in rap, but which are rooted in South Asian concerns: the words decry the caste system, promote social and religious harmony between communities and so on. This musical scene is dominated by men, and could be accused of ambiguity in its descriptions of relationships between the sexes (Apache Indian, a British Punjabi band, sang a number called *Arranged Marriages*, which was very popular in India as well as in the diaspora communities in both the United Kingdom and the United States, about wanting a wife who would make *roti* [a kind of bread] and serve him *seva kari*). The point of interest point in our discussion, however, is the power of neo-*bhangra* to appeal across ethnic and religious divides. It would be unreasonable to expect this music to be the only or even the principal force for constructing an identity across all barriers but at least it enables young South Asians to get together. This could be a preliminary stage before the construction of a more structured and thought-out movement. These relationships forged between young people in their mutual love of neo-*bhangra* bring together groups not only of South Asian origin, but also from other ethnic strands, such as young African–Americans. Young South Asians do not share their parents' fierce prejudices towards these groups (see Chapter 9). As for Muslims in particular, Philip Lewis has pointed out that the very committed young *bhangra* groups in the United Kingdom, such as Naseeb and Fun-da-mental, use words taken from the preaching of Farrakhan and Malcolm X in their songs.[47]

'NRIs', or 'Non Resident Indians'[48] and their former homeland: mutual perceptions

The way in which immigrants construct their identity is often influenced by their view of the former homeland, by the success they have had in becoming integrated into the host society, and by the likelihood of their ever returning to their country of origin. Another crucial factor is whether they came from the majority or from a minority group in the home country.

NRIs vs. South Asia: an ambivalent nostalgia

The experience of migration can often lead to excess, either in idealizing or in denigrating the former homeland. Many immigrants have very strong feelings of longing for their former home. They visit frequently, are assiduous in reading any articles about South Asia in American and ethnic newspapers, and react strongly to any criticism of their former homeland; some even become active politically.

Many others, however, become very critical of their former homeland. This process partly owes probably to the need to feel justified in emigrating. The most secular Pakistanis and Bangladeshis draw on the following list to incriminate their respective countries: illiteracy, corruption, political instability, the politicization of religion, bureaucratic inefficiency, economic inequalities, discrimination against women. More religious immigrants emphasize different issues: conspicuous consumption and heterodox religious behaviour ('*Fatiha* instead of *salat*,' was the complaint of 'Mujib', a Jama'at-i-Islami sympathizer – an ICNA leader called it 'soft Islam'[49]), social discrimination (especially the disdain with which people of lower social status are treated, 'Sitara' complained). Religious and non-religious alike criticized political life and the social system.

The attitude of Indian Muslims towards India is affected by the minority status of the group. Some (researchers, and Indian Muslims themselves) say that most have little affection for their former home, unlike not only the Hindus, but also the Pakistanis and the Bangladeshis.[50] There is certainly some truth in this. However, a distinction should be drawn between North-Indian and South Indian Muslims, who nearly all say emphatically that they are still fond of their former homeland, especially the non-Urdu speakers who, like 'Bashir', are very supportive of India in such thorny matters as the Kashmir question. There is also a difference according to generation. The younger

immigrants are less influenced by the nationalist idealism of the years following independence, and are therefore less nostalgic than their parents. Strength
of religious feeling is also a factor: Qur'anic law encourages Muslims not to
become attached to a particular country, so the more committed will be less
inclined to homesickness. The geographical origin may also matter: the distinction is no longer between South Indian Muslims and North Muslims, but
between Muslims from different regions of India. The Muslims of Aligarh, for
example, who chose to stay in India at Partition, are still very loyal to their
homeland. Immigrants from Hyderabad, on the other hand, who were in
some cases strongly opposed to the incorporation of the state of Hyderabad
into India, are more ambivalent, and indeed sometimes fiercely critical of
India. Personal experiences are bound to influence individuals' views of their
former homeland. An important issue here is whether the individual suffered
from discrimination. Even the immigrants from Hyderabad are able to express
homesickness for India, its culture, its inhabitants, 'whatever the imperfections
may be,' and can say they are trying to distinguish between 'love of a homeland' and 'what happens to Muslims when they are in a minority' (as I was told
by Najma Sultana of the AFMI, herself an immigrant from Hyderabad).

Perceptions are also different between parents and children, both in meaning and content. For the first generation, their perception of the homeland can
affect how well they become integrated into the United States, whereas for the
second generation, it is more likely to affect how much they want to preserve
their cultural identity. In terms of content, the younger generation say they
appreciate the sense of family and community, the value of hospitality, the historical and cultural riches of their respective homelands. However, they
complain about the poverty, the social inequalities, the corruption, the relative
lack of freedom (a problem for girls especially) and . . . the mosquitoes. These
thoughts are not so different from those of tourists visiting the subcontinent.
Another interesting side of young people's views is the relationships that
develop between them and their cousins, who are the same age but living in
South Asia. They see themselves as more independent and progressive but
some also describe their cousins as very westernized, so that in fact they do not
feel that they are very different.

Immigrants, and to a lesser extent their children, feel that they have a duty
towards their former homeland and are sincere in their belief that they can
contribute not only financial help (in the form of 'remittances' and investments) but also political help. In the case of Indians, this is mainly observed
among Hindus, but a number of Muslims feel the same, even if their sphere of
influence is more restricted, as in the main they hope to help to improve the
condition of their fellow Muslims. Pakistanis also express a desire to help the
development of their former homeland. Evidence for this is ample in the

lobbying organizations they have created since the early 1990s, including the Pakistan American Congress (PAC) and the Pakistani Physicians' Public Affairs Committee (PAK-PAC).[51] However, there is considerable distrust of politicians in Pakistan, so that expatriates are reluctant to send money to Pakistan for fear that it will find its way into the wrong pockets, either within the government or in other official bodies. This probably explains why, in the wake of the Indian and Pakistani nuclear trials in May 1998, and the economic sanctions imposed by America in particular, Pakistani immigrants were enthusiastic in applying pressure on the American government to help their former homeland, but they were less keen to respond to Prime Minister Nawaz Sharif's pleas for financial help. Indians, on the other hand, responded generously to such appeals for help.

South Asia vs. NRIs: 'East or West, India is the Best'?[52]

It seems that South Asian countries[53] view expatriates with a rather dubious eye. There is admiration, even pride at the way their former compatriots have made such an economic and social success of their move, but also grounds for annoyance and irritation: the most promising students have left (especially those from the IIT, the Indian Institute of Technologies[54]); the NRIs are arrogant; they return and spend money extravagantly and ostentatiously both in building second homes and in celebrating marriages – for the local population this can mean, as it has in the city of Bangalore in India, that the cost of living has risen; businessmen in India fear that they may, for example, be bought out by expatriates who have made a lot of money;[55] there are dark rumours about marriages and dowries involving immigrants (see Chapter 4); immigrants have a propensity for a heightened religiosity (whether they are Hindus, Muslims or Sikhs); immigrants returning on visits are likely to be ungracious about living conditions in the subcontinent, which are still difficult (heat and dust, poverty and mosquitoes), although they had lived in similar conditions before emigrating.

In spite of all this, South Asians are still very interested in their emigrants both in the United Kingdom and in the United States, witness the growing number of short stories and novels on the subject,[56] and recent Bollywood films such as *Dilwale Dulhaniya Le Jayenge* ('The bride will belong to the one who loves her'), *Pardes* ('Foreign land'), *Ao, Ab Laut Chalen* ('Come, let's go home now'). It is worth noting that all these films treat of the loss of cultural identity and finish with the return of the immigrant to India. These films, especially the first two, were immensely popular both in the subcontinent and in the United States.

Socially and economically, expatriates and their consumerism speed the evolution of their former homeland towards westernization. In this, they are important contributors to worldwide globalization.[57] This is exacerbated by the enthusiasm with which the economic intervention of expatriates is welcomed by South Asians in the homeland. India, in particular, was for a long time reluctant to allow this but has, since the early 1990s, relaxed its attitudes to NRIs: they are now favourably considered for visas, in negotiations to buy land or invest, for opening bank accounts, and so on. The former Indian Prime Minister, Narasimha Rao (1991–96) went so far as to invite NRIs to model themselves on the Chinese diaspora. The chief ministers of states in the Indian Union, such as Keshubhai Patel (Gujarat) or Chandrababu Naidu (Andhra Pradesh) are nowadays keen to visit America to invite those who have emigrated from their states to come over and invest back there.

Conclusion

It seems that relationships between Muslims and Hindus in the United States are typically distant and possibly growing more so. The social and political rivalries of the subcontinent have disappeared but this does not seem to bring population groups together in diaspora. Hindus and Muslims alike who have heightened nationalist feelings which find expression in increased religious fervour, exclude the other from their field of identification. This phenomenon does not confirm, for all that, the culturalist or the primordialist approach, but it does support the thesis of Sudhir Kakar, who writes that the instrumentalist analysis is not a sufficient explanation for the tensions between religious communities in the subcontinent, and that the psycho-social dimension is also of crucial importance. The role of the leaders of immigrant communities needs also to be taken into account: out of personal ambition, and/or for political reasons, they tend to instrumentalize ethnic and/or religious allegiances and to emphasize the individuality of their community, fostering therefore the formation of separate identities. They tend, as do leaders in the former homeland also, to obscure the shared history and the mutual relationships which have bound these communities together for centuries.

Our analysis of relationships between South Asians has also shown that belonging to the same religion encourages affinities, but this in itself is not sufficient to create one cohesive group. Other variables, such as language and region of origin (as seen in the phenomenon of the twice-migrants) can be powerful extra influences.

When it comes to relating to the former homeland, there are indeed prejudices on either side, but in spite of this a mutual interest and a pattern of exchanges develop between the expatriates and those who stayed at home, and these are facilitated as globalization increases.

THE HOST SOCIETY

Perceptions, discrimination and other reactions

Mutual perceptions: stereotypes die hard

South Asian perceptions of Americans

I asked 'Mirza', the Bangladeshi newspaper vendor, if he liked the United States. He replied: 'No. All the negative things I heard in Bangladesh about the United States have turned out to be true, the violence, the immodesty . . .' I tried again: 'Is there really nothing you like in the United States?' After a long silence, he answered with a laugh, 'No, nothing.' 'Mansur', the other vendor, suggested, 'The food, maybe?' and 'Mirza' retorted 'Not at all, it's much nicer in Bangladesh.' A few moments later, he did acknowledge that he approved of American cleanliness and of the discretion people displayed: 'They don't ask you about where you come from, your family and so on.'

Apart from 'Mirza', most other immigrants I interviewed on the whole had a positive image of the United States and its inhabitants. They identified the following things that they particularly valued: the freedom (the vast majority mentioned this); the opportunities to make money and to improve one's social status; the technological advances; the comfortable life; the ordered society; honesty; the value placed on intimacy and privacy; efficient systems; punctuality; people's dedication to work; cleanliness; the broad-mindedness of Americans; their discretion in not overwhelming them with questions about their ethnic and religious allegiances, their caste, their clan, their family and so on (unlike South Asians, who are very curious about these matters, even after emigrating); the social security system; the secular nature of society; and lastly the multiculturalism of American society.

These things they appreciate, but they have criticisms too: superficiality, hypocrisy, permissiveness, the disintegration of family values, criminality, alcohol, drugs, divorce, homosexuality, the lack of respect for the elderly and the way in which they are treated (they strongly disapprove of old people being put into retirement homes), the value placed on domestic pets, waste, racism (though only a minority identified this as a criticism), egocentricity, cultural imperialism and ignorance of other cultures. Politically, they are critical of American arrogance, their imperialism and their interference in the political life of other countries (except for Bosnia), the support given to conservative and dictatorial regimes (in particular Saudi Arabia), and the sale of arms.

These opinions are not related either to the degree of religious observance nor to the generation the speaker comes from. However, the more observant immigrants and the second generation tend to emphasize particular elements. The more religious mention freedom of expression and the secular nature of society, in that it gives them greater freedom to practise their own religion, even though these immigrants are in theory opposed to a secular society. 'Mujib'[1], the immigrant who sympathizes with the Jama'at-i-Islami, makes the following comment:

> It's better to live in country that is secular than in a country that isn't.
> But you don't have to believe in secular values.

As far as criticism is concerned, apart from the permissiveness of society, they identify materialism, the education system (which is expensive), the curriculum (which is Americano-centrist, in history in particular, and 'Judeo-Christian'–centrist), refusal to confront reality (illustrated by the widespread use of cosmetic surgery), elitism and racism.

The second generation also praise the United States for the freedom they enjoy, and for the diversity of cultures. Even progressive youngsters rather paradoxically echo the criticisms of the more religious immigrants, and even of the fundamentalists, in their condemnation of materialism and of the cost of an education system which promotes elitism, racism and social inequality (there are too many homeless, for example).

The issue of racism is most interesting. The majority of immigrants do not mention it, apart from the most religiously observant and some young people, who in contrast are vehement on this issue. Many immigrants more or less refuse to admit the existence of racism: this seems to arise out of a psychological need to convince themselves that they were right to emigrate, and to protect themselves from any feelings of insecurity. Also, when comparing Americans with South Asians, they see Americans as much more tolerant.

The more religious immigrants, however, guided by egalitarian ideals, both perceive and condemn racism (this is also a means to draw the major non-Muslim victims of racism into the fold of Islam). They are also more sensitive to potential slurs on Islam than secular immigrants would be. However, we have also seen that the more observant can turn a blind eye to racism, especially when it is directed at them, in order to avoid facing any doubts about their own decision to emigrate (see Chapter 3).

Young people are almost unanimous in condemning racism as one of the fundamental flaws in American society. As they have not lived in the subcontinent, they do not see why they should consider the problem as relative. The first and second generation also differ on two other issues. The first generation has internalized a more conservative discourse, so that they see American society as relatively tolerant (in particular towards African–Americans and Hispanics), whereas the second generation is more imbued with liberal thinking, and considers as racist the treatment reserved to some ethnic minorities. The immigrants who came to the United States may furthermore have expected, at least at first, to be discriminated against, perhaps more than in fact they were, so that they have grown to think of the United States as a tolerant society. Members of the second generation, on the other hand, have quickly absorbed American ways of thinking (even if they have not done so to the exclusion of other identities) and do not perceive themselves as foreigners in American society; they are more conscious than their parents of their rights, and as a result are more sensitive to discrimination, whether it is aimed at them or at other ethnic groups.

American perceptions of South Asians

We noted at the start of this study that Americans are ignorant of the subcontinent and of its inhabitants, and that they even have difficulty in distinguishing South Asians from Hispanics. As far as Muslims are concerned, Americans, and indeed many others, tend to dissociate Islam from the subcontinent, in that they associate Muslims with Arabs, and the subcontinent with Hinduism (or indeed Buddhism, as also happens in France).

As a result, South Asian Muslims find that they have two distinct stereotypes attributed to them, according to whether they are perceived as either South Asians – specifically Indians – or Muslims.

South Asians are indeed often confused with Indians, or indeed Hindus (Americans can rarely tell the difference, just like the French), even when they are Pakistanis or Bangladeshis. Before World War II, Americans mostly had negative images of India and its inhabitants, as portrayed in colonial literature (cf. Rudyard Kipling) and by American journalists (for example, Katherine Mayo[2]), which they acquired from school books (primitive tribes, good Rajahs who were loyal to the British, and bad Rajahs who plotted with the tribes against the British),[3] though nowadays the American perception of Indians has changed somewhat. Stereotypical images involving poverty, snake charmers and levitating gurus still exist, and films, such as Steven Spielberg's *Indiana*

Jones and the Temple of Doom continue to perpetuate clichés about destitute and wild Indians. Since the Spielberg film came out in the late 1980s (it was banned in India), Indians in diaspora have been asked very seriously, and this still happens, whether monkeys' brains are eaten in India.[4] Some more positive images have nevertheless also emerged, thanks largely to Mahatma Gandhi (a both mythical and stereotypical figure). The arrival from 1965 onwards of large numbers of educated Indians, who were soon to become economically successful, also helped to improve their image and that of their country. As we shall see, however, this economic success itself became a stereotype, and this has had some adverse effects on relationships both with the administration and with the host-society at large. On the whole, however, the positive clichés outweigh the negative as Americans view India itself. The television channel Eye on India broadcast in December 1995 a programme in which a journalist asked passers-by about what they thought of in relation to India: 'mystery', 'pacifism' and 'spicy food' were the three most common replies.

Pakistanis, when they are recognized as such, benefit from having a good image from the point of view of their professional achievements, but there are also negative images associated in the public mind with their homeland (its rather chaotic attempt at democracy, creation of an Islamic state . . . or indeed purely and simply complete ignorance about the very existence of Pakistan).

As far as Bangladeshis are concerned, they are not present in the United States in sufficient numbers for stereotypes to have been formulated, either positive or negative. They are, however, painfully aware that their country is a byword for abject poverty and natural disasters, in the United States and elsewhere. Since the Taslima Nasreen affair, the image of fundamentalist Islam has also been associated with this country and has gained prominence in public consciousness.

What exactly is the American perception of Islam? In many ways it is no different from the images current in many non-Muslim countries. John Esposito lists salient features: holy war and hate, fanaticism and violence, intolerance and the oppression of women.[5]

Western anti-Muslim sentiment is very ancient, and is rooted in the Crusades. The defiance of the Ottoman empire towards Western powers and colonialism[6] together reinforced this sentiment, and the current situation in many Muslim countries, where hyper-conservative or dictatorial regimes squabble for power against Islamist movements with violent tendencies, exacerbates it further.

In the United States, recent events in which the country has been involved or implicated have reinforced existing prejudices, so that Muslim immigrants who have arrived since the 1980s have been rather anxious. Such events include the Iranian revolution in 1979 and the hostage-taking at the US embassy, the Gulf war in 1991, the attack on the World Trade Center in 1993, to which list one can also add the Rushdie affair, even though the Americans were not directly involved, and lately the bombings in Kenya and Tanzania. Recent Anglo-Saxon debate on the 'Clash of Civilizations'[7] and the ambivalent findings of cultural anthropology may also be contributing to increased prejudice.

We need to establish whether the stereotypes, either ethnic or religious, have sufficient force to become the vehicles of discrimination.

Discrimination – overt or 'veiled'

Muslims from South Asia are therefore in a situation in which discrimination from the host society is likely to be directed towards them for reasons either ethnic (because they are non-White) and/or religious (because they are Muslims).

> Racists do not care if we are Indian, Arab, Pakistani, Hindu, Muslim, pacifists, terrorists. We all look the same – different from them.[8]

This sentence by Bhargavi Mandava, which she gives to an Indian taxi driver in New York, is probably accurate, but in fact we shall attempt to disentangle discrimination on religious grounds from discrimination on ethnic grounds (based on colour).

In fact, South Asians have benefited from the civil rights movement in the 1960s and their religious beliefs are protected by the constitution, but my study shows that immigrants are nevertheless suffering discrimination, both as South Asians and as Muslims.

Discrimination directly attributable to belonging to a coloured minority, in this case an Asian minority, can be experienced in a number of spheres: primarily at school and at work, and to a lesser extent in negotiating for housing or bank loans. The system of preferential treatment or positive discrimination known as 'affirmative action', which is applied in particular to university admissions, includes Asians as one of the favoured groups, but this can have its disadvantages: American universities, especially the larger ones (the Ivy League) reject applications from (South) Asians on the grounds of preferential treatment. Some universities have even instituted a system of invisible or 'silent' quotas to restrict certain minorities which are deemed to be over-represented, and this includes the South Asians.

Discrimination in the workplace, according to some South Asians, hampers their access to the higher echelons of professional life. In 1992, for example, there were more than 1,200 complaints registered by Asians of all origins at the

Equal Employment Opportunity Commission.[9] South Asians are also sometimes rejected when they apply for jobs or fired, on the grounds of their accent.

'Ashraf', an immigrant from Aligarh who is in charge of sales for an IT company, complains:[10]

> In the United States it's very difficult to hang on to a job for a long time, especially in my field. But compared to others I have a double handicap because I'm an immigrant and I have an accent. My boss has remarked on my accent several times. I'm scared he might use it as an excuse to sack me.

It should be noted that many South Asians thought on arrival in the United States that they spoke better English (because it was more British) than the Americans. They are critical of the different pronunciation of some words (*schedule, lieutenant, laboratory, either, anti*, and so on) and the spelling variations (*center* instead of *centre*, *labor* instead of *labour*, and so on). But they soon try to fit in with the American accent and intonation. Those who are still learning to do this – usually during their first two or three years in the United States – sometimes sound rather artificial, incomprehensible even. Some keep this rather unnatural accent, but after a few years most achieve an accent which, although it may not be perfect and may still betray their origins, blends sufficiently well to enable them to be less easily distinguishable from Americans.

To return to discrimination, it can also enter into negotiations to find housing or to take out a bank loan. Some immigrants complain that they have been refused housing, as indeed has happened to a number of other members of ethnic minorities, and shopkeepers and other South Asian entrepreneurs are often questioned by bank managers who need convincing that they are solvent.[11]

The label 'model minority' which is given to (South) Asians is a double-edged sword. It can count against them, for example by making it more difficult for them than for other ethnic minorities to access social services – the local and federal authorities which administer these services are not easily persuaded that members of a community which is perceived as wealthy need their help.

A second negative impact of the 'model minority' image is the racial violence perpetrated by the more disadvantaged social groups. As an ethnic group, South Asians are cornering certain markets, and this salient feature of the Asian communities aggravates hostility from the others. Some sectors are becoming monopolized by Asians, and the African–Americans and Hispanics, who are less well organized along racial lines, are being edged out. There is, for example, a detectable pattern to ethnic hostility among taxi drivers: Pakistanis versus African–Americans, Pakistanis versus Arabs, and so on. Asians are, however, less often targeted by the extreme right, who tend to attack African–Americans and Hispanics. South Asians are vulnerable, though, when they are mistaken for Hispanics. This is why some Hindu women wear the *bindi*,[12] not only for the sake of tradition, but also to avoid being taken for Hispanics.[13]

Koreans have so far borne the brunt of this type of violence (the reader will recall the riots in Los Angeles in 1992), but South Asians have not escaped entirely. The 1980s saw the start of attacks on individuals. In 1991 there were 58 incidents of racial violence towards South Asians in New Jersey (intimidation or physical attack).

In New Jersey, where there is, like in New York, a high concentration of South Asians, two gangs were particularly active in the early 1990s. The South Asians were their main target, in particular Hindus, as witnessed by the name chosen by one of the gangs, 'Dotbusters' (referring to the *bindi*). This group attacked women wearing the *bindi*. Ironically, this group had Hispanic members. As we have just seen, some Indian women wear the *bindi* specifically to set themselves apart from the Hispanics.

Aside from the social and economic reasons explained above, which give rise to jealousy and bitterness among the least advantaged groups, this violence can also be explained by the behaviour of South Asians, especially the wealthy ones, who try to identify as closely as possible with the white majority and willingly sign up to the 'thematic of dangerousness and racial inferiority' to use a phrase by Sylvia Ullmo.[14] 'Zeba', who was born in the United States, comments on her father's attitude to the African–American minority:[15] 'He behaves like a white man.' As Sucheta Mazumdar emphasizes, the *bindi* and other visible distinguishing signs betray a desire to draw a clear line between themselves and other ethnic groups. Skin colour automatically distinguishes South Asians from the white majority, so more clear signals are needed to avoid confusion with other minority groups,[16] especially the disadvantaged. It is worth noting that this recourse to visible signals is not a South Asian prerogative, but an element of American culture. Alexis de Tocqueville noted that Whites, before the abolition of slavery, made every effort not to be mistaken for Blacks, and did so all the more keenly in the 'free' states.[17]

New York also was affected by racial violence in the 1990s, perpetrated not only by economically disadvantaged groups but also by the authorities, in particular the police, who were responsible for the majority of racial violence. In 1994, in New York, Los Angeles and San Francisco, in 55 per cent of incidents in which they attacked Asians, police officers also insulted them verbally: 'Go back to China, Orientals!', 'Go back to Pakistan', 'This is not Pakistan.'

These 'nativist' reactions from Americans, who were after all themselves immigrants not so long ago, are not a new phenomenon in the United States. Today however, South Asians are not spared discrimination or racial violence, and their label 'model minority', far from protecting them, can even be turned against them. The image Americans have of India, which on the whole is favourable, is also not sufficiently potent to guarantee the safety of immigrants from that part of the world.

In spite of this, many first generation South Asians refuse to acknowledge the existence of discrimination along ethnic lines. There are two reasons for this. Firstly, it is as a way of avoiding psychosis, which, at any rate, is not justified in present circumstances. Secondly, as Arvind Rajagopal has pointed out, they are accustomed to a strongly competitive atmosphere, and they fear that if they brandish the discrimination argument, it will be seen as a cover for failure. They affect to believe, therefore, that discrimination is only aimed at more recent immigrants, who have not yet become integrated into American society.

When it comes to Islam, the image it has in American minds is shaped more by international events than by the behaviour of Muslim immigrants in the United States. Major crises in the Muslim world which in some way provoke American intervention are quite often followed by acts of vandalism against mosques or xenophobic attacks on individuals. During the Gulf war, for example, mosques and shops, especially those owned by Arabs, were torched, and women, especially if they wore the veil, were attacked. The attack on the World Trade Center in February 1993, and against the FBI building in Oklahoma in April 1995, both provoked renewed 'Muslim bashing' and 'Arab bashing'.[19]

Muslims are threatened not only by a certain ambient hostility towards Islam, which is sustained by American foreign policy, but also as immigrants. At any rate, the number of attacks on places of worship of all kinds, regardless of religion, is growing.[20]

Vandalism and racial attacks have not yet [2000] reached alarming proportions. In 1994, for example, 32 attacks against Muslims and anti-Muslim incidents were officially registered (as against 1,988 anti-Semitic incidents).[21]

In addition to acts of vandalism and aggression, Muslims suffer from discrimination. In 1996, there were 232 discriminatory acts reported (not including physical attacks), as compared to 60 in 1995.[22] The number of Muslims who make complaints has increased, so this large increase in numbers does not necessarily reflect a real growth in discriminatory acts. It should be noted, though, that South Asians are more hesitant than Arabs or African–Americans to report acts of discrimination perpetrated against them:[23] they are more recent immigrants, and they are on the whole less targeted than other groups, for the reasons explained above. Arabs are the main victims of anti-Muslim attacks, but South Asians are nevertheless fearful that anti-Arab prejudice may have negative repercussions on them also.

Most of these discriminatory incidents happen in the workplace. Some veiled women, for example, have been abusively dismissed.[24] It is difficult, though, to say that this discrimination is simply anti-Islam, since Sikhs wearing turbans, and other religious minorities wearing distinguishing signs have also suffered from it.

Civil rights protection organizations nearly always intervene in such cases, and the offending company is often forced to reverse its decision. The best-known Muslim-run organization of this type is the Council on American–Islamic Relations (see below).

Since a recent decision by the Supreme Court, however, religious groups are concerned that some rights that they have so far been guaranteed may be thrown into doubt: in June 1997, the Supreme Court repealed the Religious Freedom Restoration Act (RFRA). This act had been supported by President Bill Clinton and voted in by Congress in 1993, and it restored the principle overturned by the Supreme Court in 1990 which said that the government could only intervene in religious matters for either medical or security reasons. There was widespread rejoicing among religious groups, especially Muslims, because this new law protected, for example, those who wished to pray or wear the *hijab* at work. Now the Supreme Court has declared this law to be unconstitutional, saying that it is the job of the law courts, and not of Congress, to define the constitutional protection afforded to religion.[25]

Among those I interviewed, a certain number – nearly all from the second generation – said that as South Asians they had been the victims of open discrimination[26] in the United States, most often in the form of racist remarks: 'Indian piece of shit', 'Third-World farm animal', 'camel-jockey', and so on.

As Muslims, though, nearly all said they had never suffered from such overt discrimination, neither at work nor elsewhere. Some said that they were seen first and foremost as Indians, others pointed to the tolerance of Americans, and yet others said it was a matter of luck or fate. Even women who wear the veil said they had never been victims of this kind of discrimination. Only one, 'Sitara', complained that after the [1993] attack on the World Trade Center she was asked: 'What will your next target be?'

Things are reversed, though, when it comes to 'veiled' discrimination. Some do complain that Americans are racist towards coloured immigrants, or that they make rude comments about specific countries in the subcontinent but there are even more numerous who say that as Muslims they have been victims of more subtle forms of discrimination, or that they have been worried by a latent hostility to Islam in the United States, even if they have not themselves been directly targeted.

This is demonstrated by the tendency of some Muslims to flag up their Indian-ness, to the extent that they are on occasion keen to make a clear demarcation between themselves and Pakistanis, who in their turn sometimes try to pass themselves off as Indians. South Asian facial features vary to a surprising degree across the regions of the subcontinent, some appearing more Semitic than others, and it is these people who feel most vulnerable to being mistaken for Arabs. A number of Muslims therefore live with the anxiety of belonging to an unpopular religious minority.

For all that, the vast majority of South Asians are full of praise for the tolerance of Americans, and grateful for the opportunity to practise their religion openly and in (almost) complete freedom. They give two reasons for anti-Islamic feeling among Americans: the ignorance of the general population on the one hand,[47] and on the other the media. Some add that Muslims themselves have been their own worst enemy, unable to give a favourable impression of themselves, especially abroad but also in the United States.

'Humayun', an immigrant from Pakistan, comments on the ignorance of Americans: 'Americans know more about ETs than about Muslims.'[28]

They are unanimous in accusing the American press of being biased, including serious papers, such as the *Washington Post*, the *New York Times*, *Newsweek* or *Time*, and in considering this bias to be chiefly responsible for anti-Muslim prejudice in the United States. The papers, they say, always associate Islam and terrorism. A few examples: immediately after the arrest of Mohammed Salameh, one of the main suspects in the [1993] World Trade Center attack, the *Washington Times* carried a front-page headline '*Muslim*[29] arrested in NYC bombing'; the *Newsweek* headline after that same attack, in its 15 February 1993 issue, was '*Sunni Muslim*[30] Extremism. America, Israel, and Arab states created the Islamic militants they now fear.'[31] In fact, titles and articles in newspapers often carry phrases like 'The Sword of Islam',[32] 'Still Fighting the Crusades', 'Rising Islam May Overwhelm the West' 'The Roots of Muslim Rage', 'The Islamic War Against Modernity',[33] 'The Red Menace is Gone. Here is Islam'[34] and so on.

Television and Hollywood films are often accused of doing even more to perpetuate these stereotypes. One of the most recent films from Hollywood, *The Siege* by Ed Zwick (which came out under the title *Couvre-feu* in France in 1998), seems to me to have made a genuine attempt to portray Muslims in the United States in a different light (especially Arabs), in spite of its main theme (Islamic terrorism in New York), and yet it too conveys some stereotyping. This film portrays as one of its main characters an Arab-American who is very patriotic and inspires sympathy; he protests at the treatment of innocent people and the infringing of their civil rights in the name of security procedures (nearly all the Arab men in the city are rounded up into a stadium and an Arab-American is tortured to death). The film, above all, tries to depict Arabs as an ethnic group which is now a permanent part of American landscape. Some images, however, have provoked protest from Islamic organizations,[35] especially the recurrent image of two hands performing ablutions, used as a prelude to a terrorist attack. These organizations also objected that the American Constitution was frequently brandished, as if to convey the message that respect for the Constitution would help to clearly mark the difference between Americans on the one hand, and Arab criminals and other Muslim criminals on the other, and thus confirm American superiority.

Some American politicians are also tempted to perpetuate anti-Muslim prejudice. Patrick Buchanan, an ultra-conservative candidate at the 1996 presidential elections, declared:

> For a millennium, the struggle for mankind's destiny was between Christianity and Islam; in the twenty-first century, it may be so again. For, as the Shi'a humiliate us, their co-religionists are filling up the countries of the West.[36]

This kind of comment, directed against Muslims and immigrants, both from the media and from politicians, is still fairly rare. Most Muslim immigrants are most concerned at the veiled discrimination they see in the press, as described above, rather than by the comments of nativists who would overtly attack them for religious reasons.

The veiled discrimination they are exposed to does affect immigrants, and provokes in them a variety of reactions, which we shall examine in a moment.

On the whole, it would seem that personal discrimination against South Asians is more likely to be on ethnic grounds than on religious grounds. Yvonne Haddad remarks that South Asians may in fact suffer more than Arabs because their skin is darker.[37] As far as religious discrimination is concerned, some of those I spoke to reckoned that they suffered less because they were Indian, or, in the case of Pakistanis and Bangladeshis, because they were taken for Indians. South Asian Muslims do seem, though, to be more concerned about veiled anti-Islam discrimination, which they see notably in the press, than they are about overt discrimination on ethnic grounds.

Contrasting reactions

Few Muslim immigrants allow discrimination of any kind to affect their behaviour, but some do choose to react. These reactions tend towards two extremes: dissimulation and/or assimilation on the one hand, and on the other mobilization.

Dissimulation and/or assimilation

Some immigrants are keen above all things to become well integrated into American society, and so they choose dissimulation as their safest option. In some cases this implies assimilation.

Most who fall into this category try not to advertise their Muslim identity, and instead emphasize another identity, for example Indian. Among those I interviewed, I observed that in particular Shi'a, whether Twelver or Isma'ili (Nizari and Bohra) were likely to adopt this strategy, for two reasons: there is an old tradition in these communities of dissimulating (*taqiyya*) their identity when the community is under threat, even in their former homelands, to protect the life of the minority; also, since the Iranian revolution there has been a more explicit hostility in the United States to Shi'a. However, since the [1993] attack on the World Trade Center, Sunni have also been labelled as potential terrorists (cf. the newspapers quoted above). In most cases, this option to dissimulate does not imply a renunciation of Muslim identity: immigrants who do this continue to assert that they are Muslims, even if they do not proclaim it out loud, to practise their religion and to try to pass on their religious heritage to the next generation.

In some cases, however, dissimulation can be combined with attempts to become as far as possible assimilated into American society, by abandoning religious and even maybe ethnic identity. This kind of dissimulation often leads immigrants to change their surname. Some ethnic groups already have such surnames, or give their children such first names that do not betray their true origin – African–Americans in particular, but also the Chinese, who often have Christian first names. Other ethnic groups have surnames with ethnic or religious connotations, and they choose for their children first names with the same connotations (Hispanics and South Asians especially). South Asian Muslims therefore have surnames which immediately mark them out as different from the white majority.

A small minority choose to change their names, which administratively is fairly straightforward in the United States. This is done in a variety of ways. A very few take on a completely new name, some simplify their existing name or adopt a diminutive, especially for the first name (Bill for Bilal, Jim for Jamil, Alan for Ali, and so on), some move a letter in the name, alter the pronunciation or the placing of an accent.

Among the South Asian Muslims I met, only one 'Khan' had changed his name to 'Kahn'. However, I cannot resist the temptation to quote two other examples, one an Iranian (ex-Muslim Shi'a) and the other a family of Hindus from Kashmir. The Iranian, a very Americanized man called Hameed whose appearance and American accent could easily allow him to pass for a White, chose to be called 'Ham'. A non-Muslim who was meeting him for the first time, as I was, asked him 'Doesn't it worry you that people call you "bacon"?' He retorted 'I hope they'll think I'm a Hamilton. If I say my name's Hameed, people change that to Ahmed or Hamed . . . Sounds like a terrorist.'

In the case of the Kashmiri family, rather than taking on a diminutive they have played around with the pronunciation. The father's name was Hari Kaul, and he was introducing himself to people as 'Harry Cole.' His wife's name was Priti ('Pretty') and they had called their son Neel ('Neil').

Some people have changed their name, however, not out of a desire to dis-simulate or become assimilated but because they carry names that Americans find difficult to pronounce and they are tired of hearing them mispronounced. In some cases the American authorities actually request that an individual changes his name. A Kashmiri Muslim called Rathore told me that when he arrived in the United States in the 1960s, the immigrant service officer asked him to change his name, which he thought was too complicated for Americans, though in fact the immigrant refused.

Individuals can also opt to change their name for professional reasons – for example shopkeepers, professionals, such as doctors or lawyers, who might fear that too 'foreign-sounding' a name might frighten off potential clients. Also for professional reasons, restaurants owned by Pakistanis and Bangladeshis capitalize on India's positive image and portray themselves as 'Indian' restau-rants, calling themselves 'Gandhi' or 'Anand', as they do in France.

When it comes to naming children, some choose typically Muslim names, but other prefer an ambiguous choice, choosing biblical names, such as Adam, Dayan, or Sarah, and opting for the Judeo–Christian pronunciation and even spelling (Abraham instead of the more Islamic Ibrahim).

Mobilization

Instead of assimilation or dissimulation, some immigrants choose rather to rally together not only to oppose discrimination, but also to combat ignorance, and to raise their community's profile. This mobilization can appear rather like a promotional campaign for the Islamic religion and its adherents. They aim to make themselves more familiar to Americans, in part to attract new converts, but mainly because Muslims feel that Americans have negative images of Islam through knowing so little about it. Muslims hope ultimately to become as accepted as are Christians and Jews.

In order to raise their profile in American society and to overcome prejudice, Muslims use a variety of strategies.

1. They engage in interfaith dialogues with Jewish and Christian represen-tatives. We saw earlier that the Islamic Center of Long Island is active in this

field, and that it has a policy of establishing closer links with the Jewish community. Various other Islamic centres are making similar overtures to encourage dialogue with Christians.

2. They make the most of the tradition, respected in most American universities, of celebrating ethnic diversity. An 'Islamic Awareness Week' has thus been instituted in New York. For a whole week, Islamic associations invite Muslim and non-Muslim students to a series of meetings on the Islamic religion and on events worldwide affecting Muslims. Each meeting happens in a different university, one at Columbia, one at Long Island University and others elsewhere. In November 1995, for example, topics discussed included the status of women in the Muslim world (the talk given was apologetic – see Chapter 6), the peace process in Bosnia and the issue of Palestine (these two subjects were treated in a more polemical spirit, as the titles given to the meetings suggest: 'Liberating the Dome of the Rock' and 'Bosnia's Peace Process').

The interesting feature of this is that religion is 'ethnicized' – though this may not be the intention – by adopting the 'Islamic week' pattern used for *ethnic* celebrations in American universities. The Muslim World Day Parade gave rise to the same comment, in that the people of New York see the event as ethnic rather than religious. The Muslim students may not be specifically seeking to ethnicize Islam, indeed that phrase could create confusion (an ethnicized Islam could designate the Islam of a specific group rather than universal Islam), and yet Muslims who advocate pan-Islamism might well see this ethnicization as a means to encourage Islamic unity. In other words, these Muslims are aspiring to create a united and coherent ethnic group, transcending individual cultures (and indeed ethnic groups). This attempt to ethnicize religion is not unique to Islam: the Hindus, under the leadership of the Vishwa Hindu Parishad (World Hindu Council)[38] in particular, have tried to achieve the same object, in order to promote unity.[39] In the United Kingdom, Muslims officially requested in 1988 to be counted as an ethnic group – as Sikhs and Jews are – in order to be protected from discrimination by the Race Relations Act 1976. This request was refused, because the British authorities argued that in the light of the diversity of their languages and geographical origins they could not justifiably claim the status of an ethnic group.[40]

3. Muslims are developing their relationships with the press, with two objectives: they hope to raise their profile in the United States and to counter the veiled discrimination aimed at them. To this end, Islamic centres and their organizers invite the media to come and cover religious events, such as the Id. Organizations such as the ICNA have also started to make contact with journalists: they invite them to meetings and give the view of the organization on current affairs in the Muslim world or affecting the Muslim community. Contact with the media can also be in the form of press communiqués which

aim to give the Muslim position on specific events (such as the [1993] attack on the World Trade Center). It is worth noting that in taking on these tasks organizations such as the ICNA are bidding to be seen as the mouthpiece of the Muslim community, and they act as if the community were presenting a united front, which is in fact far from the truth.

4. They set up organizations whose specific aims are to combat discrimination and/or to raise the profile of Islam in the United States.

The organization which is most energetic in its fight against anti-Islamic discrimination in the United States is undoubtedly the Council on American–Islamic Relations (CAIR). It was set up in June 1994, and its current [2000] president is a Palestinian called Nihad Awad.[41] The CAIR is based in Washington and is officially represented in about 20 states, one of which is New York. The organization has been given the nickname 'Hijab Defence League', as one of its main activities is to defend the wearing of the Islamic veil (especially in the workplace), but it shot to fame in 1997 with the Nike shoes affair, which concerned some shoes carrying an inscription uncannily like 'Allah' written in Arabic. After a four-month intensive campaign (in which the Internet was a major tool) that spread far outside America (Malaysia, for example, confiscated all Nike products, and the Saudi Chamber of Commerce threatened to boycott all Nike shoes), the CAIR won his case, the suspect shoes were withdrawn from the market, and Nike apologized to the Muslim community.

One other organization deserves mention, the National Council on Islamic Affairs (NCIA), which has been attempting for a number of years to raise the profile of Islam in the United States. It was set up in the 1960s in New York, and its membership brings together Muslim intellectuals, professors, lawyers and businessmen. Its objective, according to its president, Ghazi Khankan[42] (whom we have already met as the co-ordinator of communication and interfaith dialogue at the ICLI, the reader will recall), is to establish relationships with the host society and to propagate Islam. The NCIA had for many years concentrated its efforts on the situation in the Middle East, and had been successful in drawing the attention of the press to events there. Since the early 1990s, it has been campaigning in various ways to bring the Muslim community into the American public eye, in New York in particular. It has recently met with success in a symbolic way. The NCIA had lobbied for the star and crescent to be put up in December in all the public places where a Christmas tree and a candelabra (*menorah*) for Hanukkah are erected. In December 1995, the organization failed to convince the New York railway authorities (Metro-North Railroad) to erect the star and crescent alongside the Christmas tree and the *menorah* in Grand Central Terminal, the major Manhattan station. The president of Metro-North Railroad, Donald Nelson, in fact decided to remove the

Christian and Jewish symbols, arguing that as 500,000 people used the station every day, it was impossible to please everyone.[43] The NCIA was more successful with Venture Fund 44 Inc., which agreed to put the Muslim symbol alongside the Christian and Jewish ones in the entrance hall to their premises in the heart of Manhattan. The owners of the building at first refused, but then gave in when the NCIA threatened legal action. The NCIA used two decisions of the Supreme Court, 'Rosenberger v. University of Virginia' and 'Ohio's Pinette Case', which ruled that if some religious symbols were permitted (such as the Christmas tree – for all that it is not in fact Christian) in a public place, it was not permissible to refuse to display other symbols expressing ideas of the same type.[44] It is worth noting that banks such as Chase Manhattan, Citybank and about 20 other institutions, subsequently on their own initiative added the star and crescent to their usual decorations.[45] Then NCIA began legal proceedings against the postal service in Manhattan and the New York City Board of Education, citing the same two cases. The Board of Education gave way in June 1997 and allowed Muslim students to make and display star and crescent symbols in schools during December, just as Christian and Jewish children do with their respective symbols. In order to achieve its object, the NCIA had to prove to the authorities that the symbols were cultural rather than religious, since public schools are secular. Mohammad Mehdi, the general secretary of the NCIA, convinced them that the symbol had cultural aspects, since the position of the stars around the moon represented to Arabs their way of navigating in the desert, and the crescent symbolized the start of the lunar month.[47] The Board of Education on the same occasion granted the two Id festivals as public school holidays, which means that now Muslim students can legally miss school for the Ids. Note that here again, as in each attempt to gain recognition in New York, Islam has to present itself, willingly or not, from an ethnic and cultural standpoint rather than a religious one.

In December 1983 the ICNA launched a 'USA Muslims Day', an annual celebration which they fixed on the third Friday in December, so between Hanukkah and Christmas, which would aim to be an opportunity for Muslims to express appreciation to their new homeland, and to inform both their children and Americans about the contributions Islam has made to civilization. The USA Muslims Day is a festival where families exchange good wishes and children receive presents. In reality, however, none of the families I met celebrated this festival – they preferred to observe *Maulid* or the Id as a substitute for Christmas.

In June 1990, in the wake of a series of acts of discrimination towards the Islamic community that year, a Muslim lobby was set up, the American Muslim Council (AMC). One of these incidents was that the FBI refused to recruit a Pakistani: the FBI argued that because of the rigidity of the requirement to pray at set hours, and the prohibition for a Muslim to take orders from a woman, this Pakistani man would be unable to carry out his professional activities.[48]

Aside from fighting discrimination, the AMC[49] says its main objectives are to make Muslims in the United States more politically aware and to lobby in Washington. The organization has its base in the American capital, and claimed in 1998 to have 19 branches across America and 300 active members (half of whom are paid). The AMC appears to work across ethnic divides, from my observations when I visited its headquarters: South Asians, Arabs, African–Americans, Malaysians and other Indonesians were all working together. The organization was originally financed by Kuwait, which took considerable interest in Muslims in the United States (as a body which could lobby in its favour) after the Gulf war. In fact, following the example of Warith Deen Muhammad's American Muslim Mission, the AMC supported American intervention in the Gulf.

The AMC has been occupied in the last few years denouncing discrimination against Muslims in the United States (in prisons, schools and so on), and anything that could be seen as reinforcing discriminatory behaviour (for example, it led an active campaign against the passing of the House Omnibus Counterterrorism Act in 1995[50]). It also regularly lobbies the United States government in support of Muslims worldwide, while being loudly and clearly critical of any terrorist activities perpetrated by Muslims, hence claiming the status of a respectable and moderate organization.

In spite of the existence of an organization such as the AMC, there is as yet little in the way of large-scale political involvement from Muslim immigrants, especially the South Asian immigrants. Any political involvement on their part tends to relate to their former homeland, which demonstrates how much they still feel involved in it, and that the fact of immigration is still very recent. It could be said that discrimination, especially on religious grounds, and the relatively low profile of South Asians and/or of Muslims were potential rallying forces for political activity. However, the conditions for effective political action (unity within the ethnic or religious group affected, alliances between groups, a high rate of electoral participation, systematic contact with politicians, the ability to portray the group as indigenous rather than foreign) are not yet fully in place, so that any political action by immigrants is limited in its effectiveness.

Conclusion

It would appear, then, that Muslims and especially their community leaders, are making many efforts to become better accepted in the United States. In real terms, the impact of organizations which are combating invisibility and discrimination is limited. However, the Muslim community in the United States is gradually becoming better coordinated and following the example set by other ethnic groups which also use the lobbying technique. We have also seen confirmation of the idea that a religious group needs to become ethnicized (a Muslim lobby) if it is to be successful in making a mark on the American landscape.

CONCLUSION

Islam as an identifier?

The debate on the concept of identity, which is still subjective, elusive, and in transition, has not yet reached a conclusion. For some it is an 'imaginary'[1] construction, for others an 'illusory'[2] one, and indeed it does seem to be flexible, fluctuating in time and space according to circumstances. Even though it is to a large extent subjective since it is a matter of belief rather than a palpable reality, it is nonetheless a useful concept as illustrated by its remarkable (and even redoubtable) efficiency.[3]

In diaspora, the concept of identity can take on a particularly important role as a panacea for the challenges of modern life and for the existential void created by the relative failure of secular ideologies.

The population groups we have been examining, Muslims from South Asia, have in the recent past experienced identity conflicts which have resulted in the creation of separate nation states: Pakistan and Bangladesh. These conflicts have been religious as well as ethnic in character and they are still alive within the Indian Union (communalist tensions between the Muslim minority and the Hindu majority), in Pakistan (ethnic and sectarian conflicts which threaten the cohesion of the country), and in Bangladesh (competition between secular and communalist forces in defining the national identity).

South Asian Muslims have emigrated (and still emigrate) taking with them the emotional baggage of these ethnic and/or religious identifications, even if the main reason for emigrating is economic rather than political.

They settle in the United States, the paradigmatic immigrant country, where each new minority has had to define and negotiate its identity, religion being one of the most significant markers. This sacralization of identity is promoted by the way in which religion is seen as an identifying symbol in the host society. South Asian Muslims are included in this process and religion has become an important element in their self-definition.

The prominence accorded to religion can be explained in a number of ways, the first of which is the American context. Most ethnic minorities in the United States (Irish, Greek, Jewish and so on) had traditionally viewed religion as a key element in establishing their identity and adapting as a community. As Lacorne has noted: 'religious practices are inextricably linked to ethnic identification.'[4] The United States also offers a degree of freedom to Muslims which they would probably not experience anywhere else (not even, or indeed especially not, in Islamic countries[5]). Religious freedom in the United States is similar to that which prevails in India, where all religions are treated equally. Muslims are therefore able to live as committed a religious life, or nearly, as any other religious group among Americans, in particular conservative Christians. Nevertheless, they do sense a feeling of veiled discrimination towards them. This leads to a paradoxical situation. On the one hand, American tolerance in religious matters enables Muslims to practise their religion more or less openly, and not to need to resort to discreet and hidden ways as is the case in France (at least among the first generation[6]). On the other hand, anti-Muslim prejudice in the American population, which is fed by the media and reinforced by international events, exacerbates the religious sentiment of Muslims, and in reaction ('reactive ethnicity'[7]), they become more committed to Islam. In this they are on the same path as their European peers, who see Islam as an effective means to 're-establish their scorned identity'.[8]

The arrival of children, and especially their maturation, can cause serious anxiety among parents, who fear that their offspring will become excessively westernized. This encourages a renewal of religious commitment among the parents, who use it as a palliative measure and even as a brake to attempt to slow down this process of westernization.

A third category of explanation is the general tendency, in the United States as elsewhere, among both minority and majority population groups, to emphasize the group's own identity in the face of increasing globalization. The Muslim world feels particularly threatened by the spectre of uniformity and the uncertainties of modern life and the last few years it has deployed a number of strategies to safeguard its identity. Religion has been one of the most obvious ways to respond to the 'quest for meaning and continuity which need to be rediscovered beyond discontinuity.'[9] The subcontinent has not escaped this process, by a long way.

As Peter Van der Veer emphasizes, nationalism is encouraged by its dialectic relationship not only with religion but also with migration: the experience of migration is a challenge to identity, and as such it engenders nationalistic activism.[10] The Sikhs are probably the most striking example of this in their campaign for Khalistan ('the country of the pure', an independent territory claimed by the Sikhs) which has greater support among Sikhs in diaspora (especially in the United Kingdom and in Canada) than in the Punjab. Hindus also, though to a lesser extent, display an increased level of nostalgia for their former homeland. The nationalist right in India has not met with much success in its efforts to establish a dialectic between the national community and the religious community. These attempts have been more successful among Hindus in diaspora (we have already seen how Hindu nationalists have had an impact on the immigrant community), because religion feeds nationalism and nationalism sets itself up as a part of religion.[11]

Muslims from India being already part of a minority, this reduces the importance of identification to the nation, as a geographic space. They therefore have recourse to other identifiers, among which religion has a crucial importance. Pakistanis already see a close correlation between religion (Islam) and nation (Pakistan), religion being the official *raison d'être* of their (former) nation.

Nation and ethnicity

This analysis should not, however, hide the national and ethnic aspects of identity. For instance, we saw how there was a difference between the first immigration wave from Bangladesh, which was more marked by nationalist ideology, and the second wave, more marked by religious feeling. These two tendencies are not mutually exclusive, and attachment to the Bangladeshi heritage remains important, both to the political manifestation (the nation) and to the cultural manifestation (the language). Bangladeshis have chosen to establish separate organizations from Hindu Bengalis and yet they have not chosen to draw markedly closer to other South Asian Muslims.

As for Pakistanis, their relationship to religious feeling is in reverse order of significance to their immigration waves. Those who played a crucial role in setting up religious institutions in the United States, as we have seen, were immigrants in the 1960s and 1970s, at a time when fundamentalist parties, and especially the Jama'at-i-Islami, had a higher profile than they now have. Pakistani students who emigrated at that time were the bearers of this ideology. Pakistan is now much bruised by ethnic conflict and the people are weary of seeing their political leaders hiding behind religion in order to draw attention away from the difficulties the country is facing. The Jama'at-i-Islami is marking time in its political life. The more recent immigrants from Pakistan, on the other hand, have a more intense interest in their national identity, if not in their ethnic identity. They see their Pakistani origins as their principal identification, and religion is taking a back seat (as is demonstrated by the fact that they say of themselves that they are first and foremost Pakistanis). True, any recent immigrant, especially those who are from the majority group in their former homeland, see that country as a central element of their self-definition.

Bangladeshi immigrants in their behaviour would suggest the opposite thesis, but Pakistani immigrants would tend to support it. Michel Oriol has written:

> One cannot address the culture of immigrants without referring in theory and in practice to the way in which identities, historically established in the original country, continue to evolve.[12]

I was unfortunately not able to meet many Pakistanis who had only recently arrived in the United States. They are often among the most disadvantaged, economically speaking, and they tend to stay away from members of the host society and also from their own community, which stigmatizes them and accuses them of being a burden and of undermining their good image. Therefore I have had to make do with hypotheses in this area. Further research on this population at a later date will enable me to confirm or reject these hypotheses. It will also be illuminating to study the changing nature of the group's identity, since it could happen that over time religious feeling will move into the ascendant over ethnic or national feeling as a means of identification.

To return to the link between nation and migration, the case of Kashmiris is also interesting. As their stay in the United States grows longer, Kashmiris seem to become more fiercely in favour of independence, and more hostile towards India. On the other hand, the most recent Kashmiri immigrants, who, though they have sometimes been themselves (or their family have been) victims of the actions of the Indian army, tend to relativize the issue and are not as hostile to India as their peers of the earlier immigration wave.

The same phenomenon can be observed in the mutual feelings of Pakistanis and Indians (especially Hindus). A longer period as immigrants does not seem to make them more able to relativize conflicts, but rather to coincide with exacerbated nostalgic sentiment, provoking a return to the more fiercely negative image of the 'Other' (which in this context is not the host society but the (former) *frère-ennemi*). The longest-established immigrants were admittedly those who lived through Partition, but this in itself is not a sufficient explanation: the dialectic between nation and migration is also present. There is an apparent paradox here between this observation and the hypothesis advanced above that among recent Pakistani immigrants national feeling was stronger than religious identity. But in fact the more established immigrants, by flagging up their Muslim identity rather than their identity as Pakistanis may stress on what distinguishes them from the host society but at the same time they are proclaiming what differentiated them for so long from the 'Other', legitimizing hence the very creation of their former homeland. Since the relationship between communities is seen through the prism of religion, the Indian in this context is (necessarily) perceived as the Hindu.

This dynamic is also to be found in the relationship of some Indian Muslims to Hindus in the United States but not necessarily in their relation to India. This brings us back to the concept of double minority which we first examined in the Introduction. The issue is to evaluate the impact on Indian Muslims that having been a minority in the former homeland has on the construction of identity and on the success of integration into the host society. Indian Muslims I interviewed on the whole felt that the experience of coming from a minority was an asset in adapting to a non-Muslim society, while yet being able to preserve their identity. As they come from a country where attitudes to religion are very similar to those in their host country, Indian Muslims even feel that they are at an advantage over other Muslims (especially those from Pakistan and from Arab countries) in that they have experience in negotiating the practicalities of integration and in preserving their ethnic and religious heritage. Their minority status in India, as we have seen, was not a major reason for emigration, but it explains why they do not feel the power of the 'myth of return'. It would be going too far to draw a parallel with the Armenians in France, for whom being a stateless people has been a justification of the impulse to become assimilated,[13] (Indian Muslims are not stateless), but there is a similarity between the Armenians and the Indian Muslims who, more than other South Asians, feel that their survival is strongly dependent on their ability to become integrated into the host society.[14] It would be wrong, though, to lay too great an emphasis on the desire of Indian Muslims to become totally assimilated – like other South Asian communities, they are keen to maintain their ethnic and religious traditions.

Some have in fact tended to reproduce in the United States behaviour of withdrawal adopted in India, isolating themselves, especially 'morally', from the host society. In India and now in America, these individuals behave as if they were closing their eyes to the fact that they are members of a minority, and paradoxically develop the feeling of belonging to the majority, not by attempting to become assimilated, but by convincing themselves of their moral superiority. This attitude is often a reaction to the phobia created when it seems their offspring might become too much absorbed by American culture.

The issue of double minority raises other questions as well as those of integration and the safeguard of ethnic and religious traditions: on the one hand immigrants can compare their situation in India with that in the United States, and on the other there is the relationship with India itself.

Some immigrants see little importance in this idea of double minority, or they take it to mean something else: these are people who did not have the sense of being in a minority before they left India, or maybe only felt that this was true in the area of religion. They then see the concept as describing them in the American context, were they are in the minority both as an ethnic group and as a religious group. Others, on the contrary, feeling little affection for India, are critical of the way minorities are treated there, when they compare the complete religious freedom they feel they enjoy in the United States. The more pessimistic compare themselves to the stateless, who are a minority anywhere and cannot boast of any homeland (or of a 'mythical elsewhere'[15]) when they are threatened with aggression to the person or to their identity.

In terms of the more direct relationship with India, emigration tends in some people to exacerbate their community loyalty (this applies also to those who did not feel they were in the minority before they left India), in that they have a heightened sense of the difficulties their fellow Muslims are facing in India. For most, this goes no further than a sentimental reaction, but for a few this leads them to mobilize their efforts in their new country and together to denounce any infringement of the rights of Muslims in India. In a more positive sense, the community also tries to provide relief for the economic and social position of Muslims in India (for example, by sending funds to develop education).

In closing this section, let us remember that the concept of identity is a fluid one, dependent on context, multi-faceted and also relative.[16] Indian Muslims, like other South Asian Muslims, and indeed like any other human being, are many-sided in their identity, and the person they are talking to, and the circumstances, are factors in which side is foremost at any given time. In the United States, the ethnic and religious side of their identity will be emphasized, and according to circumstances either the ethnic or the religious aspect will be dominant. On visiting their former homeland, they will adopt a more American identity. To paraphrase Jean-François Bayart,[17] in the United States someone from Aligarh will describe himself as an 'Aligarhwalla'[18] when talking to a 'Lucknowwalla', as a 'UP-walla'[19] when talking to a Gujarati, as an Indian when talking to a Pakistani, as a Muslim when talking to a Hindu, as a South Asian when talking to a Chinese,[20] as an Asian when talking to a Hispanic,[21] as a coloured minority when talking to a White, as a White when talking to a Black,[22] as a Sunni when talking to a Shi'a, as a parent when talking to his child,[23] as a doctor when talking to his patient . . .[24]

Is Islam transformed by immigration?

As we have seen, South Asian Muslims attach great importance to the perpetuation of their religious heritage. What happens here, however, is not a mere transplantation. There are a number of indicators to show that new characteristics are born, both in individual practice and in the collective exercise of religion. The role of the various agents (in the widest sense, meaning here both people and places) also appears to change.

The basic precepts (the Five Pillars of Islam) are unchanged in their application on the whole, though here and there minor adjustments or modifications unavoidable at any rate in a non-Muslim country, are made owing to the process of migration. The Ramadan fast, which has a social dimension, is still the most widely respected ritual, as elsewhere in the world. *Zakat* is an opportunity for a community which has generally experienced remarkable economic prosperity to express its gratitude to God. Donations are made not only to the needy in the community, but also to secular and Christian charitable organizations in the United States, a sign that the Muslim immigrants wish to be fully involved in their new country. This is shown also by the increasing number of Muslims wanting to be buried in the United States. The canonical pilgrimage is being accomplished at a younger and younger age, and the advantages offered to pilgrims by specialized agencies rather look like the special offers of classic travel agents.

Festivals are celebrated, if not in an Americanized way, then at least in a way that has adapted to the immigrant situation. The Id and/or *Maulid*, depending on families, tend to be celebrated in a way that is reminiscent of Christmas, with gifts handed out to children. USA Muslims Day, between Hanukkah and Christmas, is a new festival which has been introduced, as a way of making a mark on the American calendar. Add to this the Muslim World Day Parade, which is an opportunity for Muslims to celebrate their specificity, and also to demonstrate their identity as one 'ethnic' group (we shall return to this point) among others.

At a more fundamental level, emigration to the United States has changed the traditional roles of women and of the mosque. In the subcontinent, the involvement of women in religious life rarely went over the threshold of the home, but women in diaspora are now involved in the life of the mosque: they go there for prayers on a Friday (though less than do Arab or African–American women), they take part in Sunday conferences, giving even speeches, either to mixed audiences or to women only, depending on the liberality of the mosque management board. In some mosques, they are included on the board of management. Women who wear the veil, so the more 'Islamized', are also included in this autonomization process, in that wearing the *hijab* is seen as a deliberate act, an expression of militant religion and is also a vehicle enabling women to legitimize their presence in the public sphere.

Mosques are also changing, in that they have made considerable borrowings from churches and synagogues, both in role and in their running. They have become social meeting places, offering alternative and secure space of socialization to expatriates in search for bearings, through the strengthening of social relationships and the reinforcement of religious traditions. They are a place for immigrants to express their frustrations, their disappointment, their fears, but also their hopes, their expectations (all this either in confidence to the imam, or alternatively in the weekly meetings organized in most mosques). The imitation of churches and synagogues is also evident in the laying on of services on Sundays (prayers, sermons, meetings) and of Sunday schools, in the running of summer camps by the mosques, in the celebration of weddings within the mosques, in the committees providing aid (social, psychological or even financial help) to the faithful, and so on.

This change in the role of the mosque is mirrored in the change of role of the imam. He does not simply lead prayers, but in many ways models his work on that of priests, pastors and rabbis. His new roles include administrator, marriage guidance counsellor and public relations officer for the community. Haddad and Lummis also note that the imam is elected by members of the mosque and can be sacked by them, another symbol of the new freedom enjoyed by Muslims in diaspora.[25]

Another measure of the Americanization of Islam is the increasing use of gadgets and advanced technology by zealots: stickers, mugs, car registration plates all proclaiming 'I love Islam', CD-ROM transcriptions of the Qur'an, strip cartoons glorifying Islam, imams walking around their mosques clutching their mobile phones, and so on.

This gadgetization (which is coupled with merchandizing) is an element of the proselytizing efforts of Muslims, who are adopting American methods and idioms (or what they perceive to be such) to present the faith. One of the ICNA brochures, for example, is entitled *You Must Know This Man Muhammad*. The United States, where several ethnic minorities are relegated to the bottom of the social scale, are a particularly fertile ground for proselytization, Muslim or otherwise.

These signs of Americanization are in truth merely external and instrumental. Do they, however, conceal a change in Islam at a deeper level?

The answer seems to be in the affirmative, even if the process is still only in its infancy. Muslims in the United States confronted with a diversity equalled only at the Mecca pilgrimage, see the legitimacy of their customs called into question, when other Muslims maintain that their different customs are equally Islamic. The first generation have kept a 'traditional' view of their faith (maintaining the practice they followed in their former homeland), but a handful of immigrants are wondering whether there is a need for a reformulation of religion. The great diversity within the community is seen by some as an obstacle to cohesion and efforts are being made to homogenize the religion. There are no signs so far of a homogenized Islam but a few straws in the wind, though as yet only symbolic, suggest that a kind of standardization might be on the way. We noted the replacing of the Persian words traditionally used in South Asia with Arabic terms for any word with strong religious connotations (*Khuda Hafiz* becomes *Assalamu'alaikum*, *namaz* is replaced by *salah* or *salat*). Some immigrants acknowledge that this change has happened because they were influenced by those around them, but others claim to have made a deliberate choice, saying that only Arabic has a religious legitimacy. Some words with religious connotations are also being pronounced with an Arabic accent. This phenomenon can be especially observed among the second generation (the more observant of them only). So young South Asians are heard pronouncing words like *alhamduliliah* or *subhanallah* with as Arabic an accent as they can manage, often with an American intonation. Most South Asian children, it should be said, learn Arabic as if it were a dead language, the language of the canonical texts (like Catholic children studying Latin in their catechism classes). Only a small minority of particularly committed young people, those who are involved in Islamic movements, learn to speak Arabic as a living language.

We have noted on a number of occasions that Arabic is growing in importance, and taking over from Urdu – although Urdu has been for long the language of Islamic culture in the subcontinent – both in sermons and in religious education. Even English is preferred to Urdu: it is not only a language that most will use in everyday life, it also has the cachet of universality. Urdu meanwhile is seen as the language only of one particular culture, and now out of step with the expectations of immigrants from different backgrounds and with young people to whom it may no longer be a familiar language. In British mosques, the use of Urdu or Arabic is a matter of debate, even on occasion of conflict,[26] but in the United States the matter has not been an issue for many years (except in the Barelwi mosques, a very small minority, where the sermon is still preached in Urdu).

Another sign of nascent homogenization is clothing. This is mainly true of the more militant among the Muslim community, who see the external signal given by clothing as a remarkable way of advertising their otherness. The obvious example here is the veil worn by women. Some, even of the first generation, choose to wear the *hijab* rather than the more South Asian *dupatta*, which they perceive as more cultural, or the *burqa*, which they perceive as too traditional and impractical. The second generation especially, though, are becoming more homogeneous: the *hijab*, worn above a pair of jeans or a long skirt, and trainers, is becoming the 'uniform' of young women who want to question the values of modernity (here in the sense of 'Americanization') which they see as having destructuring effects on identity systems, and their response to this is both existential and prescriptive. But a paradox here should be underlined: in order to combat the uniformization process of modern societies, these girls are standardizing their physical appearance based on a reconstructed model (*hijab* instead of *dupatta*), a reconstruction born of and into the diaspora context.

These signs of homogenization, given through clothing and through language, fit the pattern of (neo)-fundamentalist movements.[27] In countries which are either Muslim or have large Muslim minorities, these movements promote the elimination of cultural aggregates, which are seen as innovative (*bid'at*) and/or as creating divisions between believers.[28] It should be kept in mind that it is the sympathizers and committed members of the Jama'at-i-Islami who have been very involved in setting up the religious infrastructure in the United States. This seeking after standardization is not only seen among (neo)-fundamentalists, however. Other religious leaders of a more modernist character encourage their faithful to challenge ethnic and cultural idiosyncrasies. The unity that this will enable will be a necessary requisite if they are to carry force when standing their ground in American society.

Admittedly, calls by the leadership to abandon the cultural baggage of religion has little impact on the majority of South Asians: they see religion as an essential element of their identity, but they also place a high value on their cultural heritage. There is, however, a growing trend among families to abandon the *Fatiha* tradition (which is seen as a *religious* tradition in the subcontinent, but it is defined by both the fundamentalists and the modernists as *cultural*) and the rituals associated with the veneration of saints, so that their religious practice is simpler. The American context favours this move: there are very few sanctuaries, so patterns of religious behaviour from the subcontinent cannot easily be reproduced. The higher educational level of immigrants is also a factor here. According to Van der Veer, ritual is 'a form of communication through which a person discovers his identity and the significance of his actions'.[29] In the United States, identity is defined through confrontation with others, which includes not only non-Muslims, but also other Muslims from different traditions. This would tend to explain why ritual is becoming more dogmatic, more text-based, since the sacred Text is the ultimate frame of reference for all believers, and can unite them from all cultural backgrounds. 'Identity implies the elimination and rejection, even if only temporarily, of anything which might divide. It imposes a common uniting core, or maybe several, and apart from these any other experiences must be seen as secondary,' wrote Denis-Constant Martin.[30] The defining common core here is religion.

We should note that the process of homogenization is not a systematic one. It can operate almost spontaneously or automatically, witness the decreasing importance of the Islamic schools of jurisprudence. In New York, as we saw, only the Barelwi mosque made an issue of belonging to the Hanafi school, whereas all the other mosques we examined were happy to welcome Muslims of diverse allegiance. The Indian Muslim scholar Shah Waliullah (1702–63) advocated that the schools of jurisprudence should become unified – it seems that the diaspora is bringing this about in the United States, although for now the 'new' school of jurisprudence is as yet ill defined.

These efforts at homogenization, whatever their real impact on the community, are in dialectic with the ethnicization of religion which is evidenced through the various ways in which Islam is working to make its mark on the host society: the Muslim World Day Parade, Islamic Awareness Week, even the efforts of Muslims to set themselves up as a political lobby, all these demonstrate this. The ethnicization of religion meets the need to standardize Islam, but it is also in keeping with the perception of the host society, which by seeing members of a religious group as one homogenous whole, tends to create a distinct category.[32] 'They [the host society] describe us . . . They have the power of description, and we succumb to the pictures they construct,' says Saladin Chamcha, the main character of the *Satanic Verses*.[33] This process of ethnicization happens on an individual level as well as within the social context. In the American context, although the concept of secularism is fluid and religion is important, in fact only ethnicity is officially recognized in the political process: pressure groups, census classifications, and even the Manhattan parades are all governed by ethnicity.

Attempts at 'ecumenism' can be observed in other minorities, in the United States or elsewhere, living in diaspora. Hindus, for instance, living in the United Kingdom or in North America, work at overcoming their regional diversity and to homogenize their different traditions into one that can be shared by all members of the population. The idea of a 'Hindu' temple, when in fact Hindus are divided into castes and sects, and pray to chosen specific deities, is an artefact of diaspora.[34] This phenomenon is characteristic of the symbolic construction that happens in the shaping of any community.

To finish this analysis of the specific characteristics of Islam in America, we shall examine the transformation of meaning undergone by three fundamental concepts of Islam: *hijrah*, *da'wah*, and *jihad*.

As we have seen, *hijrah* is a theoretical option for Muslims living as a minority when they feel their religious life is restricted. Another alternative is *jihad* (to which we shall return). For Pakistanis and Bangladeshis, emigration has been a reversal of *hijrah* (from a Muslim to a non-Muslim country). This does not raise major theological problems: most immigrants moved to the United States to improve their standard of living, and they do not even think about the issue. The minority who do give thought to the matter draw attention to the freedom enjoyed by Muslims in the United States, and to the tremendous opportunities for proselytization. For Indian Muslims, there is no theological problem, since they were already in a minority before emigration. They do however give thought to the matter, but in relation to the situation they have left behind: was emigration the right way to deal with the problems faced by Muslims in India? Recent articles in *The Message International*, in reaction to a *fatwa* from an Indian mullah forbidding his community to emigrate, revealed a variety of opinions.

One invoked the official protection of religious rights in the Indian Union, which *de facto* excludes *jihad* as an option. In the face of oppression, migration is then the only option available.[35] Indian Muslims can in this way justify their presence in the United States. The other article, published a little later, was critical of the first and supported the mullah. The writer reminded the readers that the most highly educated of the population are the most likely to emigrate. The Muslim minority had already lost its elite during Partition, leaving it leaderless, and this scenario was in danger of being repeated, when in the current situation it is precisely a strong leadership that is needed.[36] It appears that the concept of *hijrah* is a continuing topic of debate, whether theological or political, given that migration is a constant element of Muslim history.

In the United States, as in any country where Muslims are a minority, *hijrah* also has a second aspect, to which we referred in the Introduction: the idea of a withdrawing, either spiritually or physically, from society, into a community made up only of Muslims living according to the faith.[37] Various words have been forged to describe this phenomenon in Europe and in India, which point to earlier (in India for example) and contemporary (in Europe since the immigration of significant numbers of Muslims, and in contemporary India) experience: 'interior *hijrah*',[38] 'micro-*umma*',[39] 'utopian Medinas',[40] 'little Medinas', 'inverse ottoman *millat*'[41] and so on. The American situation suggests that if there is a *hijrah*, its most likely forum for this type of community space is the mosque, and not only those mosques whose leaders advocate isolationism, but also those which encourage Muslim immigrants to be integrated into American society. The role of the mosque as an alternative social space, as we have seen, is an element here. In fact, only a tiny proportion of South Asian Muslims have opted for a 'micro-society' form of existence, the vast majority are actively engaged in becoming integrated and accepted into American society. Even members of the Tablighi Jama'at, in some ways the supreme example of a withdrawn community, are only partially able to retreat, since their compulsion to practice *da'wa*, the other principal defining characteristic of the group, demands that they make contact with the *kafir*. Admittedly, missionaries from this movement tend to concentrate their efforts on members of the Muslim community (in an effort to bring back straying sheep).

Attempts in the United States to create little Medinas are reminiscent of the work done by Muslims in Europe, though the matter has a higher profile in Europe, where the conditions of integration for Muslims are different.

Nadine Weibel divides Muslims in Europe into two distinct categories. The first, which is in the majority, are those who advocate a 'cultural' Islam, kept within the boundaries of the individual or the family, and which is conciliating to the host society.[42] Those in the second category advocate an 'active' Islam, which affirms its faith by proclaiming it: 'Islam exhorts the believer to remember Allah in all circumstances, so everyday life is sacralized, in that the sacred is found in all things, to the point of obsession.'[43] As is the case in Europe, most Muslims in the United States belong to the first category, advocating a cultural Islam, while a minority are in the second category, professing an active Islam (the Tablighi Jama'at, the Salafi, the ICNA) and in effect they sacralize their everyday life. Although the dividing line between all these categories is porous, an intermediate category seems to be however emerging in the United States. It includes those Muslims for whom Islam is of first importance, and yet they do not display obsessive behaviour relating to the sacralization of everyday events. This category openly claims its Islam-ness, and does not see it as a barrier to dynamic participation in the host society. It includes those who are keen to make their mark in America within the existing democratic and secular structures (in which religion is kept within the private sphere). The ultimate outcome is the setting up of a political lobby, despite the implication that religion is thereby ethnicized. The ICLI leadership, for example, would fall in this category: it includes Muslims who can aspire to be legitimate leaders (in the eyes both of their own community and of the host society) of the Muslim community in the United States.

The second alternative available to Muslims in minority is *jihad*. As we have seen, this carries two meanings: firstly, an effort within oneself to reach a particular goal, and secondly, a holy war. Holy war does not seem to be credible on American soil. The [1993] attack on the World Trade Center made this kind of claim, but it was almost unanimously condemned by Muslim immigrants. *Jihad* in its first sense has more meaning in this context, in particular with reference to immigrants. Immigration carries a theoretical threat to Islamic identity, so a Muslim immigrant in a minority community has to accomplish *jihad*, a personal effort to remain faithful to Islamic precepts. This sense of *jihad* is of significance to most South Asian Muslims (even if they have not necessarily thought about the issue in these terms).

For a small minority of active members of mosques and organizations, since the issue of winning over the host state is irrelevant in diaspora, *jihad* has given place to *da'wa*, which has an important role in these institutions. This is true not only of the Ahmadiyya (their doctrine is opposed to the principle itself of holy war) and the Tablighi Jama'at (for whom proselytizing has always been a core activity) but also of progressive mosques like the ICLI, and for the ICNA. The Jama'at-i-Islami has followed this path in most western countries, and in India.[44] Should we therefore conclude, together with Marc Gaborieau and Christian Troll, that *da'wa* has become the *jihad* of Muslim activists in countries where Muslims are a minority?[45] In the American context this would seem to be so. It remains to be seen whether this *jihad*, which is the new *da'wa*, conceals political objectives. It is too soon to know. From my observations of various

Muslim organizations in New York, the main objective of activists for the moment is to ensure that Muslim immigrants and their offspring are kept safe within Islam. There is, however, a very small minority, which, fed by its conviction of the superiority of Muslim values, does dream of a Muslim America.

Is there then an incompatibility between Islam and the integration of Muslims into the United States? In other words, does Islam hamper integration? In order to answer this question, we shall not examine reasons within Islam which could weigh heavily on one side or the other. Rather, we shall try to evaluate the aptitude to integrate shown by the population groups we are examining, looking at the current situation of Muslims in the United States and the role played in that by their religious institutions.

The analysis of socio-economic data led us to the conclusion that South Asian Muslims have structurally integrated into American society, unlike Muslims in Europe. Immigrant Muslims want at the same time to maintain and perpetuate their ethnic and religious traditions, just like other ethnic groups in the United States, and in particular in New York. An essential element in this is the tolerant attitude of Americans (in spite of prejudice against Islam and Muslims, which is just as strong in the United States as in Europe), as it reduces the risk of isolation. As Denis Lacorne has noted, there has not yet been a 'scarf affair' in the United States.[46] Muslims are therefore able to practise their religion openly on the whole, despite a few practical difficulties. Islam has a role in providing structure and stability, and in this it does the same as other religions (Catholicism, Judaism and more recently Hinduism, for example), giving encouragement to immigrants as they seek to become involved in American society. As Olivier Roy has emphasized, 'religion provides a transverse identity which does not contradict other allegiances and allows the use of a different set of codes.'[47]

When we look at religious institutions, the very fact that they have been built is an expression of the desire to settle and become a part of the American scene. Most leaders, especially in the mosques, are agencies of integration: in their sermons and weekly meetings they encourage the faithful to respect the laws of the host society, and especially the secular principles (while at the same time urging them to maintain their religious heritage), and not to stray outside the boundaries defined by the State. These leaders use English (which they prefer to the vernacular, and even to Arabic) which further reinforces the message. In Europe, there is often a problem in defining the degree of autonomy of religious institutions from their original home country,[48] but this is a less acute issue in the United States. It is true that in most cases imams are still 'imported', and some institutions are still funded by external agencies (not necessarily in the home country of the community, since the Gulf countries play an important part here). Many mosques, however, are doing their best to become autonomous, especially financially. The relative wealth of South Asian immigrants is an asset here.

The leadership in a number of mosques is attempting to change the focus of their immigrant congregations. Traditionally, they have been much concerned with political and religious developments in their former homeland, and with the position of Muslims worldwide, and the hope is to engage their interest in more local issues. This does not mean ignoring the life of Muslims internationally, but the leaders are most concerned to help Muslims in the United States to become integrated, both by adapting to the requirements of the local society and by taking a full part in the life of the host country, which together will enable them to make their mark on American society. Jews are considered a model in this respect: they are 'strongly attached to their ethnic and cultural traditions', and they 'have successfully integrated without losing their identity,'[49] and they have a significant impact on American society.

We should note here the particular case of the sectarian minorities, such as the Nizarian and the Ahmadiyya: these two groups are still linked to leaderships outside the United States. These external leaderships, however, have always encouraged immigrants to integrate, though they also ask them to safeguard their particular religious (but not ethnic) ways of life. The Bohra, on the other hand, might seize the opportunity offered in diaspora to take a step away from an authoritarian leadership.

To end this section on integration, an apparent paradox: in some sense, the more immigrants display an increased level of religious observance, the more they seem to want to declare themselves Americans. I felt that the more religious of those I spoke to were perhaps more keen to proclaim their American identity (even if it took second place to their Islamic identity) than those who were still very attached to their ethnic and cultural heritage. The former have a feeling of gratitude towards the country which has given them a freedom they would not easily find elsewhere; they have little attachment to the 'myth of return'; they experience little homesickness for their former homeland (even Pakistanis and Bangladeshis), in fact they are critical of the 'home' version of Islam, which they see as too much bound up in local culture. 'Sitara', who prays at her place of work, says:

> My Pakistani identity is just that I wear the *shalwar kameez*, and I eat Pakistani food. Otherwise, I feel more American than Pakistani. I try to be as sensible as possible and not get all emotional like other Pakistanis . . . I went to Disneyworld in Florida, dressed as a Muslim (*sic*), and I had a good time. I am an American Muslim, and proud to be so. It's a feeling that makes me very happy.

These rather euphoric sentiments are more noticeable among women, and this is probably due to the greater freedom they enjoy in their new country, a freedom they would not easily achieve in the former homeland.

Islam is therefore a ground for pride rather than embarrassment, a determining characteristic rather than a place to hide and, for the first generation, a help to integration – in contrast, in Europe, this stage of immigration is a life lived at a basic level, in silence and almost in shame.[50]

For young people, the issue is not so much one of integration as of preservation of cultural heritage. Identification with Islam is an important part of this process, even if it implies a redefinition of religion, a phenomenon which is also experienced by their peers in Europe, incidentally. This redefinition meets for them two major needs: they wish to distance themselves from the quietist devotional lives their parents lead, and they feel the need to rationalize their religion. For some, this can lead to scepticism but others develop a need for greater spirituality and for a more universal version of the religion[51] which would transcend their parents' dogmatism (the parents value the security of respecting set rules) and their attachment to ethnic identifiers. However, there are as yet no major mystical groups emerging in the United States, so it has so far been a woolly desire. A third category can also be detected, which tends towards (neo)-fundamentalism: it is not devoid of rationalism, but is more inclined to a militant approach to religion.

These categories have in common that they engender an individualization of the relationship to religion, even though Islam is an eminently 'community' religion.[52] Young people are picking and choosing elements from Islam to help them in their quest for meaning and personal harmony. Religion has become an ethical reference point and practical observance has become less significant as a result. Jocelyne Cesari has analysed this phenomenon in Europe, and she underlines the 'secularized usage of religion'.[53] Other young people, the more militant ones, aspire to a strict Islamic way of life, in rigid submission to its doctrines. In study groups, they read the sacred texts in the light of their needs and pay very little heed to the teaching of the traditional religious authorities (whose usefulness to them is limited to teaching them Arabic, and in particular the pronunciation of literary Arabic). The reconstruction of religion in these various ways, symptomatic of modernity is one that can be seen across continents, and young Muslims in the United States have much in common with young Muslims in Europe especially.[54] There are, however, differences in their social and economic situations, and young South Asians particularly have high levels of education. They are therefore also close in their experiences to neo-orthodox Jews (and Christians), as described by Régine Azria, who recruit among the middle classes educated and qualified young people who have been disappointed by 'the failure of secular ideologies and are in search of new ideals'.[55] These young Jews are well integrated into society and active in 'matters in the city'.[56] There is among young Muslims in the United States a similar aspiration and indeed it is becoming a reality.

These new ways of being religious practised by young people can cause alarm among their community leaders, especially the older ones. Maulana Naseem, the imam at the ICNA, makes the following remark about 'American Islam':

> That ['American Islam'] is an unfortunate expression. There is a renewal in religion, but it sometimes comes in funny ways. One young man came to see me to ask how to become a *shaikh* [meaning here a scholar, a doctor of religion]. He had chosen to ignore all forms of *tafsir* [an exegesis, a commentary on the Qur'an], and had drawn up his own *tafsir*.

The United States can appear to immigrants as a country favourable to the establishment of a united *umma*. The path to a utopic pan-Islamism, however, is strewn with obstacles, of which the most significant are the ethnic divisions. Religion plays a crucial role in the construction of identity, but it cannot erase cultural allegiances to such an extent that an American Islam will be established. The first generation has, however, made some initial moves towards such a form of Islam. The following generations, as cultural differences gradually recede, will help an American Islam to come to birth, even if pan-Islam is not yet possible. Members of the first generation, aware that they are hampered by prejudice, are full of admiration for the way in which the second generation are able to transcend social and ethnic barriers, and they look to them to bring about the realization of the dream of a united *umma*.

American Muslims and Islamic renewal

The privileged position of Muslims in the United States begs the question of whether they will be able to play a part in the 'modernization' of Islam.

By modernization, I mean a rational understanding of Islam which would, in the light of the Qur'an, encompass contemporary mutations and the new situations which are challenging Muslim populations.[57] In other words, an understanding of Islam that would be able to combat the ideological and social stagnation that seem to characterize the Muslim religion at the present time.

Comparing the state of Islam in the nineteenth century and the twentieth century, Jo Maïla wrote:

> In the [nineteenth] century, there was a terrific renewal of critical
> thought . . . and yet [twentieth] century Islam is strained, tense, and
> curled in on itself, anxious only to justify itself.[58]

The present immobility can obscure the fact that not long ago there were attempts to reform Islam: in the nineteenth century, under the influence of Jamal al-Din al-Afghani and of Muhammad 'Abduh, reformers advocated *tajdid* (renewal), a return to the canonical scriptures, and a parallel reform of interpretation, through a revival of *ijtihad* (abandoned some 900 years earlier).[59] Muhammad 'Abduh advised in particular that the university of Al-Azhar (a famous institution, more than a thousand years old) should be reformed, introducing modern sciences and rationalism, and abandoning the technique of learning by heart. This impulse had started even earlier in the subcontinent, where scholars such as Sayyid Ahmad Khan campaigned that a more rational approach to religion should be adopted, without losing sight of the fundamental tenets of the faith.

In the twentieth century, on the other hand (or at least the second half of it[60]), Islam has been plunged into lethargy, and Muslims feel disorientated between on the one hand the dogmatism of the *'ulama*, and on the other hand the fanaticism of the fundamentalists, in which the rapprochement between these two sides[61] is a further source of confusion.

Many Muslims in the United States are aware of this dilemma and they are looking at the need for Islamic revival. They know they are well equipped for this task: the community has the highest concentration of graduate Muslims in the world. Economically, they are probably second only to the Arab states in the Gulf. They enjoy a level of freedom which, in conjunction with the above two assets, has enabled them to establish independent Islamic institutions.

Debates in a number of organizations and Islamic magazines still focus on the preservation of religious identity but they also engage with other issues, such as the relationship between Islam and democracy, Islam and secularism, the status of women in Islam (this subject is often the preserve of women themselves) – and thus show that they do take interest in sensitive issues. The professional activities undertaken by a number of these women, especially South Asian women, have given them an independence which enables them to participate on an equal (or nearly) footing with men in meetings in the more progressive mosques. Muslims are not abandoning the Islamic mould, however, as these discussions are legitimized (whether consciously or not) by the religious legacy: *ijtihad*, although not officially available, is nevertheless an essential tool for any individual facing new or unique circumstances. As Nimat Barazangi has remarked, Islam judges believers on their individual actions, and by so doing leaves them a fairly generous room for manoeuvre in reshaping their 'Islam-ness'.[62]

The diversity of Muslims in the United States is seen by some as a synonym for division and therefore as a barrier to internal cohesion, and yet others (they are still a small minority) see this plurality as an asset in the attempt to democratize religion. The latter would rather see a network of mutual support than the establishment of a utopian and all-encompassing pan-Islamism. They fear that to use Islam as a force for homogenization might bring about a new form of acculturation.

Veiled discrimination is still complained of by many Muslims. This can lead to tension, and therefore make the community withdraw into itself. To counteract this, a few people are trying to enter the public arena and combat the prejudices of the host society.

It may be an illusion to think that Muslims can transform American society (and yet that is a central tenet for the proselytes) but it is not unrealistic to hope for a modernization of Islam. Muslims are on the right lines here: they are aware of their many assets, and hope to be a model community for Muslims worldwide.[63] One man in the United States has already attempted to begin modernizing Islam.[64] He is the Pakistani intellectual Fazlur Rahman (1919–88), who taught Islamic thought at the University of Chicago from 1969 until he died. In one of his key works, *Islam and Modernity*,[65] Rahman criticized medieval scholars for their unbending and static interpretation of the Qur'an and the Hadis, and this criticism could apply today as well. He recommends that Muslims re-evaluate the Qur'an, not as a set of rigid laws, but as an ethical and moral framework, able to equip them for the new realities.[66] We have yet to see whether Rahman's baton will be picked up in the United States.

Alain Dieckhoff has said that the *aggiornamento* of Islam will come about on the banks of the Seine and the Thames. One might be tempted to add 'or on the banks of the Hudson River'.

AFTERWORD[1] (FEBRUARY 2002)

The attacks on 11 September 2001 in New York and Washington, carried out by members of an Islamic network, killed several thousand people and plunged the American population into terror. They also thrust Islam, and Muslims living in the United States, into the limelight.

It is as yet too early to know whether these events will drastically change the position of Muslims in American society as it has been described in this book, or even to measure the impact on the Muslim community. It is possible, however, to look at the attacks made on Muslims since 11 September, and the immediate reactions both of the host society and the Muslim community.

The immediate shockwave

When the first plane crashed into the World Trade Center (WTC), Muslims, like all Americans and the rest of the world, thought at first that there had been an accident. When the second plane hit the second twin tower, Muslims, like everyone else, realized that this was a terrorist attack. They nearly all say that they then prayed to God, 'Allah, please may it not be Muslims!' In the first few days after the attacks, Muslims in the United States were thrown into a state of panic. Even before the involvement of their co-religionists was confirmed, they knew that they would be the target of angry Americans, just like when the WTC was attacked for the first time in 1993, or just like when the Oklahoma bombing happened in 1995, and the Muslims were immediately blamed, though in that case the accusation was wrong. The people I spoke to remember the first few hours after the attack. They were astounded and saddened by the catastrophe, but also fearful of possible reprisals by the American population. Many stayed at home that day, and the following days. Women who wear the veil were particularly careful to stay out of the public eye; some even stopped wearing the veil, at least for a few days, or maybe even a few weeks.

Panic spread not only among Muslims but also among those who might be taken for Muslims: Arab Christians, South Asian Hindus, Sikhs, especially as one of their number was assassinated in Arizona, and Hispanics. A fact worth noting is that Hindus (Sikhs are a particular case) felt just as insecure and fearful as South Asian Muslims. We shall come back to this.

At any rate, several hundred persons across the United States were assaulted either physically or verbally after the events on 11 September. Not surprisingly, the people most frequently targeted by these racist aggressions seem to have been those who – Muslim or not – wore distinctive religious signals, such as women wearing veils, or Sikhs wearing turbans. It is a strange paradox, perhaps, that these attacks happened less in New York than elsewhere. In Manhattan, the heart of the tragedy, the number of incidents was particularly low. One could not however help noticing that nearly all the ethnic restaurants and shops displayed the American flag, sometimes together with the motto (particularly appropriate to the circumstances) 'United We Stand' – a sign of solidarity no doubt, but also, it would appear, an attempt at protection from any potential attacker. Although there are no statistics to confirm this, yet according to many South Asians I spoke to, and from my own observations, it seems that the most cosmopolitan areas of New York, such as Manhattan itself, or where there is a high concentration of immigrants, such as Jackson Heights or Jamaica, were the areas which were least touched by this kind of racial violence. One young Indian woman, a Muslim who wears the veil, and a student at Columbia, told me that after 11 September she kept her veil on when in Manhattan, but took it off whenever she went to visit her parents in a Long Island residential suburb. When I went to a particularly 'ethnic' neighbourhood of Jamaica, where South Asians, Hispanics and African–Americans all live side by side, I was struck by the number of women wearing the veil or the *shalwar kameez*, by the Sikhs with their turbans and the Muslims with their long beards, all walking the streets, apparently not in any fear. The same was true of Jackson Heights, where none of the shopkeepers I talked with complained of any kind of violence – indeed some said, almost carelessly, that they felt quite safe in their very ethnic neighbourhood. An exception, however, to this pattern is the neighbourhood of Coney Island, in Brooklyn, where lives, as we have seen, a large Pakistani community. A man driving through in a car shot into three Pakistani restaurants, though without hurting anyone.

The number of recorded attacks varies officially from 800 to 1,200, depending on sources. These figures, however, are probably an underestimate, since a number of discriminatory acts were not reported to the police, nor to the civil rights protection organizations, nor even to Islamic organizations. The attacks came in different guises, ranging from physical aggression which could be lethal (at least two South Asians were assassinated– we have already mentioned the Sikh in Arizona– and a Pakistani man was murdered in Texas), to a glance laden with anger or even hate. Verbal acts of violence also: 'You did it!',

'Go back to your country!', and so on. In such a highly charged atmosphere as there was in the United States after 11 September, it was sometimes difficult to distinguish between real 'hate crimes' and what we might call 'ordinary' crimes. Muslims themselves (and South Asians) recognize that in the immediate wake of the dramatic events, they were not easily able to be objective about any rude remark or offensive look directed towards them. Others, however, were very critical of the American authorities if they did not follow up as racist (and therefore severely punishable) some of the attacks they and members of their community suffered. Two Pakistani journalists were physically attacked and a taxi driver had his car windows broken by a white man: the vice-consul of Pakistan in New York, when I interviewed him, told me of his regret that the police refused to register these as hate crimes.

At any rate, it would seem that physical and verbal attacks were on the whole less frequent than the magnitude of the events might have threatened. Muslims in the United States, nevertheless, remain traumatized.

American reactions

Apart from the kind of reaction I have just described, there is a detectable exacerbation, on both sides, of Muslims' and Americans' views of each other. To begin with, the host society seems to have exaggerated the stereotypes normally attached to Islam, which in any case did never enjoyed a particularly good image in the United States. All those who thought of Islam as a warrior, terrorist religion have had their views vindicated, and some have been tempted to instrumentalize the events of 11 September in order to feed a fear of Muslims and justify any repression of Muslims, as well as legitimate the war against terrorism. One young man, an Arab student of law at Columbia University, makes this comment:

> Everywhere in the press, in soaps, in films, Americans have been making dismissive and mocking remarks about Muslims and Arabs. If they said the same things about African–Americans, it would be seen as politically incorrect. But with Muslims, anything goes. After 11 September, it got worse, they use the vocabulary of Star Wars, the Empire of Evil, good versus evil, and so on.

Until now, the only Islam that was seen as a threat was far-away Islam, in Iran or the Middle East. Now the threat appears to be from inside, from the five or six million Muslims on American soil.

At any rate, prejudices have not necessarily changed, but they have become dramatically intensified. The target has also widened. Before, Arabs were the main victims of anti-Islamic stereotypes and the resulting discrimination. Now, any Muslims can be targets, whatever their ethnic or national origins. The situation of South Asians has changed. As we have seen, Pakistanis, Bangladeshis and Indian Muslims, before 11 September, were in a more comfortable position than Arabs in that they were often taken for Hindus, who have a good reputation in the United States. Now, however, this is no longer the case. Instead, it appears that all those who come from the subcontinent tend to be seen as Muslim, even Hindus and Sikhs. Discrimination (and especially violent discrimination) may therefore be aimed at any South Asian, regardless of their religion. Some Hispanics have also been targeted, insofar as they can easily be confused with South Asians. This has led to situations in which non-Muslims, feeling threatened, have had to cry out 'I'm not Muslim!' This has provoked some discussion in the South Asian community, especially among Sikhs, who are frequently the target of racial attacks and are often challenged by the police. Sikh civil rights organizations encourage their members to explain to any likely attacker, and to over-zealous police officers, or even to passengers who refuse to get on a plane while the 'turban man' is on board, the particular characteristics of their religion, without necessarily emphasizing that they are not Muslim (which would implicitly legitimize anti-Muslim discrimination).

Physical and verbal discrimination has now somewhat subsided, but Muslims still feel very vulnerable to indirect discrimination in the job market, the housing market, and so on. This situation is further aggravated by the current recession in the United States, which was itself made worse by the 11 September attacks. So when Muslims complain that they have been given notice because of their religion or their ethnic origin, employers can say, whether or not it is true, that the recession is to blame. Muslims are fearful of losing their jobs through discrimination, but they are even more fearful of failing to be taken on, and it is often more difficult to establish that discrimination is the reason. The economic slow-down, and other everyday impediments (such as the higher level of security at airports and on the roads, which lead to traffic jams and delays) are an irritation to Americans, who are consequently more likely to discriminate against Muslims, whom they hold responsible, at least in part, for the current tense and uncertain atmosphere in the United States.

The legal process is the forum where the exacerbation of American reactions is most clearly to be seen. The general anxiety in the country is being encouraged by the new laws which the government wishes to introduce. According to these laws, any foreigner suspected of terrorism would be brought before a military court, and as a result any proceedings would be ultra-quick and secret. The government currently has increased powers to make enquiries about any person suspected, however faintly, of involvement in terrorist activities, and such a person can be detained and brought to trial. According to a circular of the Immigration and Naturalization Service (INS), the Attorney General has powers to send any non-citizen back to his/her country of origin, without bringing forward any evidence, if he simply has reasonable grounds to believe that the person's activities are likely to be a threat to national security. Letters have been sent to 5,000 individuals from 26 Arab and Muslim countries who have arrived in the country since January 2000, 'inviting' them to cooperate with the authorities by answering questions about terrorist networks. The government has also introduced a new law which adds 20 days on average to the immigration procedure for people from Muslim countries or countries with a large Muslim minority (especially Pakistan, India, Egypt, Iran, Saudi Arabia, Sudan and Syria), so that immigration is now more difficult to achieve. Many South Asians dream of moving to the United States, and they are likely to be hard hit by this new measure. If an employer or a university has two applications, one from a Muslim and one from a non-Muslim, they will be likely to choose the non-Muslim, given the more lengthy immigration procedure for the Muslim candidate. The justice department has, however, offered to speed up any naturalization applications if applicants are able to provide information on terrorist networks and this measure also applies to all foreigners wishing to move to the United States.

Muslims have denounced these laws, saying they favour racial profiling, and portray all Muslims as potential threats. Yet the laws have met with little opposition in the country, which has increased the sense of insecurity among Muslims. A number of civil rights organizations are tackling the issue. On the whole, however, Americans (and a number of Muslims) are in favour of the measures and see them as a necessary evil. Universities, both administrative and teaching staff, have maintained silence, even at Columbia, and including when the FBI asked to see the files of a number of students, without the students concerned being informed. Some universities have tried to oppose the new visa regulations, but the American authorities have given them to understand that if they refuse to cooperate they would lose some or all of their visa quotas for overseas students.

The fear of these laws among Muslims is exacerbated by the fact that they have seen many of their community being arrested, often arbitrarily. More than one thousand people were thrown into prison in the weeks following 11 September. At the end of November, 641 of these were still detained, of whom one third were Pakistani (208) and 20 were Indian.[2] Only a handful were claimed to have any links with Osama bin Laden's terrorist network al-Qaida. Most of those detained were illegal immigrants or people whose visas had expired. Until now, American policy towards illegal immigrants has been fairly lenient, but this is no longer the case, at least for Muslims. Other illegal immigrants seem to continue to enjoy the same leniency, which makes Muslims all the more suspicious that they are victims of racial profiling. The Pakistani community includes quite a number of illegal immigrants, which explains the high number in the figures above. One of the major problems faced by these individuals, who are recent arrivals and on the whole not very highly educated, is that they are not familiar with their rights. They therefore fail to ask for legal representation, they do not appeal, and sign documents they have not read. Their English is often poor, and they are dependent on interpreters whose level of Urdu and Punjabi is not necessarily very good. Also, neither India nor Pakistan have signed bilateral agreements with the United States which would ensure that they were kept informed if any of their nationals were detained. Governments are generally informed only if friends or family inform the embassy or the consulate. As a result, the number of South Asian detainees was not disclosed for quite a time and this has not been to their advantage in terms of their civil rights. One Pakistani of about 50 even died in detention, apparently of a heart attack. The vice-consul in New York said that what surprised him most was that neither this man nor any of the other detainees had asked for the consulate to be informed of their arrest. He did not feel that fear of the authorities in Pakistan – a number of those concerned were illegal immigrants – was a sufficient explanation for this silence. He though it likely that those arrested had probably all, or nearly all, signed papers which were hastily produced, and that they had not really read or understood them for the reasons given above.

Muslims who have recently arrived, and illegal immigrants, are those most exposed to the current repressive policies of the American authorities, but in fact all Muslims who are not United States citizens are feeling vulnerable at present. Even Muslims who are citizens have had visits from the FBI and have been interrogated, either because they are active in Muslim organizations, or simply because their neighbours thought they saw some 'unusual' behaviour.

Muslim reactions

Muslims speak of discrimination, but they speak even more of fearing the possibility of discrimination. In neighbourhoods such as Coney Island, and among taxi drivers, many of whom in New York are Indians or Pakistanis, rumours abound about an attack on such-and-such, or that so-and-so has been arrested and interrogated by the FBI and sent home, or even about such-and-such a family which has decided to move back to Pakistan or Bangladesh. Some of those most recently arrived have indeed decided to go home again, even if they have not actually done so yet. The Pakistani consulate confirms that there has been a doubling of the number of requests for visas for Pakistan from Pakistanis who have taken American citizenship, but there is no suggestion of a massive return to the former homeland.

Muslims in the United States are nevertheless still traumatized by the situation. Many, especially those who have been in the United States for a long time, feel that the events on 11 September were an attack on them on two counts:[3] 'We are victims both as Americans and as Muslims.' There are at least two comments to make on this. Firstly, those to whom I spoke were unanimous in their unconditional condemnation of the attacks (even if some said that they were a result of American foreign policy). In some parts of the world (especially in the Muslim world), including the subcontinent, there were mixed feelings, which oscillated between condemnation and jubilation, but no such mixed feelings were to be found in America. It could of course be argued that no one in the United States would dare to rejoice openly at the attacks. However, these events will have been very costly for the American Muslim community, which on the whole is a well integrated community, wanting to share in the American Dream. The events of 11 September will have been a serious setback in their efforts to integrate into the host society. Many like to call themselves American Muslims, or even Muslim Americans. A remarkable consequence of this attitude is that Muslims in the United States are out of step with other Muslims and their (former) compatriots in other parts of the world. Moreover, as we have seen, they are suffering from discrimination in the wake of 11 September, but for some the feeling of being twice a victim is a reluctant recognition that they are ashamed that it is Muslims who were found to be responsible for the terrorist attacks.

At any rate, as far as I could tell from those I interviewed, immigrants had not ceased to feel that they belonged in the United States, especially those who had been in the country for some time, and more particularly in New York. The situation does give rise to questions about their identity: 'Can one be both a Muslim and an American patriot?' Many would say 'Yes'. For some, especially Indian Muslims who were already a minority before they emigrated, the present crisis has in some way strengthened their sense of belonging to America, even if it has revived in them some unpleasant memories, reminding them of the incidents of communal violence in India. Some say that if such a tragedy had happened in their former home country, there would have been terrible rioting against Muslims. 'I might be dead now!' one immigrant exclaimed. This rather excessive reaction can be explained, as we have seen, by the diasporic condition which brings in an exacerbated ethno-religious feeling and a hypersensitive perception of the situation of fellow Muslims who have remained in the homeland.

Regardless of their religious or ethnic origins, there is also a difference between the way South Asians see the American on the street and the American official. Few of the New York residents I talked to – although they are not rep-resentative of the rest of the United States, given the highly cosmopolitan nature of New York – complained of the attitude of Americans they knew, nor indeed of the American on the street. Some even told me with emotion of the way they had been shown support and solidarity by neighbours, friends, and shopkeepers they knew. There was much mention in the press of Jewish and Christian women who offered to do errands for their Muslim neighbours, or to take their children to school, when the women were still too afraid to leave their homes. The vast majority of Muslims continue to praise the tolerance of Americans and they are still grateful for the religious freedom they enjoy in the United States. Indeed, it would appear that so far Muslims' freedom to practise their religion has not been curtailed. The number of worshippers in some mosques had considerably gone down immediately after 11 September, but they are now back to their normal attendance, or nearly. When Ramadan started, numbers went up as they usually do. Several women who had stopped wearing the veil started to wear it again after a few weeks. Another interesting example: an Islamic centre called the Center for American Muslim Research and Information (CAMRI) has just set up an online Islamic university (STUDY-ISLAM.com). This project had been in gestation for some time and was opened in October 2001, without being in any way delayed by the terrorist attacks.

Muslims attribute the anti-Islamic prejudice and the discrimination aimed at them to the ignorance of the general population, but they are nearly unani-mous in saying that the media and government authorities are also to blame. Some did say they were grateful to George W Bush for his visit to a mosque immediately after the terrorist attacks, when he emphasized that American Muslims were just as much affected as anyone else, and then said that racist attacks against people who were Muslims would not be tolerated. Immigrants, however, are dubious about the discontinuity between the words of the presi-dent and the legal measures put in place by the government. Muslims in the United States hold the media even more responsible than the American authorities for anti-Muslim feelings among the American population. While some said, on the contrary, that for once the media had tried to paint a rather more positive picture of Islam and its followers, many had nothing but nega-tive comments to make. They have never had much confidence in the media, but their mistrust has now reached such proportions that quite a number refuse to believe any factual information about Islam or Muslim countries, whether or not it claims to be objective. As a result, some have refused to believe that people claiming to be Muslims were to blame for the events of 11 September. 'Show us evidence,' they say. Some have even gone as far as to directly or indi-rectly accuse other communities, especially the Jews, of playing a part in the attacks. This accusation cost the imam of one New York mosque his job.

There is also a difference to be noted between generations. It is not surprising to discover that members of the second generation are not contemplating returning to the former homeland, whichever ethnic group they come from. They are also more quick to denounce any discrimination and they have a more realistic attitude about those who carried out the attacks on 11 September. An effect for quite a few of the second generation is that is has aroused an awakening of their identity: they have suddenly become aware of their being Muslim. Younger children seem also to have had some psychological distress. The headmistress of an Islamic school says:

> The children are very perturbed. They ask us: 'Why don't they like us?'
> [An echo, in fact, of the question George W Bush asked, but in reverse!]

Beyond these aspects, we also observe an exacerbation in Muslims of all ages and ethnic origins of their reactions and behaviours. Those who were previously hesitant to be open about their Muslim faith are now even more reluctant to do so. Their Muslim identity is pushed into the background, and they might even try to hide it, for example by a change of name.

Those, on the other hand, who thought that a mobilizing of the community was the only way to enable Muslims to be fully accepted into American society either as citizens or as permanent residents, have now been working even harder in this direction. They have not been scaling new heights, but they have been reaping the benefit of having well-established organizations such as the CAIR, the very aim of which is to combat discrimination against Muslims. The CAIR (which, as we have seen, is led by Arabs) mobilized its troops on the day after 11 September to set up hotlines and an Internet service to record all instances of discrimination. Their representatives travelled hundreds of miles across the United States, speaking in churches, synagogues, schools and so on, to defuse prejudice against Muslims.

Few Muslim organizations in America were active to quite the same degree, but a number mobilized local forces, especially in New York. In mosques with a large South Asian membership, the Islamic Center of Long Island (see Chapter 5) was probably the field leader here. Journalists used to the good public relations of this mosque (which flew the Stars and Stripes above its dome after the terrorist attacks), descended on the ICLI in the days following the attacks both to gather reactions and to show the American people the lives that ordinary Muslims were living in the United States. Members of the Islamic centre, for their part, invited many non-Muslims (journalists, but also pastors, rabbis and other representatives of the religious communities, including Hindus, Sikhs and also teachers and students) to come and see their activities, and hear their Friday sermons. The sermons were themselves changed after the events of 11 September: an increased emphasis was laid on the incompatibility of Islam and terrorism and the 'true' definition of *jihad* was explained. The major ICLI representatives also repeatedly focused on the importance of developing relationships with non-Muslims – and demonstrated it by showing that those groups who had worked hard at engaging in inter-faith and inter-community dialogues had been less hard hit than those who had (deliberately or not) kept themselves isolated. The ICLI also asked its members, who are on the whole very comfortably well off, to donate money to the families of the victims and to the Red Cross, to give blood and so on.

The Islamic Circle of North America (ICNA) was also keen to act. As with the CAIR and the ICLI, members went into churches, synagogues and schools to explain their religion, and they collaborated with civil rights protection organizations. On their Internet site, which is one of the most elaborate among Islamic centres, they posted the following statement:

> The Islamic Circle of North America (ICNA) is extremely horrified and saddened by the tragedy in New York and Washington, DC. Our hearts and prayers are with the families of the victims of this horrible and despicable crime.

The site lists just about every article on discrimination against Muslims, and articles by American journalists on the crucial importance of distinguishing between Islam and terrorism. The web site also carried advice to Muslims immediately after the terrorist attacks, in which community leaders are encouraged to make contact with the local mayor and police officers, to meet up with leaders of other communities and organize joint news conferences with them, to give blood, and so on. Advice to those suffering discrimination (verbal attacks, for example) is to stay calm and patient and so on. A free telephone contact is given to report discriminatory incidents.

The Islamic Cultural Center of New York (ICCNY), located in Manhattan, was overrun with journalists, being the most prominent Mosque in New York, and as its imam is often interviewed. This centre, however, works along different lines from the ICLI, which was built by immigrants eager to have place for a prayer as well as a space for socializing and establishing Islam in America. The ICCNY, on the other hand, was financed and built by the government of Kuwait to meet, to begin with, the needs of Muslims working at the UN. Imams are often appointed straight from Al-Azhar and do not stay in post for very long. As a result, although many immigrants go there for Friday prayers, it in fact is rather more foreign in character than other mosques. This probably also explains why it has not done much in the way of mobilization since 11 September.

The amount of mobilization has in fact varied considerably from one organization to another, but overall it has not necessarily measured up to events of
such magnitude, particularly when one considers that Muslims in the United
States are on the whole from the well-educated and prosperous layers of society, well versed in their rights, and with institutions sufficiently well funded to
enable them to mobilize their efforts. Muslims who are however aware of
being a relatively new minority, although well integrated, but not necessarily
very popular (at least since the attacks), here considered safer to keep a low profile. Some mosques and Islamic centres have made some efforts, but little in the
way of concerted action has been noted since more mobilization was at local
level – a phenomenon characteristic of Islam in the American context. On the
national level, an umbrella organization called the American Muslim Political
Coordination Council (AMPCC), which covers four of the largest Islamic
organizations (the American Muslim Alliance, the American Muslim Council,
the CAIR and the American Public Affairs Council[4]) has been active in holding many meetings with the media, politicians and civil rights protection
organizations, but the efforts on the whole have not been particularly visible or
significant. One consequence has been that Americans have criticized Muslims
for what they saw as a weak reaction in their denunciation of the terrorist
attacks. Some Muslim leaders, in response to these accusations, admitted that
their initial concern was to reassure their own community which was in shock
and fearful, rather than to rush to make statements on American television.
These same leaders argued that if they had denounced the attacks straight
away, when in fact Muslims were the immediate suspects, they would in some
way have been confirming the guilt of their fellow Muslims, at a time when
there was as yet very little evidence to support the accusation. This recalls
what we saw earlier about the reluctance among many Muslims, especially in
the first generation, to believe that Muslims could be involved in terrorist
attacks. Other community leaders disputed these criticisms, and thought they
had been prompt in denouncing the attacks – they said that the fault lay with
the media, who were slow to broadcast their opinions. All these recriminations
are testament to the mutual suspicion between Muslims and the media, and
also suggest that the American population as a whole are still very suspicious of
their Muslim minority.

Nearly all Muslims, however, clergy and lay people alike, are unanimous in
their view that the current crisis is an ideal opportunity to make Islam better
known to Americans. A few have proselytizing intentions, but most are simply
keen to combat prejudice. Some are even exultant, as never before have the
Qur'an and books on Islam been sold in such numbers in the United States!

Here again there is a difference in approach between first and second generation. The second generation are aware of the importance of denouncing

the attacks and of making Islam better known, but they are quicker to express their exasperation than their elders. The president of the Muslim Student Association at the University of Columbia, a young Indian Muslim woman born in the United States, exclaims:

> Why do I need to justify myself about these attacks, always to say where I stand on the matter, to repeat that Islam and terrorism are incompatible, as if that weren't self-evident? People ask me why Muslims would do a thing like that. Simply because I am a Muslim, I am supposed to know what drives those people? Did all Christians in the United States have to justify themselves after what Timothy McVeigh[5] did?

The current crisis gives rise to a few more observations. While Indian Muslims are no doubt relieved to be in a country where they are not the most exposed minority, they have probably shown a greater propensity to keep a low profile than the Pakistanis, on account of the reflexes inherited from the subcontinent. The Pakistanis, however, have also been relatively slow to mobilize as an ethno-national group. Thus, whereas the Indian lobby in Washington has been very busy, for example in having organizations such as the Jaish-e Mohammad or the Lashkar-e Taiyyaba denounced as terrorist by the American authorities, and in exerting pressure on the Indian government to take stronger measures against the Pakistani government after the attacks on the parliament in Kashmir, and more recently in Delhi, the Pakistani lobby, for its part, has not mobilized in any perceptible way.

Another observation is that the terrorist attacks have certainly not bridged any gaps between Muslims of different social classes, far from it. Prosperous and well integrated immigrants are loud in their disdain of those more recently arrived from their homelands, or fellow Muslims, some of whom are illegal immigrants facing all kinds of fears and difficulties, concentrated into neighbourhoods such as Coney Island. There have been racist attacks in this area, as we have seen, and a number of people living there are being harassed by the FBI. A Pakistani accountant, known in Coney Island as the unofficial mayor of the neighbourhood, complains:

> All these doctors and engineers do nothing to help the community. They even say, 'If they're illegal, let them go home, we don't care! . . . They even invent stories about Pakistanis in Brooklyn, saying they're all thieves. It's true that there are illegal immigrants, but let me tell you that many of them work very hard, twelve hours a day, and they are honest!

The current situation may have an interesting impact on the relationship between immigrant Muslims and 'indigenous' Muslims. South Asian prejudice towards African–Americans (whether or not they are Muslims) has not disappeared, far from it, but South Asians are now suddenly aware of ethnic profiling, which African–Americans have suffered for decades, centuries even. Until now, as we have seen, a number of immigrants have been careful to emphasize the differences between themselves and African–Americans, *the* unpopular minority in the United States, and now they find themselves to be in a similar position, or nearly.

American Muslims and the war in Afghanistan

The war in Afghanistan has been officially supported by a number of the largest Islamic organizations and associations of Muslims, such as the American Federation of Muslims from India, the Association of Indian Muslims of America, the Pakistan Federation of America, the American Muslim Congress and the American Muslim Alliance.

In private, people have rather more mixed feelings about the war. Some see it as a necessary evil, but would have liked to see more effort made through diplomatic channels first. Others, among Muslims, are clearly against the war, saying that there can be no justification for bombing thousands of civilians. Most of those I spoke to thought it was indeed a war against terrorism, for the moment at least. No one, or nearly no one, thought that this was 'a clash of civilizations' – some recalled the phrase used by the Iranian president Muhammad Khatami who, when he visited New York in November 2001, called for a 'Dialogue among Civilizations'.

As to seeing a link between the terrorist attacks and American foreign policy, many voices are raised in support of this view, although they would not use this to justify the attacks. 'Does a flawed policy call for an Armageddon in this city?' asks one of the leaders of the American Federation of Muslims from India. Muslims at the same time express the hope that Americans will learn a lesson here, and they quote Palestine, Kashmir, Chechnya, and so on.

At any rate, very few Americans mobilized in opposition to the war. This meant that Muslims who were fiercely opposed to it had little opportunity, as happened at the time of the Gulf war, to join in with expressions of pacifism. In the circumstances it was impossible for Muslims alone to mount a demonstration – it would have been seen as an anti-national act. However, there were small local demonstrations led by Americans. One such was organized by the Long Island Alliance for Peaceful Alternatives, in which the ICLI joined. In this kind of demonstration the slogans do not only refer to the war; there was also denunciation of anti-Muslim discrimination in the United States. A certain number of Islamic centres, such as the ICLI and the ICNA (which has a Relief Fund Section) also collected funds for Afghan civilians.

The attitude of South Asian Muslims, especially Pakistanis, to the role played by Pakistan in the Afghan affair and in opposing the Taliban is also very interesting. Pakistanis were almost unanimously supportive of General Musharraf. Some rejoiced openly, as they had always been keen to see closer links between the United States and their native country. Others pointed out that at any rate Pakistan had simply had no other choice. A small minority, the most religious in particular, were saddened by a situation in which one Muslim country was forced to take up arms against another. All, or nearly all, among the Pakistanis I spoke to, were very pleased that the United States had rejected (at least for now) India's offer to help in the war against terrorism. Indian Muslims are more divided in their opinions. Some admitted to being disappointed, as they would have preferred their native country to be playing a more important part alongside the United States. Some Hindus had also made vigorous initial protests against the United States allying itself with Pakistan, but they and the Indian Muslims did appreciate that for the time being Pakistan was strategically better placed than India. In fact, along with many Indians in India itself, some even added 'Let's let the Pakistanis do the dirty work!' Some others said they did not care which country the United States allied itself to.

Pakistanis and Indians also had different attitudes to the Taliban. Some Pakistanis condemned the Taliban unreservedly (especially those who had read Ahmad Rashid's book, which became a best seller in the United States) but others were less certain, and/or felt themselves to be in a dilemma. They did not necessarily agree with the doctrine of the Taliban (there were very few who had much sympathy for them), but out of a feeling of nationalism they sought to justify their native country's support to the 'students of religion' [which is what *taliban* means – Trans.]. A handful go even further, and refuse to see the Taliban as an ignominy; this is not so much a matter of ideology as the idealization of the former homeland which is typical of the experience of diaspora. If they were to admit the gravity of the problems raised by the Taliban government, they would be forced to question the wisdom of the Pakistan government which supported them for such a long time. At any rate, this has brought to the surface again the theory of an anti-Muslim plot and all the rhetoric against the propaganda put out by the American media, and some take refuge behind the claim that they did not know exactly what was going on in Afghanistan: 'Maybe it was really terrible, but maybe the situation has been exaggerated to justify the bombings?' they argue. The question of the *madrasahs* in Pakistan, some of which have gradually become hotbeds of Islamism, also provoked mixed reactions. Together with the issues we have just looked at, this attitude shows how some Pakistanis have preserved a rather ossified impression of their native land: they speak of the *madrasahs* as they were about 20 or 30 years ago, before they themselves emigrated. It is interesting to note that these issues gave rise to tension between Pakistanis and Afghans,[6] of whom the vast majority in the United States have always been violently opposed to the Taliban. 'We always told you the Taliban were awful!', they now say to the Pakistanis, almost in triumph.

The issue is rather different for Indian Muslims. Some agree with the Pakistanis that making the Taliban look diabolical is all part of a conspiracy against Islam. However, the condemnation of the Taliban and of the *madrasahs* is not a dilemma for the Indians as it is for the Pakistanis.

Regardless of their ethnic origins, women are more likely than men, unsurprisingly, to condemn the Taliban. Even more interestingly, Pakistanis of the second generation are also more able to be critical of their parents' native land, of its policies and of the *madrasahs*, and so on, and they seem to have a more objective view, even though they still have a strong attachment to the country of their ancestors.

People of all generations and ethnic origins among South Asian Muslims, and probably other groups also, have mixed reactions to the character of bin Laden himself, ranging from fascination (for a millionaire who walked away from a life of luxury to fight for an ideal) to revulsion for the destructiveness of his actions. Some condemn him outright, and yet others are still doubtful that he had actually had any part in the 11 September attacks.

Nothing has changed dramatically in the United States since 11 September, but the terrorist attacks have traumatized the American population, even more perhaps the Muslim community, to the extent that the latter is now pondering about its future in the United States. There was relatively little in the way of concerted activity to combat discrimination, which demonstrates how vulnerable the Muslims feel, even though they are keen above all else to continue to become integrated into the United States and to be accepted in American society.

It is also clear that Muslims in the United States have benefited from the fact that the war in Afghanistan has turned to the advantage of the Americans whose anger has, on this account, somewhat abated. Had the conflict become a long and difficult one, this might have led to a deep resentment among Muslims of American politics and politicians. There is still discrimination against Muslims, even if the worst of the violence seems to be over. But again who knows? If there were to be further terrorist attacks of great magnitude, things could take a turn for the worse: Americans are likely to want to tighten up their security measures in a way that will limit the civil liberties of Muslims.

If this happens, when they are already anxious about the new American laws that have been introduced, the reactions of the Muslims could become unpredictable (especially in the medium to long term). Whatever happens, this is a testing time for the United States as a democracy and for the Muslims as a minority.

GLOSSARY

alhamdulillah	God be praised
alim (pl. ulama)	scholar, theologian
Allahu Akbar	'God is great' (the *takbir* formula)
amil	leader; representative of the *Da'i* in the Bohra.
amir	leader, commander
aqida	doctrine
aqiqa	ceremony where a child's hair is shaved six days after birth
ashura	tenth day of Muharram
asr	afternoon
Assalam alaikum	may peace be upon you
aurhni	veil worn on the shoulders or the head by the Bohra
avaz	voice, noise
azan	call to prayer
barsi	commemoration of a death
batin	hidden, esoteric
bhangra	Punjabi dance
bid'at	(blameworthy) innovation
bindi	lit: 'spot'; red spot on the forehead of Hindu women
bismillah	in the name of God [the all-merciful, the most merciful]
burqa	a veil which covers the whole body except the eyes (Arabic equivalent: *niqâb*)
chhati	ceremony on the sixth day after the birth of a child
Da'i	missionary; spiritual leader of the Bohra
Dar ul islam	the abode of Islam
Dar ul harb	the abode of war
dargah	lit: door, doorstep; sanctuary of a saint
dashond	lit: a tenth; alms (isma'ili)
da'wa	lit: call, invitation; preaching
desi	inhabitant of, local of
din	faith, religion

du'a	non-ritual prayer, invocation, supplication
dupatta	veil (worn on the shoulders or the head)
Fatiha	first *sura* of the Qur'an
fiqh	jurisprudence; religious law
firman	decree
ghagra	long and full skirt
gham	pain, sadness
ghazal	poem, ode (Urdu)
ginan	liturgical chant in Gujarati (Nizari Isma'ili)
gyarhawin	lit: eleventh; rituals to commemorate the death of Abd al-Qadir Jilani on the 11th day of each month
gurdwara	Sikh temple
Hadis	the actions, words and thoughts of the Prophet, as told by his Companions and passed down by tradition
hafiz	one who has memorized the Qur'an
hajj	pilgrimage to Mecca
halal	lit: permitted; ritually slaughtered meat
halaqa	circle
halva	kind of sweet pastry
haram	forbidden
hijab	veil (which covers completely the hair, the neck and the shoulders)
hijrah	migration
Id	festivals marking the end of Ramadan
Id ul-Azha	festival celebrating Abraham's sacrifice
Idi	money given to children at the *Id*
iftar	meal to break the fast during Ramadan
ijtihad	the effort made by an individual to understand through reason, work done by lawyers in seeking answers to legal questions
imam	prayer leader; spiritual guide of the Shi'a
imambara	place where Shi'a keep their *ta'ziya* during the month of Muharram. Building where they commemorate the martyrs of Kerbala
insha'allah	'if God wills it'
isha	night
isna'Ashari	Twelver Isna' Ashari
izzat	honour, reputation
jama'at	group, party
jama'at khana	place of worship of the Isma'ili
jihad	holy war; effort to achieve a specific aim

kafir	infidel, wrongdoer
Khuda hafiz	'may God protect you'
khutbah	Friday sermon
kufi	style of Arabic calligraphy
kurta	tunic
Lailat ul-Qadr	Night of the divine decree (27th day of Ramadan, when the Qur'an was revealed)
lehanga	long gathered skirt
lungi	long skirt-like garment worn by men
madrasah	Qur'anic school, college
maghrib	sunset (prayer)
mahaul	atmosphere, environment
majlis	meeting, council
masala	mix of spices
masjid	mosque
matam	sadness caused by death; mourning
maulvi	religious teacher
mazhab	school of jurisprudence
mehndi	henna
mehr	dower
mihrab	niche in the mosque wall which shows the direction of Mecca
Maulid	anniversary of the birth of the Prophet Muhammad
millat	community of believers
minbar	pulpit
mleccha	barbarian; non-Indian; used pejoratively in India to designate non-Hindus
muezzin	the one who calls to prayer
mufti	lawyer; he pronounces *fatwa*
muhajir	migrants. The name given to Muslims who moved from India to Pakistan after Partition
Muharram	first month in the Muslim calendar
mujaddid	reformer
mukhi	Nizari leader
mukhiyani	feminine version of *mukhi*
musha'ira	meeting where poems are recited
namaz	Persian equivalent of *salah* (see below)
nan	kind of bread
nasta'liq	Persian style of calligraphy
na't	poem in honour of the Prophet
nikah	marriage ceremony

pagri	turban
purdah	lit: veil, curtain; system which maintains the segregation of women in Muslim upper classes
pir	Sufi master, saint, spiritual guide
puja	(Hindu) worship or acts of devotion to a deity
qaum	nation, community
qawwali	Sufi mystical chant
qazi	judge
rasul	law-giving prophet, messenger
riba'	loan with interest; usury
rida	veil of Bohra women
salah (or *salat*)	prayer (five times a day, one of the Five Pillars)
sama'	lit: to hear; listen to music
sawab	an action which earns its author merit
Sha'ban	eighth month of the Muslim calendar
Shab-i-Barat	festival of the dead (celebrated on the evening of the 14th day of *Sha'ban*)
Shab-i-Miraj	night journey of the Prophet Muhammad
shahadah	declaration of faith
shaikh	spiritual master
shalwar kameez	dress consisting of a tunic and flowing trousers
Shari'ah	Islamic law
shirk	idolatry, associationism
shura	principle of consultation
subhanallah	'may God be praised'
Sunnah	collection of rules for behaviour based on the words and actions of the Prophet
sura	chapter of the Qur'an
tabligh	communication of a message, sermon
tafsir	commentary on the Qur'an
tahara	(ritual) purity
tajdid	renewal
talaq	divorce
taqiyya	the act of hiding one's religious beliefs in order to protect oneself (in the Shi'a tradition)
taqwa	piety
tarawih	series of prayers performed by Sunni during the month of Ramadan after the 'isha prayer
tariqa	mystic path, in the Sufi tradition
tasbih	Muslim prayer beads
tauhid	unity of God

taziya	replica of the graves of Hasan and Hussain, carried in procession during Muharram
umma	nation; worldwide community of believers
urs	lit: marriage; celebration of the anniversary of the death of a saint
zahir	seen; exoteric
zakat	legally required alms
zikr	repetition of the name of God; a remembrance of God
zimmi	protected foreign community within an Islamic state
ziyara	pilgrimage, often to a saint's tomb (not required by law)
zuhr	midday (prayer)

BIBLIOGRAPHY

Abdalati, Hammudah, n d, *Islam in Focus*, Riyadh: WAMY (World Assembly of Muslim Youth).

Abu-Laban, Baha, 1983, 'The Canadian Muslim Community: The Need for a New Survival Strategy', in Earle Waugh, Baha Abu-Laban and Regula Qureshi, eds, *The Muslim Community in North America*, Edmonton, University of Alberta Press, pp. 75–92.

Adelkhah, Fariba, 1991, *La Révolution sous le voile: Femmes islamiques d'Iran*, Paris, Karthala.

Afzal, Omar, 1991, 'An Overview of Asian Indian Muslims in the United States', in Omar Khalidi, ed., *Indian Muslims in North America*, Watertown, South Asia Press, pp. 1–16.

Agarwal, Priya, 1991, *Passage From India: Post-1965 Indian Immigrants and Their Children – Conflicts, Concerns and Solutions*, Palos Verdes (CA), Yuvati Publications.

Ahmad, Aziz, 1964, *Studies in Islamic Culture in the Indian Environment*, Oxford, Clarendon Press.

Ahmad, Gubti Mahdi, 1991, 'Muslim Organizations in the United States', in Yvonne Haddad, ed., *The Muslims of America*, New York, OUP, pp. 11–24.

Ahmad, Mumtaz, 1991, 'Islamic Fundamentalism in South Asia: The Jamaat-i-Islami and the Tablighi-Jama'at of South Asia', in Martin E Marty and Scott Appleby, eds, *Fundamentalisms Observed*, Chicago, University of Chicago Press, pp. 457–530.

Ahmed, Rafiuddin, 1983, ed., *Islam in Bangladesh: Society, Culture, and Politics*, Dhaka, Bangladesh Itihas Samiti.

—— 1994, 'Redefining Muslim Identity in South Asia: The Transformation of Jama'at-i-islami', in Martin E Marty and Scott Appleby, eds, *Accounting for Fundamentalism*, vol. 4, Chicago, The Chicago University Press, pp. 669–705.

Anderson, Benedict, 1983, *Imagined Communities: Reflections on the Origin and the Spread of Nationalism*, London, Verso.

—— 1996, *L'Imaginaire national* [translation of 1983, *Imagined communities*], Paris, Éditions La Découverte.

—— 1998, *The Spectre of Comparisons: Nationalism, Southeast Asia and the World*, London, Verso.

Andezian, Sossie, 1983, 'Pratiques féminines de l'islam en France', *Archives de sciences sociales des religions*, 55 (1), Jan–March, pp. 53–66.

Anisuzzaman, 1995, *Identity, Religion and Recent History: Four Lectures on Bangladeshi Society*, Calcutta, Maulana Abul Kalam Azad Institute of Asian Studies.

Anwar, Muhammad, 1976, *Between Two Cultures: A Study of Relationships Between Generations in the Asian Community in Britain*, London, Commission for Racial Equality.

—— 1979, *The Myth of Return: Pakistanis in Britain*, Whitstable, Whitstable Litho Ltd.

—— 1994, *Young Muslims in Britain: Attitudes, Educational Needs and Policy Implications*, Leicester (UK), The Islamic Foundation.

Appadurai, Arjun, 1997, *Modernity at Large: Cultural Dimensions of Globalization*, Minneapolis, Minnesota University Press.

Archives de sciences sociales des religions, 1989, *L'Islam en Europe*, 68 (1) and 68 (2), 34è année, July–Dec.

—— 1995, *L'Islam en Europe*, 92, 40è année, Oct–Dec.

Assayag, Jackie, 1995, *Au confluent de deux rivières: musulmans et hindous dans le sud de l'Inde*, Paris, Presses de l'Ecole française d'Extrême-Orient.

Aziz Said, Abdul, 1981, ed., *Ethnicity and US Foreign Policy*, New York, Praeger.

Azria, Régine, 1996, 'Réidentification communautaire du judaïsme', in Grace Davie and Danièle Hervieu-Léger, eds, *Identités religieuses en Europe*, Paris, La Découverte, pp. 251 –67.

—— 1997, 'Les néo-communautarismes', in Frédéric Lenoir and Ysé T Masquelier, eds, *Encyclopédie des religions*, vol. 2, Paris, Bayard, pp. 2116–25.

Babès, Leïla, 1995, 'Recompositions identitaires dans l'islam en France: la culture réinventée', *Archives de sciences sociales des religions*, 92, Oct–Dec, pp. 35–47.

—— 1997, *L'Islam positif: la religion des jeunes musulmans de France*, Paris, L'Atelier.

Bacon, Jean, 1996, *Lifelines: Community, Family and Assimilation Among Asian Indian Immigrants*, Oxford, OUP.

Badie, Bertrand and Withol de Wenden, Catherine, 1994, eds, *Le défi migratoire*, Paris, Presses de la Fondation nationale des sciences politiques.

Baljon, J M S, 1986, *Religion and Thought of Shah Wali Allah Dihlawi*, Liden, E J Brill.

Ballard, Roger, 1994, ed., *Desh Pardesh: The South Asian Presence in Britain*, London, Hurst and Co.

Barazangi, Nimat H, 1991, 'Islamic Education in the United States and Canada: Conceptions and Practice of the Islamic Belief System', in Yvonne Haddad, ed., *The Muslims of America*, New York, Oxford, OUP, pp. 157–74.

Barrier, Gerald and Dusenbery, Verne A, 1984, eds, *The Sikh Diaspora*, Delhi, Chanakya Publications.

Barth, Fredrik, 1970, ed., *Ethnic Groups and Boundaries: The Social Organisation of Cultural Differences*, Boston, Little, Brown and Co.

Basu, Kaushik and Subrahmanyam, Sanjay, 1996, eds., *Unravelling the Nation: Sectarian Conflict and India's Secular Identity*, Delhi, Penguin Books.

Bayart, Jean-François, 1996, *L'illusion identitaire*, Paris, Fayard.

Bodnar, John E, 1985, *The Transplanted: A History of Immigrants in Urban America*, Bloomington, Indiana University Press.

Bhachu, Parminder, 1985, *Twice Migrants: East African Sikh Settlers in Britain*, London, Tavistock.

Body-Gendrot, Sophie, 1991, *Les Etats-Unis et leurs immigrants*, Paris, La Documentation française.

Boivin, Michel, 1996, *Shî'isme et modernité dans le sous-continent indien: la rénovation de l'ismaélisme sous l'imâmat de Sultân Muhammad Shâh Aga Khan (1885-1957)*, London, Paul Kegan.

Bonnafous, Simone, 1994, 'Dire et penser l'autre en France et aux Etats-Unis', in Sylvia Ullmo, ed., *L'immigration américaine: exemple ou contre-exemple pour la France?*, Paris, L'Harmattan, pp. 65–70.

Bouvier, L F and Gardner, R W, 1986, 'Asian Americans: Growth, Change and Diversity', *Population Bulletin*, 40(4), Nov, pp. 1–41.

Bowers, Herman Meredith, 1989, *A Phenomenological Study of the Islamic Society of North America*, PhD Dissertation, Ann Arbor, UMI.

Brass, Paul, 1974, *Language, Religion and Politics in North India*, London, Cambridge University Press.

—— 1991, *Ethnicity and Nationalism: Theory and Comparison*, New Delhi, Sage.

Breckenridge, Carol, 1995, ed., *Consuming Modernity: Public Culture in Contemporary India*, Minneapolis, Minnesota University Press.

Brown, William Norman, 1972, *The United States and India, Pakistan and Bangladesh*, Cambridge, Harvard University Press [3rd ed.].

Bruneau, M, 1994, 'Espaces et territoires en diaspora', *L'Espace géographique*, 1, pp. 5–17.

Burton-Page, J, 1975, 'Habshî', *Encyclopédie de l'islam*, Liden, E J Brill [1965], pp. 15–17.

Burghart, Richard, 1987, ed., *Hinduism in Great Britain: The Perpetuation of Religion in an Alien Cultural Milieu*, London, Tavistock Publications.

Campiche, Roland J, 1996a, 'La religion: un frein à l'égalité?', *Archives de sciences sociales des religions*, 95, July–Sept., pp. 5–9.

—— 1996b, 'Religion, statut social et identité féminine', *Archives de sciences sociales des religions*, 95, July–Sept., pp. 69–94.

Carré, Olivier, 1982, ed., *L'Islam et l'Etat*, Paris, PUF.

—— 1984, *Mystique et politique: lecture révolutionnaire du Coran par Sayyid Qutb, frère musulman radical*, Paris, Presses de la Fondation nationale des sciences politiques.

—— 1993, *L'Islam laïque ou le retour à la Grande Tradition*, Paris, Armand Colin.

Cazemajou, Jean and Martin, Jean-Pierre, 1983, *La crise du melting-pot: ethnicité et identité aux Etats-Unis*, Paris, Aubier-Montaigne.

Césari, Jocelyne, 1994, *Etre musulman en France: Associations, militants et mosquées*, Paris, Karthala-Iremam.

—— 1995, 'L'Islam, ultime recours', *Confluences–Méditerranée*, 16, winter, Paris, L'Harmattan, pp. 55-64.

—— 1997a, *Etre musulman en France aujourd'hui*, Paris, Hachette littérature.

—— 1997b, *Faut-il avoir peur de l'islam?*, Paris, Presses de la Fondation nationale des sciences politiques.

Chaliand, Gérard et Rageau, Jean-Pierre, 1991, *Atlas des diasporas*, Paris, Odile Jacob.

Charnay, Jean-Paul, 1977, *Sociologie religieuse de l'Islam*, Paris, Sindbad.

Chi, Tony Poon-Chiang, 1973, *A Case Study of the Missionary Stance of the Ahmadiyya Movement in North America*, Ph.D. Dissertation, Ann Arbor, UMI.

Clarke, Colin, Peach, Ceri and Vertovec, Steven, 1990, *South Asians Overseas: Migration and Ethnicity*, Cambridge, Cambridge University Press.

Clémentin-Ojha, Catherine, 1997, ed., *Renouveaux religieux en Asie*, Paris, EFEO.

Cohen, Anthony Paul, 1985, *The Symbolic Construction of Community*, Chichester, Ellis Horwood.

Cohen, Robin, 1996, 'Diasporas and the Nation-State: From Victims to Challengers', *International Affairs*, 72 (3), pp. 507–20.

Cole, J R I, 1989, *Roots of North Indian Shiism in Iran and Iraq: Religion and State in Awadh 1772–1859*, Berkeley, University of California Press.

Confluences-Méditerrannée, 1993, *Les Replis identitaires*, 6, spring, L'Harmattan.

—— 1995–1996, *Islam et Occident: la confrontation*, 16, winter, L'Harmattan.

Corbin, Henri, 1964, *Histoire de la philosophie islamique*, Paris, Gallimard.

Costa-Laroux, Jacqueline, 1989, 'De l'immigré au citoyen', *Notes et études documentaires*, Paris, La Documentation française.

Daftary, Farhad, 1990, *The isma'ili: Their History and Doctrine*, Cambridge, Cambridge University Press.

Das, Veena, 1990, 'The Imaging of Indian Women', in Nathan and Sulochna Glazer, eds, *Conflicting Images: India and the United States*, Glenn Dale, The Riverdale Company, pp. 203–20.

—— 1992, 'Time, Self and Community: Features of the Sikh Militants Discourse', *Contributions to Indian Sociology*, July–Dec, pp. 245–59.

Dasseto, Felice, 1988, 'The Tabligh Organisation in Belgium', in Tomas Gerholm and Yngve Georg Lithman, eds, *The New Islamic Presence in Europe*, London, Mansell, pp. 159–73.

Dasseto, Felice and Bastenier, Albert, 1984, *L'Islam transplanté*, Bruxelles, EPO.

Davie, Grace, 1996, 'Contrastes dans l'héritage religieux de l'Europe', in Grace Davie and Danièle Hervieu-Léger, eds, *Les identités religieuses en Europe*, Paris, La Découverte, pp. 43–62.

Davie, Grace and Hervieu-Léger, Danièle, 1996, eds., *Les identités religieuses en Europe*, Paris, La Découverte.

Delvoye, Françoise, 1994, ed., *Confluence of Cultures: French Contributions to Indo–Persian Studies*, Delhi, Manohar

Denny, Fredrick Matthewson, 1991, 'The Legacy of Fazlur Rehman', in Yvonne Haddad, ed., *The Muslims of America*, New York, OUP, pp. 96–108.

Dieckhoff, Alain, 1997, 'Logiques religieuses et construction démocratique', in Patrick Michel, ed., *Religion et démocratie*, Paris, Albin Michel, pp. 317–38.

Durkheim, Emile, 1985, *Les formes élémentaires de la vie religieuse*, Paris, PUF.

Dusenbery, Verne A, 1984, 'A Century of Sikhs Beyond Punjab', in N Barrier and Verne A Dusenbery, eds, *The Sikh Diaspora*, Delhi, Chanakya Publications, 1984.

Dweik, Bader S, 1992, 'Lebanese Christians in Buffalo: Language Maintenance and Language Shift', in Aleya Rouchdy, ed., *The Arabic Language in America*, Detroit, Wayne State University Press.

Eade, John, 1989, *The Politics of Community: the Bangladeshi Community in East London*, London, Avebury.

Eickleman, Dale F and Piscatori, James, 1990, eds, *Muslim Travellers: Pilgrimage, Migration, and the Religious Imagination*, Berkeley, University of California Press.

Engineer, Asghar Ali, 1980, *The Bohra*, New Delhi, Vikas Publishing House.

—— 1985, ed., *Communal Riots in Post-Independent India*, Delhi, Sangam Books, pp. 238–71.

Esposito, John, 1991, 'Ismail R al-Faruqi: Muslim Scholar–Activist', in Yvonne Haddad, ed., *The Muslims of America*, New York, OUP, pp. 65–79.

—— 1992, *The Islamic Threat: Myth or Reality?*, New York, OUP.

Esprit, 1993, *Face à la montée du radicalisme religieux*, 194, August–September.

—— 1996, *Le choc des cultures à l'heure de la mondialisation*, 220, April.

Fawcett and Carino, 1987, eds., *Pacific Bridges: The New Immigration from Asia and Pacific Island*, New York, Center for Migration Studies, pp. 350–70.

Fenton, John Y, 1988, *Transplanting Religious Traditions: Asian Indians in America*, New York, Praeger.

—— 1989, 'Asian Indian Intermarriage and Religion', lecture given at the *First Global Convention of People of Indian Origin*, New York, August.

—— 1994, *Religions of South Asian Immigrants in the Americas: An Annotated Bibliography*, Westport (Connecticut), Greenwood Press.

Ferris, Marc, 1994, 'To Achieve the Pleasure of Allah: Immigrant Muslims in New York City', in Yvonne Haddad and Jane Smith, eds, *Muslim Communities in North America*, Albany (NY), State University of New York Press, pp. 209–30.

x

Fischer, Michael M J and Abedi, Mehdi, 1990, *Debating Muslims: Cultural Dialogues in Post Modernity and Tradition*, Madison, University of Wisconsin Press.

Fisher, Maxine, 1980, *The Indians of New York City*, Delhi, Heritage Publishers.

Flandrin, Jean-Louis and Montanari, Massimo, 1996, eds, *Histoire de l'alimentation*, Paris, Fayard.

Friedmann, Yohanan, 1989, *Prophecy Continuous: Aspects of Ahmadi Religious Thought and its Medieval Background*, Berkeley, University of California Press.

Gaborieau, Marc, 1986, ed., *Islam et société en Asie du Sud*, coll. Purusartha, Paris, EHESS.

—— 1994, 'Late Persian, Early Urdu: The Case of "Wahhabi" Literature (1818–1857)', in Françoise Delvoye, ed., *Confluence of Cultures: French Contributions to Indo–Persian Studies*, Delhi, Manohar, pp. 170–96.

—— 1996a, 'Les musulmans de l'Inde: une minorité de 100 millions d'âmes', in Christophe Jaffrelot, ed., *L'Inde contemporaine de 1950 à nos jours*, Paris, Fayard, pp. 466–507.

—— 1996b, 'A Peaceful Jihad? Proselytism as Seen by Ahmadiyya, Tablighi-Jama'at and Jama'at-i-Islami', at the workshop: *Transformations of the South Asian Islamicate Community in the 19th and 20th Centuries*, University of North Carolina, 23–26 May.

—— 1997, 'Renouveau de l'islam ou stratégie politique occulte? La Tablighi Jama'at dans le sous-continent indien et dans le monde', in Catherine Clémentin-Ohja, ed., *Renouveaux religieux en Asie*, Paris, EFEO, pp. 211–29.

Gaborieau, Marc, Popovic, Alexandre and Zarkone, Thierry, 1990, eds, *Naqshbandis: Cheminements et situation actuelle d'un ordre mystique musulman*, Paris/Istanbul, Isis.

Gallery de la Tremblaye, Nadine, 1994, 'Les réfugiés d'Arménie en Californie', in Gilles Kepel, ed., *Exils et royaumes: les appartenances au monde arabo-musulman aujourd'hui*, Paris, Presses de la Fondation nationale des sciences politiques, pp. 399–412.

Gayer, Laurent, 1998, *Diaspora indo-pakistanaise et régulation de la conflictualité à Londres et Paris*, DEA* dissertation, Paris, Institut d'études politiques.

Geaves, Ron R, 1996, 'Cult, Charisma, Community: The Arrival of Sufi *Pirs* and their Impact on Muslims in Britain', *Journal of Muslim Minority Affairs*, 16 (2), pp. 169–92.

Gell, Simeran, 1993, 'Le double mariage: immigration, tradition religieuse et représentation de "l'amour" chez les Sikhs de Grande Bretagne', *Terrain 21*, Oct., pp. 111–28.

Gerholm, Thomas and Lithman, Yngve Georg, 1988, eds, *The New Islamic Presence in Western Europe*, London, Mansell.

Gerson, Louis L, 1981, 'The Influence of Hyphenated Americans on US Diplomacy', in Abdul Aziz Said, ed., *Ethnicity and US Foreign Policy*, New York, Praeger, pp. 19–32.

Ghalioun, Burhan, 1997, *Islam et politique: la modernité trahie*, Paris, La Découverte.

Ghayur, M Arif, 1980, 'Pakistanis', in Stephan Thernström, *Harvard Encyclopædia of American Ethnic Groups*, Cambridge, Harvard University Press, p. 768.

—— 1984a, 'Demographic Evolution of Pakistanis in America: Case Study of a Muslim Subgroup', *American Journal of Islamic Studies*, 1 (2), pp. 113–26.

—— 1984b, 'Ethnic Distribution of American Muslims and Selected Socio-Economic Characteristics', *Journal Institute of Muslim Minority Affairs*, 5 (1), pp. 47–59.

Glazer, Nathan, 1972, *Les Juifs américains*, Paris, Calmann-Lévy (translation of *American Judaism* (2nd ed.) Chicago, University of Chicago Press, 1972).

Glazer, Nathan and Moynihan, Daniel P, 1963, eds, *Beyond the Melting Pot*, Cambridge, M I T Press.

—— 1975, eds, *Ethnicity: Theory and Experience*, Cambridge, Harvard University Press.

* DEA (Diplôme d'études approfondies) is a qualification gained one year beyond a master's degree.

Glazer, Sulochana and Nathan, 1990, eds, *Conflicting Images: India and the United States,* Glenn Dale, The Riverdale Company Publishers.

Gordon, Milton, 1964, *Assimilation in American Life: The Role of Race, Religion, and National Origins,* New York, OUP.

Graff, Violette, 1982, 'Les musulmans de l'Inde', in Olivier Carré, ed., *L'Islam et l'Etat,* Paris, PUF, pp. 205–28.

Haddad, Yvonne, 1978, 'Muslims in Canada: A Preliminary Study', in Harold Coward and Leslie Kawamura, eds, *Religion and Ethnicity,* Waterloo, Wilfrid Laurier University Press.

—— 1983, 'Arab Muslims and Islamic Institutions in America: Adaptation and Reform', in Sameer Abraham and Nabeel Abraham, eds., *Arabs in the New World: Studies on Arab–American Communities,* Detroit, Wayne State University Press.

—— 1991, ed., *The Muslims of America,* New York, Oxford, OUP.

Haddad, Yvonne and Lummis, Adair, 1987, *Islamic Values in the United States: A Comparative Study,* New York, OUP.

Haddad, Yvonne, and Smith, Jane, 1993, *Mission to America : Five Islamic Sectarian Communities in North America,* Gainesville, University Press of Florida.

—— 1994, eds, *Muslim Communities in North America,* Albany (NY), State University of New York Press.

Halm, Heinz, 1995, *Le Chiisme,* Paris, PUF (translated from German into French by Hubert Hougue).

Hamid, Aslam, 1991, 'American Human Rights Activists, Legislators, Public Opinion, and the Indian Muslims', in Omar Khalidi, ed., *Indian Muslims in North America,* Watertown (MA), South Asia Press, pp. 44–7.

Handlin, Oscar, 1973, *The Uprooted: The Epic Story of the Great Migrations that Made the American People,* Boston, Little Brown, 2nd ed.

Hardy, Peter, 1972, *The Muslims of British India,* Cambridge, Cambridge University Press.

Haroon, Mohammad, 1984, *Cataloguing of Indian Muslim Names,* Delhi, Indian Bibliographies Bureau.

Hasan, Mushirul, 1994, ed., *India's Partition: Process, Strategy and Mobilisation,* Delhi, OUP.

—— 1996, 'Traditional Rites and Contested Meanings: Sectarian Strife in Colonial Lucknow', *Economic and Political Weekly,* 2nd March 1996, pp. 543–50.

—— 1997, *Legacy of a Divided Nation: India's Muslims since Independence,* Boulder (Colorado), Westview Press.

Helweg, Arthur, 1986, *The Sikhs of England,* Delhi, OUP [1979].

Helweg, Arthur and Usha, 1990, *An Immigrant Success Story: East Indians in America,* Philadelphia, University of Pennsylvania Press.

Herberg, Will, 1956, *Protestant–Catholic–Jew: An Essay in American Religious Sociology,* Garden City, New York.

Hermansen, M K, 1994, 'The Muslims of San Diego', in Yvonne Haddad and Jane Smith, eds., *Muslim Communities in North America,* Albany (NY), State University of New York Press, pp. 169–94.

Hervieu-Léger, Danièle, 1993, 'La religion aux Etats-Unis: turbulences et recompositions', *Archives de sciences sociales des religions,* 38é année, 83, July–Sept, pp. 5–10.

Hess, Gary R, 1971, *America Encounters India, 1941–1947,* Baltimore, Johns Hopkins University Press.

Hicks, Sallie M and Couloumbis, Theodore A, 1981, 'The "Greek Lobby": Illusion or Reality?', in Abdul Aziz Said, ed., *Ethnicity and US Foreign Policy,* New York, Praeger.

Hinnells, John R, 1994, 'South Asian Diaspora Communities and their Religion: A Comparative Study of Parsi Experiences', *South Asia Research*, 14 (1), spring, pp. 63–103.

Hjortshoj, Keith, 1987, 'Shi'i Identity and the Significance of Muharram in Lucknow, India', in Martin Kramer, ed., *Shi 'ism, Resistance and Revolution*, Boulder, Westview Press and London, Mansell Publishing Ltd, pp. 289–309.

Hogben, Murray, 1991, 'Marriage and Divorce among Muslims in Canada', in Earle H Waugh, Baha Abu-Laban and Regula B Qureshi, eds, *The Muslim Community in North America*, Edmonton, Alberta University Press, pp. 154–84.

Hobsbawm, Eric and Ranger, Terence, 1983, *The Invention of Tradition*, Cambridge, Cambridge University Press.

Hollister, J N, 1953, *The Shi 'as of India*, London, Luzac and Co.

Hossain, Mokarrem, 1982, 'South Asians in Southern California: A Sociological Study of Immigrants from India, Pakistan and Bangladesh', *South Asia Bulletin*, 2 (1), spring, pp. 74–83.

Hovanessian, Martine, 1992, *Le lien communautaire: trois générations d'Arméniens*, Paris, Armand Colin.

Huntington, Samuel, 1993, 'The Clash of Civilizations', *Foreign Affairs*, Summer.

Husain, Asad and Vogelaar, Harold, 1994, 'Activities of the Immigrant Muslim Communities in Chicago', in Y Haddad and J Smith, eds, *Muslim Communities in North America*, Albany (NY), State University of New York Press, pp. 231–58.

Husband, Charles, 1992, 'Les communautés musulmanes et la société britannique', in Bernard Lewis and Dominique Schnapper, eds, *Musulmans en Europe*, Poitiers, Actes Sud, pp. 105–26.

Ishi, T K, 1982, 'The Political Economy of International Migration: Indian Physicians to the United States', *South Asia Bulletin*. 2 (1), spring, pp. 40–8.

Israel, Milton, 1987, ed., *The South Asian Diaspora in Canada: Six Essays*, Toronto, Multicultural History Society of Ontario.

—— 1994, *In the Further Soil: A Social History of Indo–Canadians in Ontario*, Toronto, Toronto Organisation for the Promotion of Indian Culture.

Jackson, Paul, 1988, *The Muslims of India: Beliefs and Practices*, Bangalore, Theological · Publications in India.

Jaffrelot, Christophe, 1993, *Les nationalistes hindous: idéologie, implantation et mobilisation des années 1920 aux années 1990*, Paris, Presses de la Fondation nationale des sciences politiques.

—— 1996, ed., *L'Inde contemporaine de 1950 à nos jours*, Paris, Fayard.

Jain, Ravindra, 1998, 'Indian Diaspora, Globalisation and Multiculturalism: A Cultural Analysis', *Contributions to Indian Sociology*, 32 (2), pp. 337–60.

Jain, Sunita, 1997, 'Ram bacae, hindustani', in *Itne barso bad*, Nai Dilli, quoted in Stasik 1994.

Jalal, Ayesha, 1994, *The Sole Spokesman: Jinnah, the Muslim League and the Demand for Pakistan*, Cambridge, Cambridge University Press.

Jeffery, Patricia, 1979, *Frogs in a Well: Indian Women in Purdah*, London, Zed Press.

Jeffery, Patricia and Basu, Amrita, eds, 1998, *Appropriating Gender: Women's Activism and Politicized Religion in South Asia*, New York and London, Routledge

Jeffery, Patricia and Jeffery, Roger, 1996, *Don't Marry Me to a Plowman!: Women's Everyday Life in Rural North India*, Boulder (Colorado), Westview Press.

Jensen, Joan M, 1988, *Passage from India: Asian Indian Immigrants in North America*, New Haven, Yale University Press.

Johnson Steve, 1991, 'Political Activity of Muslims in America', in Yvonne Haddad, ed., *The Muslims of America*, New York, OUP, pp. 111–24.

Joly, Danièle, 1987, *Making a Place for Islam in British Society: Muslims in Birmingham*, Coventry, Centre for Research in Ethnic Relations.

—— 1991, 'Musulmans – Immigrants – Métropoles : la jeunesse pakistanaise musulmane de Birmingham', *Les Temps modernes: Démocratie et minorités ethniques – le cas anglais*, July–August 1991, n° 540-1, pp. 218–24.

Kakar, Sudhir, 1996, 'The Construction of a New Hindu Identity', in Kaushik Basu and Sanjay Subrahmanyam, eds, *Unravelling the Nation: Sectarian Conflict and India's Secular Identity*, Delhi, Penguin Books, pp. 204–35.

Kalam, M A, n.d., 'From the Migrants' Side: Ayodhyya and After – Reactions from a South Asian Diaspora. An Inquiry amongst the Pakistani and Indian Communities in Bradford, UK'. Not published as far as I could ascertain.

Kale, Madhavi, 1995, 'Projecting Identities: Empire and Indentured Labour Migration from India to Trinidad and British Guiana, 1836–1885', in Peter Van der Veer, ed., *Nation and Migration: The Politics of Space in the South Asian Diaspora*, Philadelphia, University of Pennsylvania Press, pp. 73–92.

Kaspi, André, Bertrand, Claude-Jean and Heffer, Jean, 1991, *La civilisation américaine*, Paris, PUF [1979].

Kaufman, Jonathan, 1989, *The Broken Alliance: The Turbulent Times between Blacks and Jews in America*, New York.

Kelley, Ron, 1994, 'Muslims in Los Angeles', in Yvonne Haddad and Jane Smith, eds, *Muslim Communities in North America*, New York, State University of New York Press, pp. 135–68.

Kennedy, Ruby Jo Reeves, 1952, 'Single or Triple Melting-Pot? Intermarriage Trends in New Haven, 1870–1950', *American Journal of Sociology*, 58, July, pp. 56–9.

Kepel, Gilles, 1994a, *A l'ouest d'Allah*, Paris, Seuil.

—— 1994b, ed., *Exils et royaumes: les appartenances au monde arabo-musulman aujourd'hui*, Paris, Presses de la Fondation nationale des sciences politiques.

Kepel, Gilles and Leveau, Rémy, 1988, eds, *Les musulmans dans la société française*, Paris, Fondation nationale des sciences politiques.

Khalidi, Omar, 1991, ed., *Indian Muslims in North America*, Watertown (MA), South Asia Press.

—— 1995, *Indian Muslims since Independence*, Delhi, Vikas.

Khan, Salim, 1981, *A Brief History of Pakistanis in the Western United States*, M A Thesis, Sacramento, California State University.

Khandelwal, Madhulika, 1995, 'Indian Immigrants in Queens, New York City: Patterns of Spatial Concentration and Distribution, 1965–1990', in Peter Van der Veer, ed., *Nation and Migration: The Politics of Space in the South Asian Diaspora*, Philadelphia, University of Pennsylvania Press.

Khosrokhavar, Farhad, 1995–1996, 'L'identité voilée', *Confluences–Méditerranée*, Paris, L'Harmattan, 16, winter, pp. 69–84.

—— 1997, *L'islam des jeunes*, Paris, Flammarion.

Kramer, Martin, 1987, *Shi'ism, Resistance and Revolution*, Boulder, Westview Press/London, Mansell.

Kodmani-Darwish, Bassma, 1997, *La diaspora palestinienne*, Paris, PUF.

Köszegi, Michael A and Melton, John Gordon, 1992, eds, *Islam in North America: A Sourcebook*, New York, Gavard Publishing.

Lacorne, Denis, 1997, *La crise de l'identité américaine: du melting-pot au multiculturalisme*, Paris, Fayard.

Lahaj, Mary, 1994, 'The Islamic Center of New England', in Yvonne Haddad and Jane Smith, eds, *Muslim Communities in North America*, Albany (NY), State University of New York Press, pp. 293–316.

Laoust, Henri, 1977, *Les schismes dans l'islam*, Paris, Payot.

—— 1983, *Pluralismes dans l'Islam*, Paris, Librairie orientaliste Paul Geuthner.

Le Bras, Gabriel, 1955, *Etudes de sociologie religieuse*, Paris, PUF.

Le Bras, Gabriel and Desroche, Henri, 1970, 'Religion légale et religion vécue', *Archives de sciences sociales des religions*, 29.

Le Espiritu, Yen, 1992, *Asian American Panethnicity: Bridging Institutions and Identities*, Philadelphia, Temple University Press.

Lelyveld, David, 1978, *Aligarh's First Generation: Muslim Solidarity in British India*. Princeton, Princeton University Press.

Lenoir, Frédéric and Masquelier, Ysé T, 1997, eds, *Encyclopédie des religions*, vol. 2, Paris, Bayard.

Leonard, Karen Isaksen, 1992, *Making Ethnic Choices: California's Punjabi–Mexican Americans*, Philadelphia, Temple University Press.

Lewis, Bernard, 1992, 'La situation des populations musulmanes dans un régime non musulman: réflexions juridiques et historiques', in Bernard Lewis and Dominique Schnapper, eds, *Musulmans en Europe*, Poitiers, Actes Sud, pp. 11–34.

Lewis, Bernard and Schnapper, Dominique, 1992, eds, *Musulmans en Europe*, Poitiers, Actes Sud.

Lewis, Philip, 1994, *Islamic Britain: Religion, Politics and Identity Among British Muslims*, London, I B Tauris Publishers.

—— 1996, 'The Search for Religious Guidance: The Predicament of British Muslims', lecture delivered at the workshop: *A Comparative Study of the South Asian Diaspora, Religious Experience in Britain, Canada and USA*, London, School of Oriental and African Studies, 4–6 November.

Lincoln, Eric C, 1991, *The Black Muslims in America*, New York, Kayode Publishing, [1961].

Lovell, Emily Kalled, 1983, 'Islam in the United States: Past and Present', in Earle H Waugh, Baha Abu-Laban and Regula B Qureshi, eds, *The Muslim Community in North America*, Edmonton, University of Alberta Press, pp. 93–110.

Maclean, Derryl N, 1989, *Religion and Society in Arab Sind*, Liden, E J Brill.

McDonough, Sheila, 1994, 'Muslims of Montreal', in Yvonne Haddad and Jane Smith, eds, *Muslim Communities in North America*, Albany (NY), State University of New York Press, pp. 317–34.

—— 1996, 'South Asian Muslims in Canada', lecture delivered at the workshop: *A Comparative Study of the South Asian Diaspora, Religious Experience in Britain, Canada and USA*, London, School of Oriental and African Studies, 4–6 November.

Madelung, Wilfred, 1977a, 'Imama', *in Encyclopédie de l'islam*, Liden, E J Brill [1965], pp. 1192–8.

—— 1977b, 'Isma'iliyya', *in Encyclopédie de l'islam*, Liden, E J Brill [1965], pp. 212–15.

Maïla, Jo, 1993, 'Avenirs de l'islam', *Esprit. Face à la montée du radicalisme religieux*, 194, August–September, pp. 59–81.

—— 1997, 'L'islam moderne: entre le réformisme et l'islam politique', in Frédéric Lenoir and Ysé T Masquelier, eds, *Encyclopédie des religions*, vol. 2, Paris, Bayard, pp. 847–62.

Malik, Iftikhar Haider, 1989, *Pakistanis in Michigan: A Study of Third Culture and Acculturation*, New York, AMS Press Inc.

Malik, Jamal, 1996, *Colonisation of Islam: Dissolution of Traditional Institutions in Pakistan*, Delhi, Manohar.

Malik, Salahuddin, 1993, 'Pakistanis in Rochester, New York: Establishing Islamic Identity in the American Melting Pot', *Islamic Studies*, 32 (4), pp. 461–75.

Mamiya, Lawrence H, 1983, 'Minister Louis Farrakhan and the Final Call: Schism in the Muslim Movement', in Earle H Waugh, Baha Abu-Laban and Regula B Qureshi, eds, *The Muslim Community in North America*, Edmonton, Alberta University Press, pp. 234–57.

Markovits, Claude, 1995, ed., *Histoire de l'Inde moderne, 1480–1950*, Paris, Fayard.

Marti, Martin E and Appleby, Scott, 1991, eds, *Fundamentalisms Observed*, Chicago, University of Chicago Press.

—— 1994, eds, *Accounting for Fundamentalism*, Chicago, The Chicago University Press.

Martin, Denis-Constant, 1992, 'Le choix d'identité', *Revue française de science politique*, 42 (4), August, pp. 582–93.

Marx, Gary, 1993, 'La cage de fer de la culture: Réflexions sur le problème complexe de la race, du racisme et des mass media', in Michel Wieviorka, ed., *Racisme et modernité*, Paris, La Découverte, pp. 60–77.

Masson, Denise, 1980, *Essai d'interprétation du Coran inimitable*, Paris, Gallimard.

Masud, Muhammad Khalid, 1990, 'The Obligation to Migrate: The Doctrine of *hijra* in Islamic Law', in Dale F Eickleman and James Piscatori, eds, *Muslim Travellers: Pilgrimage, Migration and the Religious Imagination*, Berkeley, University of California Press, pp. 29–49.

Matin, Abdul, 1996, *Muslims in India and Abroad: Caste and Ethnicity*, Delhi, APH Publishing Corporation.

Mazumdar, Sucheta, 1989, 'Racist Responses to Racism: The Aryan Myth and South Asians in the United States', *South Asian Bulletin*, 9 (1).

Memmi, Albert, 1997, 'Les fluctuations de l'identité culturelle', *Esprit, La Fièvre identitaire*, 228, January, pp. 94–106.

Metcalf, Barbara Daly, 1982, *Islamic Revival in British India: Deoband, 1860–1900*, Princeton, Princeton University Press.

—— 1996a, ed., *Making Muslim Space in North America and Europe*, Berkeley, University of California Press.

—— 1996b, 'New Medinas: The Tablighi Jama'at in America and Europe', in Barbara Daly Metcalf, ed., *Making Muslim Space in North America and Europe*, Berkeley, University of California Press, pp. 101–27.

—— 1998, 'Women and Men in a Contemporary Pietist Movement: the Case of the Tablighi Jama'at' in Patricia Jeffery and Amrita Basu, eds, *Appropriating Gender: Women's Activism and Politicized Religion in South Asia*, New York and London, Routledge, pp. 107–22.

Michel, Patrick, 1997, ed., *Religion et démocratie*, Paris, Albin Michel.

Miller, Roland, 1992, *Mappila Muslims of Kerala: A Study in Islamic Trends*, Madras, Orient Longman [1976].

Minault, Gail, 1982, *The Khilafat Movement: Religious Symbolism and Political Mobilization in India*, Delhi, OUP.

Minocha, Urmil, 1987, 'South Asian Immigrants: Trends and Impacts on the Sending and Receiving Societies', in Fawcett and Carino, eds, *Pacific Bridges: The New Immigration from Asia and Pacific Island*, New York, Center for Migration Studies, pp. 350–70.

Modood, Tariq, 1991, 'Les musulmans asiatiques de Grande-Bretagne et l'Affaire Rushdie',

Les Temps modernes, Démocratie et minorités ethniques: le cas anglais, 540–541, 46th year, July–August, pp. 111–32.

Mohammad, Aminah T, 1993, *Passage to America: Asian Indians in the United States,* master's dissertation, Paris, Université de la Sorbonne Nouvelle.

—— 1998, *Les Musulmans du sous-continent indien à New York: culture, religion, identité,* doctoral thesis, Paris, EHESS.

—— 1998, 'Le lobbying pakistanais aux Etats-Unis: une force émergente?', not yet published [2000].

—— 2000, 'The Relationships between Muslims and Hindus in the United States: *kafirs* vs *mlecchas*', in Crispin Bates, ed., *Community, Empire and Migration: South Asians in Diaspora,* London, MacMillan.

Moliner, Christine, 1994, *Expériences diasporiques et constructions identitaires: la communauté sikh de Grande-Bretagne,* DEA* dissertation, Paris, EHESS.

Montanari, Massimo, 1996, 'Modèles alimentaires et identités culturelles', in Jean-Louis Flandrin and Massimo Montanari, eds, *Histoire de l'alimentation,* Paris, Fayard, pp. 319–24.

Moore, Kathleen, 1995, *Al-Mughtaribun: American Law and the Transformation of Muslim Life in the United States,* New York, State University of New York Press.

Muhammad, Salaruddin, 1983, *Shah Walîullâh, sa vie, son œuvre,* np.

Muhlstein, Anka, 1986, *Manhattan: la fabuleuse histoire de New York, des Indiens à l'an 2000,* Paris, Grasset.

Murad, Khurram, 1986, *Da'wah Among Non-Muslims in the West,* London, The Islamic Foundation.

Nanji, Azim, 1983, 'The Nizari Ismaili Muslim Community in North America: Background and Development', in Earle H Waugh, Baha Abu-Laban and Regula B Qureshi, eds, *The Muslim Community in North America,* Edmonton, Alberta University Press, pp. 149–64.

Nasr, Syed Vali Reza, 1994, *The Vanguard of the Islamic Revolution: The Jama'at-i-Islami of Pakistan,* London, I B Tauris Publishers.

Neveu, Catherine, 1993, *Communauté, nationalité et citoyenneté. De l'autre côté du miroir: les Bangladeshis de Londres,* Paris, Ed Karthala.

Nielsen, Jorgen, 1992, *Muslims in Western Europe,* Edinburgh, Edinburgh University Press.

Nonneman, Gerd, Niblock, Tim and Szajkowski, Bogdan, eds, 1996, *Muslim Communities in the New Europe,* New York, Ithaca Press.

Numan, Fareed H, 1992, 'The Muslim Population in the US: A Brief Statement', *The American Muslim Council,* October, pp. 3–39.

Nye, Malory, 1995, *A Place for our Gods: The Construction of an Edinburgh Hindu Temple Community,* Surrey, Richmond Press.

Oriol, Michel, 1984, 'Sur la transposabilité des cultures "populaires" (ou subalternes) en situation d'émigration', in *L'immigration en France: le choc des cultures,* Dossiers du Centre Thomas More, May.

Pettigrew, T and Meertens, R, 1993, 'Le racisme voilé: dimension et mesure', in Michel Wieviorka, ed., *Racisme et modernité,* Paris, La Découverte.

Pinault, David, 1997, 'Shi'ism in South Asia', *The Muslim World,* 87 (3–4), July–October, pp. 235–57.

Piscatori, James and Hoeber Rudolph, Suzanne, 1997, eds, *Transnational Religions and Fading States,* Boulder, Westview Press.

Poston, Larry Alan, 1992, *Islamic Da'wah in the West: Muslim Missionary & the Dynamics of Conversion to Islam,* New York, OUP.

Qureshi, Regula B, 1991, 'Marriage Strategies among Muslims from South Asia', in Earle H Waugh, Sharon Abu-Laban, & Regula B Qureshi, eds, *Muslim Families in North America*, Edmonton, University of Alberta Press, pp. 185–212.

—— 1996, 'Transcending Space: Recitation and Community among South Asian Muslims in Canada', in Barbara Daly Metcalf, ed., *Making Muslim Space in North America and Europe*, Berkeley, University of California Press, pp. 46–64.

Racine, Jean, 1993, 'Rama et les joueurs de dés. Questions sur la nation indienne', *Hérodote*, 4th trimestre, 71, October–December, pp. 5–42.

Rahman, Fazlur, 1968, *Islam*, New York, Doubleday Anchor Book.

—— 1982, *Islam and Modernity: Transformation of an Intellectual Tradition*, Chicago, University of Chicago Press.

Rajagopal, Arvind, 1994, 'Better than Blacks? Or, Hum Kaale Hain to Kya Hua', *Samar*, summer issue.

René, Emilie, 1997, 'Fax, ordinateurs . . . au service de la protestation: les dessous de l'affaire Salman Rushdie', *Sciences humaines*, 17, June–July, pp. 47–8.

Rex, John, 1991, *Ethnic Identity and Ethnic Mobilisation in Britain*, Coventry, Centre for Research in Ethnic Relations.

Richard, Yann, 1991, *L'Islam chi'ite*, Paris, Fayard.

Rioux, Jean-Pierre and Sirinelli, Jean-François, 1997, eds, *Pour une histoire culturelle*, Paris, Seuil.

Rizvi, S A A, 1980, *Shah Wali Allah and His Times*, Canberra.

Robinson, Francis, 1974, *Separatism among Indian Muslims: The Politics of the United Provinces' Muslims 1860–1923*, Cambridge, Cambridge University Press.

—— 1988, *Varieties of South Asian Islam*, Coventry, Centre for Research in Ethnic Relations.

Rocher, Guy, 1968, *Introduction à la sociologie générale*, (vol. 1: *L'action sociale;* vol. 2: *L'organisation sociale;* vol. 3: *Le changement social)*, Paris, Editions HMH.

Rodinson, Maxime, 1966, *Islam et capitalisme*, Paris, Seuil.

—— 1975, 'Ghidha', *in Encyclopédie de l'islam*, Liden, E J Brill [1965], pp. 1081–97.

Ross-Sheriff, Fariyal and Nanji, Azim, 1991, 'Islamic Identity, Family and Community: The Case of the Nizari Ismaili Muslims', in E H Waugh, S Abu-Laban and R Qureshi, eds, *Muslim Families in North America*, Edmonton, University of Alberta Press, pp. 101–17.

Rouchdy, Aleya, 1992, ed., *The Arabic Language in America*, Detroit, Wayne State University Press.

Roy, Olivier, 1992, 'L'Islam en France: religion, communauté ethnique ou ghetto social', in Bernard Lewis and Dominique Schnapper, eds, *Musulmans en Europe*, Poitiers, Actes Sud, pp. 73–88.

—— 1996, 'Le néo-fondamentalisme islamique ou l'imaginaire de *l'oummah*', *Esprit. Le choc des cultures à l'heure de la mondialisation*, 220, April, pp. 80–107.

Rudolph, Lloyd and Susanne, 1995, *Religion and Ethnicity Among Muslims*, New Delhi, Rawat Publications.

Russell, Ralph, 1982, ed., *Urdu in Britain*, Karachi, Golden Block Works Ltd.

Sabagh, Georges and Bozorgmehr, Mehdi, 1994, 'Secular Immigrants: Religiosity and Ethnicity Among Iranian Muslims in Los Angeles', in Yvonne Haddad and Jane Smith, eds, *Muslim Communities in North America*, Albany (NY), State University of New York Press, pp. 445–76.

Said, Edward, 1980, *L'orientalisme*, Paris, Seuil [translation by Catherine Malamoud of *Orientalism*, 1978, New York, Pantheon Books].

Saint-Blancat, Chantal, 1995, 'Une diaspora musulmane en Europe?', *Archives de sciences sociales des religions*, 92, October–December, pp. 9–24.

—— 1997, *L'islam de la diaspora*, Paris, Bayard.

Salvadori, Cynthia, 1989, *Through Open Doors: A View of Asian Cultures in Kenya*, Nairobi, Kenway Publications [1983].

Sanyal, Usha, 1993, 'The [Re]-Construction of South Asian Muslim Identity in Queens, New York', lecture delivered at the conference *The Expanding Landscape: South Asians in the Diaspora*, New York, Columbia University, March 1993.

—— 1996, *Devotional Islam and Politics in British India: Ahmad Riza Khan Barelwi and his Movement*, Delhi, OUP.

Saran, Parmatma, 1980, *The New Ethnics*, New York, Praeger Publishers. With A Thottathil, 'An Economic Profile of Asian Indians', in Parmatma Saran, ed., *The New Ethnics*, New York, Praeger Publishers, pp. 233–46.

Sayad, Abdelmalek, 1983, 'Islam et immigration en France: les effets de l'immigration sur l'Islam', *L'Islam en Europe à l'epoque moderne*, Paris, Collège de France, September–October.

Schacht, J, 1975, 'Muhammad 'Abduh', *in Encyclopédie de l'islam*, Liden, E J Brill [1965], pp. 419–21.

Schimmel, Annemarie, 1980, *Islam in the Indian Subcontinent*, Liden, E J Brill.

—— 1994, *Deciphering the Signs of God: A Phenomenological Approach to Islam*, Edinburgh, Edinburgh University Press.

Schnapper, Dominique, 1998, *La relation à l'autre: Au cœur de la pensée sociologique*, Paris, Gallimard.

Schubel, Vernon James, 1991, 'The Muharram Majlis: The Role of a Ritual in the Preservation of Shi'a Identity', in Earle H Waugh, Sharon M Abu-Laban and Regula B Qureshi, eds, *Muslim Families in North America*, Edmonton, University of Alberta Press, pp. 118–31.

Shahid, W A R and van Koningsveld, P S, 1991, eds, *The Integration of Islam and Hinduism in Western Europe*, The Netherlands, Kok Pharos Publishing House.

Shaw, Alison, 1989, *A Pakistani Community in Britain*, Oxford, Blackwell.

Sheffer, Gabriel, 1986, ed., *Modern Diasporas in International Politics*, New York, St Martin's Press.

Slyomovics, Susan, 1995, 'New York City's Muslim World Day Parade' in Peter Van der Veer, ed., *Nation and Migration: The Politics of Space in South Asian Diaspora*, Philadelphia, University of Pennsylvania Press, pp. 157–77.

—— 1996, 'The Muslim World Day Parade and "Storefront" Mosques of New York City', in Barbara Daly Metcalf, ed., *Making Muslim Space in America and Europe*, Berkeley, University of California Press, pp. 204–16.

Sollers, W, 1989, *The Invention of Ethnicity*, New York, OUP.

Sourdel, Dominique and Janine, 1996, *Dictionnaire historique de l'islam*, Paris, PUF.

Stasik, Danuta, 1994, *Out of India: Image of the West in Hindi Literature* Deli, Manohar.

Stone, Carol, 1991, 'Estimate of Muslims Living in America', in Yvonne Haddad, ed., *The Muslims of America*, New York, OUP, pp. 25–36.

Streiff-Fenart, Jocelyne, 1987, 'Elements de réflexion pour une définition de la notion d'intégration', *Revue de l'Occident musulman et de la Méditerranée*, 43, 1st trimest re, pp. 61–66.

Sukhatme, Mahadevan I, 1988, 'Brain Drain and the IIT Graduate', *Economic and Political Weekly*, 18th June, pp. 1285–93.

Tassy, Garcin de, 1831, *Mémoire sur les particularités de la religion musulmane d'après les ouvrages hindoustani*, Paris, Imprimerie royale.

Taylor, Charles, 1992, *Multiculturalisme: différence et démocratie*, Paris, Flammarion [translation by Denis-Armand Canal of *Multiculturalism and "The Politics of Recognition"*, Princeton, Princeton University Press, 1992].

Temps Modernes (Les), 1991, *Démocratie et minorités ethniques – Le cas anglais*, 46e année, 540–541, July–August.

Thanawi, Ashraf 'Ali, n.d., *Behisthî Zewar*, Multan, Maktabah Imdadiyyah.

Thiesse, Anne-Marie, 1999, *La création des identités nationales. Europe XVIIIè~XXè siècle*, Paris, Seuil.

Tinker, Hugh, 1977, *The Banyan Tree: Overseas Emigrants From India, Pakistan, and Bangladesh*, London, OUP.

Tribalat, Michèle, 1995, *De l'immigration à l'assimilation. Enquête sur les populations d'origine étrangère en France*, Paris, La Découverte/INED.

Tocqueville, Alexis de, 1981, *De la démocratie en Amérique*, 2 vol., Paris, Flammarion.

Troll, Christian W, 1994, 'Two Conceptions of Da'wa in India: Jama'at-i-Islami and Tablighi Jama'at', *Archives de sciences sociales des religions*, 87, July–September, pp. 115–33.

Ullendorf, E, 1975, 'Habash, Habasha', *in Encyclopédie de l'islam*, Liden, E J Brill [1965], pp. 3–5.

Ullmo, Sylvia, 1994, ed., *L'immigration américaine: exemple ou contre-exemple pour Ia France?*, Paris, L'Harmattan.

Van der Veer, Peter, 1993, 'Migration and the Nationalist Imagination', seminar presented at EHESS, 29 April.

—— 1994, *Religious Nationalism: Hindus and Muslims in India*, Berkeley, University of California Press.

—— 1995, ed., *Nation and Migration: The Politics of Space in the South Asian Diaspora*, Philadelphia, University of Pennsylvania Press. 'Introduction: The Diasporic Imagination', in Peter Van der Veer, ed., *Nation and Migration: The Politics of Space in the South Asian Diaspora*, Philadelphia, University of Pennsylvania Press, pp. 1–16.

Vertovec, Steven, 1991, ed., *Aspects of the South Asian Diaspora*, Oxford University Papers on India, 2 (2), Oxford, OUP.

—— 1996, 'Muslims, the State, and the Public Sphere in Britain', in Gerd Nonneman, Tim Niblock and Bogdan Szajkowski, eds, *Muslim Communities in the New Europe*, New York, Ithaca Press, pp. 169–85.

Voll, John O, 1991, 'Islamic Issues for Muslims in the United States', in Yvonne Haddad, ed., *The Muslims of America*, New York, OUP, pp. 205–16.

Walbridge, Linda S, 1993, 'Confirmation of Shi'ism in America: An Analysis of Sermons in the Dearborn Mosques', *The Muslim World*, 82 (3–4), July–October, pp. 248–62.

Watt, Montgomery W, 1988, *Islamic Fundamentalism and Modernity*, London, Routledge.

Waugh, Earle H, 1983, 'Muslim Leadership and the Shaping of the Umma: Classical Tradition and Religious Tension in the North American Setting', in Earle H Waugh, Baha Abu-Laban and Regula B Qureshi, eds, *The Muslim Community in North America*, Edmonton, Alberta University Press, pp. 11–33.

Waugh, Earle, Abu-Laban, Bana and Qureshi, Regula, 1983, eds, *The Muslim Community in North America*, Edmonton, University of Alberta Press.

Waugh, Earle, Abu-Laban, Sharon and Qureshi, Regula, 1991, eds, *Muslim Families in North America*, Edmonton, University of Alberta Press.

Webb, Gisela, 1994, 'The Bawa Muhaiyadeen Fellowship', in Yvonne Haddad and Jane Smith, eds, *Muslim Communities in North America*, Albany (NY), State University of New York Press, pp. 75–108.

Weber, Max, 1996, *Sociologie des religions*, Paris, Gallimard.

Weibel, Nadine B, 1995, 'L'Europe, berceau d'une *umma* reconstituée ou l'émergence d'une nouvelle utopie religieuse', *Archives de sciences sociales des religions*, 92, October–December, pp. 25–34.

—— 1996, 'Islamité, égalité et complémentarité: vers une nouvelle approche de l'identité féminine', *Archives de sciences sociales des religions*, 95, July–September, pp. 133–41.

Weiner, Myron, 1990, 'The Indian Presence in America: What Differences Will it Make?', in Nathan and Sulochana Glazer, eds, *Conflicting Images: India and the United States*, Glenn Dale, The Riverdale Company.

Wensinck, A J, 1998, 'Sha'bân', in *Encyclopédie de l'islam*, Liden, E J Brill [1965], p. 159.

Werbner, Pnina, 1989, *The Migration Process: Capital, Gifts and Offerings among Pakistanis in Britain*, Oxford, Berg Publishers.

—— 1992, 'Le radicalisme islamique et la guerre du Golfe: les prédicateurs et les dissensions politiques chez les Pakistanis de Grande Bretagne', in Bernard Lewis and Dominique Schnapper, eds., *Musulmans en Europe*, Poitiers, Actes Sud, pp. 127–50.

Wieviorka, Michel, 1993, ed., *Racisme et modernité*, Paris, La Découverte.

Willaime, Jean-Paul, 1996, 'Laïcité et religion en France', in Grace Davie and Danièle Hervieu-Léger, eds, *Identités religieuses en Europe*, Paris, La Découverte, pp. 153–71.

Williams, Raymond Brady, 1988, *Religions of Immigrants from India and Pakistan: New Threads in the American Tapestry*, New York, Cambridge University Press.

—— 1992, ed., *A Sacred Thread: Modern Transmission of Hindu Traditions in India and Abroad*, Chambersburg, Anima Publications.

Wilson, Kalpana, 1993, 'Globalisation and "Muslim Belt": Reshaping of British Racism', *Economic and Political Weekly*, 19 June, pp. 1288–90.

Zaman, Muhammad Qasim, 1997, 'The Role of Arabic and the Arab Middle East in the Definition of Muslim Identity in Twentieth Century India', *The Muslim World*, 87 (3-4), July–October, pp. 272–98.

—— 1998, 'Sectarianism in Pakistan: The Radicalization of Shi'i and Sunni Identities', *Modern Asian Studies*, 32 (2), July, pp. 689–716.

Zeghal, Malika, 1996, *Gardiens de l'islam: les oulémas d'Al-Azhar dans l'Egypte contemporaine*, Paris, Presses de la Fondation nationale des sciences politiques.

Islamic publications in the United States (except periodicals)

The AMC Report *(American Muslim Council)*
American Muslim 1994 Resource Directory
Crescent School Student Handbook
ICLI Newsletter *(Islamic Center of Long Island)*
Islamic Horizon *(Islamic Society of North America)*
Monthly Da'wat (Masjid ul-Aman)
Mosques Around the World *(Ahmadiyya Muslim Association)*
Resalah *(Islamic Cultural Center of New York)* (monthly bulletin of the mosque)
Sound Vision: Helping Tomorrow's Muslims Today *(Islamic Circle of North America)*
Unveiling Prejudice: the Status of Muslim Civil Rights in the United States *(Council on American–Islamic Relations Research Center)*

Periodicals

Akhbar-e-Jahan (Pakistan)
Biswin Sadi (India).
Communalism Combat (India)

Daily News – Long Island (US)
Dawn (Pakistan)
Economic and Political Weekly (India)
Herald (Pakistan)
Hudaa (US)
India Abroad (US)
India Today (India)
International Herald Tribune (US)
Long Island Jewish World (US)
Masala (US)
The Message International (US)
The Minaret (US)
The New York Times (US)
Pakistan Link (US)
Samar (US)

Government sources

1990 Census of Population: Social and Economic Characteristics, New York. US Department of Commerce, Economy and Statistics Administration, Bureau of Census.

Fernandez, Edward W and Robinson, Gregory J, n.d., 'Illustrative Ranges of the Distribution of Undocumented Immigrants by State', US Bureau of the Census, Technical Working Papers 8.

Literature

Banerjee Divakaruni, Chitra, 1996, *Arranged Marriages*, New York, Anchor Books.

Dhanoa, Parminder, 1991, *Waiting for Winter*, Delhi, Penguin Books.

Gupta, Anu, 1995, 'Crystal Quince' in Roshni Rustomji-Kerns, ed., *Living in America: Poetry and Fiction by South Asian American Writers*, Boulder, Westview Press.

Kureishi, Hanif, 1990, *The Buddha of Suburbia*, New York, Viking.

Luthra, Punam, 1992, 'Pati Dev', in The Women of South Asian Descent Collective, eds, *Our Feet Walk the Sky: Women of the South Asian Diaspora*, San Francisco, Aunt Lute Books, pp. 257–63.

Maira, Sunaina and Srikanth, Rajini, 1996, eds, *Contours of the Heart: South Asians Map North America*, New York, Asian American Writers Workshop.

Mandava, Bhargavi C, 1996, *Where Oceans Meet*, Seattle, Seal Press.

Naqvi, Tahira, 1995, 'All is Not Lost', in Roshni Rustomji-Kerns, ed, *Living in America: Poetry and Fiction by South Asian American Writers*, Boulder, Westview Press, pp. 145–54.

—— 1996, 'Beyond the Walls, Amreeka', in Sunaina Maira and Rajini Srikanth, eds, *Contours of the Heart: South Asians Map North America*, New York, Asian American Writers Workshop, pp. 290–302.

Rushdie, Salman, 1992, *The Satanic Verses*, Dover, The Consortium [1998].

—— 1993, *East West*, New York, Pantheon Books.

Rustomji-Kerns, Roshni, 1994, ed., *Living in America: Poetry and Fiction by South Asian American Writers*, Boulder, Westview Press.

Seth, Vikram, 1993, *A Suitable Boy*, Delhi, Viking.

Sheikh, Farhana, 1990, *The Red Box*, Delhi, Rupa and Co.

Women of the South Asian Descent Collective, eds, *Our Feet Walk the Sky: Women of the South Asian Diaspora*, San Francisco, Aunt Lute Books.

APPENDICES

Appendix 1

LIST OF QUOTED PERSONS[1]

Abbas   immigrant, forties, Gujarati from East Africa, married, unemployed, Bohra. (M)

Abid   immigrant, forties, from Kashmir, married (to Saida), doctor, Sunni. (M)

Afsana   immigrant, forties, from Madras, married (to Hasan, mother of Rafiq), unemployed, Sunni. (F)

Ansar   immigrant, fifties, from Kashmir, married, doctor, Sunni. (M)

Anwar   immigrant, thirties, from Hyderabad (India), getting married, engineer, Sunni. (M)

Arbaz   born in the United States, 19 yrs old, family from Aligarh, unmarried, student, Sunni. (M)

Arshad   born in the United States, 23 yrs old, family from Karachi, unmarried, student, Sunni. (M)

Asghari   born in the United States, 20 yrs old, family from Hyderabad (India), unmarried, student, Sunni. (F)

Ashraf   immigrant, thirties, from Aligarh, unmarried, head of sales in a computer firm, Sunni. (M)

Aslam   born in the United States, 22 yrs old, family from Lucknow, unmarried, student, Sunni. (M)

Bashir   immigrant, fifties, from Kerala, married, doctor, Sunni. (M)

Faiza   immigrant, forties, from Lucknow, married, unemployed, Sunni. (F)

Farida   born in the United States, 21 yrs old, family from Bangladesh, unmarried, student, Sunni. (F)

Fazilat   born in the United States, 20 yrs old, Gujarati from East Africa, unmarried, student, Isma'ili Nizari. (F)

Ghafar   immigrant, thirties, from Bangladesh, unmarried, restaurant waiter, Sunni. (M)

Ghazala   immigrant, forties, from Karachi, married (mother of Wahida and Mahila), dentist, Sunni. (F)

Hanif   immigrant, thirties, from Punjab, married, taxi driver, Sunni. (M)

Hasan   immigrant, fifties, from Madras, married (to Afsana, father of Rafiq), engineer, Sunni. (M)

Hasina   immigrant, forties, from Hyderabad (India), married, computer analyst, Sunni. (F)

Humayun   immigrant, forties, from Karachi, married, engineer, Shi'a. (M)

Iqbal   immigrant, forties, from Aligarh, married, trained as engineer and now working as computer consultant, Sunni. (M)

Ismat   immigrant, forties, from Punjab, married, unemployed, Sunni. (F)

Kabir   born in the United States, 19 yrs old, family from Karachi, unmarried, student, Shi'a. (M)

Maliha   born in the United States, 20 yrs old, family from Karachi, unmarried (daughter of Ghazala and sister of Wahida), student, Sunni. (F)

Mansur   immigrant, forties, from Punjab, married, newspaper vendor, Shi'a. (M)

Mirza   immigrant, fifties, from Bangladesh, married, newspaper vendor, Sunni. (M)

Mujib   immigrant, fifties, from Karachi, married, engineer, Sunni. (M)

Nadim   immigrant, thirties, from Bangladesh, ex-computing student working as a grocer, unmarried, Sunni. (M)

Nighat   immigrant, forties, from Punjab, married, doctor, Sunni. (F)

Nisar   immigrant, fifties, from Punjab, married, businessman, Ahmadi. (M)

Rafiq   born in the United States, 11 yrs old, family from Madras (son of Afsana and Hasan), school student, Sunni. (M)

Riyaz   immigrant, fifties, Gujarati from East Africa, married, engineer, (Paanwala) Bohra. (M)

Rukhsana   immigrant, fifties, from Aligarh, married, doctor, Sunni. (F)

Sadat   immigrant, fifties, from Punjab, married, accountant, Sunni. (M)

Safia   immigrant, fifties, from Punjab, married, doctor, Sunni. (F)

Saida   immigrant, forties, from Kashmir, married (to Abid), doctor, Sunni. (F)

Salma   born in the United States, 20 yrs old, family from Hyderabad (India), unmarried, student, Sunni. (F)

Salman   immigrant, thirties, Gujarati from East Africa, married, shopkeeper, Bohra. (M)

Shabana   born in the United States, 21 yrs old, Gujarati from East Africa, unmarried, student, Bohra. (F)

Shabnam   immigrant, fifties, from Madras, married, doctor, Sunni. (F)

Sikandar   born in the United States, 19 yrs old, family from Bangladesh, unmarried, student, Sunni. (M)

Sitara   immigrant, forties, from Punjab, unmarried, doctor, Sunni. (F)

Sultan   immigrant, 28 yrs old, from Madras, married, engineer, Shi'a. (M)

Vikram   born in the United States, 21 yrs old, family from Gujarat, unmarried, student, Hindu. (M)

Wahida   born in the United States, 18 yrs old, family from Karachi, unmarried (sister of Maliha and daughter of Ghazala), student, Sunni. (F)

Zainab   born in the United States, 27 yrs old, family from Hyderabad (India), getting married, student, Sunni. (F)

Zakir   born in the United States, 24 yrs old, family from Punjab, unmarried, student, Sunni. (M)

Zeba   born in the United States, 20 yrs old, family from Karachi, unmarried, student, Sunni. (F)

Zeenat   born in the United States, 22 yrs old, family from Punjab, unmarried, student, Ahmadi. (F)

Zohra   born in the United States, 18 yrs old, 'UP-walli' from Guyana, unmarried, student, Sunni. (F)

Zoya   immigrant, forties, from Hyderabad (India), married, teacher, Sunni. (F)

Appendix 2

ACRONYMS

AAHOA	Asian American Hotel Owner Association
ABCD	American Born Confused Desi
AFMI	American Association of Muslims from India
AIC	American Islamic College
AIM	Association of Indian Muslims
AMASFS	American Muslim Alliance Social and Family Services
AMC	American Muslim Council
AMM	American Muslim Mission
AMSE	Association of Muslim Scientists and Engineers
AMSS	American Muslim Social Scientists
BCCI	Bank of Credit and Commerce International
BJP	Bharatiya Janata Party
CAIR	Council on American–Islamic Relations
CSA	Concerned South Asians
FIA	Federation of Indian Associations
FOB	Fresh Off the Boat
HSS	Hindu Swayam Sevak Sangh
IAFPE	Indian American Forum for Political Education
ICCNY	Islamic Cultural Center of New York
ICLI	Islamic Center of Long Island
ICNA	Islamic Circle of North America
ILA	Indian League of America
IMA	Islamic Medical Association
IMANA	Islamic Medical Association of North America
IMG	Indian Medical Graduate
IPSG	Indian Progressive Study Group
ISNA	Islamic Society of North America
ITC	Islamic Teaching Center
IIT	Indian Institute of Technology
LDC	Licensed Drivers Coalition

MCNY	Muslim Center of New York
MSA	Muslim Student Association
MSI	Muslim Savings and Investment
MYNA	Muslim Youth of North America
NRI	Non Resident Indian
PAC	Pakistan American Congress
PAK-PAC	Pakistani Physicians' Public Affairs Committee
RFRA	Religious Freedom Restoration Act
RSS	Rashtriya Swayam Sevak Sangh
SAAA	South Asian Aids Action
SALGA	South Asian Lesbian and Gay Association
SAYA	South Asian Youth Action
SCMS	Sister Clara Muslim School
VHP	Vishva Hindu Parishad (World Hindu Council)
WAMY	World Assembly of Muslim Youth
YAR	Youth Against Racism

Appendix 3

MAPS

Map 1: States of the Indian Union

CNRS - SIS - CEIAS - UMR 8564
Centre de compétence thématique « Modélisation, Analyse spatial, SIG »

Source: Geographical coordinates from ESR 1 1993 World database (DWC)
Polyconic projection system
Software: ARC/INFO version 7.2.1
Production: F. PIROT - M. LEGRAND - A. MOHAMMAD-ARIF

Map 2: Cities in South Asia

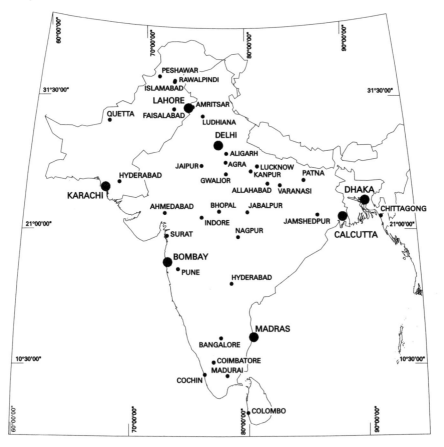

CNRS - SIS - CEIAS - UMR 8564
Centre de compétence thématique « Modélisation, Analyse spatial, SIG »

Source: Geographical coordinates from ESR 1 1993 World database (DWC)
Polyconic projection system
Software: ARC/INFO version 7.2.1
Production: F. PIROT - M. LEGRAND - A. MOHAMMAD-ARIF

● Major cities
• Other cities

Map 3: Pakistan

CNRS - SIS - CEIAS - UMR 8564
Centre de compétence thématique « Modélisation, Analyse spatial, SIG »

Source: Geographical coordinates from ESR 1 1993 World database (DWC)
Polyconic projection system
Software: ARC/INFO version 7.2.1
Production: F. PIROT - M. LEGRAND - A. MOHAMMAD-ARIF

- - - - Provincial
         border

●   Major cities

SIND Province

Map 4: Bangladesh

CNRS - SIS - CEIAS - UMR 8564
Centre de compétence thématique « Modélisation, Analyse spatial, SIG »

Source: Geographical coordinates from ESR 1 1993 World database (DWC)
Polyconic projection system
Software: ARC/INFO version 7.2.1
Production: F. PIROT - M. LEGRAND - A. MOHAMMAD-ARIF

Map 5: The United States

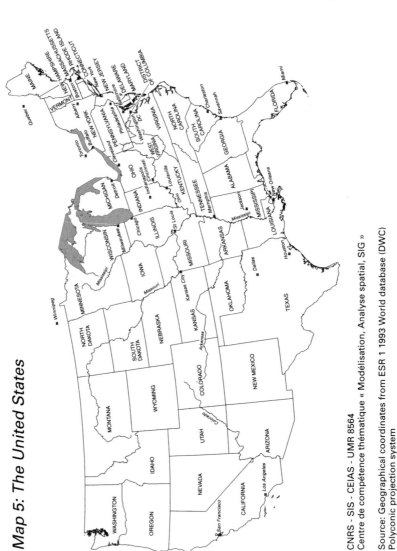

CNRS - SIS - CEIAS - UMR 8564
Centre de compétence thématique « Modélisation, Analyse spatial, SIG »

Source: Geographical coordinates from ESR 1 1993 World database (DWC)
Polyconic projection system
Software: ARC/INFO version 7.2.1
Production: F. PIROT - M. LEGRAND - A. MOHAMMAD-ARIF

Map 6: Indian population of the United States in 1990

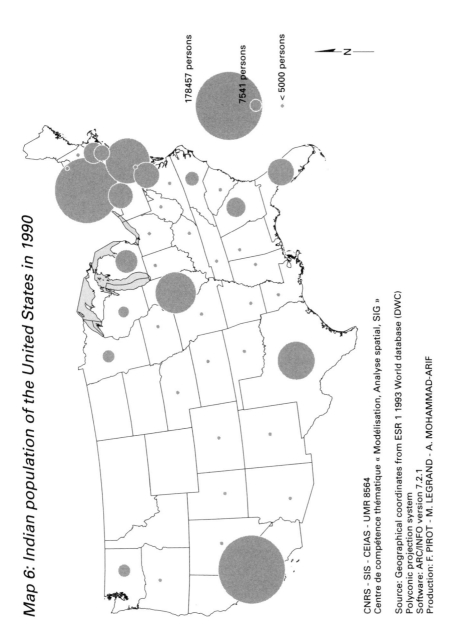

178457 persons

7541 persons

< 5000 persons

N

CNRS - SIS - CEIAS - UMR 8564
Centre de compétence thématique « Modélisation, Analyse spatial, SIG »

Source: Geographical coordinates from ESR 1 1993 World database (DWC)
Polyconic projection system
Software: ARC/INFO version 7.2.1
Production: F. PIROT - M. LEGRAND - A. MOHAMMAD-ARIF

Map 7: Mosques and Islamic Centres in New York and Nassau County (Long Island) included in research

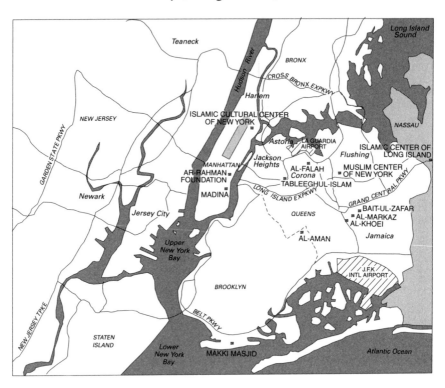

Key

al-Aman: Bangladeshi mosque
al-Falah: Tablighi Jama'at mosque
al-Khoei: Twelver Shi'ite mosque
al-Markaz: l'Islamic Circle of North America (Jama'at-i-Islami) centre
ar-Rahman Foundation: 'the taxi driver's mosque'
Bait-ul-Zafar: Ahmadiyya centre
Islamic Center of Long Island: 'the mosque of the future'
Islamic Cultural Center of New York: 'the great mosque of New York'
Madina: Bangladeshi mosque
Makki: Masjid: Pakistani mosque
Muslim Center of New York: Indo–Pakistani mosque
Tableeghul-Islam: Barelwi mosque

CNRS - SIS - CEIAS - UMR 8564
Centre de compétence thématique « Modélisation, Analyse spatial, SIG »

Source: Geographical coordinates from ESR 1 1993 World database (DWC)
Polyconic projection system
Software: ARC/INFO version 7.2.1
Production: F. PIROT - M. LEGRAND - A. MOHAMMAD-ARIF

Appendix 4

TABLES OF STATISTICS

Table 1 Total population of the United States by ethnic group (rounded figures)

	Population	% of population (1990)	% of population (1980)
Total	248,710,000	100	100
Whites	199,686,000	80.3	83.2
African–Americans	29,986,000	12.1	11.7
Asians	7,274,000	2.9	1.5
Native Americans	1,959,000	0.8	0.6
Hispanics	22,354,000	9.0	6.4
Other	9,805,000	3.9	3.0

Source: 1990 US Census of Population.

Table 2 Total population of New York City by ethnic group

	Population	% of population (1990)	% of population (1980)
Total	8,306,075	100	100
Whites	3,827,088	52.2	60.7
African–Americans	2,102,512	28.8	25.2
Asians	512,719	7.0	3.3
Native Americans	27,531	0.4	0.2
Hispanics	1,783,511	24.4	19.6
Other	52,714	11.6	10.6

Source: 1990 US Census of Population.

Table 3 Indian population by state (1990 census)

State	Number	%	State	Number	%
United States – Total	815,447	100.0	Massachusetts	19,719	2.4
Alabama	4,348	0.5	Michigan	23,845	2.9
Alaska	472	0.1	Minnesota	8,234	1.0
Arizona	5,663	0.7	Mississippi	1,872	0.2
Arkansas	1,329	0.2	Missouri	6,111	0.7
California	159,973	19.6	Montana	248	0.0
Carolina (North)	9,847	1.2	Nebraska	1,218	0.1
Carolina (South)	3,900	0.5	Nevada	1,825	0.2
Colorado	3,836	0.5	New Hampshire	1,697	0.2
Connecticut	11,755	1.0	New Jersey	79,440	9.7
Dakota (North)	482	0.1	New York	140,985	17.3
Dakota (South)	287	0.0	New Mexico	1,593	0.2
Delaware	2,183	0.3	Ohio	20,848	2.6
District of Columbia	1601	0.2	Oklahoma	4,546	0.6
Florida	31,457	3.9	Oregon	3,508	0.4
Georgia	13,926	1.7	Pennsylvania	28,396	3.5
Hawaii	1,015	0.1	Rhode Island	1,975	0.2
Idaho	473	0.1	Tennessee	5,911	0.7
Illinois	64,200	7.9	Texas	55,795	6.8
Indiana	7,095	0.9	Utah	1,557	0.2
Iowa	3,021	0.4	Vermont	529	0.1
Kansas	3,956	0.5	Virginia	20,494	2.5
Kentucky	2,922	0.4	Virginia (West)	1,981	0.2
Louisiana	5,083	0.6	Washington	8,205	1.0
Maine	607	0.1	Wisconsin	6,914	0.8
Maryland	28,330	3.5	Wyoming	240	0.0

Source: 1995–1996 Asian Indian Business Resource.

Table 4 Number of mosques and Islamic centres by state

State	Number	State	Number
United States – Total	953	Massachusetts	9
Alabama	20	Michigan	59
Alaska	1	Minnesota	5
Arizona	10	Mississippi	7
Arkansas	3	Missouri	8
California	158	Montana	1
Carolina (North)	20	Nebraska	4
Carolina (South)	13	Nevada	5
Colorado	8	New Hampshire	1
Connecticut	13	New Jersey	38
Dakota (North)	2	New York	124
Dakota (South)	2	New Mexico	6
Delaware	4	Ohio	43
District of Columbia	9	Oklahoma	8
Florida	35	Oregon	14
Georgia	35	Pennsylvania	38
Hawaii	–	Rhode Island	1
Idaho	2	Tennessee	10
Illinois	67	Texas	56
Indiana	17	Utah	3
Iowa	7	Vermont	–
Kansas	4	Virginia	17
Kentucky	10	Virginia (West)	1
Louisiana	19	Wisconsin	9
Maine	–	Washington	10
Maryland	17	Wyoming	–

Source: 1994 American Muslim Resource Directory.

Table 5 Number of Shi'a mosques by state

State	Number
Arizona	2
California	17
Florida	7
Georgia	3
Illinois	4
Indiana	2
Louisiana	1
Maryland	5
Massachusetts	1
Michigan	11
Minnesota	1
New Jersey	16
New York	14
New Mexico	1
Ohio	1
Oregon	2
Pennsylvania	1
Texas	1
Virginia	1
Washington, D C	2
Washington	1
Total	**96**

Source: 1994 Nationwide Muslim Directory

Table 6 Number of Nizari Isma'ili jama'at-khana by state

State	Number	State	Number
Arizona	1	Missouri	1
California	9	Nevada	1
Carolina (South)	1	New Jersey	1
Colorado	1	New York	4
Connecticut	1	New Mexico	1
Florida	6	Ohio	2
Georgia	1	Oklahoma	1
Illinois	3	Pennsylvania	2
Indiana	1	Texas	7
Iowa	1	Virginia	1
Massachusetts	1	Washington	1
Michigan	2	Washington, D C	1
Minnesota	1	Wisconsin	1
		Total	**53**

Source: R B Williams, 1988, *Religions of Immigrants from India and Pakistan*, Cambridge, Cambridge University Press, p. 301.

Table 7 Number of Ahmadiyya mosques and Islamic centres by state

State	Number
Arizona	1
California	2
Carolina (North)	1
Florida	1
Illinois	3
Louisiana	1
Maryland	2
Michigan	1
Missouri	1
New Jersey	2
New York	2
Ohio	2
Oregon	1
Pennsylvania	3
Texas	1
Washington, D C	1
Wisconsin	1
Total	26

Source: Mosques Around the Word, Ahmadiyya Muslim Association Publication, 1994.

Table 8 Number of Islamic schools by state

State	Number
Alabama	2
Arizona	2
Arkansas	1
California	14
Carolina (North)	2
Carolina (South)	1
District of Columbia	2
Florida	4
Georgia	4
Illinois	8
Indiana	2
Kentucky	1
Louisiana	2
Maryland	4
Massachusetts	2
Michigan	8
Minnesota	1
Missouri	2
Mississippi	1
New Jersey	6
New York	10
Ohio	2
Oklahoma	1
Oregon	1
Pennsylvania	4
Tennessee	3
Texas	9
Virginia	3
Washington	1
Wisconsin	1
Total	104

Source: 1994 American Muslim Resource Directory.

Table 9 Numbers of student organizations by state

State	Number	State	Number
California	18	Nebraska	2
Carolina (North)	8	New Hampshire	1
Carolina (South)	3	New Jersey	3
Colorado	4	New York	21
Connecticut	3	New Mexico	2
Dakota (North)	1	Ohio	9
Dakota (South)	2	Oklahoma	5
District of Columbia	4	Oregon	8
Florida	6	Pennsylvania	14
Georgia	2	Tennessee	8
Hawaii	1	Texas	8
Idaho	2	Utah	4
Illinois	10	Vermont	1
Indiana	10	Virginia	11
Iowa	3	Virginia (West)	3
Kansas	2	Washington	3
Kentucky	2	Wisconsin	6
Louisiana	6	Wyoming	1
Maryland	5		
Massachusetts	11		
Michigan	11		
Minnesota	3		
Mississippi	3		
Missouri	9		
		Total	238

Source: 1994 American Muslim Resource Directory.

Appendix 5

Web sites

American Muslim Alliance	www.mercury.hypersurf.com/~ama
American Muslim Council	www.amermuslim.org
Council on American–Muslim Relations	www.cair-net.org
India Abroad	www.indiaabroad.com
Indo-Link	www.indolink.com
Islamic Circle of North America	www.icna.org
Islamic Society of North America	www.isna.org
Pakistan Link	www.pakistanlink.com

NOTES

ACKNOWLEDGEMENTS

1. Mohammad 1998, doctoral thesis in social anthropology and ethnology.

INTRODUCTION

1. Residential suburb of New York.
2. In certain suburbs in the USA, taxis take several passengers going in different directions, within the same city, and charge the same to each passenger, whatever their destination.
3. Honorary title given to a Sikh.
4. London suburb where there is a large Sikh community.
5. 'Propaganda or action conducted by members of one religious community against members of another religious community, because of their religious affiliation'. Racine 1993, p. 26.
6. The author notes that she has opted for the word 'immigrant' rather than 'immigré' in this book to describe immigrants. This distraction, not available in English, is between someone whose status is not yet permanent ('immigrant') and someone with permanent leave to remain in a country (immigré). In support of her choice she quotes Bonnafous 1994, p.69.
7. South Asia, or the Indian subcontinent, comprises India, Pakistan, Bangladesh, Sri Lanka, Nepal, Bhutan, and the Maldive Islands. I shall be dealing in this book with immigrants only from the first three of these countries.
8. It would perhaps be more accurate to speak of the South Asian 'communities', in the plural, given the diversity that exists within this group. However, I shall stay with the singular, referring to the common geographical origin of the community. The reader is asked to bear in mind that any 'community' is a symbolic construct. Similarly, in spite of its internal diversity, I shall refer to 'the Muslim community' in the singular, in the sense of an entity, comprising groups which share a common religion.
9. Curiously, this confusion is shared by the Hispanics themselves who regularly address South Asian immigrants in Spanish.
10. Since the 1980 census, Indians from India and Native Americans have been respectively called 'Asian Indians' and 'American Indians'. It is worth noting that, until 1980, Indians were included in the 'other' Asian ethnic category, and indeed Pakistanis and Bangladeshis still are.
11. Markovits 1994. On Muslims in India, see the chapters by Marc Gaborieau.
12. Gaborieau 1996a, p. 466.
13. This term does not, in India, carry the implications it has in France of separation of church and state. It means that the state gives equal respect to all religions practised in the country.

14. Van der Veer 1994, p. 23.
15. Streiff-Fenart 1987, p. 65.
16. Ibid.
17. Cf. Herberg 1955 and Gerson 1981, pp. 23–4.
18. This definition is a synthesis of those offered by Brass (1991, p. 19) and Bodnar (1985, p. xvi).
19. Anderson 1983.
20. Hobsbawm 1983.
21. Sollers 1989.
22. The term diaspora is traditionally applied to the Jews. However, the concept has been widened to include other communities, in particular the Indian community. Cf. Chaliand and Rageau, 1991, pp. 145–54. I am taking the term to include other South Asians, Pakistanis and Bangladeshis in this case. In the same way as Indians, Pakistanis and Bangladeshis are claiming their own distinct identity. In their adopted country they have formed their own political, cultural and religious organizations; they maintain (real or imagined) links with their former home country. These characteristics of diaspora have been defined by Bruneau (1994, pp. 5–17) and re-examined by Kodmani-Darwish (1997, p. 178).
23. Van der Veer 1995, p. 7.
24. Indian National Party founded in 1980. Cf. Jaffrelot 1993.
25. Lewis 1992, pp. 11–34.
26. Ibid.
27. Sunni Islam comprises four schools of law: the Maliki is the main school followed in Africa (except in Egypt); the Shafi'i school in Arab countries and in south India; the Hanafi school in Turkey, Central Asia and in most of the Indian subcontinent; the Hanbali school in Saudi Arabia.
28. The others are Shafi'i. Twelver Shi'a, the Isma'ili and the Ahmaddiyya are also present.
29. Lewis 1992, pp 27–8.
30. Masud 1990, p. 42.
31. Sayyid 'Abd al-'Aziz al Siddiq, *Hukm al-iqama bi-bilad al-kufr wa-bayan wuju-biha fi-ba'd al-Ahwal*, Bughaz, Tangier, quoted in Masud 1990, p. 43.
32. Lectures by Professor Derryl Maclean at EHESS in March and April 1996.
33. Weibel 1995, pp. 25–34.
34. Voll 1991, pp. 205–14.
35. Herberg 1955, p. 274.
36. Glazer 1972, p. 16.
37. Sayad 1983, p. 10.
38. Ibid.
39. Ibid.
40. Not to be confused with insertion, which implies that links with the former home country are still very strong. Integration, on the other hand, means a complete and thorough settling into the host society without, however, losing a sense of distinctiveness within it. Cf. Costa-Laroux 1989, quoted in Neveu 1993, p. 237.
41. Hicks and Couloumbis 1981, p. 68.
42. Glazer 1972, p. 19.
43. Kennedy 1952, p. 56–9.
44. To quote Chantal Saint-Blancat, the title of whose paper asks if there is a Muslim diaspora in Europe. She says that Muslims in Europe, who are a vast mosaic in terms of both ethnicity and culture, are on the point of being a real diaspora.
45. Cf. in particular Leonard 1992.
46. Haroon 1984, pp. 30–2.
47. Appadurai 1997.
48. Brass 1974.

49. Bayart 1996.
50. Helweg 1990, p. 159.
51. Hovanessian 1992, p. 8.

1 ISLAM IN THE INDIAN SUBCONTINENT

1. These figures are an estimate: there are no reliable statistics in Muslim countries on the numbers within each sectarian division.
2. Cf. below.
3. I shall not discuss the Ahl-i-Hadi because I did not meet any members of this movement in New York.
4. For a thorough study of the Deobandi, cf. Metcalf 1982.
5. The official apolitical nature of the Tablighi Jama'at, which has traditionally been seen as one of its main characteristics, has recently been questioned by scholars such as Felice Dasseto and Marc Gaborieau: Gaborieau suggests that the movement's official apolitical stance is to conceal its political aims. Cf. Gaborieau 1997.
6. For a complete study, cf. Sanyal 1996.
7. Lewis 1994, pp. 36–7.
8. Troll 1994, pp. 127–30.
9. Anisuzzaman 1995.
10. 'Ali married Fatima, the daughter of Muhammad and Khadija.
11. The Shi'a doctrine of the imamate is founded on 'the permanent need of mankind for an infallible leader who is guided by God, and for an unchallenged teacher in religious matters: the imamate is therefore raised to the same level as prophethood, and the only difference between the message-giving Prophet (*rasul*) and the imam is that the latter does not pass on a divine scripture.' Definition given in Madelung 1977a, p. 1195.
12. Laoust 1977, and Richard 1991.
13. Hollister 1953.
14. On the Shi'a in Awadh, cf. Cole 1989.
15. For further details, see Hasan 1996, p. 545.
16. Ibid., p. 548.
17. Hjortshoj 1987, p. 299.
18. Hasan 1996, p. 547.
19. There is a particularly good analysis of these conflicts in modern Pakistan in Zaman 1998.
20. Gaborieau 1996a, p. 477.
21. Hjortshoj 1987, p. 292.
22. Pinault 1997.
23. Madelung 1977b.
24. On Isma'ili in the Sind, cf. Maclean 1989.
25. According to Nizari tradition, it was to Gujarat that the first *Da'i* was sent: his name was Nur al-Din but he was known in India as Satgur Nur.
26. For more details on the reforms of the Aga Khan, see Boivin 1996.
27. Meaning literally 'veil' or 'curtain', this word has taken on the sense of the segregation of women, in particular in the higher levels of Indo-Muslim society.
28. Daftary 1990, pp. 522–3.
29. Ross-Sheriff and Nanji 1991, p. 101.
30. Since the 1960s Asians, and Indians in particular, have as a group been thought of as more economically successful than the Africans.
31. Tinker 1977.
32. Halm 1995, p. 203.
33. The Hafizi, who spread through Egypt and Syria due to an official Fatimid *da'wa*, did not however survive the fall of the dynasty in 1171. Notice that *da'wa*, which literally

means 'call', 'invitation' (implication – to join Islam), takes on here the more specific sense of an invitation to join the cause of an individual, of a family, or more widely of a particular religious organization which claims the right to the imamate. Cf. Daftary 1990, p. 559.

34. Cf. below.
35. Daftary 1990, p. 291.
36. *Da'i*: literally 'he who calls', 'who invites' to the true faith. In its wider sense, it means a missionary or a preacher, but the word refers specifically to those who propagate the Isma'ili faith.
37. The classic etymological explanation of this term is that it derives from the Gujarati *vohorvu* (cf. *vyavahar*), which means 'commerce'. Isma'ilism did indeed take root amongst the shopkeepers and businessmen of the cities. A less common explanation says that the Bohra called themselves by this name in reference to their original Hindu caste, the 'Vohra'. Cf. Daftary 1990, p. 291.
38. In 1589 according to the Sulaymani Bohra.
39. I have here adopted the Indian transliteration instead of the Arabic transliteration Burhan al-Din.
40. The Sulaymani Bohra are one of the smallest Muslim communities of the Indian subcontinent. They seem not to have much of a tradition of emigrating; I did not manage to find any in New York.
41. Daftary 1990, pp. 314–5.
42. A *lungi* (a long loincloth), a *kurta* (tunic) of white muslin and a skullcap woven with gold threads and cotton for men. Women traditionally wear a *lehanga* (long gathered skirt), a *blouse* (a kind of bodice) and an *aurhni* (veil worn on the shoulders or on the head). Engineer 1993 [1980], pp. 150–1.
43. Ibid., p. 159–60.
44. The injunctions are promulgated as *firman* or religious messages sent by the *Da'i* to his community (as happens in the Nizari community).
45. Engineer 1993, p. 291.
46. I shall deal here only with the case of the Qadiyani. The Ahmadiyya have been divided since 1914 into two main branches: the Qadiyani and the Lahori. The Qadiyani stand in a direct line from Mirza Ghulam Ahmad, whereas the Lahori maintain that the founder of the sect was merely a *mujaddid* (reformer), and are opposed to the division from the rest of Islam.
47. The main review published by the Ahmadiyya still carries the same title.
48. Haddad and Smith 1993, p. 59.
49. The first Ahmadi missionary to England was a certain Khwaja Kamaluddin. Cf. Friedmann 1989, p. 15.
50. Moore 1995, p. 61.
51. *Mosques Around the World*, p. 39.
52. Haddad and Smith 1993, p. 59.
53. Cf. Chapter 5.
54. *Mosques Around the World*, p. 51.
55. *The Review of Religions*, 19 July 1920, p. 240, quoted in Moore 1995, pp. 61–2.
56. Haddad and Smith 1993, pp. 60–1.
57. A community composed probably mainly of Arabs.
58. *Mosques Around the World*, p. 51.
59. Friedmann 1989, p. 31.
60. Poston 1992, p. 112.
61. Haddad and Smith 1993, pp. 61–5.
62. Estimate given by the Ahmadiyya themselves. The figure could be much bigger than the actual numbers.
63. *Mosques Around the World* , p. 30.

64. Haddad and Smith 1993.
65. *Mosques Around the World*, p. 38.

2 ECONOMIC AND DEMOGRAPHIC PROFILE

1. Lovell 1983, pp. 94–5.
2. Ibid.
3. Dusenbery 1984, p. 4.
4. Jensen 1988, p. 101.
5. Punjabi peasants did indeed give support to Indian political refugees who were fighting the British. In 1913 the political refugees founded a party, the Ghadar. One of its objectives was to create an international network dedicated to overthrow the British domination of India. In the First World War it openly supported Germany and this hastened its decline, as its members were accused by the Americans – at the instigation of the British – of infringing the neutrality laws of the Wilson government. The leaders were arrested and condemned after the so-called *Hindu Conspiracy Trial* (1917). Cf Jensen 1988.
6. Glazer 1972, pp. 16–17.
7. Williams 1988, p. 87.
8. Ghayur 1984b, p. 55.
9. Afzal 1991, p. 4.
10. *1990 Census of Population*, sections 1 and 2, 1990, CP-1-34.
11. Williams 1988, p. 298.
12. *1990 Census*, as above.
13. Cf. Chapter 5.
14. Stone 1991, p. 28.
15. Numan 1992, p. 16.
16. Khandelwal 1995, p. 180.
17. It is possible that this percentage is an overestimate: most Muslims in India are at the lower end of the social scale, so the percentage emigrating is probably lower than the percentage of the Indian population as a whole (about 12 per cent). However, as I am unable to ascertain a more exact percentage, I shall use these figures. In the absence of systematic research on the subject, one could on the other hand equally advance that Muslims in the upper middle classes are emigrating in proportionately higher numbers from their communities than Hindus are, for example.
18. Cf. Chapter 1.
19. Afzal 1991, p. 5.
20. Ghayur 1980, p. 768. These figures correspond to the Pakistani population in the whole of America. My own interviews however confirm that Punjabis and Muhajirs are present in large numbers.
21. Ishi 1982, pp. 40–8.
22. Helweg 1990, p. 36.
23. *India Abroad* 17 January 1992, p. 21.
24. Jaffrelot 1993.
25. Anwar 1979.
26. Costume consisting of a long tunic and flowing trousers.
27. Helweg 1990, pp. 196–200.
28. In Muslim countries, it is usually the groom's family which pays the dowry. Indian Muslim families have adopted the reverse Hindu custom: the bride's family pays the dowry. Bangladesh follows the Indian custom. In Pakistan, while the Punjab and the Sind (apart from a few tribal population groups) follow the Indian pattern, two provinces (NWFP and Baluchistan) follow the Muslim pattern.
29. Muhlstein 1986, p. 130.
30. Fenton 1988, p. 35.

31. *India Abroad*, 18 October 1996, pp. 43–4.
32. Saran and Tottahil, 1980, p. 245.
33. Minocha 1987, p. 302.
34. *1990 Census of Population*, as above.
35. The figure was even lower for the whole of America (17 per cent). Ibid.
36. Ibid.
37. The figure was even higher for the whole of America (43.6 per cent). Ibid.
38. Ibid.
39. Ibid.
40. Khandelwal 1995.
41. This passage on Jackson Heights uses information from Khandelwal 1995 and from two articles in *India Abroad*, 14 August 1992 (pp. 18–23) and 31 May 1996 (p. 46).
42. Interview in June 1998.
43. Interview in June 1998.
44. *India Abroad*, 29 December 1995 and 27 December 1996, p. 30.
45. Helweg 1990, pp. 146–60.
46. Extracts from this documentary, which I saw myself in Delhi in November 1994, were published in: Bald, Vivek Renjen, 'Taxi Meters and Plexiglass Partitions', in Sunaina Maira and Rajini Srikanth, eds, *Contours of the Heart: South Asians Map North America*, New York, The American Writers' Workshop, 1996, p. 68.
47. This is rather ironical since Denzel Washington is one of the principal characters in Mira Nair's film, *Mississippi Masala*, an important theme of which was Indian prejudice vis-à-vis African Americans.
48. *Times of India*, 7 November 1999. Information gathered over the Internet.
49. Gallery de la Tremblaye 1994, p. 409.
50. 'Profile of Asian Indians: Census Information', *Asian Indian Business Resource*, 1995–6, p. 40.
51. *1990 Census of Population*.
52. Schnapper 1998, p. 197. This study re-examines work done in Chicago in the 1920s and 1930s.
53. Families with many children constitute an exception to this. As an indication, the 1990 census shows that an average Indian family (all religious groups) had 3.8 people (compared to 3.2 for the whole of New York).
54. Mohammad 1998.
55. Helweg 1986, p. 211.
56. Ibid, p. 204.
57. In 1980, the total amount of remittances sent to India was estimated at 64 million dollars. Cf. Fenton 1988, p. 46. In the same year, in New York, 30 per cent of Indian families were sending 100 dollars per month and 26 per cent were sending a greater amount than this. Cf. Saran and Thottathil 1980, p. 240.

3 RELIGIOUS PRACTICES

1. Kaspi, Bertrand and Heffer 1991, p. 63.
2. Williams 1992, pp. 256–7.
3. Charnay 1977, p. 152.
4. On Islam and the issue of secularism, see in particular Lewis 1992, pp. 11–34.
5. On the actual dichotomies between religiosity and observance, see Charnay 1977, pp. 172–6.
6. Cf. Introduction and Le Bras 1955, vol. 2, pp. 397–417.
7. Cf. in particular Williams 1988, p. 89; Husain and Vogelaar 1994, p. 256.
8. Tribalat, 1996.
9. Davie 1996, p. 59.

10. Haddad and Lumnis 1987, p. 32.
11. On the religious practice of women among Muslims, cf. Charnay 1977, pp. 162–8. On the religious practice of women among Christians and other religions, cf. Le Bras 1955, vol. 1, pp. 356–9. Cf. also Campiche 1996b, pp. 74–5.
12. Fenton 1988, p. ix.
13. The analysis which follows is based on interviews conducted both with individual members of the South Asian community in the United States – whether or not they were regular, or indeed infrequent, attenders at the mosque – and with community leaders. 'Ethnic' newspapers supplied me with complementary information.
14. Roy 1992, pp. 73–88; Tribalat 1995; Charnay 1977.
15. Cesari 1997a, p. 133.
16. Ibid., p. 123–4.
17. This Bohra does not abide by all the obligations. Cf. Chapter 1.
18. Interview in January 1996.
19. I was not able to confirm whether the Bohra really do have guesthouses everywhere in the world. But they certainly have them in places where there are religious shrines: Mecca and Medina; Kerbala and Najaf. The staff in these guesthouses help the pilgrims to carry out all the formalities and act as guides also. Cf. Salvadori 1989, p. 262.
20. Interview in December 1995.
21. In fact, she is an active member of the ICNA, an organization with close links to the Jama'at-i-Islami.
22. On the reactions to the *hijab*, see below.
23. *Riba'* will be examined in detail later.
24. This mosque will be examined in detail in Chapter 5.
25. Cf. Chapter 5.
26. For further details on Islamic food rules, cf. Rodinson 1975, pp. 1081–97 (especially pp. 1085–6 and 1093–5).
27. Cf. especially Bikhu Parekh in *India Abroad* 27 August 1993, p. 21.
28. Interview in November 1995.
29. Interview in December 1995.
30. Rocher 1968, vol. 1, pp. 96–7.
31. I interview her in November 1995.
32. I interview her in December 1995.
33. I interview her in November 1995.
34. Interview with Yvonne Haddad in December 1995.
35. Bayart 1996, p. 189.
36. Montanari 1996, p. 321.
37. Qur'an 24:31: 'And say to the believing women that they should lower their gaze and guard their modesty; that they should not display their beauty and ornaments except what (must ordinarily) appear thereof; that they should draw their veils over their bosoms and not display their beauty except to their husbands, their fathers, their husband's fathers, their sons, their husbands' sons, their brothers or their brothers' sons, or their sisters' sons, or their women, or the slaves whom their right hands possess, or male servants free of physical needs, or small children who have no sense of the shame of sex'. Cf. Masson 1980, pp. 462–3.
38. Qur'an 33:59: 'O Prophet! Tell thy wives and daughters, and the believing women, that they should cast their outer garments over their persons (when abroad): that is most convenient, that they should be known (as such) and not molested. And God is Oft-Forgiving, Most Merciful.' Cf. Masson 1980, pp. 560–9.
39. Cf. especially Jeffery 1979. On Muslim women in India, cf. also Jeffery and Jeffery 1996.
40. Cf. Chapter 1.
41. Cf. Chapter 1.

42. Interview in November 1995.
43. Weibel 1996, p. 136.
44. Interview in Madras in February 1995. 'Shabnam' was spending some time in India.
45. This is the lady doctor who performs her prayers at work in her hospital.
46. Cf. Chapter 6.
47. Interview in January 1996. My thanks to Usha Sanyal, who enabled me to meet this person.
48. Interview in January 1996.
49. Here, *maulvi* is a scholar and/or Muslim teacher of Arabic. *Saheb* is a mark of respect.
50. Adelkah 1991.
51. Weibel 1996, pp. 138–9.
52. On the *riba'* and the relationship between Islam and economic structures, cf. Rodinson 1966.
53. Haddad 1987, pp. 99–102, and my own interviews with immigrants.
54. Cf. Chapter 1.
55. On matters temporal and religious, Islamic law distinguishes five categories: obligatory (necessary), recommended, allowed, disapproved, forbidden. Cf. Lewis 1992, p. 17.
56. Interview in January 1996.
57. The first Islamic bank was opened in 1963 in Egypt. Cf. *The Message International*, December 1992, p. 27.
58. *New York Times*, 8 April 1994.
59. Marriage is examined in the next chapter.
60. 'Amreeka' is how South Asians traditionally pronounce 'America'.
61. Tahira Naqvi, 'Beyond the Walls, Amreeka', in Sunaina Maira and Rajini Srikanth, eds, *Contours of the Heart: South Asians Map North America*, New York, Asian American Writers' Workshop, 1996, p. 292.
62. Ibid, p. 299.
63. Interviews with immigrants and community leaders whose duty it was, particularly in the mosques, to lead burial rites.
64. Nielsen 1992, p. 53.
65. Cesari 1997a, p. 106.
66. Interview with Abdul Sattar Oza, head of the American office, in January 1996, in New York. The association (its founder is nicknamed 'Father Teresa' in Pakistan) is officially represented in seven countries worldwide (Bangladesh, Japan, Dubai, England, United States, Canada, Australia). The head office is in Pakistan. It is run by Memons, a merchant community originally from Indian Gujarat. The New York office opened in 1988.
67. Interview in January 1996.
68. To recite *Fatihas* is to read from the Qur'an, including the first sura (called *Fatiha*).
69. An action which earns its author merit.
70. Roy 1992, p. 79.
71. Haddad and Adair 1987, p. 33.
72. Interviews with community leaders. I took part in the Id ul-Fitr celebrations in August 1986, in a suburb of Los Angeles. A programme, *Islam in America*, broadcast by McNeil/Lehrer News Hour in August 1993, also featured this. The programme showed how the Islamic Center of Long Island celebrates Id ul-Fitr. I am grateful to Faroque Khan for introducing me to one of the journalists who made the programme.
73. *Namaz* is the Persian equivalent to *salat*, the daily prayers. *Namaz* is also used in Urdu.
74. Fisher and Abedi 1990, pp. 272–3.
75. Interview in December 1995.
76. Schubel 1991, pp. 118–31 is a most interesting article on this subject.
77. For more details on Islamic festivals, Cf. Tassy 1931, p. 321–79; Schimmel 1994. pp. 66–76.

78. Religious group claiming to be Sufi mystics. They will be described more fully further on. Cf. Sanyal 1996.
79. Persian word, *laylat al-barat* in Arabic. This ceremony pre-dates Islam. Cf. Wensinck 1998, p. 159.
80. A kind of bread.
81. A kind of sweet pastry.
82. In a way which is reminiscent of the Jewish action when praying, but in slower motion.
83. Individual prayer of supplication (different from *namaz* or *salah*, the daily prayer).
84. Interview in November 1995.
85. *The Minaret*, 21 December 1996, p. 1.
86. For more details on this, see Haddad and Lumnis 1987, p. 152–4.
87. Literally, the repudiation of a wife by her husband.

4 THE SECOND GENERATION

1. A mixture of spices.
2. 'Beurs' is a term used in France to describe young North Africans born in France [Translator's note]. Kepel 1994a, p.12.
3. Barth 1970.
4. Muhlstein 1996, p. 130.
5. *India Abroad*, 30 August 1996, p. 42.
6. *Masala*, Autumn 1996, p. 42.
7. My emphasis. *India Abroad*, 18 October 1996, p. 3.
8. Occasional articles in *India Abroad* suggest that there is sporadic violence amongst young South Asians, but these are still being described as isolated incidents: *India Abroad*, 22 November 1996, p.3
9. Joly 1991.
10. Interview in November 1995.
11. Cf. Chapter 5.
12. Glazer 1972, p. 173.
13. My italics.
14. Glazer 1972, pp. 176–7.
15. Cf Chapter 3.
16. Gupta, p. 108.
17. Helweg 1990, p. 143.
18. Interview in December 1995.
19. Interview in July 1993.
20. Bear in mind that the concepts of 'liberal', 'conservative' and 'traditional' are very relative: behaviour which appears 'conservative' in the United States can be perceived as very 'liberal' in the subcontinent.
21. Note that the study of emigrated population groups can help to define mutations in the home population in a variety of areas: food habits, attitudes to marriage, religious practices and so on.
22. This expression is used by Farhad Khrosrokhavar in reference to young North African women in France. There are observable similarities with young Muslims, whatever their ethnic origin and country of adoption. Young North African women have to compartmentalize their lives, behaving in one way with their family and in another with their French friends. Cf. Khrosrokhavar 1997.
23. Kelley 1994, pp. 140–1.
24. Interview in January 1996.
25. This is not in fact quite true for South Asians, as there is a multitude of languages in the subcontinent. In fact the only truly shared language among South Asians is English.
26. *Avaz* means voice, sound, noise.

27. *India Today*, 31 August 1989, p. 98.
28. *Desi*, literally inhabitant, in this case of India, Pakistan and Bangladesh.
29. Title of a letter to *India Abroad* from a young correspondent. Cf. *India Abroad*, 12 January 1996, p. 3.
30. Agarwal 1991, p. 4.
31. Cf. Chapter 5.
32. In particular at Columbia Universty and Queens College.
33. Cf. Roy 1992.
34. Interview in August 1993.
35. Arizona is a well-known brand of iced tea in the United States.
36. Haddad and Lummis 1987, p. 120.
37. Interview in November 1995.
38. Schubel 1991, p. 126.
39. Ibid., p. 127.
40. *Gham*: literally pain, sadness; here it denotes lamentation for the victims at Kerbala.
41. Schubel 1991, p. 128.
42. On the question of the veil in France, see Khosrokhavar 1995–6. pp. 69–84.
43. Interview in January 1996.
44. Khosrokhavar 1995–6 p. 75, and Khosrokhavar 1997.
45. Interview in January 1996.
46. Interview in December 1995.
47. Khrosrokhavar 1997, p. 314.
48. This expression was used by a French Minister for Education (François Bayrou at the time) during the 'Islamic scarf affair' which sent shock-waves through the French education system in the autumn of 1989.
49. Interview in December 1995
50. Interview in December 1995.
51. Khrosrokhavar 1995–6, p. 78.
52. Qureshi 1991, pp. 183–212.
53. Ibid., p. 204.
54. The Parsis, or Zoroastrians, practice strict endogamy (marriage within the community), or very nearly, in the subcontinent, which has the effect of limiting the numerical growth of the community.
55. Cf. Seth 1993.
56. Interview in July 1993.
57. Cf. Joly 1987, p. 214–18.
58. Naqvi 1995, p. 145–54.
59. Interview in January 1996.
60. Cf. Chapter 3.
61. Helweg 1990, pp. 186–7.
62. Qureshi 1991, p. 204.
63. Mandava 1996, p. 197.
64. Interview in November 1995.
65. *Ghagra*: a long, full skirt.
66. For comparison, see Gell 1993.
67. As demonstrated by the kinds of homes (very spacious and in smart neighbourhoods) and cars (Mercedes and BMWs and so on) which they either own or aspire to own.
68. Most of my interviews with young people or their families were about unmarried young people. It is therefore difficult to give figures on how important the dowry is to Muslim immigrants from South Asia. A good short story on this theme is Luthra, 1994, pp. 257–63.
69. Haddad and Lummis 1987, pp. 40–1.

5 ISLAMIC INSTITUTIONS

1. American Muslim Resource Directory 1994, p. 92.
2. Haddad and Smith 1994, p. xx.
3. *New York Times*, 4 May 1993.
4. Ferris 1994, p. 210.
5. *New York Times*, 25 February 1993 and Daily News-dong Island, 28 December 1995.
6. Moore 1995, p. 105.
7. Ahmad, G M 1991, p. 12.
8. Larry Poston studied 72 Europeans and Americans who converted to Islam. They converted after observing the behaviour of a Muslim friend or acquaintance. Only one person converted through the activity of a missionary. Poston 1992, p. 179.
9. Haddad and Smith 1994, p. xviii; Moore 1995, pp. 106–7.
10. On Sayyib Qutb, see Carré 1984.
11. Haddad and Smith 1994, p. xxi.
12. Interview with Yvonne Haddad, November 1996.
13. Fenton 1988, p. 192.
14. Haddad 1983, p. 73.
15. Husain and Vogelaar 1994, pp. 245–6.
16. *The Minaret*, January–February 1993, p. 72.
17. Thanawi (n.d.) p. 29.
18. *India Today*, 28 February 1997, p. 12; *Communalism Combat*, February 1997, 30, pp. 1–3.
19. Lewis 1994, p. 101.
20. Interview with Yvonne Haddad, November 1996.
21. *Mosques Around the World*, p. 51. Russell is presented here as the first Ahmadi in the United States; Haddad and Smith 1993, p. 59: these authors do not question the theory that Russell was the first Ahmadi in the United States. They claim that Russell was not corresponding with Kur but rather with Ghulam Ahmad himself.
22. Ferris 1994, p. 210; Poston 1992, p. 163. Webb also appears in the *Who's Who* of the *American Muslim Resource Directory 1994*, p. 183, although this directory definitely does not include the Ahmadiyya in its definition of orthodox Islam.
23. Ferris 1994, pp. 210–11.
24. Ibid., pp. 211–12.
25. Ibid., pp. 212–14.
26. Ibid., pp. 215–16.
27. Ibid., pp. 214–15.
28. On Al-Azhar and in particular on the sermons preached there, cf. Zeghal 1996, pp. 165–228.
29. Interview with the imam of the mosque in November 1995. Supplementary information from *Resalah*, March 1994, p. 3.
30. *New York Times* (17 February 1967; 2 January 1968; 28 October 1984; 29 May 1987, 15 September 1988; 26 September 1988; 21 October 1988) quoted in Ferris 1994, pp. 218–19.
31. Lawyer who pronounces *fatwas*.
32. The one who calls to prayer.
33. Haddad 1978, p. 80; Abu-Laban 1983, p. 87.
34. Interview in December 1995.
35. The call to prayer is given from the doorway of the building for practical reasons, as there is no other way to be heard by the worshippers, and not for ideological reasons. The Barelwi prefer this method because their leader, Ahmad Riza Kahn Barelwi, said that in the time of the Prophet, of Abu Bakr and of Umar, the *azan* was given from the door of the mosque. Cf. Sanyal 1996, p. 190.
36. *Muslim Center of New York, Souvenir Breaking Ceremony and Fund Raising Dinner*, 2 May 1989.

37. *The Message International,* November–December 1996, p. 13
38. The vice-president of the mosque, Muhammad Tariq Sherwani, whom I interviewed, did not say what sum was given.
39. *India Abroad,* 13 September 1996, p. 47.
40. I carried out this study through weekly interviews with about 20 active members of the ICLI, and by reading their bulletin, and various other documents (brochures, invitations, publicity, etc.) between November 1995 and January 1996.
41. The Shah Bano affair happened in India, starting in 1985. Shah Bano, who has now died, was a Muslim woman repudiated by her husband who obtained, thanks to the High Court, the grant of a living allowance. A number of Muslim organizations protested against what they considered to be an attack on Islamic law. They won their cause in 1986, when the then government passed the *Muslim Women (Protection of Rights) Bill,* which does not require anymore that Muslims follow the law relating to living allowances.
42. *ICLI Newsletter,* pp. 3–4, and *Long Island Jewish World,* 10–16 September 1993, p. 3 and pp. 18–19.
43. Some of the mosques whose membership is largely recently arrived Pakistani immigrants, especially those in Brooklyn (for instance, the Coney Island mosque), are run along lines rather similar to the Bangladeshi mosques described here.
44. See below.
45. Hinnells observed this phenomenon in the Parsi people; Hinnells 1994, p. 81.
46. Bhachu 1985.
47. Walbridge 1993.
48. Russell 1982, p. 32.
49. Dweik 1992, p. 117.
50. The same phenomenon can be observed in France.
51. During colonization, the British thought of Arabic as one of the classical languages of India, on a par with Sanskrit. Arabic, however, could not be called the cultural language of Indian Muslims, unlike Persian: the vast majority, even of literate people, could neither speak or write in Arabic. Cf. Zaman 1997.
52. On the issue of Persian, see Gaborieau 1994; Ahmad 1994, pp. 223–34.
53. This figure is almost certainly an underestimate for Indian and Pakistani Shi'a. Given the impossibility of a matter of census of religious minorities, I cannot provide a more accurate figure.
54. Interviews in December 1995 with the imam, his secretary and the librarian.
55. Sabagh and Bozorgmehr 1994, pp. 445–73.
56. Amongst secularized Iranians, as amongst the early Bangladeshi migrants, a sense of religious identity has not completely disappeared under an ethnic identity. These Iranians have maintained an identity distinct from Jewish or Bahai Iranians. Ibid.
57. See Chapter 3.
58. Williams 1998, pp. 211–16; Nanji 1983; Ross-Sheriff and Nanji 1991, pp. 101–117.
59. Telephone interview with Hanif Hamdani.
60. Williams 1988, p. 301.
61. McDonough 1996.
62. Nanji 1983, pp. 160–3 and Williams 1988, pp. 211–215.
63. Telephone interview in January 1996 with Moin Muhiuddin, the nephew of the present *Da'i,* who lives in Pennsylvania.
64. Telephone interview with Moin Muhiuddin.
65. Interview in January 1996.
66. *Mosques Around the World,* p. 133.
67. Interview in January 1996.
68. At Port-of-Spain (Trinidad), an Ahmadi woman, Dr Anesa Ahamad, preached the Friday sermon to a mixed congregation in 1994, a first in Islamic history. *India Abroad,* 18 August 1995, p. 11.

69. Interview in January 1996.
70. Chi 1973, p. 79.
71. Under the influence of Sufism and in an effort to counteract vigorous Christian pros-
    elytism, Ghulam Ahmad devised his own theory on *jihad* and made it one of the
    central tenets of Ahmadi religious thought: he reinterpreted *jihad* to mean an exclu-
    sively defensive war, or a war waged with the pen. His rejection of the aggressive
    'holy war' formula attracted much criticism from orthodox Muslims.
72. Chi 1973, p. 133.
73. Husain and Vogelaar 1994, p. 244.
74. *Resource Directory of Islam in America 1994*, pp. 107–111, and my own observations.
75. *Crescent School: Student Handbook*, p. 21.
76. Lewis 1994; Lewis 1996.

6 ISLAMIC MOVEMENTS

1. Bowers 1989, pp. 107–08.
2. Ibid, p. 111.
3. Ahmad 1991, p. 15
4. *Resource Directory of Islam in America*, pp. 113–18.
5. Abdalati, n.d. Abdalati's work was published for the first time in 1963 by the Al-
   Rashid mosque in Canada, and since then many new editions have been brought out.
   Many Muslim leaders considered that it is the best presentation of Islamic ideals and
   of the objectives of the Canadian Islamic community. It is also available in the United
   States. Abdalati was an Egyptian who qualified at Al-Azhar after studying for a Masters
   at McGill University and for a doctorate at Princeton. Cf. McDonough 1996.
6. A reminder that *da'wa* means invitation.
7. Schacht 1975 pp. 419–21; Laoust 1983, pp. 385–434; Sourdel 1996, pp. 303 and 704.
8. Johnson 1991, p. 113
9. Zeghal 1996, p. 225.
10. Poston 1992, pp. 139–40.
11. Fashionable expression drawn from the work of Abdalatif. Cf. McDonough 1996.
12. Williams 1988, p. 97.
13. Ismail Al-Faruqi advocated a modern Islam and good relationships between Christians
    and Muslims. He was one of the most respected Muslim scholars and activists in the
    United States, in both the Muslim and non-Muslim communities, until his violent
    death in 1986. For a biography of Al-Faruqi, see Esposito 1991.
14. Bowers 1989, pp. 180–9.
15. Interview with a representative of the MYNA in New York.
16. Bowers 1989.
17. The MSA is not affiliated to the ICNA.
18. Sanyal 1993.
19. Interview in January 1996 with Zahid Bukhari, president of the New York branch.
20. Islamic Circle of North America, *The Charter and By-laws*, 1994, p. 4.
21. The number of South Asian Muslims in United States is about 100,000. According to the
    Canadian census of 1991, there were 253,260 Muslims in Canada, of all ethnic origins.
    Islam is therefore in third position, in terms of numbers, behind Christianity and Judaism.
22. It is worth remembering that the leaders of organizations tend to inflate the numbers
    of their followers and sympathizers.
23. It seems, however, that in Pakistan the Jama'at-i-Islami is beginning to enlarge its
    social base, and even to welcome non-Muslims. Cf. Amélie Blom, 'Les partis et mou-
    vements islamistes au Pakistan', a contribution to the Pakistan group (a collaboration
    between the Centre d'études de l'Inde et de l'Asie du Sud and the Centre d'études et
    de recherches internationales), 6 January 1998.

24. *The Message International*, September 1990 and August 1996.
25. *The Message International*, June 1990, p. 9.
26. *The Message International*, August 1996, p. 24.
27. Until the Gulf war, the Jama'at-i-Islami received large financial donations from Saudi Arabia, which even financed the setting up of the Islamic Foundation in England. But as the Pakistani Jama'at-i-Islami supported Iraq during the Gulf War, the Saudis removed their financial backing. Nasr 1994, p. 60.
28. Interview in January 1996.
29. On this institution, see Metcalf 1982, pp. 335–47.
30. *The Message International*, September 1990, p. 15.
31. Troll 1994.
32. Ahmad 1991, p. 459.
33. *The Message International*, January 1991, p. 23.
34. Interview with Tariq Khan, responsible for publicity and for magazine circulation.
35. *The Message International*, August 1997.
36. Information from the Sound Vision catalogue, *Sound Vision: Helping Tomorrow's Muslims Today*, 1995.
37. Ibid.
38. Carré 1984, p. 32.
39. Murad 1986, quoted in Poston 1992, p. 205.
40. Ibid, p. 84.
41. Robinson 1988, p. 20.
42. Nasr 1994, p. 15.
43. Ibid, p 149.
44. Gaborieau 1997, p. 215.
45. I went to Al-Falah in January 1996 and spoke with the imam (a Punjabi Pakistani) and a Puerto Rican convert. The Tablighi Jama'at is well known for its deep reluctance to give any details on its internal organization. My experience in New York confirms this, as the imam was very reluctant to talk. I was able to collect further details in a telephone interview with the director of the mosque in September 1997.
46. It is worth noting that the Gujaratis are particularly active in the Tablighi Jama'at. They are, for example, the dominant force in the European centre at Dewsbury. Metcalf 1996a, p. 112.
47. Ahmad, Mumtaz, 1991, pp. 457–530.
48. Metcalf 1998.
49. Kelley 1994, p. 149.
50. Hermansen 1994, p. 183.
51. Gaborieau 1997, p. 222.
52. Expression taken from Derryl Maclean.
53. On Canada, cf. McDonough 1994, p. 324; on England, cf. Lewis 1994, pp. 89–101.
54. Gaborieau 1997, p. 216.
55. Metcalf 1982, p. 313.
56. 'Remembrance', in which the divine name or sacred formulas are repeated. This is a Sufi technique for spiritual concentration.
57. A poem sung in praise of the Prophet.
58. Geaves 1996, p. 173.
59. Ibid.
60. Interview in January 1996.
61. It would appear that the Barelwis also recruit among businessmen. Ibid, p. 174.
62. Plural of *fatwa*. Sanyal 1996, pp. 167 and 177.
63. Metcalf 1982, p. 308.
64. As far as I am aware, no *Pir* belonging to the Barelwis tradition has emigrated or has been 'imported' to New York.

65. Abd al-Qadir al-Jilani, who was born in Iran and is now buried in Baghdad, was the founder of the Sufi order of the Qadiris. Although Ahmad Riza was also affiliated to the Chishti, Naqshbandi and Suhrawardi movements, he was particularly devoted to Jilani. Sanyal 1996, p. 128.
66. *Sama'*: 'listen to music'. Some Sufis value this technique for inspiration or contemplation.
67. Sanyal 1996, p. 112 and p. 148.
68. The Chishtiyya movement was founded by an Indian Sufi, Mu'inu'd-Din Chishti (1142–1236), and it is one of the largest Sufi movements in the Indian subcontinent.
69. Sanyal 1996, p. 117.
70. Metcalf 1982, pp. 307–08.
71. Sanyal 1996, p. 212.
72. McDonough 1994.
73. The Sufi order was founded by Muhammad ibn Muhammad Baha'ad-Din Naqshband (1317–89) from Bukhara. Cf. Gaborieau, Popovic and Zarkone 1990.
74. I owe my information here entirely to Webb 1994.

7 THE EMERGENCE OF A 'UTOPIAN UMMA'?

1. Haddad 1978, p. xxviii.
2. Anisuzzaman, pp. 45–6.
3. Ibid., p. 45.
4. Telephone conversation with Amin Hasin, vice-president of the Isma'ili American Council, in Washington, DC in December 1995.
5. Telephone conversation with Amin Hasin.
6. Telephone conversation with Amin Hasin.
7. Telephone conversation with Moin Muhiuddin.
8. Interview with Nazir Ayaz and Mukhtar Ahmad Cheema.
9. In the sense of relationship with other ethnic communities (between South Asian Muslims and Muslims from areas other than South Asia).
10. Interview with Yvonne Haddad in November 1995.
11. Rex 1991, p. 103.
12. Interview with Yvonne Haddad in November 1995.
13. 'They are Muslims, but still . . .'
14. 'Habash' in Arabic refers to the land and people of Ethiopia. Cf. Ullendorf 1975, pp. 3–5.
15. Burton-Page 1975, pp. 15–17.
16. Jain 1994, p. 53.
17. Marx 1993, p. 62.
18. Williams 1988, pp. 142–3.
19. Kaufman 1989; Kepel 1994a.
20. On black Islam, cf. Lincoln 1991.
21. Mamiya 1983, pp. 245–51.
22. *The Message International*, October 1993, p. 37.
23. Interview with Zaheer Uddin, then General Secretary of the ICNA, in November 1995 and June 1998.
24. Cf. Blom, Dissertation in preparation.
25. René 1997, pp. 47–8.
26. Rex 1991, pp. 106–07.
27. This kind of statement can be heard in most mosques and Islamic centres.
28. Rex 1991, p. 107.
29. Werbner 1989, pp. 127–49.
30. Kepel 1994a, p. 74.
31. Cf. especially the October 1990 issue.

32. *The Message International*, October 1990, p. 22.
33. Interview in November 1995.
34. However, all the people I interviewed in 1995–9 were still young adolescents in 1990–1.
35. Interview in December 1995.
36. Cf. Chapter 4.
37. The American Muslim Mission, the ICNA, the ISNA, the National Community, the Majlis Shura of New York, the Bosnia Action Committee of Chicago, the American Muslim Council, the Michigan Islamic Council, the Balkan Muslims Association, the Islamic Medical Association.
38. Other actions taken to help the Bosnian people included sending financial help to families and the sponsoring of children by Islamic centres such as the ICLI, by taking them into families in the United States.
39. *The Message International*, April 1991, pp. 9–10; April 1992, pp. 15–28.
40. Interview with Habibullah Mayar in January 1996.
41. Slymovics 1995, pp. 159–60.
42. Ibid., pp. 173–4; interview with Habibullah Mayar.
43. Ibid., p. 171.
44. *Islamic Horizons*, July–August 1999, p. 12.

8 IDENTITY AND ETHNICITY

1. *Mleccha* or *malishth*: a barbarian, a non-Indian. This pejorative term describes non-Hindus, in particular Muslims.
2. Cf. Introduction.
3. Engineer 1985, pp. 238–71.
4. Brass 1991, p. 15.
5. This thesis was defended notably by Francis Robinson. Cf. Francis 1974. Robinson argued that Hindus and Muslims were distinct civilizations destined to develop into separate nations once political patterns had been established.
6. Kakar 1996.
7. The BJP even managed to seize power in India in February 1998 and again in September 1999.
8. 'Hindu-ness'. This concept is the foundation for nationalist Hindu ideology.
9. Interview with Sucheta Mazumdar in June 1995.
10. The AFMI was created in 1990. Its main objective is to improve the position of Muslims in India. It organizes annual conferences in India and in the United States, bringing together activists to discuss the problems faced by fellow Muslims. Interview with Najma Sultana in January 1996.
11. A worldwide Hindu organization. The VHP was founded in 1964 to promote the Hindu religion. Cf. Jaffrelot 1993.
12. *India Abroad*, 13 August 1993, p. 25.
13. Association of National Volunteers. This paramilitary organization was started in 1925 at Nagpur by K B Hedgewar. It promotes a nationalist Hindu ideology. Jaffrelot 1993.
14. *India Abroad*, 26 July 1996, p. 8.
15. Ibid.
16. The American branch of the Sangh Parivar (lit. 'the family of the Organization'), which is the name given to the whole network of nationalist Hindu organizations.
17. Cited in *Communalism Combat*, February 1997, p. 9.
18. Van der Veer 1994, p. 4.
19. *India Abroad*, 12 December 1992, p. 3.
20. *India Abroad*, 15 January 1993, p. 4.

21. *India Today*, 31 August 1993, p. 48c.
22. *Frontline*, 10 September 1993. pp. 10–16; *India Abroad*, 31 August 1993, p. 48c–d; *India Abroad*, 13 August 1993, p. 25–6.
23. *India Abroad*, 13 August 1993, p. 25.
24. Cf. Chapter 3.
25. Hamid 1991. p. 44.
26. Cf. Chapter 4.
27. Kalam n.d. Not published as far I could ascertain.
28. Fisher 1980.
29. Cf. especially Miller 1992, pp. 173–6 in particular.
30. Interview in January 1996.
31. Malik, I H 1989.
32. Interview in August 1993.
33. Interview in July 1993 in Boston, in a restaurant named 'The Rose of Kashmir', owned by Sikhs and employing Bangladeshi waiters!
34. Cf. especially Kale 1995; Jain 1998, pp. 337–60. I am indebted to Eric Meyer for drawing my attention to this latter article.
35. This expression is taken from Le Espiritu 1992.
36. *India Abroad*, 14 May 1993, p. 26.
37. *India Abroad*, 7 March 1997, p. 2. Shortly before his death, he took on the role of ambassador for rapprochement, at least in musical terms, between India and Pakistan. He denounced the prohibition which prevented Indian artists from performing in public in Pakistan. Cf. *India Abroad*, 29 August 1997, p. 40.
38. Lewis 1996, pp. 14–15.
39. Das 1992, pp. 245–59. I am indebted to Christine Moliner for drawing my attention to this article.
40. *India Abroad*, 16 September 1994, p. 3.
41. *India Abroad*, 16 August 1996, p. 46.
42. Cf. Chapter 4.
43. Interview in November 1995.
44. Wilson 1993, pp. 1288–90.
45. Kalam, n.d., p. 5.
46. *India Abroad*, 5 November 1993, p. 32.
47. Lewis 1994, p. 180.
48. Used here in the widest sense, so including also Pakistanis and Bangladeshis.
49. In other words, popular Muslim practices take on a greater importance than respect for Qur'anic prescriptions (in this case ritual prayer). Cf. Chapter 3.
50. Interview with David Lelyveld in November 1995. Lewis 1994, p. 60, emphasizes this with reference to Gujarati Muslims in the United Kingdom.
51. Mohammad 1998.
52. Title of a song from the commercial Hindi film *Judva* (David Dhawan, 1997).
53. I shall confine my remarks here to India.
54. Sukhatme 1988.
55. Weiner 1990, p. 250.
56. Short stories on South Asians in diaspora are published fairly regularly in *Akhbar-e-Jahan* (Pakistan) and *Biswin Sadi* (India).
57. This point deserves to be studied separately.

9 THE HOST SOCIETY

1. Cf. Chapter 7.
2. Das 1990, pp. 212–17.
3. Hess 1971, p. 3.

4. Banerjee Divakaruni 1996, p. 268–9.
5. Esposito 1992, p. 5.
6. Said 1980; Esposito 1992; Confluences-Méditerrannée 1995–6.
7. Huntington 1993.
8. Mandava 1996, p. 197.
9. *India Abroad*, 28 May 1993, p. 23.
10. Interview in August 1993.
11. Information gained from a number of issues of *India Abroad*.
12. Crimson dot on the forehead of Hindu women (in theory once they are married).
13. Fenton 1988, p. 22.
14. Ullmo 1994, p. 14.
15. Interview in December 1995.
16. Mazumdar 1989, p. 51.
17. Tocqueville 1981, pp. 457–8.
18. Rajagopal 1994, p. 8. Note that Arthur and Usha Helweg believe on the contrary that immigrants put forward the discrimination argument in order to hide failure. Or more accurately, the Helwegs say that this is used by immigrants to justify themselves to their families in the subcontinent. They also say that some immigrants claim discrimination in order to access rights available to disadvantaged minorities. Cf. Helweg 1990, pp. 188–92.
19. Moore 1995, p. 103; Williams 1988, p. 90; Lahaj 1994, p. 311. Interview with Yvonne Haddad in November 1995.
20. The reader will recall the burning of African–American churches in various areas in the United States in 1996. Hindu temples have also been attacked, as far back as the 1970s.
21. *India Abroad*, 1 December 1995, p. 26.
22. Unveiling Prejudice 1997, p.4
23. An investigation by the Council on American–Islamic Relations Research Center showed that of those who complain, the most are Arabs (45 per cent), then African–Americans (25 per cent). South Asians trail far behind (Pakistanis 13 per cent, Indians 2 per cent, Bangladeshis 2 per cent). Ibid p. 5.
24. *India Abroad*, 9 August 1996, p. 40
25. *India Abroad*, 4 July 1997, p. 44.
26. I am borrowing here the terminology used by Thomas Pettigrew and R Meertens, 'overt' (or direct) discrimination and 'veiled' (or indirect, insidious) discrimination [the terms used in French are 'flagrante' and 'voilée' respectively – Translator's note]. These authors were more specific in their use of the term racism (overt and veiled). Pettigrew and Meertens 1993, p. 109.
27. And yet, as Dominique Schnapper notes (Schnapper 1998, p. 133) 'it would not be right to conclude, as many well-intentioned thinkers have done, that prejudice is born only out of ignorance, and that if they knew each other better, people would cease to be prejudiced.'
28. Interview in August 1993.
29. The italics are mine.
30. The italics are mine.
31. Cited in *The Message International*, March 1993, p. 17, and April 1993, p. 19.
32. Cited in Esposito 1992, p. 168.
33. Ibid., pp. 4–5.
34. *New York Times*, 21 January 1996, pp. S1, S6.
35. *International Herald Tribune*, 7–8 November 1998.
36. Cited in Esposito 1992, p. 175.
37. Haddad and Lummis 1987, pp. 81–2.
38. Cf. Chapter 8.

39. Van der Veer 1993.
40. Vertovec 1996, p. 177.
41. Interview in June 1998.
42. Interview in December 1995.
43. *Daily News*, 28 December 1995.
44. *The Minaret* (New York), 1 January 1996, p. 14.
45. NCIA Report, 22 December 1995.
46. *The Message International,* July 1997, p. 12.
47. *India Abroad*, 11 July 1997, p. 40.
48. AMC brochure: *American Muslim Council: Our First Five Years,* 1990–5, p. 7.
49. Interview with Atif Harden, at that time director of the AMC, in June 1998.
50. This bill, which was branded as McCarthyist by its critics, allowed the government to carry out surveillance on, and to imprison for up to ten years, people who were carrying on legal activity, but working – even if it could be proved that they were unaware of the fact – for organizations which were at the same time engaging in illegal activity elsewhere; it also allowed the expulsion of any immigrant suspected of terrorism or of association with terrorist organizations, where this might be demonstrated with evidence not necessarily available to the person in question.
51. Mohammad 1998.

CONCLUSION

1. Memmi 1997, p. 100.
2. Bayart 1996.
3. Memmi 1997, p. 102.
4. Lacorne 1997, p. 47.
5. The Ahmadiyya, for example.
6. Sayad 1983, p. 10.
7. Barth 1970.
8. Azria 1997, p. 2122.
9. Ibid., p. 2117.
10. Van der Veer 1994, p. xii.
11. Ibid., p. 84.
12. Oriol 1984, p. 46, cited in Neveu 1993, p. 319.
13. Hovanessian 1992, p. 38.
14. Ibid.
15. Neveu 1993, p. 237. ['Ailleurs mythique' in French – Translator's note.]
16. Bayart 1996, p. 98.
17. 'A Saint-Malo man will describe himself as a Malouin to a man from Rennes, as a Breton to a Parisian, as a Frenchman to a German, as a European to an American, as a White to an African, as a worker to his boss, as a Catholic to a Protestant, as a husband to his wife, as a patient to his doctor.' (Ibid., pp. 98–9).
18. Meaning an inhabitant of or someone from Aligarh.
19. 'Uttar Pradesh-walla'.
20. 'South Asian', as we have seen, is however a fairly ill-defined identity.
21. 'Asian', in fact, is even less clearly defined than South Asian.
22. A reference to the strong feelings South Asians have about skin colour.
23. A reference to the need parents feel to have their authority respected by their children, and so to persuade their children to keep their religious and ethnic heritage alive.
24. A reference to the significant numbers of medical practitioners in the South Asian community.
25. Haddad and Lummis 1987, p. 23.
26. Roy 1996, p. 88.

27. Ibid.
28. Ibid.
29. Van der Veer 1994, p. 84.
30. Martin 1992, p. 587.
31. On Shah Waliullah, cf. Rizvi 1980 and Baljon 1986.
32. Please bear in mind that South Asian Muslims are more often seen by Americans as 'Indians', or even as 'Hindus', rather than as Muslims.
33. Rushdie 1992, p. 168.
34. Cf. especially Nye 1995, pp. 51 and 64; Van der Veer, 1995, p. 10.
35. *The Message International*, September–October 1996, pp. 11–12.
36. *The Message International*, March 1997, pp. 10–11.
37. Voll 1991, pp. 209–13; Roy 1996, pp. 94–5.
38. Roy 1992, p. 82.
39. Weibel 1995, p. 28.
40. Lectures given by Professor Derryl Maclean at the EHESS in March and April 1996.
41. Under the Ottoman Empire, each *millat* had its own religious leader, who was responsible to the state for the payment of taxes and the maintaining of public order. This system guaranteed the freedom of religious minorities. A reversal of this situation would imply that immigrant Muslims would enjoy a dispensation similar to that granted to *dhimnu* in Muslim countries. Cf. Waugh 1983, pp. 22–3 and Roy 1996, pp. 94–5.
42. Weibel 1996, p. 135.
43. Weibel 1995, p. 26.
44. Gaborieau 1996b, p. 15 and Troll 1994,
45. Gaborieau 1996b, pp. 15–18.
46. Lacorne 1997, p. 42.
47. Roy 1996, p. 107.
48. Cf. especially Nielson 1992, pp. 12–129.
49. Saint-Blancat 1995, p. 13.
50. Babès 1995, p. 44.
51. As with young Muslims in Europe. Cf. Babès 1995, pp. 38–43.
52. Sayad 1983, p. 10.
53. Cesari 1995, p. 58.
54. Cf. special issue on Islam in Europe in *Archives de sciences sociales des religions* 1995; Davie and Hervieu-Léger 1996.
55. Azria 1996, p. 264.
56. Ibid., p. 267.
57. Maïla 1997, p. 847–62.
58. Ibid., p. 847.
59. Zeghal 1996, p. 66.
60. In the first half of the twentieth century there were some notable scholars, such as Abul Kalam Azad (1888–1958) and Muhammad Iqbal (1938–).
61. Zeghal 1996, especially the last chapter (pp. 328–63).
62. Barazangi 1991, p. 164.
63. They organize conferences on this topic. One of these, in November 1994 at the ICLI, was entitled 'The Role of American Muslims in the Global Islamic Renaissance'.
64. He was criticized for this by fundamentalists in Pakistan, which is why he left Pakistan for America in 1968. He achieved recognition at the University of Chicago, which persuaded Pakistan to invite him on an official visit, and show him honour. Cf. Denny 1991, pp. 97–8.
65. Rahman 1982.
66. Denny 1991, p. 104–05.
67. Dieckhoff 1997, p. 336.

AFTERWORD

1. This Afterword was written after I had carried out some research in New York in November 2001. I was taking part in some research by the Delhi Centre for Human Sciences, in collaboration with the Centre d'Etudes de l'Inde et de l'Asie du Sud (Paris). I would like to express particular thanks to Frédéric Grare and Marc Gaborieau. I would also like to thank all those in New York who answered my questions with the greatest patience and good will, as indeed they always have done, in spite of the very tense current situation. I would especially like to mention Faroque Khan, Naeem Baig, Zaheer Uddin, Ramzi Qaseem, Najma Sultana and Asghar Choudhri.
2. *Dawn*, 29 November 2001.
3. I don't mean by this people who lost a friend or relative in the attacks.
4. The first of these has a majority of South Asian members, the remaining three a majority of Arabs.
5. Timothy McVeigh planted the bomb in the Oklahoma FBI building.
6. It is not known how many Afghans live in the United States. They are mostly concentrated on the West Coast. Estimates for New York vary from 6,000 to 20,000. Afghan immigrants have set up two mosques in New York, both in Queens.

APPENDIX 1

1. The people listed in this section are those to whom I have given nicknames. Others feature in the index.

INDEX

This index covers the main body of the text as well as the appendices and notes, but not the glossary or bibliography. It is written in word-by-word order, where a space precedes a letter, eg. American Muslim Mission precedes Americanization.